THE ACTS OF THE APOSTLES

I - 13

CALVIN'S COMMENTARIES

CALVIN'S COMMENTARIES

THE ACTS OF THE APOSTLES

I - 13

Translators
JOHN W. FRASER
and
W. J. G. McDONALD

Editors
DAVID W. TORRANCE
and
THOMAS F. TORRANCE

WILLIAM B. EERDMANS PUBLISHING COMPANY
GRAND RAPIDS, MICHIGAN

THE PATERNOSTER PRESS
CARLISLE

Published jointly in the United States
by Wm. B. Eerdmans Publishing Co.
255 Jefferson Ave. S.E., Grand Rapids, Michigan 49503
and in the U.K. by The Paternoster Press
P.O. Box 300, Carlisle, Cumbria CA3 0QS

First paperback edition published 1995

Printed in the United States of America

00 99 98 97 96 95 7 6 5 4 3 2 1

The Acts of the Apostles 1-13 – Volume 6

Eerdmans ISBN 0-8028-0806-9

British Library Cataloguing in Publication Data

Calvin, Jean
Acts of the Apostles. – 1-13 – New ed. –
(Calvin's New Testament Commentaries
Series; Vol. 6)
I. Title II. Fraser, John W.
III. McDonald, W. J. G. IV. Series
226.607

Paternoster ISBN 0-85364-712-7

Published in Great Britain by Oliver and Boyd, Edinburgh

INTRODUCTION

Chief Editions of John Calvin's Commentary on the Acts of the Apostles

I. Latin

First Edition, Volume I, dedicated to Christian III, King of Denmark. John Crispinus, Geneva, 1552. Volume II dedicated to Prince Frederick of Denmark. John Crispinus, Geneva, 1554.

Second Edition, Complete Commentaries on the Acts of the Apostles, revised, and 'enriched with a large addition', and with Indices. Dedicated to Nicolas Radzivil. Crispinus, 1560; another edition by Crispinus 1560, with title, 'John Calvin's Two Books of Commentaries on the Acts of the Apostles'. Others: Nicolaus Barbirius and Thomas Courteau, 1564; Eustace Vignon, 1573 and 1584; John Vignon, 1609.

Amsterdam Edition, 1667. (Not included in Prolegomena of C.R.)

Amsterdam Edition of Calvin's N.T. Commentaries, edited by A. Tholuck, Vol. IV. Berlin, Gustav Eichler, 1833.

Corpus Reformatorum, Volume LXXVI. *Johannis Calvini Opera quae supersunt Omnia.* Edited Baum, Cunitz and Reuss. Volume XLVIII. *Opera Exegetica et Homiletica*, Volume XXVI. Brunswick, 1892.

II. French

First Edition, Volume I, 1552. Volume II, 1554. Geneva, Philbert Hamelin. Commentaires sur les quatre évangiles et les Actes. Geneva. Badius, 1561; Bourgeois, 1562; Blanchier, 1563.

Commentaire de Iean Calvin sur les Actes des Apostres. 1562. (No place or printer.)

Paris Edition, 1854.

III. English

The Commentary of M. Iohn Calvin upon the Actes of the Apostles. Faithfully translated out of Latine into English for the great profite of our countrie-men, by Christopher Fetherstone, student in Divinitie. London, G. Bishop. 1585.

Commentary upon the Acts of the Apostles by John Calvin, edited from the original English translation of Christopher Fetherstone by Henry Beveridge, 2 volumes, Edinburgh, Calvin Translation Society, 1844.

INTRODUCTION

Text and Translation

This translation has been made from the Latin texts of Tholuck and C.R. It has been compared at certain places with the French of Blanchier's edition, printed at Geneva 1563, from the copy in the National Library of Scotland, Edinburgh.

The first four chapters have been translated by the Rev. W. J. G. McDonald, B.D., Edinburgh.

Dedicatory Epistles

The letter to the Second Edition is given first and in full, because it contains much of the substance of the letters to the First Edition. The first letter to the First Edition is not translated *in extenso*, but omissions and divergences from the letter to the Second Edition are noted in a following and separate section. In the third place the second letter to the First Edition is translated in its entirety.

Use of Scripture

The Revised Version is used for the text at the head of each section, with margin readings inserted in brackets, or referred to in footnotes, where necessary, particularly when these are followed by Calvin. Occasionally Calvin's text omits what RV includes, e.g. 9.20, 'in the synagogues'. In the commentary itself, because Calvin often paraphrases Scripture, or quotes it freely, the RV is used when it agrees with his Latin, otherwise his Latin is used. At the beginning of the commentary on each verse the RV is generally followed, but, where required, Calvin's Latin is translated.

Scripture References

Tholuck includes many that are not in the C.R. text. These have been incorporated in this translation, and some have been added by the translators.

Abbreviations

C.R.	*Corpus Reformatorum*, as above.
Tholuck	Edition of A. Tholuck, as above.
Vulg.	Latin Vulgate (*Editio minor* of Henry J. White, has been used. Oxford/British and Foreign Bible Society, London, 1911.)
Lewis and Short.	*A Latin Dictionary*. Oxford.

Manse of Farnell,
Brechin, Angus
28th February 1964

JOHN W. FRASER

THE DEDICATORY EPISTLE TO THE SECOND EDITION

JOHN CALVIN

TO

THE MOST ILLUSTRIOUS PRINCE

THE LORD NICOLAS RADZIVIL

DUKE IN OLIKA, PALATINE OF VILNA

SUPREME MARSHAL AND HIGH CHANCELLOR

OF THE GREAT DUKEDOM OF LITHUANIA, ETC.

A LORD TO BE HIGHLY ESTEEMED

I MUST briefly give my reason for deleting the names of the kings to whom I had dedicated these commentaries, so that the change may not incur the charge of inconsistency with some ignorant men. For although I still owe the memory of the dead father the veneration which it deserves, and I honour the son with all due respect, yet the insolence of certain men forced me to expunge their names in this second edition. For they have been roused to fierce hatred of me, and while they are afraid that the majesty of kings may procure some favour for my writings, they make it known that the kings were extremely displeased that their own name was mixed up with a doctrine of the sacraments that they condemn. Whether that is true or not I leave undecided, but in fact it does not interest me, since I have sought neither private gain nor favour for myself. But because it would be unbecoming and shameful for me to force writings on unwilling readers, when they find plenty who are willing, it has been worth while making it public now that such an idea never entered my head, but that I did expect more kindness than I have experienced. There can certainly be no complaint if I remove myself from the contempt of those who are disdainful of my services, and allow them to enjoy those pleasures of theirs, which they desire and with which they amuse themselves.

Indeed it is to good advantage that I have chosen to substitute you, most illustrious Prince, for two men; both because I consider you a most deserving person to have his name appear in the spiritual building of the temple of Christ; and because I have no fear that you will also honour this book of mine with the same good-will that you did not hesitate to show towards me in the kindest of letters. But now, leaving the consideration of private kindness aside, I shall rest on the other aspect. In addition I may justifiably and very well apply to you what I had to say to the other previously. And in fact it is not my intention to celebrate in this place the splendid virtues by which you have acquired the highest authority and unparalleled favour with the most serene King of Poland. My mind is rather inclined to an exhortation, the substance and aim of which will be this, that just as you embraced the pure teaching of the Gospel with alacrity at the beginning, just as you endeavoured, with vigour and greatness of spirit, to maintain the true worship of God up to now, you may go on with the same perseverance right to the bitter end of this course.

When you knew that to many people there is nothing more detestable than to be candid in the profession of piety, and to be openly devoted to it, it was, nevertheless, a sure mark of rare virtue that, as soon as the truth of the Gospel of Christ dawned upon you, you did not hesitate to provoke their ill-will against you by giving your allegiance to it. And those services, which you did not cease to render for the fostering and increasing of the Church in its beginning, deserve great praise; although this sedulousness was by no means acceptable with several noblemen, and on all sides produced a great deal of ill-will for you. But because difficulties that are just as arduous remain for you, it is important to make up your mind continually to surmount them, until you come to the end of the final act. And it must be done with all the more diligence, since many princes, although they see the horribly corrupt state of the Church, yet do not dare to attempt any remedies, because the danger that they fear from newness, once evil things have been driven out of ancient and undisturbed possession, hinders them, and keeps them back from functioning. Some think that it is absurd and foolish to touch incurable diseases. Others, because of some sort of indefinable perverseness, run away in terror from all reformation. But it would be superfluous to discuss those obstacles which surround you, with you to whom they are all too well known. Yet whatever assaults Satan inflicts upon you, and with whatever fights and struggles he exercises you, it is never permitted to grow weary in this sacred warfare, for which you have volunteered under the banner of Christ.

Moreover, however willing you may be of yourself, it will, I hope, be neither disagreeable nor useless for you to have the favourable progress of your ready zeal helped and advanced by this aid, which the Lord offers to you by my hand. As often as things in the world seem to be turned upside down, no more suitable or firmer support can be found for strengthening consciences than, when, placing the Kingdom of Christ before our eyes as we now see it, we consider what the pattern (*ratio*) and nature of it was, and what sort of state and condition it had, in the beginning.

When we talk about the Kingdom of Christ, we must take note of two things in particular, first, the teaching of the Gospel by which Christ gathers the Church to Himself, and by which He governs it when it has been gathered; secondly, the actual fellowship of the godly, who, having been united among themselves by the sincere faith of the Gospel, are truly regarded as the people of Christ. It is better to become thoroughly acquainted with the living picture of both these things, which Luke clearly draws in the Acts of the Apostles, by reading the whole book, than to believe either my account of it, or that of anyone else. For although the Son of God has always reigned from the very beginning of the world, yet it was after His revelation in the flesh, and the publication of His Gospel, that He began to set up a judgment-seat plainer to see than ever before (*illustrius solito tribunal*), as a result of which He now too appears in the highest degree conspicuous (*maxime conspicuus*). If we turn our eyes to this book (*huc*) we shall feast them, not on an empty picture (as Virgil says about his Aeneas), but on the sound knowledge of those things from which we must seek life. And to revert to what I intended to speak about, this is the best refuge for consciences, where, amidst those tumults and commotions by which the world is shaken, they may rest at peace. Finally, this meditation alone will never cause to happen to us what experiences prove far too often, viz. the truth of the statement that Ennius made long ago about the majority of men, 'wisdom is abolished, as often as something is done by force'. For if, when the heat of battle was at its greatest and fiercest, the harmonious music of pipes had so much influence on the Spartans, that it calmed the ferocity innate in that warlike people, and tempered the violence, which, on that occasion, runs riot and gets out of hand, even in people who are otherwise gentle of nature, how much better and more effectively will the Kingdom of Christ bring this about by the heavenly music of the Holy Spirit? And I say this because it not only tames savage beasts, but makes lambs out of wolves, lions and bears, because it turns spears into pruning-hooks, and makes swords into ploughshares.

Therefore, most illustrious Prince, in presenting to you the kind of moderating influence that the need of the times demands, I believe that this service will not be unacceptable to your excellency, the very essence of which is equitableness, so that you may realize with certainty that it provides encouragement of a particularly fitting and useful kind to look to the origin of the Church as Luke describes it. For in it both the wonderful power of God under the shame of the cross, and the unflagging endurance of the servants of God under a huge burden of troubles, shine out, and the very success, incredible by worldly standards, brings forth fruit from both in the greatest abundance. Finally, missing out the rest of the things which it is better to find out from reading Luke himself, I shall mention one thing, which is particularly appropriate to earthly princes and the chief governors of kingdoms and nations. When the power of the whole world was in opposition, and all the men, who had control of affairs then, were in arms to crush the Gospel, a few men, obscure, unarmed and contemptible, relying on the support of the truth and the Spirit alone, laboured so strenuously in spreading the faith of Christ, avoided no toil or dangers, remained unbroken against all attacks, until at last they emerged victors. Accordingly there is no excuse for Christian princes, distinguished as they are by a certain authority, since God has provided them with the sword for the defence of the Kingdom of His Son, being at least just as spirited and faithful in the discharge of such an honourable task. Again, it is not for me to say how faithful and skilful an interpreter I have been. The work will be fruitful for all, I certainly hope.

Indeed, most illustrious Prince, again I must ask you, even implore you both privately to yield yourself completely to the sovereignty of Christ, in accordance with the auspicious beginnings you made before, and to be not only a faithful and indefatigable helper, but also a standard-bearer, in advancing the Kingdom of Christ among so many noblemen, who are commended, both by the splendour of their birth, and the excellency of their virtues. God has thought the kingdom of Poland worthy of an extraordinary privilege and honour, in that the majority of the nobility have finished with ungodly superstitions, which are corruptions and debasements of the worship of God, and unanimously desire the right kind of godliness, and a properly constituted Church order. And it is well known that these men were greatly helped by your influence. But too many struggles still remain for them and you, for you to give yourselves up to ease and rest like veteran soldiers.

In the first place, although no external enemy may cause you annoyance, there will be more than enough to do against internal troubles. You have already found out by experience how Satan is equipped with a variety of tricks for hatching plots to shatter the holy concord among the brethren, in which the safety of the Church consists. Certainly there happens among you what is usual everywhere, that trouble-makers force their way in when things are in disorder, and when they see a few men, and weaklings at that, being molested by an immense multitude, and the truth, which is hidden under dense clouds of misrepresentations, being defended by them with difficulty, they take them by surprise all the more easily, as if by tunnelling under them. And with this subtlety that master of all deceits assuredly sets about the ruin of the Church, not only by breaking apart and tearing to pieces the unity of the Church, but by falsely burdening the name of Christ with a bad reputation, because the assembly of the godly, with which those impudent rascals mix themselves up, seems to be something like sinks and bilges holding all the dregs of society.

So, while Stancarus, a man of turbulent nature, is spreading his mad ideas among you for the sake of his ambition, with which he is completely inflamed, as a result of this a dispute has broken out, which threatens to make some break away (*dissipationem aliquam*); and you have been exposed to the reproaches of many men, because it was believed that his sect was being extended further. Now, look, on the other hand, at a certain physician, George Brandata, who is worse than Stancarus, because he is imbued with a more detestable error, and cherishes more secret poison in his mind. For that reason the easy-going attitude of those, among whom the impiety of Servetus has suddenly acquired so much favour, deserves more blame. For although I am convinced that they are free from those perverse and sacrilegious doctrines, yet they ought to have been more cautious, so that this fox might not sneak his way into their fellowship. Because pests of this kind will never be lacking, and Satan will never cease to bring forward into the front line of battle those champions who are devoted to him, to throw the foremost ranks of the Gospel into disorder, we must persevere and stand ready for battle. And to meet greater evils, a proper and well-ordered method of government must be established by you, for it is the reliable protector of holy peace. For as it is well known that purity of doctrine is the soul of the Church, so we may justifiably compare discipline to the sinews, by which the body is bound and connected together, and so preserves its strength.

Now, on the other hand, the dishonesty of other enemies ought to whet your zeal. I am speaking about the heralds of the Roman Antichrist, who, to deceive the ignorant, continually trumpet the word 'Church' with high-sounding voices. About the Church there is no controversy between us, in that its authority ought to be worthy of reverence by all the sons of God. But here is the exception. Under the false pretext of honour they make the vague (*umbratile*) name of 'the Church' subject to their own caprice, while we, on our part, revere the Church from the heart, so that in our view it is extremely sinful to profane its sacred name. Not to mention other godly ministers of sound and pure doctrine I myself have already dealt with this question before this in several places, almost to the point of being sick of it. When mention is made of the Church, whose Head is the Son of God, and how He, who is the fountain of eternal life, always quickens it by His Spirit, how ridiculous it is to produce a body without a head, and so a dead body.

The Pope's sycophant hirelings cry out that they have the Church. Whether their boast is true or not can be found out in no better way than by considering the Head. It is surely evident that it is cut off from the body by their sacrilegious violence. For how will Christ retain the place of Head, deprived of all His power, dispossessed of His sovereignty, and stripped of His authority? The Heavenly Father appointed Him Head of the Church on this condition, that He may rule all men, from the greatest to the least, by the teaching of His Gospel; that He may be the only Priest to propitiate the Father Himself continually for us, just as He once appeased His wrath by the sacrifice of His death; that the death of the same one may be a perpetual atonement for sins, His blood the only means of cleansing, His obedience a complete satisfaction; that He may be the only Intercessor by whose pleading our prayers are heard; that He may be a faithful defender and guardian to shield us by His protection; that having subdued the vices of our flesh He may remake us in righteousness and holiness; and that He alone may begin and perfect in us the blessed life. If the Papists have left Him with any of those things they may certainly have the Church on their side. But if the Pope, oppressing consciences with a harsh and exceedingly cruel tyranny, has taken away the supreme power from Christ; if he has introduced a form of government altogether alien to the teaching of the Gospel; if he has invented a new and exotic sacerdotal office, so that he, a mortal man, takes it on himself to be the reconciler between God and the world; if he has devised daily sacrifices which may take the place of the death of Christ; if he has discovered a thousand victims to atone for sins; if he has brought counterfeit cleansing waters (*lavacra*) out of Lake Avernus, to dry up the blood of the Son of God; if he has put innumerable patrons in His place; if he has torn into a thousand pieces the righteousness which must be sought completely from Him; if he has set up man's free-will instead of the Holy Spirit; then nobody need be in any doubt that the true Christ is banished far away by the Papists. I have said that it is a dead body that the Papists exhibit for the body of Christ, for the reason that they have abolished the teaching of the Gospel, which is the true soul of the Church, and the only thing that gives it life, and they yet grandly proclaim some vague indefinable 'Church'.

We say openly, how, among them, the purity of doctrine has been corrupted, yes, and polluted with monstrous errors. They not only plead the excuse of the imperfect state of the Church, when they defend all corruptions, but, besides, they complain that grave and undeserved injury is done to the Church by us, because we say that it is in the wrong. But, in the first place, there should have been an examination of doctrine, so that the Church may then be recognized. Those fair and honest judges wish what is spuriously entitled 'doctrine' to have the force of prejudice for concealing the difference. And that is surely no excuse for deceiving; for with what illusions would they attempt to mislead even those of poor vision in such a great light? But because they consider this licence to tell lies as part of their tyranny, they seem to themselves to be ruling in accordance with their own desire, only when they are abusively mocking at miserable souls.

We need not go far for an example. In our time we have now the Tridentine Fathers, now those of Bologna, although disputing in hostile manner among themselves, yet frothing out their empty canons on both sides. And of course if assent is given to their principles both sides will be ready to triumph. I do not know how many bishops and abbots sit there, perhaps a hundred horned beasts. If the choicest flower of the whole nation flourished there, it would nevertheless be nothing other than an impious conspiracy against God. But now, after the Pope collected the bran and refuse of his impure and offensive flock into a single pit, will a representative church suddenly emerge from it? And are they not yet ashamed to be calling a 'holy, general and lawful Council' what does not even deserve to be described as the useless and comical masquerade of a Council? But as for us, to whom the promise is given that the Antichrist who sits in the temple of God must be destroyed by the breath of the mouth of the Lord, let us not cease to refute this shameful and meretricious impudence with that inviolable Word, which they scoff at so boldly, so that it may be made clear to all what difference there is between the chaste bride of Christ and the disgusting harlot of Belial, between the sanctuary of God and the brothel of Satan, between the spiritual household of the godly and a pig-sty, and, finally, between the true Church and the Roman Curia. No more certain or clearer proof of this situation can be produced either by Euclid or Archimedes, than if one were to compare the Church, such as it is described by Luke, with the Pope's synagogue. And I am certainly not so hard as to wish that disorderly chaos, from which both the natural order and human reason shrink completely, to measure up to the norm of the apostles, angelic and heavenly as that is. If they were only to point out anything there that has any affinity with them, they would certainly be at liberty to triumph over me. But since everything is contrary to that norm, even if the majority of men may deliberately turn a blind eye, at any rate with the whole of heaven applauding, we will be allowed not only to condemn their foolish pride fearlessly, but also freely to expose it to ridicule. At the same time a great consolation sustains us, that, when the Papists superciliously oppose us with the title of 'the Church', we however know that we are fighting only with the professed enemies of Christ.

Indeed the first thing to wish for is that the most Serene King, who, through His wisdom, recognized the faults of the Roman Curia long ago, may order the destruction of those useless bulls, with which the Council makes a show from a distance, and may at last apply His mind more freely to the serious and complete restoration of the Church. Yet no delay ought to prevent each one of you making an effort, to the utmost of his ability, to increase those beginnings, which started to spring up so auspiciously.

Farewell, most distinguished Lord, and most Illustrious Prince. May the Lord always direct you by His Spirit; may He increase your dignity in every way, and bless your godly undertakings right to the end.

GENEVA, 1st August 1560

THE DEDICATORY EPISTLES TO THE FIRST EDITION[1]

NOTES; AND EXTRACTS FROM THE FIRST LETTER

THE First Edition appeared in two volumes. The first was dedicated to King Christian III of Denmark and dated 29 February 1552, the second to his son Frederick, dated 25 January 1554. Calvin refers to this in the letter to Frederick. 'When I began to expound the Acts of the Apostles two years ago, I divided my commentaries into two volumes, so that the first, dedicated to your father, and the other in fact to you, might see the light of day under favourable auspices. My reason for doing that was that I thought it would be suitable to connect you with the narrative of that history, which embraces the very beginnings of the Christian Church right from its actual birth, and then its advances and increases, so that the precise resemblance of the reborn Church, which the Lord has committed to your protection, may encourage you more and more in the right course of duty.'

The first letter repeats much of what is found in the fuller letter to Radzivil in the Second Edition. The beginning and ending are different, and other divergences are noted here.

The first letter begins:

'Most Excellent King, when, long ago, according to the Law's regulation, the sacred trumpets sounded for the Jews, as they went forth to battle, I understand that it was done, not only that the people might not dare to undertake any war, or carry on those that they started, without the auspices of God; but also so that forgetfulness of God, which is especially fatal at that time, might not steal upon minds terrorized by the clash of arms, as usually happens. For with our nature, frail and fickle as it is, nothing is easier than for all our senses to be engrossed by the cares of the world, which completely alienate us from God. I include many things under "cares of the world". Fear of dangers discourages some; vain hopes of new things seduce others; some are carried away by ferocity; others give themselves over to unbridled licence; despair drives some almost to madness; others degenerate through the persistence of misfortunes into an almost

[1] These are found in C.R. Vol. XLII, *Calvini Opera* Vols. XIV and XV, *Thes. Epistolicus.* Vol. V Letter 1607, and Vol. VI Letter 1901.

stony hardness; the passion for violent action (*grassandi*), beyond what is lawful, drives others headlong. Thus almost all become divorced from God (*profanescunt*), molested as they are by a variety of corrupting influences. But as things are now in confusion everywhere, I believe that scarcely ever has there been a time, when there was more need for the minds of the godly to be awakened by that sacred trumpeting which I have mentioned, so that the noisy uproars all around them may not finally overwhelm them with insensibility. For what historians report, that those who live by the Nile cataracts are dull of hearing on account of the continuous violence of the rushing water, happens with far worse effect in this connexion, viz. that a fatal torpor follows deafness of the soul. There is one remedy, if the heavenly trumpets are resounding constantly in our ears. But we see how many shamefully deprive themselves of such a great blessing, either by surrendering themselves to lassitude through laziness, or even by voluntarily bringing lethargy on themselves. Certainly the heroic power of your mind, most potent King, has formerly raised you too high for you to need to be aroused from another place, as if you were a sluggard; no, and what is more, as far as those obstacles that I have noted are concerned, your attentiveness to hearing the voice of God is said to be such as can be a remarkable example of alacrity to others.'

Common material begins at the sentence beginning, 'Moreover, however willing' on page [2] of the Radzivil letter, and stops at 'equitableness', in the first sentence of the paragraph beginning on page [3]. It resumes with the paragraph beginning 'Now' on page [5]. But in the letter to Christian this first sentence begins slightly differently: 'Now, on the other hand, look also at this. The dishonesty of our enemies encourages, or rather forces me, to dedicate this work to you. I am speaking etc.'

The paragraph beginning on page 7 commences differently in the letter to Christian: 'Swollen with this ferocity the Tridentine Fathers are still, today, putting out their canons in foaming waves.' The paragraph on page [8] beginning 'Indeed the first thing' is omitted.

The letter to Christian ends:

'But may your Majesty grant me this confidence, so that godly readers may enjoy this work of mine under the auspices of your Majesty, until the other, remaining part is published in its own good time, under the name of your son, for whom I have intended it.

'Farewell, O King, most wise and most distinguished by a pre-eminence in all virtues. May the Lord establish the throne, on which He has set you, right to the end.'

Historical background to the second letter is provided in notes in C.R. When King Frederick I died in 1534 there was a dispute that year, and for a time after, about the succession. Some of the chief men favoured Christian, then a prisoner, others John, the younger son of Frederick. The former defended the Reformation cause, the latter the Catholic tradition. In 1542 King Christian III had caused Frederick his son, a boy of eight, to be elected to share the royal authority with him. Frederick succeeded on the death of Christian in 1559.

Both these letters were omitted from the Second Edition for the reason given at the beginning of the letter to Radzivil. But in the Prolegomena to Acts of C.R. another reason is given. 'If our author believed that with the presentation of this work the favour of those princes could be won for himself and his theology, this hope greatly deceived him. For in that very year, 1554, Evangelicals, who were driven out of England by Queen Mary and were seeking asylum for themselves among foreigners, were cruelly turned away from Denmark at the instigation of Lutheran ministers. Therefore, when in the year 1560 the Commentary on Acts was again submitted to the press, the author offered the new edition to another patron, Nicolas Radzivil.' A note to the letter to Frederick also states: 'It is clear that when he wrote this he had not yet found out about the reception in Denmark of John a Lasco and the English exiles.'

DEDICATION TO THE SECOND PART OF THE COMMENTARY ON THE ACTS OF THE APOSTLES

FOR THE MOST SERENE KING-ELECT OF DENMARK AND NORWAY, FREDERICK, THE MOST EXCELLENT SON OF KING CHRISTIAN

JOHN CALVIN
PRAYS FOR THE ROYAL SPIRIT OF WISDOM AND FORTITUDE FROM THE LORD

O RENOWNED KING, after the Kingdom of Denmark had been for long shaken by many serious disturbances, it was due to the singular blessing of God that not only has it been completely pacified more quickly than men might have hoped and supposed, but it preserves its own status today with all its affairs constituted in the best order. It increases the value of this happy situation that, in the midst of those upheavals of wars and disagreements, by which we see almost the whole Christian world shaken or in a ferment, it enjoys the gladness of peace. It is a matter of such great importance for noble and wise princes to be set over the world by God, both to curb the whole force of injustice by their power, and to establish a proper form of government at home by their prudence and equity. Since the most Serene King, your Majesty's father, excels in both these ways, Denmark could not have looked after its own interests in a better or wiser way than by taking to herself as King one on whom he had already conferred the honour and right of kings by generation.[1] But so that such an extraordinary blessing of God might not be lost through the death of one man, as usually often happens, the succession of his son was added, to preserve the situation for a long time, for he would continue and establish the order admirably set up under the father's auspices. Sometimes it does indeed happen that sons are not only unlike their fathers, but that when they have gained power, either by some sort of perverseness

[1] *C.R. note:* In 1542 the father, King Christian III, had caused him to be elected to share the royal authority with him, when he was still a boy of eight. He succeeded on the death of the father in 1559.

or foolish emulation, or by contentions and disagreements in the court, they allow themselves just as much freedom to violate the father's laws, as if they were eagerly attacking the greatest of enemies. But God has generously provided for the kingdom of Denmark in this respect, that you are a most outstanding king, with the heroic stamp of your father's nature, educated in his most virtuous discipline, having embraced the way of life delivered by him from hand to hand, as the saying goes, and think of nothing else but following in his footsteps. However you have not only been chosen to be his successor to assume the office left vacant by his death, but also both adopted by his living and distinguished judgment, and given by the providence of God as an aide, on whose shoulders part of the burden may lie. And I do not doubt that among the principal gifts of God, with which he is splendidly adorned, he justifiably counted this, that a son was given to him, not only one to whose fidelity he may safely entrust his kingdom, but one from whose services he may now receive other fruits in very great abundance, as well as feeling a certain alleviation. Although one can imagine nothing more suited to the general well-being of the people than this holy agreement, there also falls to your Majesty's lot, as an individual, a welcome chance to bear witness to your godliness, because, by playing a secondary role to a very good king without envy, by showing yourself obedient and deferential to him, as is right, you draw from all the godly, because of your modesty, praise that is just as valuable as the glory of bearing rule is commonly regarded.

Now indeed the fruit of that blessing extends more widely than to the kingdom of Denmark, because after receiving the support of another protector, the kingdom of Christ is putting down deeper and firmer roots there. That King Christian was true to his name in actively and magnificently defending the true worship of God there is no need to tell. This one thing seems to me to be a clear enough example. Although many princes see the horribly corrupt state of the Church, yet they do not undertake any reform, because being in ancient and also undisturbed possession, they are hindered and kept back from functioning, by the danger that they fear from newness.[1] But, O King, when things were just beginning, and were still either in confusion or doubt,[2] your father was just as undaunted as pious in

[1] A sentence that is very similar is to be found on page 2 of the letter to Radzivil.

[2] *C.R. note:* When King Frederick I died in 1534 throughout that year, and after, there was a dispute about the succession among the chief men of the Kingdom, some preferring the captive Christian, others John the younger son of Frederick. Of these the former defended the Reformation, the latter the Catholic tradition.

making it his entire concern that pure religion might flourish among the Danes, purged of the filth of superstitions. Now, most noble King, all declare that you are inflamed with an eagerness like his to retain and preserve its purity. And one would wish the Danes to pay proper attention to this unbroken sequence of divine grace. We see that Christ has shown Himself to many countries in this time of ours; and that where He has been unworthily received He has transferred the seat of His Gospel elsewhere. Therefore those whom He has deemed worthy of that special favour, that He makes known the hope of a firm abode with them in the future, ought to be all the more eager to make an effort to devote themselves to Him completely.

But to come to myself. When I began to expound the Acts of the Apostles, two years ago I divided my commentaries into two books, so that the first, dedicated to His Majesty, your father, and the other to you indeed, might see the light of day under favourable auspices. My reason for doing that was that I thought it would be suitable to connect you with the narrative of that history, which embraces the very beginnings of the Christian Church right from its actual birth, and then its advances and increases, so that the precise resemblance of the reborn Church, which the Lord has committed to your protection, may encourage you more and more in the right course of duty. For even if I do not mention these things, there was the quite heroic courage which was known and famous in the case of your father, but your own ardour does not need incentives; yet even if I do not mention how beneficial encouragement may be in a task that is so immense and difficult, in the common weakness of human nature, in the midst of so many of Satan's obstacles, he was well enough instructed by the mistress of experience, and you, O King, are learning every day that you do not need the advice of my words. Your Majesty will surely realize that it is encouragement[1] of a particularly fitting and useful kind to look to the origin of the Church as Luke describes it. For in it both the wonderful power of God under the shame of the cross, and the unflagging endurance of the servants of God under a huge burden of troubles, shine out, and the very success, incredible by worldly standards, brings forth fruit from both in the greatest abundance.

Finally, missing out the rest of the things which it is better to find out from reading Luke himself, I shall touch on one thing which is appropriate for a royal personage. When the power of the whole world was in opposition, and all the men, who had control of affairs then, were in arms to crush the Gospel, a few men, obscure, unarmed and contemptible, relying on the support of the truth and the Spirit alone,

[1] From this point to 'I certainly hope' can be found on page 3f of the letter to Radzivil.

laboured so strenuously in spreading the faith of Christ, avoided no toil or dangers, remained unbroken against all attacks, until at last they emerged victors. Accordingly there is no excuse for Christian princes, distinguished as they are by a certain authority, since God has provided them with the sword for the defence of the Kingdom of His Son, being at least just as spirited and faithful in the discharge of such an honourable task. Again, it is not for me to say how faithful and skilful an interpreter I have been. The work will be fruitful for all, I certainly hope. But if your Majesty will not be unwilling to take a taste I am confident that this work will not be disagreeable to him.

May the Lord keep the Most Excellent King, your father and yourself safe together for a very long time; may He continue to direct you with the Spirit of wisdom and fortitude; may He enrich you more and more with an abundance of all blessings; and always preserve peaceful rule under your control.

GENEVA, 25 January 1554

THE THEME OF THE ACTS OF THE APOSTLES

So that all the godly may give more attention and diligence to the reading of this history, it is worth while noting briefly how much benefit may be derived from it.

The highest praise for a history by secular writers is to call it an 'instructress of life'. If a narrative of events, which only gives guidance in connexion with men's deeds, as to what ought to be avoided, and what followed, merits such a splendid description, what title will the sacred histories deserve? For not only do they regulate the external life of man so that he may obtain commendation for virtue, but, what ought to be of more value to us, they also show that God has cared for His Church from the beginning, that always He stood by, a just vindicator, for those who turned to Him for support and protection, that He was gracious to, and easily moved by, miserable sinners. By instructing our faith in this way they raise us up higher than the heavens. I say nothing about their commending the general providence of God; the distinguishing of the true worship of God from counterfeit cults; their failing at no point to separate vices and virtues. However I refrain at present from repeating those descriptions which commonly belong to the sacred narratives. I am merely mentioning those things which are peculiar to this book which we have undertaken to investigate.

The things that Luke sets down here for our instruction are great things and of extraordinary benefit. At the beginning when he reports that the Holy Spirit was sent to the apostles, he not only confirms that Christ was true to the promise He made, but he teaches that He also remembers His own, and is the perpetual Governor of His Church, because the Holy Spirit has descended for that purpose. From that we learn that spatial distance does not prevent Christ from being always present with His own, as He promised. The beginning of the reign of Christ, and, as it were, the renewal of the world is being depicted here. For even if the Son of God had already gathered some of the Church by His preaching before His departure from the world, yet in fact the Christian Church began to exist in its proper form (*legitima forma*) only when the apostles were endowed with new power, and preached that that unique Shepherd had both died and been raised from the dead, so that by His guidance all who had previously been wandering and scattered might come together into the one sheepfold. Therefore both the origin and the progress of the Church, from the Ascension of Christ, by which He was declared the supreme King of heaven and earth, are reviewed here for us.

Moreover there is apparent in it both the astonishing power of Christ and the efficacy and force of the Gospel itself. For in it Christ has furnished clear proof of His divine power, because, through men of no importance and endowed with no skill, He brought the whole world into submission to Himself so easily by the sound of the Gospel, despite the fact that Satan rose up in opposition with so many hindrances. In it we also see the incredible power of the Gospel, because, in face of the resistance of the whole world, not only did it win through, but with the greatest honour brought all that seemed invincible into obedience to Christ. Therefore more was achieved by these few contemptible little men against all the stormiest commotions of the world, with the humble sound of the human voice, than if God had thundered openly from heaven.

But on the other hand the Holy Spirit warns us that the Kingdom of Christ never raises itself without Satan furiously setting himself against it, and employing all his contrivances either to overthrow it or to shake it to its foundations. And we are certainly taught not only that Satan resists Christ like the enemy he is, but that almost the whole world, carried away by the same madness, makes every effort not to grant the rule to Christ. Yes, and what is more, it must be established that when ungodly men are in an uproar against the teaching of the Gospel, they are both serving in Satan's army, and being whipped up into such a blind fury by his cunning. That is the reason for so many grave disturbances, so many hostile conspiracies, so many infamous attempts by the ungodly to impede the course of the Gospel, which Luke reports throughout. Finally, just as the apostles found out from actual experience that the teaching of the Gospel is fire and sword, so we must learn from what they discovered that, due to the inflexible ill-will of Satan, and the fatal stubbornness of men, it will always be the case that the Gospel is involved in many attacks and struggles, and that that situation stirs up horrible disturbances.

But of course on the other hand Luke reports that the apostles nevertheless carried out with invincible courage and steadfastness what they knew was commanded them by God; and at the same time he calls to mind how well they tolerated having to swallow innumerable, vexatious, loathsome and insulting things, how patiently they endured savage waves of persecution, and, finally, how calmly they put up with abuses and hardships of every kind. Surely by such examples we are given lessons in endurance. For since the Son of God has announced that the Cross will always be associated with His Gospel, there is no cause for us to deceive ourselves with a vain hope, as if the situation of the Church here would always be peaceful and flourishing. Therefore let us also prepare ourselves to put up with similar things. But this tremendous consolation is added, that just as God long ago marvellously saved His Church when it was afflicted and crushed in so many ways, so He will also come to our help today. For certainly, since the whole of this book teaches that, when the Church is continually surrounded by death, it is protected by the hand of God alone, God Himself in this way is setting before our eyes His extraordinary providence in procuring its safety.

Furthermore several of the apostles' speeches are repeated here. These deal with the mercy of God, the grace of Christ, the hope of blessed immortality, the invocation of God, repentance and the fear of God, and other principal points of the heavenly teaching, in such a way that we need not look anywhere else for the whole substance of the faith.

Finally, leaving aside an explanation of the sound and pure teaching at the present time, if it is particularly worth our while and beneficial for us to know these things, viz. to understand what sort of beginning the Christian Church had, how the apostles entered upon the preaching of the Gospel, what successes they had, and at the same time in what battles they were engaged, how they persisted, strenuously and resolutely, in the midst of so many obstacles, how, while under the ignominy of the Cross, they splendidly triumphed over all the pride of the world, how wonderfully God helped them, then it is right that this book be especially commended to us. For if it were not in existence, then the knowledge of such great things would either have been buried, or enveloped in darkness, or involved in doubt. For we see that Satan directed all his ingenuity to the end that nothing about the things done by the apostles might remain extant, except what was defiled with lies, so as to render suspect everything said by them, and finally to expunge from the minds of the godly all memory of that age. For he incited crazy men or cunning mockers to spread obnoxious tales with suppositious names, and the absurdity of these deprived genuine histories of credit also. Thus the booklets, which were circulated about Peter and Paul under the name of Linus, contain such disagreeable dirges, that all they can do is make the worldly laugh, and irritate the good. Similarly the fictitious argument of Peter with Simon Magus is so ridiculous that it brings shame on the Christian name. We must pass the same judgment about all that farrago which is found in the preface to the *Recognitions* and *Homilies* of Clement, and quoted in the rhapsodies of Gratian. They deceive the ignorant, with their pretence of ancient names; and, as if they were oracles, dishonest men boast of them, in a supercilious and impudent fashion when in fact they are scandalous dirges. Satan has taken advantage of this licence in lying, so that after the Ascension of Christ into heaven we may have no certainty. So if this record of Luke's was not in existence Christ could have appeared to have left no effect of His death and resurrection on earth, after He had been lifted up to heaven. For everything would have vanished along with His body. We should not know that He was received into heavenly glory in such a way that He maintains His rule on earth. We should not know that the teaching of the Gospel was published by the ministry of the apostles to reach even to us from them, although through a variety of hands. We should not know that they were inspired by the Holy Spirit not to teach anything except what was of God, in order that our faith might rest on the firm truth of God. Since this book without question originated from the Spirit Himself, and takes away our doubt about these matters, I now confirm once again what I justifiably said before by way of preface, that it must be regarded by us as a kind of vast treasure.

CHAPTER ONE

The former treatise I made, O Theophilus, concerning all that Jesus began both to do and to teach, until the day in which he was received up, after that he had given commandment through the Holy Ghost unto the apostles whom he had chosen. (1-2)

1. Before passing on to the events which followed the ascension of Christ, Luke brings together in summary the matters which he dealt with in the preceding volume, in order to link the volumes together. He offers this brief description of the history of the Gospel—that it is the narrative of what Jesus did and said during the time when He was upon earth. Now the common interpretation, that in Christ holiness of life was prior and the teaching was secondary, is far from being the mind of Luke. It is true that the way of life of a good and honourable teacher ought to be so ordered that his life speaks before his tongue—otherwise he is in no way different from a play-actor—but Luke rather recalls what he said near the end of his gospel, that Christ was a prophet mighty in deed and word, whose excellence consisted in what He did no less than in what He said (Luke 24.19). Yet there is little difference between these two passages. For the mightiness of the works which is extolled in the earlier passage has the miracles in view: but in this passage 'to do' has in my opinion a wider application, so as to comprehend all the mighty acts which belonged to His ministry, among which the death and resurrection hold first place. For the function of the Messiah was to consist not in teaching alone, but that He should make peace between God and men, and be the Redeemer of the people, the Restorer of the kingdom and the Author of eternal felicity. All these things, I say, as having been promised of the Messiah, were looked for at His hands.

Now we see that the sum of the Gospel comprises these two parts—the teaching of Christ and His acts—in that He not only brought to men the embassy committed to Him by the Father, but also accomplished in deed all that could be required of the Messiah. He inaugurated His Kingdom, He reconciled God by His sacrifice, He expiated the sins of men by His own blood, He subdued death and the devil, He restored us to true liberty, He won for us justice and life. But that all that He did and said might be ratified, He attested Himself by His miracles to be the Son of God. So the words 'to do' extend also to the miracles; but they must not be restricted to these only.

From this we must note that those who simply know the bare history have not the Gospel, unless there is added a knowledge of the teaching, which reveals the fruit of the acts of Christ. For this is a holy knot, which may not be dissolved. Therefore whenever mention is made of the teaching of Christ, let us learn to join to it the works as seals by which its truth is established and its effects shown forth. On the other hand, in order that the death and resurrection of Christ may be profitable for us, and that His miracles may have their value, let us be equally attentive to the words that He speaks. For this is the true rule of Christianity.

Concerning all that Jesus began . . . I have no objection to the interpretation of some, that Luke here said 'concerning all' rather than 'all' absolutely; for it is possible to deal with the works and teaching of Christ to a certain degree, but to cover the entire sequence, so that the record should be complete, would be an excessive burden. As John says, the world would not contain the books (John 21.25). It is also to be noted that Luke says that he began his history from the beginning of the work of Christ. But after setting forth Christ's nativity, he at once passes over to His twelfth year and after briefly telling of His disputation in the Temple he passes over eighteen years in silence and finally enters upon the proper account of the deeds of Christ.

It is therefore evident that only those acts and words, which have a bearing upon the substance of our salvation, are noted here. For from the time Christ came forth into the world clothed in our flesh, He lived privately at home until the thirtieth year of His age, when the Father invested Him with a new part. God wished the earlier period of His life to remain hidden, that knowledge of the things which build up our faith might be held in greater esteem by us.

Former speech (*sermonem*). I choose to translate thus, because *λόγον ποιεῖσθαι* as Budaeus noted, has the same meaning for the Greeks as 'to make or deliver a speech' has for the Latins. A contrast is implied with this second section, which the evangelist is beginning, so that we understand that he has undertaken to write upon a new theme.

2. *Until the day*. Therefore the ascension of Christ to heaven is the conclusion of the narrative of the Gospel. He ascended, that He might fill all things, says Paul (Eph. 4.10). Our faith gains other advantage thereby but it will be sufficient at this point to note that every aspect of our redemption was wholly and perfectly completed at the moment when Christ ascended to the Father, and that Luke therefore, in this narrative, fully performed his task with regard to the teaching and works of Christ. And the words 'received up' are used, that we may know that He did in fact depart out of this world, lest we should give

assent to the fantasies of those who consider that no change of place was involved in the ascension.

Commandment through the Holy Ghost. By these words Luke reminds us that Christ though He departed from the world did not thereby abandon His concern for us. For in establishing a perpetual government in the Church, He gave proof of His will to provide for our salvation. Indeed He has given assurance of His intention to be present in power and succour (*praeesse et adesse*) to His own people even to the end (Matt. 28.20)—even as in truth He is present by His ministers. Luke means therefore that Jesus did not depart without first having provided for the government of the Church, whereby we recognize His concern for our salvation. And this providence of Christ Paul clearly noted in the passage quoted above—'that he might fill all things, appointing apostles, evangelists, pastors etc.'. But these commands, which he says Christ gave to the apostles, I understand of the preaching of the Gospel; just as it is the custom to provide ambassadors with certain instructions to guard against their rashly going outwith the intention of the one who has sent them. And all this is set out to commend the teaching which the apostles gave.

For greater clarity, let us take the points one by one. In the first place, he says they were chosen by Christ, so that we may be assured and convinced of their calling. He is not here setting in opposition the calling of God and the merits of men, but simply affirming that they were raised up by God, and did not presumptuously take upon themselves this function. It is true, indeed, that they were elect by grace; but now the question arises of the point to which Luke's thought is tending. Now I affirm that his object is no other than that we should be convinced of the divine calling of the apostles so that we should learn to have regard, not to men, but to the Son of God from whom the call comes.

This must always be a maxim in the Church, that no one may claim honour for himself. Secondly, he says that they were instructed by Christ what they were to do: as if he were saying that they did not utter their own inventions but they faithfully delivered what was enjoined them by their heavenly Master. And in order that what Christ commanded them might receive the greater reverence, he adds that this was done by direction of the Holy Spirit. And this, not because the Son of God, who is eternal Wisdom, required to be guided by any other, but because He was also man, that no one should think that what He delivered to the apostles came forth from a human spirit, he recalls us expressly to the authority of God. Just as the Lord Himself so often affirmed, that He taught nothing except what He received from the Father, and therefore declared that His teaching was not His own. He makes clear therefore that in the preaching of the Gospel there is nothing which derives from man, but it is a divine ordinance of the Spirit to which the whole world must be subject.

To whom he also shewed himself alive after his passion by many proofs, appearing unto them by the space of forty days, and speaking the things concerning the Kingdom of God: and, being assembled together with them, he charged them not to depart from Jerusalem, but to wait for the promise of the Father, which, said he, ye heard from me: for John indeed baptized with water; but ye shall be baptized with the Holy Ghost not many days hence. (3-5)

3. *To whom etc.* This he adds to establish faith in the resurrection as a matter most necessary to know, without which the whole Gospel falls to the ground and there is no faith left. Put briefly, the entire authority (*maiestas*) of the Gospel collapses unless we know that the living Christ speaks to us from the heavens. It is of this that Luke is most mindful. That the truth of this should be put beyond doubt, he declared that it was established by many tokens. What Erasmus, following an old commentator, calls 'arguments' I translate 'proofs'. For that is the name given by Aristotle, in the first book of his *Rhetoric*, to the necessary element in signs.

As I said before, Christ bore witness to His resurrection by many evident signs, which served instead of necessary proofs, so that His apostles might have no doubt on the matter. Again, he does not enumerate these signs and evidences except to say that He was seen by them on several occasions over a period of nearly a month and a half. A single appearance might have incurred a measure of suspicion, but in showing Himself to them so often, He left no room for doubt. By this means, too, He put an end to the reproach of ignorance, which He had attributed to the apostles, lest it should discredit their preaching.

He spoke the things concerning the Kingdom of God. He tells us again that the apostles were well taught by the one and only Master before they took upon them to teach the world. Therefore, whatever they set forth by speech or writing concerning the Kingdom of God were speeches uttered by Christ. Now in this word he sums up the aim of the teaching of the Gospel, namely that God should reign in us. The beginning of this Kingdom is regeneration, the end and fulfilment of it is blessed immortality. Progress between the two consists in a fuller advance and increase of regeneration. For greater clarity let us note, first, that we are born and live as strangers to the Kingdom of God until God refashions us into a new life. Therefore we may properly set the world, our flesh, and all that is in the nature of man in opposition to the Kingdom of God. For the natural man is wholly occupied about the things of this world; here he seeks his felicity and his final good. Meanwhile we are in exile from the Kingdom of God; and God is, as it were, banished from us: but Christ by the preaching of the Gospel lifts us up to meditation upon the life to come. To do this, He corrects and reforms in us our earthly affections, and so, having stripped from us the vices of our flesh, He separates us from the world. And just as eternal death awaits all who live according to the flesh, so, in so far as our inner man is renewed that we may go forward in the life of the Spirit, we draw nearer to the perfection of the Kingdom of God, which is participation in the glory of God. God therefore wills to reign in us now, that He may at length make us partakers of His Kingdom. From this we gather that Christ spoke chiefly about the corruption of mankind, about the tyranny of sin, whose bondslaves we are, of the curse and condemnation of eternal death to which we are all subject: and also of the means of regaining salvation, of the remission of sins, of the denying of the flesh, of spiritual righteousness, of the hope of eternal life, and other topics of that kind. And if we wish to be rightly instructed in the Christian religion, we must apply our study to these things.

4. *Gathering them together* (*congregans eos*), *he charged....* They had already done the work of apostles previously, but only for a short time, limited by their proclamation to awakening the Jews to hearing their Master. So that command to teach which Christ had earlier laid upon them while He lived with them on earth (Matt. 10.7) was a kind of preparation for the apostolate which was to come, but for which they were not yet ready.

Before the resurrection of Christ they therefore had no regular office (*ordinarium munus*) laid upon them, but they roused their own people, as I have said, like heralds, to give audience to Christ. At length, after the resurrection, they were created apostles who published abroad the doctrine committed to them throughout the whole world. As to the fact that, when they had been appointed, Christ still commanded them to hold back from fulfilling the office, this was not done without good reason. Indeed many reasons may be adduced why it should have been so. It was no long time since they had shamefully deserted their Master, and many signs of their unbelief were still fresh. By suddenly forgetting all the teaching they had so fully received, they had shown clear evidence of gross spiritual ignorance. They were guilty, too, of a slothfulness of spirit which could only be cured by postponing the promised grace with a view to whetting their desire for it. But we must observe that the principal reason was that the Lord appointed beforehand a certain time for the sending of the Spirit so that the miracle might be the more striking in our eyes.

Thereafter He left them idle for a time in order that He might better set forth the magnitude of the task which He was about to commit to them. The truth of the Gospel is confirmed to us thereby because the apostles were forbidden to set themselves to the preaching of it until time had passed and they had been duly prepared. Moreover they were bidden to stay together because they were all to have the one Spirit given to them. If they had scattered, their unity would not have been so clearly seen. Though they were scattered abroad afterwards in many places, yet because their message was what they had imbibed from the one fountainhead, it was almost as though they spoke with one mouth. Furthermore it was fitting that they should begin to preach the Gospel at Jerusalem that the prophecy might be fulfilled, 'there shall go a law out of Zion, and the word of the Lord out of Jerusalem' (Isa. 2.3). Although the participle *συναλιζόμενος* can be translated in different ways Erasmus' translation seems right, because the meaning 'gathering together' agrees best with the context.

To wait for the promise. It was right that those who would soon afterwards lay the yoke of Christ upon the world, should first be accustomed to obedience. Surely they have taught us by their example that work or rest from work should be at the Lord's pleasure alone. For if the whole warfare of our lives is waged under His banner and leadership, surely He ought not to have any less authority over us than any earthly commander has in his army. Therefore, since military discipline involves that no one moves unless ordered by his commander, it is not lawful for us either to set out or to attempt anything until the Lord gives the signal; and as soon as He sounds the retreat, we must halt. We are warned moreover that we are the partakers of the gifts of God through hope but we must observe the nature of hope, as it is here described. For hope is not that which a man invents presumptuously for himself, but only that which is grounded upon the promise of God. Therefore Christ does not allow the apostles to look for whatever is pleasing to themselves, but expressly adds 'the promise of the Father'. Moreover He makes Himself the witness of this, because we ought to have such assurance that, although all the instruments of Hell rise up against us, this should remain fixed in our hearts—'In God we have believed'. 'I know', says Paul, 'whom I have believed' (II Tim. 1.12). Here He puts them in mind of what is written in John chapter 14.16-17, 'I will pray the Father and He shall give you another comforter, that he may continue with you: I mean the Spirit of truth' etc.

Again, 'These things have I spoken unto you while I am with you; the Spirit whom the Father will send in my name, he will teach you all things,' etc. (John 14.25f). Again, 'When the Spirit of truth is come, whomI shall send you from my Father, he will bear witness of me' (John 15.26). Again, 'If I go away I shall send you a Comforter, who will reprove the world' (John 16.7f). And He had said long before, 'He that believeth on me, out of his belly shall flow rivers of living water' (John 7.38).

5. *Because John baptized with water.* Christ repeats this to His apostles from John the Baptist's own words. For some of them had heard from the mouth of John what the evangelist reports: 'I indeed baptize you with water but he that cometh after me shall baptize you with the Holy Ghost, and with fire.' Now Christ declares that they shall indeed perceive that the words of John are true. Furthermore, this is of great importance in confirming the preceding sentence; for the argument is drawn from the office of Christ (*ab officio Christi*). Namely, John was sent to baptize with water; he fulfilled his functions as became a servant of God. To the Son it is given to baptize with the Spirit; it remains therefore for Him to perform His duty. It must be that He should fulfil what the Father commanded Him, the work for which He came down to earth. But it seems absurd that what was spoken in general of the grace of regeneration should be confined to the sending of the Spirit visibly. My reply is that Christ did not baptize with the Holy Spirit only at the time when He sent Him under the form of tongues of fire. He had before this conferred this baptism on the apostles, and He baptizes all the elect thus daily. Because the sending of the Holy Spirit in so spectacular a manner was a symbol of the hidden grace wherewith the Lord continuously inspires His elect, it is appropriate that He should apply to it the testimony of John. Besides the fact that the apostles did not receive the Spirit for themselves alone but for the benefit of all the faithful, there was also mirrored forth the universal grace of Christ towards His Church, while He poured forth the gifts of His Spirit in full measure. Although therefore Christ daily baptizes the elect of his Father there is no reason why He should not set forth this evidence, memorable before all others, so that the apostles might know that from John they had received only the beginning—but not a vain beginning—for now the fulfilment of that baptism was at hand. The conclusion commonly arrived at from this and similar passages that there was a distinction between the baptism of John and that of Christ is frivolous. There is no dispute here about baptism, but simply a comparison between the person of John and the person of Christ. When John said that he baptized with water, he was not setting forth the nature of his own baptism but who he himself was, so that he should not take to himself what belonged to Christ. So also today ministers ought to speak of themselves only in such a way as to acknowledge Christ as the Giver of all which they set forth in baptism, and leave nothing to themselves

except only the outward administration. For when baptism is entitled the laver of regeneration (Titus 3.5) a washing from sin, participation in the death and burial of Christ, and ingrafting into His body (Titus 3.5, Rom. 6.4), there is no declaration thereby of what the man is doing who administers the external sign, but rather what Christ is doing, who alone makes the sign effectual. We must always make this distinction lest by adorning men we rob Christ. It may be asked however why He named John at this point rather than anyone else. First, it is clear enough that John professed himself the minister of the baptism of water and Christ the Author of the baptism of the Spirit. Secondly, because it was proper that John should decrease and Christ increase; and thirdly, because John was hitherto held in such esteem among the apostles that the glory of Christ might in some measure have been obscured. Therefore Christ, to recall them to His own person, tells them that John ministered to them only the external baptism, yet He assures them too lest they should doubt regarding the promise. For they held John in great respect and so they were persuaded that the baptism which they had received from his hands was not in vain. Now if one might expect that the efficacy and fruit of it could be looked for from Christ, then the apostles were surely right to hope for the fulfilment of what John had prefigured.

So ought we to consider that the baptism of water which we received from the hands of men was not in vain, because Christ who ordered that to be done will do His part to baptize us with the Spirit. So faith draws a true connexion from the external sign to the internal effect, yet without attributing either to the sign or to the minister more than is proper, but in the sign looking to the promise which is of Christ and recognizing Him as the only Author of grace. Let us therefore observe such a balance that the honour due to Christ is in no way diminished and yet let us hope for that fruit from our baptism which is here noted.

By saying that it will be 'before many days', He quickens their expectation. So it follows that there was no need to lament the death that so soon produced such precious fruit. And let us note this also, that the word 'baptism' is used in this place in other than its normal sense in order that the contrast between Christ and John may be complete. Similarly Paul, after setting down the law of works, that there may be a parallel on the other side uses 'the law of faith' instead of 'faith' (Rom. 3.27).

They, therefore, when they were come together, asked him, saying, Lord, dost thou at this time restore the Kingdom to Israel? And he said unto them, It is not for you to know times or seasons, which the Father hath set within his own authority. But ye shall receive power, when the Holy Ghost is come upon you: and ye shall be my witnesses both in Jerusalem and in all Judaea and Samaria, and unto the uttermost part of the earth. (6-8)

6. He points out that apostles were gathered together when this question was posed, to show us that it was not raised through the foolishness of one or two but through the concern of all. Yet their blindness is remarkable, that when they had been so fully and carefully instructed over a period of three years, they betrayed no less ignorance than if they had never heard a word. There are as many errors in this question as words. They ask Him concerning the Kingdom; but they dream of an earthly kingdom, dependent upon wealth, luxury, outward peace and blessings of this nature. And while they assign the present as the time for restoring this Kingdom, they desire to enjoy the triumph before fighting the battle. Before setting hands to the work for which they are ordained they desire their wages; they also are mistaken in this, that they confine to Israel after the flesh the Kingdom of Christ which is to be extended to the farthest parts of the world. The whole question is at fault in this, that they desire to know things which are not right for them to know. No doubt they were well aware of what the prophets had said about the restoration of the kingdom of David, for they had often heard Christ speaking of this, and it was a common saying that in the depths of the captivity of the people every man's spirit was revived by the hope of the Kingdom to come. They hoped that this restoration would take place at the coming of the Messiah, and so the apostles, when they saw Christ raised from the dead, at once turned their thoughts to this. But in so doing they betrayed what poor progress they had made under so good a Master. Therefore Christ in His short reply briefly reprimands their errors one by one, as I shall presently indicate. To 'restore' in this passage means to set up again that which was broken down and disfigured by many ruins. For out of the dry stock of Jesse should spring a branch, and the tabernacle of David which was miserably laid waste should rise again.

7. *It is not for you to know, etc.* This is a general rebuke of the whole question. For it was an intrusion for them to desire to know what their master desired to remain hidden. Yet this is the true means of gaining wisdom that we should be prepared to advance as far along the road of learning as our Master desires us to go in teaching us, and we should willingly remain ignorant of the matters which He keeps from us. But since we are almost all by nature given to a foolish and vain curiosity, to which presumption is quickly added, let us observe

cheerfully this admonition of Christ by which both faults are corrected. To grasp His meaning we must observe the two elements which He holds in conjunction: 'It is not for you', He says, 'to know the things which the Father has set within His own authority.' He is speaking about times and seasons; but since the same principle applies in other things we should accept this as a universal precept, that we are to be content with what God reveals and regard it as unlawful to inquire about what He does not reveal. This is the true mean between the two extremes. The Papists, to cover their gross ignorance, maintain that they do not embark upon the hidden mysteries of God—as though the whole of our religious faith rested upon anything else than the hidden mysteries of God. If we are to have nothing to do with the hidden mysteries of God we must take leave of Christ and His Gospel. In this matter, as I said, we must observe a mean. We must desire to learn as much as our heavenly Master will teach us: but let no one presume to grasp after what He wishes to keep hidden from us, so that we may be wise, but with sobriety. So whenever we are vexed with this foolish desire of knowing more than we ought, let us remember this saying of Christ, 'It is not for you to know.' For unless we are minded to burst in against His will and commandment this will be constraint enough to restrain our wayward inclinations. Now regarding the foreknowledge of times and seasons, Christ condemns only such probing as goes beyond the limit set by God's revelation. This is noted in the second section, as I called it: 'which the Father has set within His own authority'. Indeed God has in His own power (Gen. 1.14) winter and summer and the other seasons of the year, cold and heat, fair weather and foul. But because He has promised (Gen. 8.22) that the course of the seasons shall be unchanging, He is not said to have kept in His own power what He has revealed to men. Such matters as philosophers or farmers have come to understand by their art, by learning, by judgment, or by experience, God is not described as having kept to Himself, since He has in a sense put all that into their hands. We must hold the same view regarding the prophets. For it was their function to know the things which God reveals. But we are to remain in ignorance regarding the secret course of events, for time to come. There is nothing which holds us back more from our duty than excessive concern and curiosity in this field for we always want to make our decisions in the light of what the outcome will be. But the Lord keeps the outcome dark and instead prescribes for us the duties which we have to do. From this a tension develops, because we do not willingly allow God to have that which is His own, namely, the government and direction of future events, but we involve ourselves in a strange and distressing anxiety. In a word, Christ forbids us to arrogate to ourselves those matters which God claims as His own. Among these is the foreknowledge of those matters whose ordering God has taken to Himself, according to His own pleasure, far contrary to our own thoughts and beyond the understanding of our minds.

8. *Ye shall receive power.* As the best means of bridling their curiosity, Christ calls them back both to the promise of God and to His commandment. Curiosity arises usually from idleness or from distrust. Distrust is cured by meditating on the promises of God—His commandments tell us how we ought to occupy ourselves and employ our studies. Therefore He orders the disciples patiently to wait for the promise of God and to be diligent in executing the duty which God has commanded them. Meanwhile He rebukes their impatience in grasping too hastily for those things which are the special gift of the Holy Spirit, and with which they had not yet been endowed by Him. They had begun the wrong way when, being called to go on warfare, they desired to lie at ease and avoid the hardships. By saying 'Ye shall receive power' He advises them of their weakness, lest before the proper time they should pursue things which they are unable to attain. It can be read in either of two ways: 'You shall receive the power of the Spirit', or, 'When the Spirit comes upon you'. The latter, however, is more suitable because it expresses more fully their own inadequacy, until such time as the Spirit comes upon them.

'*Ye shall be my witnesses.*' By this one statement He corrects two errors. For He shows that they must fight before they can hope to triumph: and that the nature of Christ's Kingdom is other than they thought. Therefore He says 'Ye shall be my witnesses': in other words the farmer must work before he can reap the harvest. We are to gather from this that we must fix our attention at present on the way by which we are to attain the Kingdom of God instead of engaging in subtle speculation on the conditions of the life to come. There are many who inquire of the nature of their future blessings, when they come to be received into heaven: but they take no heed to the means by which they are to arrive there. But in the first instance they must renounce the world. They reason regarding the nature of the future life which they are to enjoy with Christ: Meantime they do not give thought to this—that we must be partakers of His death, that we may hereafter live with Him (II Tim. 2.11). Let every man therefore apply himself to the work which lies to his hand: let us all fight stoutly under the banner of Christ: let us go forward manfully and tirelessly along the path to which we have been called, and God will give the fruit in due time.

There follows another correction when He declares that they will be His witnesses. He meant by this to banish from the disciples' minds a false impression regarding the earthly kingdom: for that, as He points out in a few words, consists in the preaching of the Gospel. They have no cause therefore to dream of wealth, luxury, power in the world or any other earthly thing when they hear that Christ is reigning when He subdues the world to Himself by the preaching of the Gospel. It follows from this that His reign is spiritual and not after the pattern of the world. The apostles' assumption regarding a worldly kingdom (*de carnali regno*) proceeded from the error common to their whole nation. It was not surprising that they all laboured under this delusion. For when we apply to it the measure of our own understanding what can we conceive that is not gross and earthly? So it happens that like the beasts our senses attract us to what appeals to our flesh, and we grasp rather at what is at hand. So we see that the Chiliasts (i.e. those who believed that Christ would reign on earth for a thousand years) fell into a like error, and so took all the prophecies which describe the Kingdom of Christ figuratively on the pattern of earthly kingdoms, and applied them in the manner that would most profit the flesh, whereas it was God's purpose to raise their minds to higher things. As for ourselves, lest we be entangled in like errors, let us learn to apply our minds to hear the Gospel preached, which prepares a place in our hearts for the Kingdom of Christ.

In all Judaea. First He shows that it will not be the work of a day, when He appoints them to cover the whole world with the teaching of the Gospel. Furthermore He indirectly refutes the false opinion which they held of Israel. They thought that only those were Israelites who were of the seed of Abraham according to the flesh. Christ bears witness that they must reap in Samaria also, which, though close at hand, was far off in outlook. He shows that all the other regions which were far distant and separated from God must be gathered in to the people of God, to become partakers of the same grace. The magnitude of the gulf separating Jews and Samaritans is well known (John 4.9). Christ orders that, the wall of separation being broken down, they should make of both one body (Eph. 2.14), that His Kingdom should arise in every place. By naming Jerusalem and Judaea which the disciples had experienced to be full of deadly enemies, He advises them of the considerable trouble and hardship that await them, so that they may cease to think of speedy triumph. And it must cause them no little fear to set out in the midst of so many cruel enemies and rouse their rage. Now He assigns priority to the Jews, as being in a sense the firstborn (Exod. 4.22): yet He calls all the nations without distinction, which formerly had been strangers to the hope of salvation. Hereby we learn that the Gospel was preached in every place by the express command of Christ, that it might reach even to us (Eph. 2.7).

And when he had said these things, as they were looking, he was taken up; and a cloud received him out of their sight. And while they were looking stedfastly into heaven as he went, behold, two men stood by them in white apparel; which also said, Ye men of Galilee, why stand ye looking into heaven? This Jesus, which was received up from you into heaven, shall so come in like manner as ye beheld him going into heaven. (9–11)

9. The reader may learn from the *Institutes* of the benefit that has come to us by the ascension of Christ. Yet because it is one of the chief articles of our faith Luke gives particular care to proving it. Indeed the Lord Himself wished to put it beyond all doubt by ascending so openly to heaven and by other circumstances establishing the certainty of it.

For if He had vanished secretly the disciples might indeed have stood rigid in astonishment, but now, standing as they are on an elevated spot with an unhindered view on all sides, they see the One whom they know so well, and to whom they have even now been listening, being raised on high, and, while their eyes follow Him, being carried away in a cloud, there is no room for them to doubt of His Ascension to heaven. The angels also are there to bear witness. It was necessary for our sakes that the narrative should be set down so meticulously, so that we should know that the Son of God, though nowhere visible in the world, yet lives in heaven. This seems to be the reason why the cloud concealed Him before He entered into His celestial glory, so that the disciples, content with what they had seen, might not inquire further. From them we learn that our minds are of too limited capacity to rise to the full measure of the glory of Christ. Therefore let this cloud be the means of restraining our presumption as was the smoke which was continually before the door of the tabernacle in the days of the Law.

10. *Two men.* He calls the angels this because they appear in the form of men, for, although it could be that they had in fact the bodies of men, regarding which I would not take issue on one side or the other, yet it is certain that they were not men; yet because this metonymy occurs frequently in Scripture, especially in the first book of Moses, I shall not delay further on it. Their white garments were an indication of special distinction and authority, for God meant thereby to distinguish them from ordinary men, that the disciples might be more attentive to what they said, and that we in our day might know that this vision was given them by God.

11. *Men of Galilee.* I do not share the view of those who think that this name was given to the apostles in a slighting manner, as if the angels were rebuking their sloth and dullness. In my opinion it was to make them more attentive to those whom they had never seen before and who yet addressed them as if they knew them well. Yet they seemed to be receiving an undeserved rebuke for looking up into heaven. For where else should they seek for Christ? Do the Scriptures not repeatedly exhort us to this? The answer is that they were not rebuked because they looked up towards heaven; but because they desired to behold Christ, when a cloud had been interposed to prevent them from seeing Him with their bodily senses. And again, because they hoped that He would return soon that they might enjoy the sight of Him again, whereas He ascended to heaven to remain there until such time as He should come a second time to judge the world. Let us therefore learn from this passage that Christ is not to be sought either in heaven or upon earth other than by faith; and also that we must not desire to have Him present with us bodily in the world. For the man who clings to either of these ambitions often moves further away from Him. So their astonishment is made a ground of censure, not for its own sake but in so far as they were overwhelmed by the strangeness of the event: just as we are often carried away in wonder at the magnitude of the works of God, but we fail to apply ourselves to considering for what purpose they were done.

Jesus which was received up. There are two parts of this sentence. The first is that Jesus was received up into heaven that they should not foolishly yearn to bring Him back to earth. The other is at once added by way of consolation regarding His second coming. From the conjunction of these two and from each separately, there comes a sound argument for refuting the Papists and all others who imagine that Christ is corporeally present under the symbol of bread and wine. For when Christ is said to be taken up to heaven, spatial distance is clearly indicated. I grant that the word 'heaven' is taken in various ways: sometimes for the air, sometimes for the whole system of the spheres, sometimes for the glorious Kingdom of God where the majesty of God has His proper abode, however much He fills the world. Wherefore Paul places Christ above all heavens (Eph. 1.21) because He is above the whole world and holds the highest station in that habitation of blessed immortality: 'For He is more excellent than all the angels, over whom He is Head.' But this is no reason why He may not be absent from us, and that by this word 'heaven' there may not be meant a separation from the world. However much they may protest, it is evident that 'heaven' into which Christ was received is set over against the fabric of the world. His being in heaven therefore means that He is outwith the world.

But first, we must examine what the purpose of the angels was. For then we shall judge more perfectly what the words mean. The angels wish to recall the disciples from desiring the bodily presence of Christ. It was for this purpose that they said He would not come again until He came to judge the world. This is the object of appointing the time that they should not look for Him in vain too soon. Who can fail to see that these words indicate that He is corporeally absent from the world? Who can fail to see that we are forbidden to desire to have Him upon the earth? They think to avoid this by a cunning quibble when they say that in that day He will come visibly but that now He comes every day invisibly. But the point at issue here is not the form of His presence: the apostles are simply taught that Christ must remain in heaven until He appears at the Last Day. The desire for His corporeal presence is condemned as absurd and perverse. The Papists claim that while He is not present in bodily form in the sacrament the body of His glory is present supernaturally and by a miracle: but we must reject as frivolous and childish their inventions concerning the body of His glory. They invent for themselves a miracle, having no scriptural warrant. The body of Christ was already glorious when after His resurrection He talked with His disciples. This took place through the extraordinary and secret power of God. Yet notwithstanding, the angels forbid us to desire Him again after that manner and say that He will not so come to men, until the last day. Let us therefore keep their commandment, and not seek to draw Him down from heaven by our own inventions, and let us not think that He will be accessible to our hands or to our other senses more than He is to our eyes. I speak always of His body. Their claim that it is infinite is an absurd dream, and may be safely rejected. Nevertheless I willingly confess that Christ is ascended that He may fill all things: but I say that He is spread abroad everywhere in the power of His Spirit, not in the substance (*essentia*) of His flesh. I grant moreover that He is present with us both in the Word and in the Sacraments. Nor is it to be doubted that all are truly made partakers of His flesh and blood, who by faith receive the symbols of His flesh and blood. But this partaking (*communicatio*) has nothing in common with the ravings of the Papists, for they produce Christ upon the altar in such manner as Numa Pompilius called down his Jupiter Elicius or as witches bring down the moon from heaven with their incantations. But Christ in extending to us the bread in His Supper invites us to heaven that by faith we may receive life through His flesh and blood. This does not take place in such manner that His flesh is transferred into us that we may live thereby, but He transmits (*transfundit*) His strength (*vim*) to us by the secret power of His Spirit.

Shall so come. As I said, all sorrow at the absence of Christ is assuaged, indeed wholly removed, when we know that He will come again. The object of His coming is to be marked at once: that He will come as a Redeemer, and will gather us with Himself to blessed immortality. He does not now sit idle in heaven (as the gods of Homer are depicted, concerned only with their delights); so too He will not appear again without profit. So the single-minded awaiting of the coming of Christ must both restrain the importunate desires of our flesh and support our patience in all adversity, and also refresh our weariness. It has this effect only among the faithful, who believe that Christ is their Redeemer; for to the wicked it brings nothing but fear and dread. And though they now mock when they hear of His coming, yet they will be compelled to behold Him sitting upon His judgment seat, whom now they will not deign to hear speak. Furthermore it is frivolous to inquire about what clothes we believe Him to have worn then, and whether He will be clothed in the same way when He comes again. As for what Augustine mentions in his Epistle to Consentius (*Epist.* 146), I do not intend to make a refutation: what I have no clear solution for, is best left alone.

Then returned they unto Jerusalem from the mount called Olivet, which is nigh unto Jerusalem, a sabbath day's journey off. And when they were come in, they went up into the upper chamber, where they were abiding; both Peter and John and James and Andrew, Philip and Thomas, Bartholomew and Matthew, James the son of Alphaeus, and Simon the Zealot, and Judas the son of James. These all with one accord continued stedfastly in prayer with the women and Mary the mother of Jesus, and with his brethren. (12-14)

12. Passing on to another incident, He shows that the disciples when they returned to Jerusalem lived together in one room. It was the upper part of a house which was let out to tenants; the more commodious part was retained by the owners. By using this expression Luke shows that they were confined in constricted quarters. The inconvenience of this however had not split the company. They might have lived in greater comfort apart, but they could not part company before they had received the Spirit. The mention of the distance adds credibility to the narrative—unless perhaps he wishes to indicate by this that they were not alarmed by the fear of danger from returning and living together in one house, even though the house not being large and the space insufficient for the number of disciples some considerable noise might arise. *A sabbath day's journey*

was two miles. This estimate agrees with the passage in John 11.18, where he says that Jerusalem was distant from Bethany almost fifteen furlongs, which consists of about one thousand nine hundred paces. Mount Olivet was situated beside Bethany. There was no Sabbath day's journey prescribed in the Law, for in the Law the Lord simply bids them rest on the Sabbath day (Jer. 17.24). But because the Jews could not easily be restrained from hasting about on the Sabbath day on their own business (as we find the Lord Himself complaining that they bore burdens out at the gates (Jer. 17.24)), it is therefore to be assumed that it was determined by the common council of the priests, with a view to curbing this indiscipline, that no one should travel more than two miles on the Sabbath. Although Jerome in his *Reply to Algasia* says that this discipline derives from two Rabbis, Attriba and Simon Heli.

13. *Where they abode.* Some have translated 'where they were abiding', as though they were accustomed to dwell there, but I am of opinion that they began at that time to use that hired room, until such time as the Holy Spirit should come upon them. The Papists go beyond themselves in absurdity in deducing the primacy of Peter, because he is the first of the apostles to be named there. Although we admit that he was first among the twelve it does not follow that he was made ruler of the whole world, but if he is chief of the apostles on the ground that his name comes first in the list, I will similarly infer that the mother of Christ was inferior to the other women because her name is here left to the last; which they will never admit, as too obviously absurd. Wherefore unless they wish to expose their papacy to the mockery of all men they must cease from embellishing it with such puerilities. But what is their object? They want to prove from the Scriptures that there is another head of the Church second to Christ. There is not a single syllable in the Scriptures to support their theory. It is not surprising therefore if they eagerly seize hold of certain passages here and there which however they will drop of their own accord, even if no one dashes them from their hands. Let us turn from this to mark what Luke's intention is. Because the disciples had fallen away and basely deserted Christ, everyone where his fear drove him, they deserved to be treated like deserters and runaways and to lose their status. Therefore that we may know that by the will of the Lord they were gathered together again and restored to their former position, Luke records all their names.

14. *With their wives.* Some translated 'the women', and think he means those who accompanied Christ. I have no desire to dispute with anyone, but I do not hesitate to choose what I regard as the more probable. I admit that the word which Luke uses can be taken in

either sense but the reason why I think he speaks of wives is that since Paul bears witness that they were later accustomed to take their wives around with them (I Cor. 9.5), it is hardly likely that they were at that time separate from them. For it is much easier to stay still in one place than to be constantly on the move and changing one's abode. Again, when they were looking for the speedy coming of the Spirit, why should they deny their wives a share in so great a blessing? Peter's wife was to be a helper to him shortly afterwards. We must assume the same of the others. These women needed heroic fortitude and steadfastness if they were not to fall short. Who could believe then that they were separated from their husbands during the time when they awaited the power of the Spirit? But if one keeps the general term, 'the women', it is reasonable to suppose that those who were married were included in the company. Howbeit Luke wishes in passing to point out to us how greatly their outlook had changed for the better. For whereas before the men had fled in terror and panic, now the very women are gathered together with them, fearing no danger. He includes the mother of Christ with the other women, though John is said to have kept her at his own home. But as I said before, they had come together now only for a short time. There is no doubt that afterwards they went their own ways. As for the word 'brethren', it is well known that by the Hebrews all kinsfolk are covered by the term.

All these continued. Here he shows that they were waiting with expectancy for the Spirit. This was the purpose of their prayer, that Christ would send His Spirit, as He had promised. We gather from this that the only true faith is that which stirs us up to call on God. The assurance of faith is quite a different thing from carelessness. The Lord surely does not convince us of His grace that our minds may become indifferent, but rather to stimulate our desire to pray. Moreover faith is not a sign of doubt but rather a testimony to our confidence, because we ask the Lord to grant to our prayers the things which we know He has promised. So it is right that, after their example, we should be instant in prayer, that we may gain daily increase of the Spirit. Increase, I say, because before we can conceive any prayer we must receive the first fruits of the Spirit. For He is the only Master who can truly teach us to pray aright and who not only teaches us the words to say, but also governs our inward affections (Rom. 8.26).

Furthermore Luke expresses two essentials for true prayer, namely, that they persevered, and were of one mind. This was an exercise of their patience in that Christ kept them in suspense for a time when He could have sent the Spirit at once. So God often delays and seems to let us languish, to teach us the habit of perseverance. The impatience of our prayers is a harmful, even a baneful, disease; so it is no surprise if God corrects it. Meanwhile as I say, He trains us to be constant in prayer. Therefore if we wish not to pray in vain let us not be wearied by delay. As for the concord of their minds, it stands in contrast to the scattering which fear had caused before. Yet it may readily be gathered even from this how necessary it is to pray generally, as Christ commanded everyone to pray for the whole body, and in common, as if each prayed in the character of all: Our Father, give us this day, etc. Whence does this unity of tongues come, but from one Spirit? Wherefore when Paul in Romans 15.6 wishes to give the Jews and the Gentiles a right form of prayer He banishes all division: 'that we may', he says, 'being all of one mind, with one mouth glorify God'. And truly we must all be brethren and agree together as brethren if we are to call God Father.

And in these days Peter stood up in the midst of the brethren, and said (and there was a multitude of persons gathered together, about a hundred and twenty), Brethren, it was needful that the scripture should be fulfilled, which the Holy Ghost spake before by the mouth of David concerning Judas, who was guide to them that took Jesus. For he was numbered among us, and received his portion in this ministry. (Now this man obtained a field with the reward of his iniquity; and falling headlong, he burst asunder in the midst, and all his bowels gushed out. And it became known to all the dwellers at Jerusalem; insomuch that in their language that field was called Akeldama, that is, The field of blood.) For it is written in the book of Psalms, Let his habitation be made desolate, and let no man dwell therein: and, His office let another take. Of the men therefore which have companied with us all the time that the Lord Jesus went in and went out among us, beginning from the baptism of John, unto the day that he was received up from us, of these must one become a witness with us of his resurrection. (15-22)

It was right that Matthias should be chosen in the place of Judas, that the treachery of one man might not seem to have shattered or destroyed the institution once appointed by Christ. Not without due care did He at the beginning choose twelve to be the premier heralds of His Gospel. For when He stated that they would be judges of the twelve tribes of Israel, He showed that this had been done expressly that they might gather into one faith the tribes of Israel dispersed through the whole world. But after the Jews refused the grace offered to them, it was right that there should be gathered out of every nation of the world the Israel of God. Therefore this was, as it were, a sacred number; had it been diminished through the wickedness of Judas, the preaching of the Gospel would have then possessed, and would today possess, less authority, as being defective in its origins. Thus although Judas had, so far as in him lay, assailed the institution of Christ, it yet stood firm and intact. The traitor perished, as he deserved; but the order of the Apostles continued unbroken.

The company of names (*turba nominum*). It is uncertain whether by this expression he means men, to whom the term strictly applies, since women are taken as included under their husbands' names, or whether he takes names to mean individuals, as the Hebrews use the word 'souls'. It is also doubtful whether they were accustomed to attend daily at the room where the apostles lived or whether they lived there continuously with them. For the place would hardly have been big enough to furnish the necessities of life for such a number. To me at least it is more likely that Luke states the number at this point to let us know that they were all present together at the time when Peter made his address; from which we may conjecture that they were not always present. Though I affirm nothing with certainty, I rather incline to the probable assumption that the whole Church was called together when they had an important matter to deal with. The words 'standing up' point in the same direction.

16. *It was needful that the Scripture should be fulfilled.* Because Peter addresses the company, the Papists count him head of the universal Church; as if no one could speak in the assembly of the faithful without forthwith being made Pope. We admit indeed that in every gathering someone must have first place; so in this case the apostles gave the honour to Peter. But what reference has this to the Papacy? So let us pass from this and consider what the Spirit speaks by the mouth of Peter. He begins by saying that the Scripture had to be fulfilled, lest anyone's mind should be troubled by the dreadful fall of Judas. For it seemed wholly inconsistent that one who had been chosen by Christ for so exalted a position should have fallen so grievously at the outset of his course. Peter clears away this stone of stumbling by declaring that it had been foretold in Scripture. From this we may adduce a warning of great relevance for daily life, namely, that we should ascribe this distinction to the prophecies of Scripture, that they are able to quell apprehensions that suddenly arise. For nothing disturbs us more than when we rest upon our own understanding and thereby create for ourselves petty causes of offence, which God would readily deal with if we had the conviction that nothing is irrational which He has foreseen, and ordained, and indeed foretold, with a view to strengthening us. Yet Judas may not be excused on the ground that what befell him was prophesied, since he fell away not through the compulsion of the prophecy but through the wickedness of his own heart.

Peter's sermon is in two parts. Firstly, he disposes of the difficulty which devout minds might have found in the fall of Judas; whence also he derives an exhortation that the rest may learn to fear God. Secondly, it remains for them to choose another in Judas' place. He establishes both by the witness of Scripture.

Which the Holy Ghost foretold. Such expressions of speech procure a greater reverence for Scripture, when we learn that David and all the prophets spoke solely under the direction of the Spirit, so that they themselves were not the source of the prophecies but rather the Spirit who used their tongues as an instrument. Since therefore our dullness is such that we ascribe far less authority to Scripture than we ought, we should take careful note of expressions of this kind and make ourselves familiar with them, that our faith may be confirmed by constantly remembering the authority of God.

17. *Adopted.* Literally, numbered. He says that he had been one of their number, to indicate that the empty place should be filled to keep the number intact. This bears upon what follows, that he had obtained a part in the ministry. For it follows from this, that the body would be, as it were, maimed, if that part of it were lacking. It was staggering that a man whom Christ had elevated to such distinction should have fallen headlong to such destruction. This circumstance aggravates the atrociousness of the crime and warns the others to beware and to fear. We cannot doubt that the disciples remembered Judas with great grief and bitterness: but Peter refers expressly to the excellence of his office, that they may be the more attentive and concerned to seek the remedy.

18. *Now this man.* I think it probable that this account of the death of Judas was inserted by Luke, and I therefore set it within a parenthesis to distinguish it from the address of Peter. For what object was there in recounting what the disciples well knew? Further it would have been absurd to declare before them that the field bought with the proceeds of the betrayal was called by the Jews in their own tongue, Aceldama. It is trifling to reply, as some do, that Peter was saying this to the Galileans, who had a different language from the Jews. In pronunciation indeed they differed somewhat, but not so that they did not readily understand one another—just as the inhabitants of Paris do those of Rouen. Besides, how could the word Jerusalem be suitably used, when Peter was delivering his sermon in that place? Why should he interpret in Greek among Jews a word of their own mother-tongue? Therefore Luke himself inserts this sentence, in case readers ignorant of the events should find Peter's words obscure.

He possessed a field. This word can signify two things. But here, to my mind, it means 'possess' rather than 'acquire'. But I leave it open, since it is of little consequence which sense is adopted. Luke uses this expression, not because Judas either had use of the field, or bought it himself (for it was bought after his death), but meaning that his burial, branded with eternal shame, was his reward for his falsehood and wickedness. For he did not so much sell Christ as his own apostleship for the thirty pieces. He did not obtain the money; he only possessed the field. Moreover it came to pass through the wonderful providence of God that the common name of the field marked with open infamy the priests who had bought the innocent blood from the traitor. He says that the Hebrews called it this in their tongue, because he was a Greek by race. And he names as the Hebrew tongue that which the Jews employed after the exile in Babylon, a mixture, namely, of Syrian and Chaldean.

20. *It is written in the Book of Psalms.* He removes by the authority of Scripture any offence which might have been created by the falling away of Judas. It might indeed appear as if the meaning of this passage had been distorted, in that, firstly, David prayed that this might befall, not one man in particular, but his enemies in the plural, and, secondly, that Peter seems to be falsely applying to Judas words spoken about the enemies of David. My reply is that David speaks at that point about himself, that he may describe the condition of Christ's Kingdom. In this Psalm, I say, is contained the general image of the whole Church, which is the Body of the Son of God. Therefore the matters set down there had to be fulfilled in the Head—and were so fulfilled, as the Evangelists testify. Now to the objection that the words spoken against the enemies of David are not appropriate to Judas, the reply is that they are the more appropriate because David does not in that passage regard himself as a solitary figure, cut off from the Body of Christ; but rather, as a member of the Body of Christ and moreover bearing His image, he stands forth in the name of Christ. Whoever understands that this character (*singularem personam*; Fr. *cette condition*) was laid upon David to be a figure of Christ will not be surprised that all that was prefigured in David should be applied to Him. So although he comprehends the whole Church, he begins at the Head, and describes in particular what Christ is to suffer at the hands of wicked men. For we know from the teaching of Paul that whatever evils the godly suffer are parts of the afflictions of Christ, and are intended for the fulfilling of them. This order or connexion was observed by David, or rather by the Holy Spirit, who wished by the mouth of David to teach the whole Church. Now whatever is said regarding the persecutors of Christ in general is rightly applied to their standardbearer, that, as he stands out in impiety and wickedness, so his punishment should be known and marked. To the further objec-

tion that the Psalms offer cursings and not prophecies, and that therefore Peter was in error in concluding that they were bound to be fulfilled, the answer is simple. For David was not moved by any corrupt or vicious disposition of the flesh towards seeking vengeance; but he had the Holy Spirit as his Guide and Director. Therefore whatever he prayed for, under the inspiration of the Spirit, has the force of prophecy, because the Spirit requires no more than what God has determined in Himself to perform and wishes to promise to us. In that Peter cites two different testimonies from the Psalms, the first is to the end that Judas, together with his name and family, should be destroyed (Ps. 69.26) and his place be empty, and the second, which he takes from Psalm 109.8, that another should be chosen to take his place. There may appear to be a contradiction—a waste habitation, and succession. Yet the fact that the Spirit says in the former passage only that the adversaries of the Church are to be removed and their place left empty and without inhabitant does not preclude a later successor taking the empty place. Indeed this increases the gravity of the punishment, that the office which was taken from the man who was unworthy is given to another.

And his bishopric. The Hebrew word could not be translated more fitly. פְּקֻדָּה has the meaning of administration, so called from the idea of overseeing. Those who interpret the word as 'wife' are refuted by the context. The reference to his wife follows in the next verse, that she should be made a widow. So after wishing that the wicked man may be deprived of his life, he adds that he should be robbed of his honour; not only so, but that another should succeed, thereby doubling the punishment, as I said before. And in the passing he notes indirectly that the treacherous and evil man of whom he speaks should not be one of the common herd, but one endowed with a position, from which nevertheless he is to fall. From this passage we are to learn that the wicked who persecute the Church of God will not escape scot-free. This wretched end awaits them all.

21. *We must therefore.* What he now brings in seems at first sight to be far-fetched. For if David spoke of transferring the bishopric of Judas, it does not at once follow that a successor should be elected by the disciples. Yet because they knew that they had the charge laid upon them of ordering the Church, as soon as Peter has shown them that it was God's will that this should be done, he rightly infers that it is they who ought to execute the matter. For since God is pleased to use our agency for maintaining the government of the Church, as soon as we are assured of His will, we must not delay but diligently perform whatever our ministry demands. That was, beyond all controversy, the duty of the Church; just as, when we hear today

that those whose behaviour is improper and wicked are to be put out of office and replaced by others, the Church must take this work in hand. So it was unnecessary to raise any question about a matter on which there was no doubt.

Therefore let us always be mindful to consider what our duty is, that we may be ready to obey the Lord. Then when he speaks of making an Apostle, he says he must be a witness of the resurrection: which shows that there is no apostleship without preaching of the Gospel. This makes it evident how vain the popish bishops are, who wear only dumb masks and yet boast that they are the successors of the Apostles. I grant that Peter here requires an eye-witness of the kind that St John confesses himself to be when he says, 'He which saw it beareth witness' (John 19.35). For this is of great weight in strengthening faith. Yet Peter, in appointing himself and his colleagues preachers (*praecones*) of the resurrection, puts them under the stringent obligation to teach. He names the resurrection, not because they are to bear witness to that alone, but because, firstly, in that is comprehended the preaching of the death of Christ, and secondly, we have in that the end and completion of our redemption; also it carries with it the heavenly authority of Christ and the power of the Spirit in protecting His own, in establishing justice and equity, in restoring order, in abolishing the tyranny of sin, and in putting to flight all the enemies of the Church. Let us understand therefore that there is no question of matters which essentially belong together being excluded. Yet let us observe that the resurrection is mentioned in place of the rest, as being the chief point (*primarium caput*) of the Gospel—as Paul also declares (I Cor. 15.17). But were the Apostles alone witnesses to the resurrection? Was not this common also to the rest of the disciples? For it seems as if Peter attributes this position to the Apostles alone. I reply that this title is given to them because they were chosen particularly for this purpose and held first place among those charged with this mission. Though the chief witnesses, they were not the only ones.

All the time. He begins at the time when Jesus began to show Himself to the world. This, as I said earlier, is to be carefully noted. For He lived quietly and privately till nearly His thirtieth year. For He would not make Himself known further than was necessary for our salvation. Therefore when the time came for Him to begin the work for which the Father had appointed Him, He came forth like a new man, lately born. No one can fail to observe the force of this for curbing our curiosity. The whole life of Christ might have been an admirable mirror of more than absolute perfection; and yet to keep our study and meditation upon those things which are most essential for us to know, He chose to lead the greater part of His life buried in obscurity. Who now would dare to wander forth without Christ, when He has accommodated the knowledge of His own person to the building up of our faith? 'To go in and out' is used by the Hebrews to mean living among men and engaging in the normal events of life. In this sense citizens are said to go in and out by the gates of the city; so John 10.9—'If any man enter in by Me, he shall go in and out, and shall find pasture.' Although in II Chron. 1.10, it seems to be a mark of rule and government.

And they put forward two, Joseph, called Barsabbas, who was surnamed Justus, and Matthias. And they prayed, and said, Thou, Lord, which knowest the hearts of all men, shew of these two the one whom thou hast chosen, to take the place in this ministry and apostleship, from which Judas fell away, that he might go to his own place. And they gave lots for them; and the lot fell upon Matthias; and he was numbered with the eleven apostles. (23-26)

23. Only one was to be chosen in the place of Judas; they put forward two. It may be asked why they were not content with one. Was it because they were so like that they could not discern which was the more fit? This would surely not have been adequate reason for them to allow the matter to be decided by lot. And it seems also that Joseph was held in greater estimation. Or was it that there was a difference of opinion? This is highly unlikely, and is rendered untenable by the striking testimony that Luke gave a short time before to their unanimity. Finally it is not to be thought that they should mar the election of the apostle with such dissension. But the lot was introduced rather for this reason, that it might be known and witnessed to that Matthias was not to much chosen by the votes of men as appointed by the judgment of God. For there was this difference between the apostles and pastors, that whereas the pastors were chosen simply by the Church, the apostles must be called by God. Thus Paul in the preface to his epistle to the Galatians declares himself to be an apostle 'neither of men nor made by man'. Therefore as the distinction of this office was so great, it was fitting that in the election of Matthias, however well men had done their duty, the final decision should be left to God. Christ had appointed the others with His own voice; if Matthias had been adopted into their ranks by the choice of men alone, his authority would have been less than theirs. A middle course was adopted, whereby the disciples offered to God those whom they thought to be the best and He should choose to Himself the one whom He knew to be most fit. Thus God, by the outcome of the

lot declared that He approved the apostleship of Matthias. Now the disciples might seem to have acted rashly and irregularly in entrusting so important a matter to chance. For what certainty could they gain thereby? I reply that they had recourse to the lot only under the inspiration of the Holy Spirit. For although Luke does not say it was so, yet since he has no desire to accuse the disciples of rashness but rather makes it plain that the election was lawful and approved by God, I therefore affirm that they took this step under the guidance of the Holy Spirit; even as beyond doubt their whole course of action was dictated by the same Spirit. But why do they not pray that God should choose whom He would out of the whole multitude? Is not this to rob God of His freedom, when they limit Him to their choices and in a sense make Him subject to them? But anyone who will take time to consider the matter will clearly recognize from the sense of Luke that the disciples would have dared to do nothing, which they did not know to be their duty and to have been commanded them by God. As for those who raise difficulties, we shall let them go their own way.

24. *In praying they said.* Literally, 'Having prayed, they said'. But there is no obscurity in the sense, for he simply wished to say that they prayed in the terms that follow. He does not repeat all the words of the prayer, but is content briefly to give the essence of it. So although they were both honourable men, pre-eminent in holiness and all the virtues, yet because the most important of all qualities is integrity of heart, which God alone can know and judge, the disciples pray that God will bring to light that which is hidden from men. This same course is required today when choice of a pastor is being made. For though we are not to appoint two men for the one position, yet because we are so often liable to be deceived, and because the discerning of spirits comes from God, we must always ask God to show us whom He wishes to have as ministers that He may control our plans. Here we may also learn the importance that must be given to integrity in the choice of pastors. For, without that, learning and eloquence and every other distinction are insubstantial as smoke.

25. *Ministry and apostleship.* Because the word 'ministry' carries no honour with it, he adds 'apostleship' which carries greater dignity, though the sense will be clearer if you interpret it as 'the ministry of the apostleship'. There are frequent instances of *hypallage* in the Scriptures. Luke assuredly intended that to the task there should be linked the dignity of the office (*praestantiam muneris*), so that the reverence and authority accorded to it might be the greater. And yet he sought to give warning also that the apostles were called to a heavy duty.

26. *They gave their lots.* We must not at this point engage in a long discussion about lots. Those who think it wrong to cast lots at all fall into error partly through ignorance, partly because they do not understand what is signified by the word 'lot'. There is nothing which men do not corrupt through their vanity and presumption, and so it has come to pass that lots have been overtaken by abuse and superstition. For divination by lot is altogether devilish. But when governors divide provinces among themselves, and brothers their inheritance, it is then lawful. Solomon is a clear witness to this, when he places God in control of the outcome. 'The lots (he says) are cast into the bosom, and the judgment of them cometh forth from the Lord' (Prov. 16.33). This ordinance is no more depraved by corrupt usage than genuine astrology is by the vain and counterfeit devices of the Chaldeans. The Chaldeans use the name of astrology as a cloak for their wicked curiosity and thereby bring into disrepute a science that is both useful and praiseworthy. The so-called fortunetellers are guilty of the same; but it is our business to distinguish between the lawful use and the corrupt. He says the lots were given, so that they might be put into an urn or one of their laps and then drawn out. It is to be noted that the word 'lot' is differently understood at this point. For when it is said earlier that Judas obtained part in the ministry, the meaning was (according to the normal usage in Scripture) that a portion was allotted to him by God. Later reference is made to the lot in the strict and literal sense. It is however probable that, since the word גּוֹרָל is commonly used in both connexions in Hebrew, Peter intended to refer to what they were about to do and Luke regarded it in the same way.

The lot fell upon Matthias. It turned out as no one expected, for we may gather from what went before that he was less thought of than the other. For apart from the fact that Luke gave the first place to the other man the latter was also distinguished by two surnames, a mark of the high estimation in which he was held. He was called Barsabbas, i.e. the son of an oath, or, of quiet, and so called from the quality itself as though he were a kind of mirror either of faithfulness and blamelessness, or of a gentle and humble nature. The other surname is a mark of singular honesty. This man therefore in the judgment of men was the superior; but God preferred Matthias to him. This teaches us not to boast if we are exalted to the heavens in the opinion of men, and by their choice are reckoned outstanding men; we must rather have regard to being approved of by God, who alone is the lawful Judge, by whose judgment we stand or fall. This also may often be observed that God passes over the man who is of highest distinction in the sight of men, that he may cast down all pride in the flesh. By adding 'he was reckoned among the rest', he cleanses the lot-taking from every questionable mark of presumption, because the Church embraced him, as chosen by God, upon whom the lot had fallen.

CHAPTER TWO

And when the day of Pentecost was now come, they were all together in one place. And suddenly there came from heaven a sound as of the rushing of a mighty wind, and it filled all the house where they were sitting. And there appeared unto them tongues parting asunder, like as of fire; and it sat upon each one of them. And they were all filled with the Holy Spirit, and began to speak with other tongues, as the Spirit gave them utterance. (1-4)

1. *And when the day of Pentecost was now come* ('fulfilled', *compleritur*). 'To be fulfilled' is used for 'to arrive'. For Luke a second time bears witness to their constancy, when he says that they all stood in the same place until the time appointed for them. This is the significance of the adverb 'together'. Furthermore, we have touched above on the reason why the Lord delayed the coming of the Spirit for a whole month and a half. The question is why He sent Him particularly upon that day. I do not wish to contradict the interpretation of Augustine that, as the Law was given to the people of old fifty days after Passover (*Pascha*), written by the hand of God on tables of stone, so the Spirit, whose work is to write that Law in our hearts, the same number of days after the resurrection of Christ, who is the true Passover, fulfilled what had been prefigured in the giving of the Law (I Cor. 5.7). But inasmuch as He insists upon this subtle interpretation as though it were fundamental, in the *Quaest. in Exodun* and in the *Epistola II ad Januarium*, I could wish for him a greater sobriety and modesty. Nonetheless let him find satisfaction in his own interpretation, while I shall adopt one that is sounder, namely, that it was upon a feast-day, when a great multitude always gathered at Jerusalem, that the miracle was performed, that the fame of it might be the greater. And certainly by this cause it was spread abroad even to the furthest bounds of the earth, as we shall see presently. With the same purpose Christ often went up to Jerusalem on feast-days (John, chapters 2, 5, 7, 10, 12), so that the mighty works (*virtutes*: Fr. *vertus & miracles*) which he wrought might be the more widely known, and that in the greater gathering of people there might be greater fruit for His teaching. Similarly Luke later reports that Paul hastened with a view to reaching Jerusalem before the day of Pentecost: not on religious grounds but because of the greater profit to be gained from larger numbers (Acts 20.16). Therefore in the choice of the day God

had regard to the usefulness of the miracle; that the news of it might, in the first place, be more widely talked of in Jerusalem at a season when the Jews were more inclined to give thought to the works of God, and secondly, be spread abroad to the remotest lands. It was called the fiftieth day, the reckoning being made from the feast of the firstfruits.

2. *And there came*. The gift had to be visible in order to stir up the disciples through the bodily senses. For such is our dullness in appreciating the gifts of God that unless He first aroused all our senses His power would pass us by and vanish unrecognized. This therefore was to prepare them and to help them to understand that the Spirit promised by Christ was come. Yet it was not so much for their benefit as for ours, even as the appearance of the cloven and fiery tongues had its meaning rather for us and for the universal Church than for them. For God was able to have furnished them with the power necessary for preaching the Gospel without the addition of any sign. They themselves might have known that it was not by accident nor by their own efforts that they were so suddenly changed; but these signs which are here recorded were destined to be profitable to all ages —as we today know they are to us. Now we must briefly observe the analogy (*analogiam*) of the signs. The violence of the wind had the effect of making them afraid. For we are never rightly prepared to receive the grace of God unless the vain confidence of the flesh has been mastered. For as by faith we have open access to Him, so it is humility and fear that open the door for Him to come to us. He will have nothing to do with proud and careless men who please themselves.

It is a common thing for the Spirit to be indicated by 'wind'. For Christ Himself when giving the Spirit to the apostles, blew upon them (John 20.22); and in Ezekiel's vision there was a whirlwind and a wind (Ezek. 1.4). Indeed the word Spirit itself is a transferred word. Because that hypostasis of the divine essence which is called the Spirit is incomprehensible in itself the Scripture borrows the word for the blast of the wind: because it is the power of God, breathed forth as it were by Him into all His creatures. The appearance of tongues is restricted to this event only. For just as the figure of a dove which descended upon Christ was an appropriate indication of Christ's nature and office, so now God chooses the sign which is in keeping with the thing signified, namely, to show forth the working of the Holy Spirit in the apostles which afterwards followed. Diversity of tongues would have been an obstacle to the wide dissemination of the Gospel. So if the preachers of the Gospel had spoken one language only, all men would have thought that Christ was confined to a small corner of Judaea. But God found a way for the Gospel to break forth when He gave the apostles distinctive tongues, so that they might spread through all peoples what He had delivered to them. This reflects the marvellous goodness of God, in that a punishment for human pride was transformed into a means of blessing. For what cause was the diversity of tongues but that the wicked and lawless designs of men might be brought to nothing (Gen. 11.7)? But now God furnishes the apostles with a diversity of tongues that He may call back lost and wandering men into the blessings of unity. These cloven tongues made every man speak the language of Canaan as Isaiah foretold (Isa. 19.18). For whatever language they speak they all with one mouth and one Spirit call upon the same Father in heaven (Rom. 15.8). I said that this was done for our sakes, not only because we have reaped the fruit, but also because we know that the Gospel did not light upon us by chance, but by the appointment of God. For He gave the apostles diversity of tongues to the end that no nation should fail to share in the doctrine committed to them; and by this the calling of the Gentiles is confirmed. This serves also to establish the truth of their doctrine, for we know that it is no human invention when we learn that the Spirit dwelt in their tongues.

We must now state the meaning of the 'fire'. It was beyond all doubt a token of the efficacy which the word of the apostles would carry. Otherwise even if they had sounded forth to the uttermost parts of the earth, they would only have beaten the air ineffectually. The Lord shows therefore that their voice is to be as fire, to kindle the hearts of men, for the burning up and consuming of the vanity of the world and the purging and renewing of all things. They would never otherwise have dared to enter upon so difficult a task, had the Lord not assured them of the power that would attend their preaching. So it came about that the apostles' teaching did not simply sound in the air, but pierced the minds of men and filled them with the warmth which came from heaven. This power was shown forth not in the apostles' words alone but is still revealed daily. So we must beware, lest we should be like stubble when the fire burns. Furthermore the Lord gave the Holy Spirit once to His disciples in visible shape, that we may be assured that the Church will never lack His invisible and hidden grace.

And it sat. The sudden change to the singular makes it questionable whether he is speaking of the fire. He said that there appeared tongues as of fire: but then follows, 'it sat upon them', but I take this to refer to the Spirit. For it is common in Hebrew to express in the second clause a substantive which has been omitted in the first. This is an example: it sat upon them and they were all filled with the Holy

Spirit. Now we know that Luke, though he wrote in Greek, uses many Hebraic turns of speech. In using 'tongues' of the Holy Spirit, he is in line with Scripture, for John also calls the dove by the same name (John 1.32): for it was the Lord's will to bear witness to the presence of His Spirit by a sign of this kind. If it were merely an empty sign there would be no reason to give it the name of what was signified. But where the reality is conjoined, it is appropriate that its name should be given to the sign which presents it to our apprehension. The fulness of the Spirit, with which he says each one was endowed, does not signify an equal measure of gifts in each one, but rather the excellence which would be sufficient to enable each to execute his office.

4. *They began to speak.* He shows what the effect was that followed at once and also to what use this gift of tongues was to be applied, but because soon afterwards Luke notes that strangers from many lands marvelled because every one of them heard the apostles speaking in his own tongue, some think it likely that they did not speak in a number of languages but that they all understood what was spoken in one tongue, as well as if they had heard their own. They think therefore that the one set of sounds was distinctively applied to the hearers. They base their conjecture on the further fact that Peter delivered one sermon among a multitude gathered together from many races, who could not have understood his language, unless another voice different from that which proceeded from his mouth had come to their ears. But we must first notice that the disciples spoke in strange tongues; the miracle would otherwise have been wrought not in them but in the hearers. The imagery therefore which He used earlier of the coming of the Spirit would have been false, the Spirit being given not to them but to the hearers. We hear again how Paul gave thanks to God, because he speaks with diverse tongues (I Cor. 14.18). Indeed he justifies both the knowledge and the use of them. He had not attained this skill either by his own study or industry, but he had it by the gift of the Spirit. In the same place he affirms that it is a special gift, with which all are not endowed. From this I take it as evident that the apostles had the understanding of various tongues given to them so that they might speak to the Greeks in Greek, and to the Italians in Latin, and thereby have true communication with their hearers. I make no decision on whether a second miracle was added, whereby Egyptians and Elamites understood Peter speaking in the Chaldean tongue as if he were uttering diverse voices. There are some suggestions which would lead to this conclusion, yet they are not so certain as to be beyond argument. For it may be that they spoke in diverse tongues as they happened to

meet men of different language and as opportunity offered, and that one spoke in one language, another in another. At all events it was evidently a miracle when they saw various languages come readily to them. As for Peter's address it might have been understood by the majority, wherever they were born, because it is likely that most of those who came together to Jerusalem would be acquainted with the Chaldean tongue. But again there is nothing unreasonable if we should say that he spoke in other tongues also. I have no desire to engage in long dispute over this matter, if only this is established beyond question, that the apostles truly changed their speech.

Now there were dwelling at Jerusalem Jews, devout men, from every nation under heaven. And when this sound was heard, the multitude came together, and were confounded, because that every man heard them speaking in his own language. And they were all amazed and marvelled, saying, Behold, are not all these which speak Galilaeans? And how hear we, every man in our own language, wherein we were born? Parthians and Medes and Elamites, and the dwellers in Mesopotamia, in Judaea and Cappadocia, in Pontus and Asia, in Phrygia and Pamphylia, in Egypt and the parts of Libya about Cyrene, and sojourners from Rome, both Jews and proselytes, Cretans and Arabians, we do hear them speaking in our tongues the mighty works of God. And they were all amazed and were perplexed, saying one to another, What meaneth this? But others mocking said, They are filled with new wine. (5-13)

5. *Now there were dwelling at Jerusalem.* When he calls them religious men, he seems to suggest that they came to Jerusalem to worship God: even as God, in all the time after the dispersion, raised His standard as it were in that city and gathered thither such seed as remained, because the temple there was still in active use. Yet in passing he shows who it is that benefit from the miracles by which God declares His power. For wicked and profane men either laugh at them or are indifferent to them, as we shall see presently. Furthermore he wanted to cite as witnesses those whose testimony would carry greater weight on account of their godliness. By saying 'from every nation' he means that they came from different and widely scattered countries. Further on he names the countries which are widely distant from one another, such as Libya and Pontus, Rome and Parthia and Arabia and so on. This serves to make the miracle yet more impressive. For the Cretans and the men of Asia who lived as neighbours might have had some interchange of language. But the same could not apply to the Italians and Cappadocians or between the Arabians and the men of Pontus. This also was a work of God deserving to be recalled and marvelled at, that amid a dispersion of such terrifying proportions He

not only preserved a remnant in every place but also caused foreigners to join themselves to an afflicted people who seemed on the point of extinction. For although scattered far and wide in their places of exile, so divided from one another as almost to inhabit separate worlds, they were yet kept united by their faith. He does not unadvisedly call them devout and God-fearing men.

6. *When this was noised abroad.* In the Greek Luke says, 'when this sound was uttered'; but his meaning is that the report of it was spread abroad and caused a great multitude to come together. If one after another in various places and at various times had heard the apostles speaking in different tongues, the miracle would have been less striking. They all came together to one spot, that the diversity of tongues might be the more apparent by immediate contrast. There is the further circumstance to be noted, that everyone knew what was the apostles' native land, and that moreover they had never left it so as to be able to learn foreign languages. So by their speaking indiscriminately, and as occasion offered, one in Latin, one in Greek, one in Arabian, and every one of them changing his language, the work of God was thereby made more evident.

11. *The mighty works of God.* Luke notes two points which caused the hearers to marvel: firstly, that the apostles were formerly ignorant and unlearned men, born in a district of no repute, yet now they discoursed profoundly of the things of God and of heavenly lore; and secondly, that they had suddenly been endowed with new tongues. Both points were worth noting, because had the speech poured forth been foolish and ill considered, it would not have had the effect of impressing their minds; and the majesty of what was happening should have led them to a deeper consideration of the miracle. Although they give due honour to God by their astonishment, yet the principal fruit of the miracle consists in their asking questions, and thereby showing that they wished to learn more. Otherwise their amazement would have done them no good. Assuredly wonder at the works of God should be linked with reflection and a desire to understand.

13. *Others mocking.* This shows the extent of men's blindness as well as their wickedness when Satan has taken away their senses. In this miracle the majesty of God could scarcely be more clearly seen than if He were Himself visibly to come down from heaven. Anyone with a drop of sound understanding in him must surely be shaken even to hear of it. How beast-like then must men be who see with their eyes and yet mock and essay by their jests to scoff at the power of God. Yet this is what happened. There is nothing too wonderful for men who are touched by no concern about God to turn to mockery,

for they of set purpose harden themselves in their ignorance even in matters that are as clear as day. And it is a just punishment that God brings upon such pride in delivering them to Satan to be driven headlong into blind madness. Wherefore we need not marvel that there are so many today who in the midst of light remain blind, when they are deaf to such clear teaching and wantonly refuse the salvation offered to them. For if the wonderful works of God, whereby He marvellously sets forth His power, are subjected to the mockery of men, what shall become of teaching which to them seems only common fare? Luke does not imply that those who laughed were wholly degraded and beyond hope but means rather to show the effect of this miracle upon the mass of men. And indeed it has always been so in the world, for there are few who have been touched with the true feeling for God as often as He has revealed Himself. It is not surprising; for religion is a rare virtue, and a virtue which few men have, and yet it is the beginning of understanding. Yet though the greater part of men are hard and stiff necked and refuse to consider the works of God, yet these works are never without fruit, as this narrative shows.

But Peter, standing up with the eleven, lifted up his voice, and spake forth unto them, saying, Ye men of Judaea, and all ye that dwell at Jerusalem, be this known unto you, and give ear unto my words. For these are not drunken, as ye suppose; seeing it is but the third hour of the day; but this is that which hath been spoken by the prophet Joel; And it shall be in the last days, saith God, I will pour forth of my Spirit upon all flesh; and your sons and your daughters shall prophesy, and your young men shall see visions, and your old men shall dream dreams: yea and on my servants and on my handmaidens in those days will I pour forth of my Spirit: and they shall prophesy. And I will shew wonders in the heaven above, and signs on the earth beneath; blood and fire, and vapour of smoke: the sun shall be turned into darkness, and the moon into blood, before the day of the Lord come, that great and notable day: and it shall be, that whosoever shall call on the name of the Lord shall be saved. (14-21)

14. *But Peter standing up.* By the words 'standing up' Luke indicates that an important speech was made in the assembly. For speakers rose to address the people that they might be better heard. The point of the speech is that he deduces that Christ has now been revealed through the gift of the Holy Spirit which they saw.

But in the first place he refutes the error of the view that the disciples were drunk. The refutation rests upon probability, for men are not usually drunk in the morning. As Paul says 'those who are drunk, are drunk in the night' (I Thess. 5.7) for through shame they shun the light. And surely the disgrace of this vice is such, that they are right in doing so. And yet this argument has not always been true; for Isaiah inveighed against those who in his day rose early to follow drunkenness (5.11). Even today there are many who like hogs as soon as they rise from sleep pass to drinking, but because this is not a common custom among men Peter says it is not likely in this case. Those with any knowledge of antiquity know that the civil day from the rising of the sun to sunset was divided into twelve hours, so that the hours were longer in summer and shorter in winter; therefore what would be with us the ninth hour in the morning and in summer the eighth was among the men of old the third. Peter dismisses lightly the allegation of drunkenness because too serious a defence was unnecessary. So he takes the facts to be beyond question and is concerned rather to quieten the mockers than to instruct them. He refutes them not so much from the circumstance of the time of day as from the testimony of Joel. In saying that that which was foretold had now come to pass, he rebukes their ingratitude in not recognizing so signal a blessing, promised in time past, and now present to their eyes. As to His upbraiding all with the fault of a few this is not in order to make them all guilty of the same fault but, because a fit occasion was offered by their mockery to teach them altogether, He does not neglect the opportunity.

17. *It shall be in the last day.* By this evidence he proves that the Messiah is already revealed. It is true that Joel does not expressly mention the last days, but as he tells of the perfect restoration of the Church, it is beyond question that that prophecy refers to the last age alone (Joel 2.29). Therefore Peter's words agree with the intention of Joel but he adds this phrase simply for clarity's sake that the Jews may know that the Church, at that time in ruins, could only be restored through being renewed by the Spirit of God. Furthermore because the renewing of the Church would mean the beginning of a new age Peter refers it to the last days. And surely this was familiar doctrine to the Jews that all the great promises concerning the blessed and well ordered state of the Church should not be fulfilled until Christ by His coming should restore all things. So it was not to be questioned among them that what was cited from Joel referred to the last time. Now by the last days, or the fulness of time, is meant the stable condition of the Church through the manifestation of Christ.

I will pour forth of my spirit. He intends to prove, as was said already, that the Church can only be repaired by the giving of the Holy Spirit. So he accuses them of dullness since, though they all looked for a speedy restoration, they did not give consideration to the means by which it would come about. Now when the prophet says 'I will pour out', he clearly meant by this word to indicate the full abundance of the Spirit. We must take the words 'I will pour forth of my Spirit' (or, from my Spirit), as if he had said simply, 'I will pour forth my Spirit'. For these latter words are the words of the prophet. But Peter follows the Greek which translates the Hebrew word את as ἀπό. So it is futile to engage here in subtleties, because whatever changes are made in the words, the prophet's meaning must be retained. Nevertheless, when God is said to pour out His Spirit, I maintain it must be so taken that from His Spirit He causes an infinite variety of gifts to flow out to men, as though from a single spring which can never run dry. For Paul bears witness, that there are diverse gifts, but One Spirit (I Cor. 12.4). We learn from this a valuable doctrine, that God can give us no more excellent gift than the grace of the Spirit, and that indeed all else is worth nothing without this. For when God desires to promise in the shortest form to give salvation to His people, He declares He will give them the Spirit. From this it follows that we can obtain no good things until we have the Spirit given us. It is in truth the key which opens to us the door for us to enter into all the treasures of spiritual blessings, and even into the Kingdom of God.

Upon all flesh. The significance of this general statement is made clear from what follows. First is given the inclusive phrase 'all flesh': and then the qualification by which the prophet indicates that there shall be no distinction of age or sex but that God admits all without distinction to partake of His grace. The words 'all flesh'—because young and old, men and women, are included. It may be asked why God promises to His people, as though it were some novel and unheard of thing, what he was wont to bestow upon them through all ages from the beginning, for there was no age that did not have its share of the grace of the Spirit. The answer to this question is set out in these two phrases: 'I will pour out', and 'upon all flesh'. For a double antithesis is to be noticed here between the Old and New Testament times. For the pouring out, as I said, signifies great abundance, whereas, under the Law, the distribution was more sparing. For this reason also John says that the Holy Spirit was not given until Christ ascended into heaven. 'All flesh' means an infinite multitude whereas the Lord formerly granted full participation in His Spirit only to a few. Furthermore in the comparison of the two we do not deny that the fathers under the Law were partakers of the self-same grace as we are: but the Lord shows us to be above them, as indeed we are. I repeat that all godly men from the foundation of the world were endowed with the same Spirit of understanding, of righteousness, and of sanctification, with which the Lord today illuminates and regenerates us; but there were only few who then had the light of knowledge given to them, if they are compared with the great multitude of the faithful, which Christ at His coming quickly gathered together. Again, their knowledge was obscure and slender, and veiled, as it were, compared with the knowledge which we today have out of the Gospel, where Christ, the Sun of Righteousness, shines with full mid-day brightness. This is not to deny that a few so excelled in faith that they are perhaps without equal at the present day, but their understanding savoured nonetheless of the tutelage of the Law. For it is always true that godly kings and prophets have not seen or heard those things which Christ has revealed by His coming (Matt. 13.17, Luke 10.24). So Joel commends the excellence of the New Testament, by foretelling that the grace of the Spirit will be more abundant in its day, and furthermore that more men will be partakers of it.

And your sons shall prophesy. By 'prophesy' he means to indicate a gift of intelligence of a rare and singular kind. The sentence immediately following is to the same effect, 'Your young men shall see visions, and your old men shall dream dreams.' These were the two normal means by which the Lord usually revealed Himself to the prophets, as we learn from Numbers 12.6. For in that passage the Lord separates Moses from the normal run of prophets, by saying 'I appear unto my servants by a vision or by a dream, but with Moses I speak face to face.' We see therefore that the general statement is followed by way of confirmation by two examples. But the meaning is this that they will all be prophets, as soon as the Holy Spirit is poured out from heaven. To the objection, that nothing of the sort happened, either among the apostles themselves or among the whole multitude of the faithful, I reply that it was a common custom of the prophets to foreshadow the Kingdom of Christ under images appropriate to their own day. When they speak of the worship of God they name the altar, the sacrifices, the offering of gold, silver, and frankincense. Yet we know that altars now have passed, and that the sacrifices which were used under the Law are abolished, and that the Lord requires at our hands some higher thing than earthly riches. This is true indeed; but the prophets, in adjusting their style to the fashion of their own time, comprehend, under figures which were familiar to people of the time, the same things which we now see set forth in a different guise: just as elsewhere when He promises to make priests of Levites, and Levites of the common people (Isa. 66.21), he means simply this, that in the Kingdom of Christ every man, however mean, shall have an honourable standing. To gain the true and accurate meaning of this passage therefore we must not take too literally words which are derived from the old economy of the Law, but we must seek the simple truth, shorn of metaphor. And that truth is that the apostles through the sudden inspiration of the Spirit discoursed prophetically, that is, under Divine influence and exceptionally, concerning heavenly mysteries. The word 'prophesy' therefore signifies simply the rare and excellent gift of understanding: as if Joel should say that under the Kingdom of Christ there should not be merely a few prophets to whom God would reveal His secrets, but that all men should be endowed with spiritual wisdom to the extent of excelling in prophetic gifts. As it is written also in Jeremiah: 'Every man shall no longer teach his neighbour, because they shall all know me from the least up to the greatest' (Jer. 31.34). Now Peter by these words invites the Jews whom he is addressing to be partakers of the same grace, as though he should say, 'God is prepared to pour out far and wide the Spirit which He has poured on us. There is therefore nothing, unless from your side, to hinder you from receiving with us of this abundance.' As for ourselves, let us understand that the words spoken then to the Jews are true for us today for, although the visible gifts of the Spirit have ceased, God has not yet withdrawn His Spirit from His Church. Wherefore, by this same promise, He offers the Spirit daily to us all without exception. Thus if we are poor and needy it is only through our own slothfulness; and it is evident that those who keep back the ordinary Christian man or woman from the knowledge of God are wicked and sacrilegious enemies of the Spirit, forasmuch as God not only admits women as well as men, young as well as old, but indeed invites them by name.

18. *On my servants.* By these words the promise is restricted to those who worship God, for God does not make His Spirit a common thing, as He would do if He were to make it general to the unbelievers and mockers. It is undeniable that as it is by the Spirit that we are made servants of God so we are not His servants until we have received the Spirit; but it is those whom God has adopted into His own family and has designed by His Spirit to serve Him whom he afterwards furnishes with new gifts. Again, the prophet was not looking at his own period, but intended only to make this grace apply to the Church. So long as the Church was restricted to the Jews it is they to whom the honourable titles of servants and handmaidens of God are given. But as soon as God broke down the dividing wall and gathered to Himself the Church from every quarter, as many as are received into the fellowship of the covenant are called by the same name. Only let us remember that the Spirit is appointed especially for the Church.

19. *I will show wonders.* In the first place we must see what is meant

by this great day of the Lord. Some expound it in terms of the first coming of Christ in the flesh: others refer it to the last day of resurrection. I agree with neither. In my view the prophet covers by the term the whole Kingdom of Christ. And so he calls it the 'great day', from the time that the Son of God began to be manifested in the flesh, that he might lead us into the fulfilment of His Kingdom. And so he indicates no one particular day but regards this day as beginning at the first preaching of the Gospel, and as extending to the final resurrection. Those who restrict it to the period of the apostles are influenced by the connexion which the prophet makes between this clause and the preceding one. But there is nothing unreasonable in this, because the prophet points to the time when these events began, despite the fact that there is a continuous progress in them until the end of the world. Furthermore he speaks metaphorically in saying that the sun shall be turned into darkness, and the moon into blood, meaning thereby, that the Lord will show tokens of His wrath throughout the whole fabric of the world, which will make men swoon with fear as though all nature was being fearfully changed. For as the sun and moon witness to us of God's fatherly favour, while in their courses they give light to the earth, so on the other side the prophet foretells that they shall be messengers of God's wrath and displeasure. This is the second section of the prophecy. For after he dealt with the grace of the Spirit poured out upon all flesh, lest anyone should imagine that the whole world would be prosperous and quiet, he adds that in the days of Christ the world would be troubled and beset by great fear, as Christ Himself warns us more fully in Matt. 24 and Luke 21. But this is the more effective for setting forth the grace of God in that, when destruction threatens all things, whosoever calls upon the name of the Lord is sure of salvation. By the darkening of the sun, by the blood streaming from the moon, by the black vapour of smoke, the prophet meant to represent that wherever men turn their eyes, whether upwards or downwards, there would, as he has said, be apparitions galore to cause fear among men. This is as much as to say that the world was never in a more miserable state and that there were never so many dreadful tokens of God's wrath. From this we may gather how immense is the goodness of God, who provides a present remedy for such dire evils, and again, how perverse and ungrateful to God are those who do not flee to a sanctuary of salvation which is so close and accessible. There is no question that, by setting forth this dreadful picture, God's intention is to stir up all the godly that with a still more fervent desire they may seek for salvation. It is for the same purpose that Peter quotes it, so that the Jews may know of the dreadful calamities in store for them unless they receive the grace of the Spirit that is offered to them. It may be asked, however, how the revelation of Christ can be associated with such an overwhelming flood of ills, for it may seem absurd that He should be the sole pledge of the love of God towards mankind in whom the Heavenly Father lays open all the treasure of His goodness, pours out indeed the bowels of His mercy towards us—and yet that by His coming the wrath of God should blaze forth more violently than ever, so as to consume heaven and earth in a single conflagration. But we must first notice that because men are too slow to receive Christ they must be whipped on by various afflictions. Secondly, as Christ calls to Himself those who labour and are weighed down with ills, we need to be subdued by much misery, to learn humility thereby (Matt. 11.28). For it is out of prosperity that men rear the horns of pride. For the man who counts himself happy cannot but violently despise Christ. In the third place, because we are set more than we ought upon seeking the security of the flesh, whence it arises that many tie the grace of Christ to the present life, it is right for us to learn to turn our thoughts into a different channel that we may know that the Kingdom of Christ is spiritual. Therefore God subjects us to many miseries according to the flesh, to teach us that the blessings of Christ are heavenly. This leads us to seek our felicity beyond this world. Moreover, men bring miseries upon themselves by their ingratitude. For the servant who knows his master's will, and does not obey it, is deserving of heavier punishment (Luke 12.47). The more personally (*familiarius*) the Father deals with us in Christ the more our ungodliness increases and breaks out into open rebellion; so that it is not to be wondered at if at the appearing of Christ there appear also many signs of God's vengeance since men by their wicked contempt more grievously provoke God against themselves and arouse His wrath. Surely the fearfulness of the day of Christ is secondary, whether God wills to correct our dullness of spirit, to subdue us who are still unwilling to be taught, or to punish our ingratitude; for in itself that day brings with it nothing that is not pleasurable, but the contempt of God's grace rightly provokes Him to a wrath which is to be trembled at.

21. *Whosoever shall call upon.* A notable passage.

For as God urges us forward like lazy donkeys by threats and intimidation to seek salvation, so after wrapping heaven and earth in darkness, He yet reveals a way whereby salvation may shine before our eyes: namely, if we shall call upon Him. For this circumstance must be carefully noted. If God simply promised salvation it would be great enough, but far greater that He should promise it amid the manifold chasms of death. When, He says, all things are in turmoil and possessed by the fear of death, only call upon Me and you shall be saved. So however much a man may be overwhelmed in the gulf of misery there is yet set before him a way of escape. We must also observe the universal word, 'whosoever'. For God admits all men to Himself without exception and by this means invites them to salvation, even as Paul deduces in Rom. 10, and as the prophet had earlier recorded. 'Thou Lord who hearest prayer, unto Thee shall all flesh come' (Ps. 65.2).

Therefore since no man is excluded from calling upon God the gate of salvation is set open to all. There is nothing else to hinder us from entering, but our own unbelief. It is, I say, all men, to whom God reveals Himself through the Gospel. But just as salvation is sure through calling upon the name of God, we must likewise gather that if we do not call upon Him we are thrice miserable and undone. And yet since our salvation is grounded upon our calling upon God, there is nothing thereby taken away from faith, since this invocation is based upon faith. There is also another circumstance no less worthy of note, that the prophet indicates that this calling upon God belongs particularly to the last days. For although He desired to be called upon in every age since He showed Himself in Christ to be the Father we have access more easily to Him. This ought both to increase our confidence and to strip from us our heedlessness. The Lord Himself reasoned that this privilege should make our eagerness to pray twice as great: 'Hitherto have ye asked nothing in My Name; ask, and ye shall receive' (John 16.24); as if He should say, 'You prayed hitherto even though there had not appeared in flesh a mediator and advocate: but now when you have Me to plead your cause how much more eagerly should you do so '

Ye men of Israel, hear these words: Jesus of Nazareth, a man approved of God unto you by mighty works and wonders and signs, which God did by him in the midst of you, even as ye yourselves know; him, being delivered up by the determinate counsel and foreknowledge of God, ye by the hand of lawless men did crucify and slay: whom God raised up, having loosed the pangs of death: because it was not possible that he should be holden of it. (22-24)

22. *Jesus of Nazareth.* Now Peter applies to his object the prophecy of Joel: that the Jews may thereby understand that the time of restoration had come and that Christ was given to them to this end. For this promise could be fulfilled only by the coming of the Mediator. Now this is the proper use of all the gifts which we have through Christ—that they should lead us to Christ, as to the source of all. But Peter approaches this gradually. He does not begin by immediately declaring that Jesus was the Christ, but simply says that He was a Man

sent from God and proves this by His miracles. Thereafter he adds that when He had been put to death He rose from the dead. So it appears more and more clearly and fully that He was not some one of the prophets, but the very Son of God, who was promised as the restorer of all things. Take this then as the first section, that Jesus of Nazareth was a Man approved by God by manifest testimonies so that He could not be despised as some base or obscure person. The old translator did well to render ἀποδεδειγμένον by 'approved'. Erasmus is in error in thinking that he read it otherwise, and he himself did not express the meaning of Luke by translating it, 'exhibited'. For seeing the word means to the Greeks, to show: so that the mathematicians also entitle the proofs whereby they set a thing before men's eyes, ἀποδείξεις (i.e. demonstrations), Luke's meaning was that Jesus did not come unknown and without testimony or approbation but that the miracles which God wrought through Him had the effect of bringing Him honour and glory. For this reason he says that He was revealed to the Jews, because God desired His own Son to be accounted excellent and great among them. It is as though he said that miracles were not designed for other peoples, but only for the Jews, that they might recognize that Jesus was sent to them from God.

By mighty works. He calls miracles by three different names. And because God displays His power in them in a new and unwonted manner, or at least arouses great wonder by them, they are rightly called mighty works. For we are generally more moved when something remarkable happens. Thus they are also called wonders, since they cause us astonishment. Again, they are called signs, because the Lord does not wish the minds of men to be fixed there, but to be lifted up higher, and so directs them to a more distant end. He uses the three terms, the more to exalt the miracles of Christ, and by multiplying the terms to drive men to give consideration to them. Further he does not make Christ the Author of them so much as the Agent, because as we said he wishes to go forward by degrees. Nevertheless, the question may be asked whether miracles are sufficient as an effective proof, since it is in this way that sorcerers might procure credit for their impostures. My answer is that Satan's illusions are far different from the power of God. Christ says elsewhere that the kingdom of anti-Christ will consist in wonders, but, He adds immediately, in lying wonders (II Thess. 2.9). If the objection is raised that we cannot easily distinguish them, because he says that they will have such appearance as to deceive, if possible, the very elect (Matt. 24.24), I reply again that this error proceeds only from our own defects (because we are so dull and unobservant). For God shows His own power clearly enough. Therefore in the miracles which God displays there is sure enough corroboration both of the doctrine and of the ministry if only our eyes are open to see. If the proofs are not strong enough for the wicked so that they are often deceived by the false miracles of Satan, the cause must be their own blindness. But whoever has a pure heart perceives God with the purity of inward vision as often as He shows Himself. Nor can Satan deceive us except when through the wickedness of our hearts our judgment is corrupted and our eyes blinded or glazed by our own dullness of vision.

23. *Him ye did slay*. He mentions the death of Christ for this reason especially, that the resurrection might be more assuredly believed. Among the Jews it was well known that Christ had been crucified. So His rising again was a mighty and wonderful token of divine power. Meanwhile, to prick their consciences with the feeling of sin, he says that He was killed by them; not that they crucified Him with their own hands but because the whole people with one voice demanded His death. And although many of the audience whom he is addressing did not consent to that wicked and godless act of cruelty He is right in charging the nation with it, since they had all defiled themselves by their silence or by their heedlessness. There was no room either for a defence of ignorance, since earlier He had been openly shown forth by God. This guiltiness therefore which He lays upon them is a first stage towards repentance.

By the determinate counsel. He removes the stumbling block, that at first sight it seems unaccountable that the man whom God had so greatly enriched should afterwards be laid open to every kind of indignity and suffer so shameful a death. Since therefore the Cross of Christ generally disturbs us when we see it first, Peter advises us that Christ suffered nothing by chance or because He lacked the power to deliver Himself, but because it was thus appointed by God. For the knowledge of this alone that the death of Christ was ordained in the eternal counsel of God cuts off all occasion of foolish and wicked cogitation, and removes the stumbling-blocks which might otherwise be created. For we must be assured that God decrees nothing rashly or in vain; from which it follows that there was just cause for which He would have Christ suffer. This same knowledge of God's providence is a stage toward considering the purpose and fruit of the death of Christ. For in the counsel of God we are at once met by this, that the Just was subjected to death for our sins, and that His blood was the price of our death.

Here is an important passage regarding the providence of God, that we may know that that providence governs our life as well as our death. Luke is speaking of Christ; but in His Person we have a mirror which represents for us the universal providence of God, which extends through the whole world, and yet shines especially upon ourselves who are the members of Christ. Luke deals here with two doctrines, the foreknowledge and the decree of God. And although the foreknowledge is first in order, because God sees what He wills to determine before He determines it, Luke makes it secondary to the counsel and decree of God, so that we may know that God wills or resolves nothing which He has not long before directed to its particular end. Men often decree a multitude of matters rashly, because they do so without forethought. But to teach that God's counsel is never divorced from reason, Peter couples with it His foreknowledge. Now we must distinguish these two, and with the greater care, because many are deceived at this point. They pass over the counsel of God, by which He governs the whole world and grasp at His bare foreknowledge. This is the source of the common distinction that although God foresees all things, He yet lays no necessity upon His creatures. It is indeed true that God has knowledge of this or that for the reason that it will happen; but, as we see, Peter teaches that what befell Christ was not only foreseen by God but was decreed by Him. From this we may deduce a general doctrine that God shows forth His providence no less in governing the whole world than in ordaining the death of Christ. It therefore belongs to God not only to foreknow the future, but of His own will to ordain what He will have take place. This second point was declared by Peter when he said that Christ was delivered by the certain and determinate counsel of God. Therefore the foreknowledge of God is not the same as the will of God, whereby He governs and orders all things.

There are some, of sharper insight, who admit that God not only foreknows but by His beck and nod governs whatever happens in the world. They imagine however a confusion of rule, as if God gave liberty to His creatures to follow the course of their own nature. They say that the sun is ruled by the will of God, because it performs its function which God once appointed for it in giving light to us. They think that in the same way man has free will left to him because his nature is disposed to a free choice of good and evil. But those who think thus imagine a God who sits idle in heaven. The teaching of Scripture is very different which ascribes to God a special authority in every matter including the actions of men. Yet we must consider for what purpose the Scripture teaches this. For we must beware of foolish speculations whereby we see many carried away. It is the work of Scripture to exercise our faith, that we may know that we are protected by the hand of God lest we be subject to injury at the hand of Satan and of the wicked. It is good for us to embrace this single truth, for Peter has no other object in this passage. We have indeed an example set before us in Christ, that we may be wise with sobriety. For there is no question that His flesh was subject to corruption, after the manner of nature. But by the providence of God it was delivered from corruption. If anyone asks whether the bones of Christ could be broken, it cannot be denied that by nature they could be, and yet that no bone could be broken because God had so appointed (John 19.36). By this example I say we are directed to give first place to the providence of God, to keep within our own appointed limits and not to invade rashly the secrets of God where our sight cannot penetrate.

By the hands of the wicked. Peter would seem to suggest that the wicked obeyed God, from which one of two absurdities would follow: either that God is the author of evil, or that men do not sin whatever evil they commit. Concerning the second, I would reply that the wicked are very far from obeying God, in whatever way they execute what God in His own counsels has appointed. For obedience springs from a voluntary affection, and we know that something far different is true of the wicked. Again no one obeys God except the man who knows His will. Obedience therefore depends upon the knowledge of the will of God. Furthermore God has revealed His will to us in the Law. Therefore only those men obey God who do what is agreeable to the Law of God, who, again, submit themselves willingly to His government. We see nothing of this kind in any of the wicked whom in their ignorance God drives to and fro. No one then would say that they are to be excused for the reason that they obey God, for the double reason that we are to seek the will of God in His Law and that they desire as far as they can to resist God. As for the other point, I deny that God is the author of evil because this expression carries certain implications. For a wicked deed is judged according to the end at which it is aimed. When men commit theft or murder, they sin in being thieves or murderers; in theft and murder there is a criminal intention. But God who uses their wickedness stands on a different level. His object is far different, for He wishes to chastise the one and exercise the patience of the other: but in this He never declines from His own nature, that is, from perfect righteousness. So then when Christ was delivered by the hands of wicked men and was crucified it came to pass by the appointment and ordinance of God. Treachery however which is wicked in itself and murder in which such wickedness is found must not be thought to be the works of God.

24. *Having loosed the pangs of death.* By 'the pangs of death' I understand more than bodily feeling. Those who faithfully consider the nature of death, hearing that it is the curse of God, must conceive that by death the anger of God is shown. This gives rise to dread and

terror which create greater misery than death itself. Moreover Christ died on this condition, to take our guilt upon Himself. The inward fear of conscience which made Him so afraid as to sweat blood when He presented Himself at the judgment seat of God caused Him greater horror and distress than all the torments of the flesh. But the words of Peter that Christ wrestled with sorrows of this kind and was victorious have this effect, that believers ought not now to be afraid of death, for the nature of death is not as it was in Adam, because by the victory of Christ the curse of God is swallowed up (I Cor. 15.54). We still feel the prickings of sorrow, but they do not wound us grievously while we hold up the shield of faith. He adds an explanation that it was not possible for Christ to be mastered by death inasmuch as He is the Author of life.

For David saith concerning him, I beheld the Lord always before my face; for he is on my right hand, that I should not be moved: therefore my heart was glad, and my tongue rejoiced; moreover my flesh also shall dwell in hope: because thou wilt not leave my soul in Hades, neither wilt thou give thy Holy One to see corruption. Thou madest known unto me the ways of life; thou shalt make me full of gladness with thy countenance. Brethren, I may say unto you freely of the patriarch David, that he both died and was buried, and his tomb is with us unto this day. Being therefore a prophet, and knowing that God had sworn with an oath to him, that of the fruit of his loins he would set one upon his throne; he foreseeing this spake of the resurrection of the Christ, that neither was he left in Hades, nor did his flesh see corruption. (25-31)

25. The resurrection of Christ which was attested by clear and reliable prophecies and which could be gathered from the unbroken line of the prophets' teaching had to be proved to the Jews as though it were altogether strange and novel. Yet this is not surprising. For we see that, often as Christ had inculcated this into the disciples, they profited little from it. Yet they did retain certain principles of true doctrine which might have opened the way for them to the knowledge of Christ, as we shall presently see. Because therefore the gift of the Spirit was the outcome of the resurrection of Christ, Peter proves by the testimony of David that it was necessary that Christ should rise, that the Jews might thereby know that it was He who was the Author of this gift. He takes it as understood by all, that He was raised from death to live, not for Himself, but for His own. Now we see the direction of Peter's thought that this, which was in fact foretold so long before, should not be regarded as something new; moreover

that Jesus is Christ because David prophesied of Him, as of the Head of the Church.

First of all we must see whether this passage in the Psalms is wholly to be understood of Christ, as Peter maintains. Thereafter, if there is anything in the text worth noting, we shall consider it in its place. Peter alleges that what is spoken here does not refer to David: 'Thou wilt not suffer thy Holy One to see corruption' (Ps. 16.10), for David's corpse suffered corruption in the grave. It might appear to be a frivolous argument. It might quickly be objected that the word is not to be stressed since David intended simply to exempt himself from destruction. So in whatever way corruption affected him there is no hindrance to his foretelling that he was safe from the danger of it, knowing that the Lord would deliver him. Indeed it seems to be a repetition of the previous sentence, as is common in the Hebrew tongue. This being so, the sense is plain that God will not suffer him to come under the power of death or to be consumed by it. This interpretation is confirmed by the use of the word שאול, where we read 'hell', and of שחת, where we read 'corruption'. Both these words signify the grave. Thus David is made to say twice that he would be delivered from death by the grace of God. Finally he makes the same statement in Ps. 49.15, 'God shall redeem my soul from the hand of hell.' So too on the other side when he speaks of the wicked he takes 'going down into the grave' for 'destruction'.

I would reply to this briefly that there is something more referred to here than the general deliverance of the godly. David indeed promises that God will be his eternal Deliverer, in life as in death. He would not have gained much to have been once delivered from one danger, unless he had hoped that by the protection of God he would be safe even to the end; but he speaks of such safety as is superior to the common lot. Surely the words sound as though he is glorying in a new and singular privilege. I admit that there is repetition and that the two clauses deal with the same theme: 'thou shalt not leave my soul in hell', and 'thou shalt not suffer me to see corruption'; but this is not simply to be understood of God's will to deliver His Holy One from eternal destruction. For freedom from corruption is specifically promised. I am not concerned that שחת signifies the grave, as does שאול in the earlier clause. Though I would not quarrel about words we must have regard to the etymology. When therefore the grave is called שחת because it brings corruption upon the human body there is no doubt that that was the quality of it that David had in mind. By this word therefore it is not so much the place, but the condition of putrescence, which is expressed. The sense is that God will not suffer Him of whom the Psalm speaks to rot in the grave.

Since David was not exempt from this necessity, it follows that the prophecy was not truly or perfectly fulfilled in him.

The circumstance itself makes clear that the Psalm is to be interpreted wholly of Christ. For seeing that David was one of the sons of Adam, he could not escape that universal condition of mankind, 'Dust thou art, and unto dust thou shalt return' (Gen. 3.19). The grave stands open, I say, for all the sons of Adam to swallow them up and consume them, so that no man can exempt himself from that corruption. As we behold ourselves separated from Christ, we see awaiting us a grave which threatens us with corruption. So too if David is separated from Christ, the statement that he will be preserved from the grave cannot be true of him. When therefore he boasts that he shall be free from the grave, so far as corruption is concerned, it is beyond question that he places himself within the Body of Christ, wherein death was overcome and its kingdom abolished. But if David promises himself exemption from the grave on no other grounds than that he is a member of Christ, it appears from this that this freedom must begin with Christ as the Head. Every man of sound judgment must recognize that this is a valid argument. God subjected all mankind to corruption; therefore David, inasmuch as he was numbered among men, could not escape it. And it cannot be doubted that since among the Jews to whom this address was given it was an unquestioned assumption that the restoration of all things was to be looked for at the hands of the Christ alone, they would the more readily acquiesce in the words of Peter, because they saw that the content of the words could have no other application than to the Messiah. They had not reached such a point of impudence, not at least those who are mentioned here, as to dispute on matters which were beyond argument. For at this time, God had provided His disciples with listeners who were godly men, prepared to learn. They sought the Messiah in the Old Testament. They knew that a type of the Messiah was figured in David. There was among them religion and a reverence for Scripture. And yet today the impudence of almost that whole people is such as to make men despair of them. Whatever pressure is applied to them, they evade it. Where there is no way out they still break through. When they are overcome they still refuse to yield. And there is no doubt that this shamelessness and wilfulness is a punishment for their ungodliness. But let us return to Peter's sermon.

As David not only declares that God will be his deliverer but mentions the particular form of his deliverance, namely, that he shall not be subject to the corruption of the grave, Peter correctly gathers that the reference cannot properly be to David, since his body did suffer corruption in the grave. But as this was a hard saying for the Jews to hear, he softens it by a circumlocution. He does not deny outright that this prophecy had been fulfilled in David, but indirectly implies as much in saying that like all other men he lies consumed in the grave. Now David's prophecy concerning Christ was such as to offer a consolation applicable both privately to himself and, by extension, to the whole body of the Church. The wholeness and perfection which belongs to the Head is subsequently shared out abroad among all the members. There is no doubt that David in this passage spoke of himself, but only in so far as he beheld himself in Christ, as in the mirror of life. He has regard first to Christ; thereafter he turns his eyes to himself and to the other believers. So we have in this place described to us a general doctrine concerning the nature of faith, the spiritual joy of conscience, and the hope of eternal deliverance.

I beheld. We must hold this principle. If we desire to have God present with us, we must set Him before our eyes; and that even before He shall appear, for the eye of faith penetrates far further than the length of our present experience. It is therefore of the nature of faith to set God always before it as a Guide in every perplexity and danger, for there is nothing which so sustains us as to know that God is present with us; even as the belief that He is not present often casts us down and in the end dismays us utterly. David adds that he did not take heed to the direction of God in vain. He says 'He is at my right hand', whereby he indicates that there is no danger of His ever deceiving us or our faith, when we hold Him present with us; for we shall always be aware of His ever-present help. Faith, in hoping for the help of God, ought to outstrip all that we gather from experience and the senses; but as soon as it ascribes to God the glory of beholding Him in His Word, although He be absent and invisible, it will be overwhelmed by the outcome. For the measure of faith is not adequate to comprehend the infinite greatness of the power and goodness of God. He draws a parallel from those who, to prop up the weak or strengthen the fearful, join themselves to their side.

Should not be moved, is not to be thrown down and lose courage but remain as it were firm and sure footed, as in Ps. 46.5, 'God is in the midst of her, therefore she shall not be moved'. For although often the godly are sorely shaken, yet, because they come to themselves again, they are said to continue firm. There is therefore no reason why they should be afraid of falling, who are upheld by the help of God. Conversely those who place their strength anywhere other than in God will be shaken by the slightest breath of wind, and before even a slight onset of temptation will fall to the ground.

26. *Therefore my heart was glad.* Joy of the soul, gladness of speech,

and quiet assurance (*securitas*) of the whole body follow upon confident trust (*fiducia*). For unless men have lost all feeling, they must be anxious and distressed, and thus miserably tormented, so long as they feel themselves destitute of the help of God. But that sure trust which is placed in God not only delivers us from anxiety but fills our hearts with a wonderful joy. That is the joy which Christ promised in full measure to His disciples and which He testified could not be taken from them (John 16.22; 17.13). He expresses the magnitude of this joy when he says that it cannot be held in but will burst forth into the language of exultation. כבוד indeed signifies glory: but here and in many other passages it is taken for 'the tongue'. And so the Greek rightly translated it. The quietness of the 'flesh' refers to the quiet assurance of the whole man, which the protection of God affords us. It matters not that the faithful have their peace continually disturbed and are brought into alarm. For just as in the midst of distress they nonetheless rejoice, so there are no troubles so great as to take their quietness of spirit from them. To the objection that the peace of the faithful has its abode in the spirit and is not a peace of the flesh, I reply that they have a peace of body, not because they are exempt from trouble but because they believe that God cares for them wholly, and that not only their souls shall be saved through His perfection but their bodies also.

27. *Because thou wilt not leave.* To leave the soul in hell is to allow it to be overcome by destruction. Two different words are used each of which means the grave in Hebrew. Because שׁאל means to demand, I suppose שׁאול is used for hell, because death is insatiable; hence also the translation, 'Hell hath enlarged her soul'; and again, 'They set open their mouth like hell.' And because the other word שחת is derived from *corruption* or *consuming*, that quality is to be considered, just as David noted it. The questions which are raised by some at this point regarding the descent of Christ to hell are in my view out of place as being remote from the thought and purpose of the prophet. For the word *soul* (*anima*) means not so much the spirit which belongs to an immortal being (*essentia*), as the life itself. For when a man is dead and lies in the grave, the grave is said to have dominion over his life. The Greek translation, *holy*, is in Hebrew וחסיד, which correctly signifies *gentle*; but Luke did not regard this as it was not relevant to the present purpose. Furthermore gentleness is so often commended among the faithful because it is proper for them to imitate and resemble the nature of their Father.

28. *Thou madest known to me.* He means that He was restored from death to life by the grace of God, for he regards his re-emergence to life as a gift granted by the special blessing of God. This was so

completely fulfilled in Christ that there was nothing lacking in perfection. Yet the members have their limitations. Therefore Christ was exempt from corruption, to be the firstfruits of those who rise from death (I Cor. 15.20). We in our turn shall follow Him at the last but first we shall be turned into dust (I Cor. 15.42). The next words —that he should be filled with gladness by the countenance of God— agree with the words 'show us Thy face, and we shall be saved' (Ps. 80.3); again, 'the light of Thy countenance is shown upon us; Thou hast put gladness in my heart' (Ps. 4.6-7). For it is only the pleasantness of God's countenance which can not only make us glad, but quicken us; on the other hand, when His face is turned away or troubled we cannot but faint.

30. *Being therefore a prophet.* He gives two reasons to show that it is not surprising that David should speak of matters that would come to pass long after his own time. The first is, that he was a prophet. Now we know that to the prophets things to come and matters far removed from the knowledge of men are revealed. It is therefore unjust to measure their words by the common yardstick which we apply to the words of other men, since under the direction of the Spirit they reach beyond the distant courses of the years. Therefore they are also called seers: because placed, as it were, upon a lofty watch-tower they behold things which by reason of their remoteness are hidden from other men. The second reason is, because Christ was promised especially to him. This was so universally accepted as an axiom among the Jews that as often as mention was made of Christ, they forthwith had the Son of David on their lips. These arguments are not such as necessarily to prove that this prophecy is to be interpreted in terms of Christ; nor was that Peter's intention; but he wished in the first place to prevent the contrary objection, how David could have such skill in foretelling a matter which he could not know. Therefore he declares that David knew Christ both by prophetic revelation and by a promise made to him personally. Moreover the principle which Paul lays down, 'Christ is the end of the Law' (Rom. 10.4), was highly reckoned among men of sound judgment. Thus no man doubted that the aim of all the prophets was to lead the godly by the hand to Christ. Therefore whatever notable or remarkable utterance they made was commonly regarded as referring to Christ. We must also observe that Peter's reasoning was sound, when he assumed that David was not ignorant of what was the point of supreme importance in all revelation.

God had sworn with an oath. God swore, not only that He might make David believe His promise but that the promise itself might be the more highly regarded, and it is here repeated with the object, as

I think, of making the Jews consider the great importance of a promise which God had marked in such a way. The same admonition is profitable for us also, for there is no question that the Lord meant to stress the excellence of the covenant by the insertion of a solemn oath. Meanwhile it is an acceptable remedy for the infirmity of our faith to see the sacred name of God set before us like a pledge, that His words may be more faithfully believed. The words, *according to the flesh*, indicate that in Christ there was something more noble than flesh. Therefore Christ, as man, came forth from the seed of David, but in such manner that He retains His divinity; and so the distinction between the two natures is clearly expressed; since Christ is called the Son of God according to His eternal Being, in the same manner as He is called the seed of David according to the flesh.

This Jesus did God raise up, whereof we all are witnesses. Being therefore by the right hand of God exalted, and having received of the Father the promise of the Holy Ghost, he hath poured forth this, which ye see and hear. For David ascended not into the heavens: but he saith himself, The Lord said unto my Lord, Sit thou on my right hand, till I make thine enemies the footstool of thy feet. Let all the house of Israel therefore know assuredly, that God hath made him both Lord and Christ, this Jesus whom ye crucified. (32-36)

32. *This Jesus.* After proving by the testimony of David that Christ must rise again he says that he and the rest of his associates were with their own eyes witnesses of this resurrection. For the context will not allow the word *raised up* to be taken in any other sense. Therefore it follows that what David had foretold concerning the Christ was fulfilled in Jesus of Nazareth. Thereafter he speaks of the fruit or outcome of this. For in the first place he had to show that Christ was alive. Otherwise it would have been absurd and incredible that He should be the author of so great a miracle. Nevertheless he also shows us that Christ did not rise for His own sake alone, but by pouring out His Spirit to make the whole Church partaker of His life.

33. *By the right hand of God.* The *right hand* is used to mean either the hand or the power, as elsewhere in Scripture. He means that it was a wonderful act of God to exalt His Christ, whom men had thought to be destroyed by death, to such a pinnacle of glory.

The promise of the Spirit, for 'the Spirit who was promised'. For He had often before promised the Spirit to the apostles. Peter therefore means that Christ had obtained from God the Father the power to fulfil what He had promised. And He gives the full words of the promise, so that the Jews may know that this did not happen suddenly but that the words of the prophet, spoken long before the event, were now verified. Furthermore, reference to obtaining it of the Father is to be applied to the person of the Mediator. It can truly be said either that Christ sent the Spirit from Himself, or that He was sent from the Father; from Himself, because He is eternal God; from the Father, because, inasmuch as He is man, He receives from the Father what He gives to us. Peter's words are wisely suited to the understanding of the ignorant to prevent anyone asking an inappropriate question concerning the power of Christ. And surely, since it is the office of Christ to direct us to the Father, this form of words is most suitable for godly use, whereby Christ, set as it were between God and ourselves, delivers to us with His own hands the gifts which He has received from the hands of the Father. Moreover we must observe this sequence whereby He says that the Spirit was sent by Christ after He was exalted. This agrees with those sentences: 'The Spirit was not yet given because Christ was not yet glorified' (John 7.39); and 'Unless I go hence, the Spirit will not come' (John 16.7). It was not that the Spirit began at that time to be given, for the holy fathers were endowed with Him from the beginning of the world; but that God deferred giving this more plentiful abundance of grace, until He had established Christ on His princely seat; and this is signified by the word *poured out*, as we saw a little earlier. For by this means the power and effect of Christ's death and resurrection are sealed; and we also know thereby that we have lost nothing by His departing out of the world because, though He is absent in body, He is present with us in a better way, namely, by the grace of His Holy Spirit.

34. *For David.* Although they might readily gather from the effects which they saw with their eyes that the power had been given to Christ, nevertheless, that they might be the more convinced of His glory, He proves by the testimony of David that it was appointed long ago by God that Christ should be exalted to the highest honour. For the words, 'sit at the right hand of God' mean the same as to hold supreme authority, as will later be more fully shown. Before repeating the prophecy he shows that it is relevant only to Christ. Therefore to make the sense clearer, the sentence must run: 'David declares that it was ordained by God that a King should sit at His right hand.' Now this does not apply to David who was never elevated to such distinction. Therefore he speaks this of Christ. Moreover there should have seemed to be nothing novel in what had been foretold to the Jews by the oracle of the Holy Spirit. It appears from this in what sense Peter denies that David ascended into heaven. He is not speaking in this passage of whether the soul of David was received into blessed rest and the heavenly dwelling, or not: but the ascending into heaven covers all that Paul teaches in

Eph. 4.9, where he places Christ above all heavens, that He may fill all things. A discussion regarding the state of the dead is therefore here quite out of place. For Peter is establishing only this, that the prophecy concerning the sitting at the right hand of God was not fulfilled in David, and therefore the truth of it must be sought elsewhere. And since it can be found nowhere but in Christ, the conclusion is that the Jews, warned by prophecy, know that that is shown to them in Christ which was foretold them so long before. It is true indeed that David reigned by the command of God and was in some sense God's representative (*vicarius*), but not so that he should be above all creatures. This 'sitting' therefore, is applicable to nobody unless he be supreme over the whole world.

The Lord said to my Lord. Since this is the lawful means of exercising power, that the King (or whatever other name the ruler holds) recognizes that he is ordained by God, David therefore declares that the commandment to reign was given to Christ by name (Ps. 110.1); although he said that He did not take the honour to Himself presumptuously, but only obeyed the command of God. Now we must see whether Peter's reasoning is sound. He gathers that the words apply to Christ because the sitting at the right hand of God is not true of David. It seems that this might be refuted, because David reigned by the specific command of God, in His name, and by His help; which is to sit at the right hand of God. But Peter takes for granted what is true and what I have already touched on, that a wider and more majestic government is here spoken of than that which David enjoyed. For although he was in the seat of God (*vices Dei*) and represented Him in his rule, yet this power is far inferior to being exalted to the right side of God. Now this is attributed to Christ, because He is placed above all principalities, and above every name that is named, not only in this world, but in the world to come (Eph. 1.21). Seeing that David is far inferior to the angels he holds no station so high as to be regarded as next to God. For one must ascend far above all heavens to come to the right hand of God. Thus no man is rightly and properly said to sit there save only He who surpasses all creatures in His degree of honour. One who resides among the creatures, although he be reckoned in the order of angels, remains far below that exalted position. Finally the right hand of God is not to be sought for among His creatures, but surpasses even all the heavenly principalities.

Furthermore the content of the sentence itself is of great importance. The King is bidden in it to bear supreme rule, until God shall have laid low all His enemies. Now, although I grant that such an honourable title of authority can be applied to an earthly ruler, it cannot be said that David reigned until such time as all his enemies were subdued. For from these words we rightly gather that the Kingdom of Christ is eternal. But the kingdom of David was not only temporal, but was frail, and of short duration. Moreover when David died he left many enemies surviving him in various places. He had won many notable victories, but he was far from subduing all his enemies. Some of the neighbouring peoples he made tributaries of his, others he routed or destroyed: but what is this compared with universal conquest? Finally, we may prove from the total context of the Psalm that nothing other than the Kingdom of Christ can be understood. Passing over other points, what is written here regarding eternal priesthood bears no relation to the person of David. I know that the Jews mutter that kings' sons are elsewhere called כהנים. But here he is dealing with the priesthood, as it is ascribed by Moses to the King Melchizedek. And a new kind of priesthood is established by a solemn oath. Therefore we must not here imagine anything common or ordinary. Now it would have been wickedness for David to intrude himself into any part of the priest's office. How then could he be called a greater כהן than Aaron, and consecrated by God to all eternity? But because it is not part of my present plan to expound the whole Psalm, let this reason which Peter gives be enough, that He is made Lord of heaven and earth, who sitteth at the right hand of God. As for the second part of the verse, regarding the putting of His enemies under His feet, read my remarks upon I Cor. 15.25.

36. *Therefore let all the house of Israel know.* The house of Israel confessed that the Christ who was promised would come; but they did not know who He was. Therefore Peter concludes that Jesus, whom they had treated so shamefully, for whose very name they had such hatred, is He whom they ought to acknowledge as their God and to reverence. For he says God has made Him Lord and Christ; in other words, you must look for no other than Him whom God has created and given. Furthermore he says that this title is His because God the Father gave Him this honour. He joins the title Lord with the word Christ, because it was commonly understood among the Jews that the Redeemer should be anointed, on the principle that He was the Head of the Church and that supreme power for ordering all things was given to Him. And he addresses the whole House of Israel, as though to say: whosoever will be reckoned among the sons of Jacob and look for the promise, let them know for sure that this is He, and none other. He uses the word *house* because God had separated the people of that name and family from every other people, and he says ἀσφαλῶς, or, for a surety, not only that they may rest their sure confidence in Christ, but that he may take away all occasion

of dubiety from the many who are often so ready to doubt even on matters which are beyond question. At the end of his speech he upbraids them again because they crucified Christ, that they may be afflicted with deeper pangs of conscience and thereby seek a remedy. And now since they know that Christ is the anointed of the Lord, the Governor of the Church, and the Giver of the Holy Spirit, the accusation carries the greater weight. For their putting of Him to death was not only marked by an excess of cruelty and wickedness but was also a testimony to an unspeakable disloyalty towards God, to sacrilege and ingratitude, and, in the last resort, to apostasy. But it was necessary for them to be wounded in this way, lest they should have been slow to seek for medicine. It is true that they did not crucify Him with their own hands, but it is more than enough to make them guilty, that they asked to have him put to death. These same words serve to accuse us too, if by making mock of Him as the apostle says (Heb. 6.6) we crucify within ourselves Him who is even now glorified in heaven.

Now when they heard this, they were pricked in their heart, and said unto Peter and the rest of the apostles, Brethren, what shall we do? And Peter said unto them, Repent ye, and be baptized every one of you in the name of Jesus Christ unto the remission of your sins; and ye shall receive the gift of the Holy Ghost. For to you is the promise, and to your children, and to all that are afar off, even as many as the Lord our God shall call unto him. (37-39)

37. *They were pricked in their heart.* Luke now tells us the outcome of the sermon, so that we may know that the power of the Holy Spirit was shown forth not only in the diversity of tongues, but also in the hearts of those who heard. He notes a double effect: firstly, that they were touched with a feeling of grief; secondly, that they were obedient to Peter's counsel. This is the beginning of repentance. This is the entrance to godliness, to feel grief for our sins and to be wounded by an awareness of our evildoing. For as long as men are heedless they cannot give the attention they ought to doctrine. For this cause the Word of God is compared to a sword (Heb. 4.12), because it mortifies our flesh, that we may be offered as a sacrifice to God. But to this pricking of heart there must be added a willingness to obey. Cain and Judas were pricked in heart, but despair kept them back from submitting themselves to God. For the mind that is oppressed by dread can do nothing else but flee from God. Surely when we are told that a contrite spirit and a humble heart are a sacrifice acceptable to God, what is in mind is a voluntary pricking of the heart. For the heart-searching of the wicked is mingled with great disquiet, but we

are to have our confidence sure and our heart strong with the assurance of salvation, that we may be prepared to commit ourselves to God and to follow whatever He may command. Every day we see many pricked, who yet fret and murmur or else furiously resist and in consequence go raging mad. The very reason of their going mad is that against their will they are aware of such prickings. They alone profit from prickings of this kind who are willing to be made sorrowful and are prepared also to seek a remedy from God.

38. *Peter said.* From this we learn that those who ask at the mouth of the Lord and offer themselves to Him to be ruled and taught never go away empty. For that promise can never fail: 'Knock and it shall be opened unto you' (Matt. 7.7). Whoever therefore is truly prepared to learn, the Lord will not deny His godly desire; for He is the best and most faithful of masters, if only He has pupils prepared to study and to learn. We need not fear therefore that He will allow us to lack wise counsel, if only we are attentive to hear Him and do not refuse to embrace whatever He may teach us. Let us also allow ourselves to be governed by the counsel and authority of those men whom He gives us to be our teachers. Thus the quick and prompt obedience of those who wait upon the apostles is because they are persuaded that they are sent from God to show them the way of salvation.

Repent. There is a greater emphasis in the Greek word, for it signifies the conversion of the mind, that the whole man may be renewed and made another man. This is to be carefully noted because this doctrine in the days of the Papacy was miserably corrupted. For they practically transferred the name of repentance to certain external rites. They do indeed babble something about the feigned contrition of the heart, but they touch upon that aspect only slightly. They lay weight especially upon the outward exercises of the body, which would be of little worth even if there were no corruption in them. But they inculcate practically nothing else but false and trifling things, wherewith men are wearied to no purpose. Wherefore let us know that this is the true repentance, when a man is renewed in the spirit of his mind as Paul teaches (Rom. 12.2). There is no doubt that Peter preached at length of the force and nature of repentance, but Luke only touches on the main points and does not record the words of the address that he delivered. This much we must understand, that Peter first exhorted the Jews to repent, and thereafter lifted them up with the assurance of forgiveness. For He promised them the remission of sins. Now these, as we know well, are the two divisions of the Gospel; and therefore when Christ wishes briefly to relate the content of the doctrine of the Gospel, He says that in His name are to be preached repentance and remission of sins (Luke 24.47). Furthermore because we can be reconciled to God only by the intercession of the death of Christ, and our sins cannot be purged and done away other than by His blood, Peter recalls us to Him by name. He puts baptism in the fourth place as the seal by which the promise of grace is fulfilled.

We have therefore in these few words almost the sum total of Christianity: namely, that a man renouncing himself and the world devotes himself wholly to God; secondly, that he is delivered by the free forgiveness of sins from guilt involving death and adopted into the number of the children of God. And as we can obtain none of these things without price, the name of Christ is placed before us, as the only foundation of faith and repentance. This also we must note, that the repentance that has its beginning when first we turn to God must be continued throughout our life. This message therefore must continually be heard in the Church, 'Repent' (Mark 1.15). Not that those who desire to be accounted faithful, and have their place already within the Church, are to make a beginning in this, but that they are to continue to proceed in it; although many take upon themselves the name of faithful men, who have never even begun to repent. We must therefore hold this order of teaching, that those who up to now have lived to the world and to the flesh should begin to crucify the old man, that they may rise to newness of life; while those who have already entered upon the course of repentance should continually press forward towards the mark. Furthermore, because the inward conversion of the heart ought to bring forth fruits in the life, repentance cannot rightly be taught, unless works are required; not those frivolous works which alone are thought of value among the Papists, but such as are sound testimonies to blamelessness and holiness.

Be baptized every one of you. Although in the context of the passage baptism here precedes remission of sins, yet it follows in order, because it is nothing else but a sealing of the blessings, which we have through Christ, that they may be established within our consciences. Therefore after Peter spoke of repentance he called the Jews to the assurance of grace and the hope of salvation. So afterwards, Luke, in a sermon of Paul's, joins faith and repentance in the same sense as he here places the remission of sins. This is rightly done, for the hope of salvation consists simply in the free imputation of righteousness, and we are counted just, freely before God, when He forgives our sins. And as I said before that the doctrine of repentance has a daily use in the Church, we must so also regard the remission of sins which is continually offered to us. And surely it is no less necessary to us through the whole course of our life than at our first entrance into the Church. So it would profit us nothing to be once received into favour by God, unless this embassy of His, as it were, should be continually maintained, 'Be reconciled unto God, because he was made sin for us who knew no sin, that we might become the righteousness of God in him' (II Cor. 5.20).

Moreover the Papists so corrupt and adulterate this other part of the Gospel that they quite exclude the remission of sins which was to be obtained through Christ. They confess that sins are freely forgiven in baptism, but they will have them redeemed through satisfactions after baptism. And although they mingle the grace of Christ with this, because they wrap it up in human merit they hereby overthrow the whole teaching of the Gospel. First they take from men's consciences the certainty of faith; thereafter, by dividing the forgiveness of sins between the death of Christ and the satisfactions performed by ourselves, they completely rob us of the benefit of Christ. For Christ does not reconcile us to God in part, but completely; neither is there any forgiveness of sins to be obtained through Him which is not total and complete. The Papists are in great error in this matter, for they restrict baptism to the time of birth and the life that went before, as if the significance and power of it did not even extend to the time of death.

Let us know therefore that forgiveness of sins is grounded in Christ alone, and that we must not think of any other expiation than that which He has performed by the sacrifice of His death. And for this cause, as we said, Peter declares His name, whereby he indicates to us that none of these things can be rightly taught, unless Christ is set in the midst so that the effect of this doctrine may be sought in Him. There is no need for long exposition, where He bids them be baptized for the remission of sins. For although God once reconciled men to Himself in Christ, not imputing unto them their sins (II Cor. 5.19), and now imprints in our hearts by His Spirit faith in this reconciliation, yet, because baptism is the seal whereby He confirms to us this benefit (*baptismus sigillum est, quo hoc beneficium nobis confirmat*), and so the earnest and pledge of our adoption, it is worthily described as given to us for the remission of sins. For in that we receive Christ's gifts by faith, but baptism is a help for confirming and increasing our faith (*fidei confirmandae et augendae baptismus adminiculum est*), the remission of sins, which is a result of faith, is joined to it as to the lesser means. Furthermore we must not extract a definition of baptism from this passage, because Paul touches upon only a part of it. Thus our old man is crucified by baptism, as Paul teaches, that we may rise unto newness of life (Rom. 6.4, 6). And again, we put on Christ Himself (I Cor. 12.13), and the Scripture teaches everywhere that it is a sign of repentance. But because Peter is not discoursing openly in this passage of the whole nature of baptism, but in speaking of the forgiveness of sins indicates in passing that the confirmation of it is in baptism, there is nothing strange in his omitting the other part.

In the name of Christ. Although baptism is no empty figure but a true and effectual testimony; notwithstanding, lest anyone should give credit for what is offered therein to the element of water, the name of Christ is clearly expressed, so that we may know that the sign will be profitable to us only if we seek the power and effect of it in Christ and know that we are washed in baptism, because it is the blood of Christ which washes us. We gather also that Christ is the goal to which baptism points us. All men therefore gain benefit from their baptisms, by the degree to which they learn to look to Christ. But the question arises—was Peter entitled to change the form prescribed by Christ? The Papists think so, or pretend to do so, and claim the liberty thereby to alter or abrogate the institutions of Christ. They admit that nothing of substance has been changed but they regard the Church as free to change whatever it desires as regards the form. But their argument on this point can easily be refuted. In the first place we must hold that Christ did not give the apostles magic words to be used for incantation, as the Papists imagine, but He summed up the whole mystery in a few words. Then again I maintain that Peter is not speaking in this passage of the form of baptism but simply declaring that the whole efficacy of baptism is contained in Christ; although Christ cannot be grasped by faith without the Father by whom He was given to us and the Spirit by whom He renews and sanctifies us. The answer consists simply in this, that it is not a fixed formula of baptism that is being dealt with here, but the recalling of the faithful to Christ, in whom alone we obtain all that baptism prefigures to us. For we are cleansed by His blood, and we enter upon a new life by the benefit of His death and resurrection.

Ye shall receive the gift of the Holy Ghost. Because they were smitten with astonishment when they saw the apostles suddenly begin to speak in foreign tongues, Peter says that they will be partakers of the same gift if they pass over to Christ. The supreme gifts were the remission of sins and newness of life; but this was something extra, in order that Christ might show His power in them by some visible gift. This passage ought not to be taken to refer to the grace of sanctification which is conferred upon all the godly in common. He promises them the gift of the Spirit of which they saw an example in the diversity of tongues. Therefore this does not strictly apply to us. For since it was the inauguration of His Kingdom that Christ meant to set forth by these miracles, they lasted only for a time; but because the visible graces which the Lord distributed to His own mirrored forth that Christ was the Giver of the Spirit, the words of Peter—'Ye shall receive the gift of the Spirit'—apply in a measure to the whole Church. For although we do not receive the Spirit to the end that we may speak with tongues, or be prophets, or cure the sick, or work miracles, yet is He given to us for a better use, that we may believe with the heart unto righteousness, that our tongues may be trained to true confession (Rom. 10.10) that we may pass from death to life (John 5.24), that we who are poor and empty may be made rich, and that we may sound victorious against Satan and the world. Therefore the grace of the Spirit will always be conjoined to baptism, unless a hindrance arise on our part.

39. *For to you is the promise.* This has to be specifically said, that the Jews might be certain that the grace of Christ belongs to themselves as well as to the apostles. Peter proves it by showing that the promise of God was intended for them. We must always pay attention to this, that the will of God is made known to us in no other manner than by His Word. But it is not enough to have the Word in its general sense, unless we know that it is meant for ourselves. Therefore Peter says that the blessings of God which the Jews see in him and his fellow-disciples were promised to themselves. It is a necessary requirement for a firm faith that every one is fully convinced that he is included in the number of those whom God is addressing. In a word, this is the true rule of faith, when I am thus persuaded that salvation is mine because the promise that offers it applies to myself. A wider confirmation is added, when the promise is extended to those who before were afar off. For God had made the covenant with the Jews. If the power and effect of it are now extended to the Gentiles also the Jews need not doubt that they will find the promise of God firm and sure.

We should note these three stages, that the promise was made first to the Jews, and then to their children, and finally that it is to be imparted to the Gentiles. We know the reason why the Jews are preferred before the others; for they are the first begotten in the family of God (Exod. 4.22), and were indeed set apart from all others by a special privilege. Therefore Peter observes the correct order in giving the pre-eminence to the Jews. The addition of their children derives from the word of the promise: 'I will be thy God, and the God of thy seed after thee' (Gen. 17.7), where God reckons the children with the fathers in the grace of adoption.

This passage therefore sufficiently refutes the Anabaptists who deny baptism to the children of the faithful while they are still infants, as though they were not members of the Church. They attempt evasion by giving an allegorical meaning, and interpreting children as those who are spiritually begotten. But this gross presumption is of no profit to them. It is evident that Peter spoke thus because God adopted one nation as peculiarly His own. And circumcision bears evidence that the right of adoption was shared even by infants. Therefore as God made a covenant with Abraham when he was not yet born, because he was the seed of Abraham, so Peter teaches that all the children of the Jews are covered by the same covenant because the word continues in force which says, 'I will be the God of your seed'.

And to those who are afar off. Last of all are mentioned the Gentiles, who were formerly strangers. Those who refer it to the Jews who were driven into distant countries are completely in error. Peter is not speaking of distance in terms of place but of the distinction between Jews and Gentiles; for the Jews were the first to be joined to God by reason of the covenant and so became of His family and household, but the Gentiles were banished from His Kingdom. Paul uses the same terms in Eph. 2.11, when he says that the Gentiles who were strangers to the promise are now brought near to God through Jesus Christ. For Christ has broken down the dividing wall and has reconciled both Jews and Gentiles to the Father, and by His coming has preached peace to those who were near and to those who were far off. Now we understand Peter's meaning. That he may magnify the grace of Christ, he offers it to the Jews in such a way as to show that the Gentiles also are partakers of it. So he uses the word *call*, as though to say: 'As God formerly called you together by His voice to be one people, so that same voice shall sound forth everywhere so that those who are afar off shall join themselves to you when they are called by a fresh proclamation of God.'

And with many other words he testified, and exhorted them, saying, Save yourselves from this crooked generation. They then that received His word were baptized: and there were added unto them in that day about three thousand souls. And they continued steadfastly in the apostles' teaching and fellowship, in the breaking of bread and the prayers. (40-42)

40. *And with many.* Although in what has gone before Luke has not repeated the words of Peter but only given briefly the main points, he yet shows us here again that Peter did not provide bare doctrine only but added also the stimulus of exhortation. And he indicates clearly that he laid great insistence upon this. He marks his earnestness by saying that he testified and exhorted them. For it was not so easy for them to rid themselves at once of the errors with which they were formerly infected and to cast off the government of the priests to which they were accustomed, and so it required violence to drag them out of this mire. The point of it was that they should beware of that crooked generation. For they could not be Christ's

unless they departed from His professed enemies. The priests and scribes at that time enjoyed great authority, and by wearing the mask and guise of the Church, they deceived the simple. This was for many a severe hindrance to their coming to Christ. Some again might waver and others fall away from true faith. Peter therefore declares plainly that they are a crooked generation, however they may boast in the title of the Church. He therefore bids his hearers to separate themselves from them lest they become entangled in their godless and harmful fellowship. By the words, *save yourselves*, he means that they shall surely perish if they unite themselves to such a plague. Surely experience teaches how miserably men are tossed to and fro who cannot discern the voice of their pastor from the voice of strangers; and again what a hindrance softness and slothfulness are to many who desire to remain uncommitted. So he commands them to go out from the wicked, if they desire to be saved. And this point of doctrine is not to be neglected. It would not be enough to have Christ set before us, unless we were also taught to flee those things which lead us away from Him. It is the duty of a good pastor to defend his sheep from the onset of wolves. So today, so that we may keep the people in the pure doctrine of the Gospel, we must often show and testify how much Papistry differs from Christianity and what a hurtful plague it is to be entangled with the unfaithful enemies of Christ. Peter is not to be charged with abuse, because he calls the reverend fathers who had the ordinary government of the Church in their hands at that day a *crooked generation*. For the dangers which can draw the souls to destruction are to be pointed out by their names. For men will not beware of poison, unless they know that it is poison.

41. *They then that gladly* (*qui ergo libenter*). Luke shows clearly how fruitful this one sermon of Peter's was: namely, that it gained for Christ about three thousand men. He shows too the power of faith and its nature, when he says that readily and cheerfully they embraced His word. Faith must begin with this ready and willing desire to obey. But since many show themselves at first to be very willing, who afterwards have no constancy or steadfastness, lest we should think that it was some sudden impulse that seized them, Luke proceeds to commend their perseverance; for, as he says, they willingly embraced the word of the apostles and were joined to the disciples of Christ, or ingrafted into the same Body, and continued in their doctrine. Thus we ought to be neither slow to obey, nor swift to withdraw; but we ought to cleave steadfastly and firmly to the doctrine which we so eagerly embraced. Furthermore, this example ought to cause us no little shame. For whereas there was a great multitude converted to Christ through one sermon, a hundred

sermons can barely move a few of us; and whereas Luke says that they continued steadfast, scarcely one in ten shows even a moderate desire to advance in the faith; indeed the majority soon come to loathe our doctrine. Woe, therefore, to the dullness and the fickleness of the world!

42. *In the teaching.* Luke not only commends their constancy in faith and devotion, but says also that they applied themselves steadily to those exercises which tend to the strengthening of faith; namely, that they studied conscientiously to improve themselves by hearing the apostles, that they gave themselves much to prayer, and that they were careful to maintain the practice of fellowship and of the breaking of bread.

With regard to the apostles' teaching and to prayer, the meaning is clear. Fellowship and the breaking of bread may be understood in different ways. Some think that breaking of bread means the Lord's Supper, others that it refers to alms, others again that the faithful had their meals together in common. Some think that *κοινωνία* is the celebration of the Holy Supper; I hold rather with those who believe that that is meant by the breaking of bread. For *κοινωνία*, without addition, is never found in this sense. I therefore refer it to mutual association, alms, and other duties of brotherly fellowship. The reason why I would rather have breaking of bread to be understood here of the Lord's Supper is because Luke is recording those things which constitute the form of the church visible to the public eye. Indeed, he defines four marks by which the true and genuine appearance of the Church may be distinguished. Do we seek the true Church of Christ? The picture of it is here painted to the life. He begins with doctrine, which is the soul of the Church. He does not name doctrine of any kind but that of the apostles which the Son of God had delivered by their hands. Therefore, wherever the pure voice of the Gospel sounds forth, where men continue in the profession thereof, where they apply themselves to the regular hearing of it that they may profit thereby, there beyond all doubt is the Church.

It is easy to learn from this how frivolous is the boasting of the Papists when with gaping mouths they confidently thunder out the name of the Church, whereas they have most shamefully corrupted the entire teaching of the apostles. For if what they say be fairly examined, we shall find no sound part at all; it is for the most part as unlike the apostles' teaching as darkness from light. The rule of divine worship, which ought to be sought out of the Word of God alone, is among the Papists only compounded out of the superstitious inventions of men. They have transferred to the merits of works the hope of salvation which ought to have rested in Christ alone. The invocation of God is utterly polluted with innumerable profane ravings. Whatever is heard among them is either a distortion or an overturning of the apostles' doctrine. Therefore we may refute the foolish arrogancy of the Papists with the same ease with which they cloak their works with the title of the Church. For the abiding question must be, whether they have retained the purity of doctrine, from which they are as far distant as hell is from heaven. Yet in this point they are wise enough in that they will enter into no controversy over doctrine. But we, as I have said, may freely condemn that meaningless mask, inasmuch as the Holy Spirit pronounces that the Church is principally to be discerned by this sign, whether the simplicity of the doctrine handed down by the apostles flourishes within it.

In fellowship. This section and the last follow from the first, as fruits or effects. For doctrine is the bond of brotherly fellowship among us, and also sets open to us the door to God, that we may call upon Him; and the Supper is added to the doctrine as a confirmation. Luke is therefore justified in assembling these four points to describe to us the well-ordered state of the Church. And we must endeavour to observe this order, if we wish to be truly adjudged to be the Church before God and the angels and not only to make a boast in the empty name of it before men. It is certain that he is speaking about public prayer. Therefore, it is not enough for men to make their prayers at home by themselves, unless they all assemble together to pray; in this also consists the profession of faith.

And fear came upon every soul: and many wonders and signs were done by the apostles. And all that believed were together, and had all things common; and they sold their possessions and goods, and parted them to all, according as any man had need. (43-45)

43. *And fear came.* He shows us that the sight of the Church was such as to dismay the others who did not consent to its doctrine. This happened for the preserving and developing of the Church. When a sect arises all men vigorously oppose it, and as novelty is hateful the Jews would not have allowed the Church of Christ to stand for one moment, unless the Lord had restrained them by fear, as though by a bridle. Furthermore Luke notes the kind of fear it was, not that which leads men to obedience to Christ but that which keeps them in suspense and restrained, that they dare not hinder the Lord's work. Even so there are some at the present day who are content to be ignorant of the Gospel, or at least are so entangled with the cares of this world that they cannot completely ally themselves to Christ, and yet are not so hardened but that they recognize that the truth of God is with us; they remain therefore in the middle of the road and do not support

the cruelty of the wicked, because they are afraid to strive against God. Now when he says *every soul*, he uses a synecdoche. For certainly there were many who despised the hand of God and others were not deterred by any fear from raging against the Church. But Luke's meaning is that such power of God was evident within the Church that most of the people stood dumb.

And many wonders. This section helps to explain the effect upon the people. Together with the other works of God the miracles served to make them afraid; though this was not the only reason, but one of many why they were afraid to set themselves in opposition to God, whom they understood from the miracles to be on the side of the apostles. We learn from this that miracles are not only profitable for bringing men into obedience to God but also for making the godless somewhat more amenable and taming their ferocity. Pharaoh was a signal example of desperate stubbornness, and yet we see how miracles could at times pierce his stubborn heart. In time he forgot them, but when the hand of God was heavy upon him he was compelled through fear to give way. In short, Luke teaches that by this means the Jews were held back, that the Church which might easily have been destroyed might lift up her head. And we have often experienced the same thing in our own day. He teaches that they were not only restrained by fear from daring to do the harm that they wished to the Church, but that they were also brought low in reverence, to the glory of the Gospel.

44. *And all*. Where I have translated *joined together* Luke's words are literally, *into the same*, or, *into one*, which could be taken of the place, as though he said that they were accustomed to dwell together in the same place. But I prefer to take it of their agreement together, of which he says later (4.32) that they were of one heart. So he proceeds in the proper order, in that beginning with what they thought, he goes on to their liberality which was the fruit of that. He therefore lets us see that they were truly united among themselves with brotherly love, and gave evidence of this, in that the rich sold their goods to help the poor. Now this is a striking example of love, and Luke records it so that we may learn that we are to relieve the poverty of our brethren out of our abundance.

A sound exposition of this passage is necessary, on account of fanatical spirits who devise a *κοινωνία* of goods whereby all civil order is overturned. In our own day the Anabaptists have clamoured for this, because they thought there was no Church unless all men's goods were heaped up together and everyone took therefrom as they chose. We must beware of two extremes. For many on a pretext of civil order conceal what they possess and defraud the poor, thinking that they are doubly righteous so long as they do not seize another man's goods. Others are carried away to the opposite error, desiring to have everything mingled together. But what does Luke say? Surely he notes a different system, when he says that selection was made in the distribution. To the objection that no one had anything of his own since all things were common, there is a simple answer that common sharing of this kind must be held in check in the interest of what is next stated, namely, that the poor should be relieved according as any man have need. We know the old proverb: 'All things are common among friends.' When the Pythagoreans spoke thus, they did not mean that a man was not to govern his own house privately, or that they intended wives to be held in common. So this community of goods of which Luke speaks does not do away with household government. This will be more clearly seen in chapter 4 where he names two alone who sold possessions worth so many thousands. Thus we may gather even as I have just said, that they brought forth their goods and held them in common only with the object of relieving immediate necessity. The impudence of the monks was grotesque who profess to abide by the apostles' rule, because they call nothing their own: and yet they sell nothing, show no concern if anyone is in want, but stuff their idle bellies with the blood of the poor, and have no other interest in the community of goods than seeing that they are fully and luxuriously provided for, although the whole world should starve. What resemblance have they to the first disciples, whose counterparts they would like to be thought?

And day by day, continuing stedfastly with one accord in the temple, and breaking bread at home, they did take their food with gladness and singleness of heart, praising God, and having favour with all the people. And the Lord added to them day by day those that were being saved. (46–47)

46. *Continuing steadfastly in the temple.* We must observe that they frequented the temple for the reason that there was greater opportunity and occasion offered there for furthering the Gospel. It was not the holiness of the place that drew them since they knew that the shadowy things of the Law had had their end; nor was it their desire to encourage others by their example to the worship of the temple; but because there was there a great concourse of godly men who laid aside their private cares, which might have distracted them more fully anywhere else, and sought the Lord. They were continually in the temple, that they might win such men for Christ. There may have been a further reason that influenced them, the mutual imparting of

teaching among themselves, which would have been less convenient in private houses, especially since their numbers had increased so greatly.

Breaking bread at home. Luke indicates that they did not show the signs of true piety only in public but that the course and tenor of their private lives was of the same kind. For whereas some think that in this passage the breaking of bread means the Holy Supper this seems to me far removed from Luke's meaning. He indicates to us that they used to eat together, and to do so frugally. For those who make sumptuous banquets do not enjoy such fellowship together in their meal. Again, Luke adds, *in singleness of heart,* which is also an indication of temperance. In brief, his meaning is that their method of life together was brotherly and sober. Some join gladness and simplicity of heart with the praise of God, and the context makes this probable. But because there can be no singleness of heart in praising God which is not true of every part of life, it is therefore certain that it is here mentioned with the meaning that the believers practised it everywhere. We must note also the circumstance of their situation, how they were glad and joyful, even though surrounded by many dangers. The knowledge of God's love toward us and the assurance of His protection bring with them this blessing, that we praise God with quiet hearts whatever the world may threaten. And as Luke spoke a little earlier of the public state of the Church, so now he shows the manner of life practised by the faithful, that we may learn by their example to practise a thrifty fellowship in our way of life, to cultivate simplicity in all our living, to enjoy spiritual gladness, and to exercise ourselves in the praise of God. Furthermore simplicity of heart goes a long way; but, if united with the breaking of bread, it means as much as sincere love, where men are above board with one another and do not use guile to seize personal advantage. I prefer this attitude to its opposite, that carefulness by which provident men cause themselves so much torment. For when we do not cast our cares on God our just reward is uneasiness and fear.

47. *Having favour.* It is the fruit of a blameless life, to find favour even among strangers. Yet we need not doubt that many hated them. But although he speaks generally of the people Luke means only that section which was wholesome and not infected by the poison of hatred. He means briefly that the faithful conducted themselves in such a way that because of their blameless lives they were agreeable to the people and approved by them.

The Lord added daily. By these words he shows that their diligence did not lack its effect. They strove to the best of their ability to gather into the Lord's sheepfold those who had wandered and were straying.

He says that the labour they bestowed on this was not useless or in vain because the Lord increased the Church daily. And surely the fact that the Church is diminishing rather than increasing is to be ascribed to our slothfulness, or indeed our sinfulness. But although they all strove earnestly to increase the Kingdom of Christ, yet Luke claims this honour for God alone, that it was He who brought those outside into the Church. And surely this is His own special work. For ministers achieve nothing by planting and watering, unless He makes their works effectual by the power of His Spirit (I Cor. 3.6). Furthermore it is to be noted that he says that those were added to the Church who were to be saved. He teaches that this is the way of obtaining salvation, that we should be admitted into the Church. For outside of it, just as there is no forgiveness of sins, neither is there hope of eternal life. Furthermore this is excellent comfort for all the godly, that they were received into the Church that they might be saved, as the Gospel is called the power of God unto salvation to everyone that believeth (Rom. 1.16). Now as God calls only a part, or a certain number, this grace is restricted to election, that it may be the first cause of our salvation.

CHAPTER THREE

Now Peter and John were going up into the temple at the hour of prayer, being the ninth hour. And a certain man that was lame from his mother's womb was carried, whom they laid daily at the door of the temple which is called Beautiful, to ask alms of them that entered into the temple; who seeing Peter and John about to go into the temple, asked to receive an alms. And Peter, fastening his eyes upon him, with John, said, Look on us. And he gave heed unto them, expecting to receive something from them. But Peter said, Silver and gold have I none; but what I have, that give I thee. In the name of Jesus Christ of Nazareth, walk. And he took him by the right hand, and raised him up: and immediately his feet and his ankle-bones received strength. And leaping up, he stood, and began to walk; and he entered with them into the temple, walking, and leaping, and praising God. And all the people saw him walking and praising God: and they took knowledge of him, that it was he who sat for alms at the Beautiful Gate of the temple: and they were filled with wonder and amazement at that which had happened unto him. And as he held Peter and John, all the people ran together unto them in the porch that is called Solomon's, greatly wondering. (1-11)

1. We saw before that many signs were wrought by the hands of the apostles; now Luke, according to his usual custom, cites one out of many as an example, namely, that a lame man who was crippled in his feet from his mother's womb was perfectly restored to health. He diligently assembles all the circumstances which serve to set forth the miracle. If it had been that his legs were out of joint, or a disease resulting from an accident, the cure might have been easier. But a natural defect could not be so easily put right. When he says that the man was carried, we gather that it was no trifling lameness, but that the man lay as though his legs were dead. He would be the better known to all the people from the fact that every day he begged for alms. In that he was healed and began to walk in the temple at the hour of prayer, the knowledge of the miracle would be the more widely spread abroad. There is the added testimony that on being lifted to his feet he at once leapt up and walked joyfully.

Were going up together. Since the words ἐπὶ τὸ αὐτό indicate time as much as place, the former seems more appropriate to the context but, as it is of no importance, I state no preference. The name of the ninth hour of prayer is given to the time when day began to draw towards evening. For as the day was divided, as I have said elsewhere, from the rising of the sun to its going down, into twelve hours, that whole period was divided into four parts. So by the ninth hour is meant the last portion of the day; as the first division extended to the third hour, the second from the third to the sixth, the third from the sixth to the ninth. Hence we may rightly conjecture that that hour was appointed for the evening sacrifice. Furthermore, if anyone asks whether the apostles went up into the temple to pray according to the rites of the Law, I think this less likely to be true than that it offered a better opportunity for spreading abroad the Gospel. To take advantage of this passage to suggest that we may engage in superstitious worship would be frivolous reasoning, while we are dealing with those who are ignorant and weak. The Lord appointed that the Jews should offer sacrifice evening and morning (Exod. 29.41). By this practice they were taught to begin and end the day by calling upon God and worshipping Him (Num. 28.4). Therefore Peter and John might freely come into the temple which was consecrated to God; they did not pollute themselves seeing they called upon the God of Israel, thereby testifying their godliness. Now in that the Lord desired the people of old to observe stated hours, we gather that the Church cannot do without a fixed discipline. Even today if our excessive laziness did not prevent it, it would be valuable for us to have such meetings daily. And as the apostles went up at that hour, we understand that we must neglect no opportunity for furthering the Gospel.

3. *He asked an alms.* We see how God restored health to this lame man, contrary to his expectations. Because he thought his disease was incurable, he was anxious only for sustenance. What he would never have dared to ask was given to him. In the same way God often goes ahead of us, and does not stop until He is urged by us to do so. We are not to take from this an excuse for laziness, as if God met us of His own accord and that we should idly and slothfully allow Him to do us good. We are commanded to pray, therefore let us not omit our part. But first of all, in the person of the lame man we have the example set before us of a man not yet illuminated by faith so as to know how to pray aright. Without being asked, God forestalls such men, according to necessity. When therefore He restores our souls, not just to health but to life, the cause of His working is Himself. The first stage of our calling is that He should bring to pass what does not yet exist, that He should show Himself to those who do not seek for Him (Rom. 4.17, Isa. 65.1). Moreover, however we may be taught by faith to pray to God, yet because we are not always aware

of our miseries it does not come into our minds to seek a remedy. And so the Lord applies the remedy freely and unlooked for. Finally, however much we are given to prayer, He yet exceeds our hope and our petition with His goodness.

4. *Look upon us.* Peter does not speak thus without being certain of the purpose of God. And surely with these words He bids the man hope for some singular and exceptional blessing. Yet it may be asked whether the disciples had power to work miracles as often as they wished. My reply is that they were ministers of God's power under such conditions that they attempted nothing of their own will or initiative, but the Lord worked through them, when He knew it to be expedient to do so. Thus it happened that they healed one, and not all without exception. Therefore as in other matters, so also in this, they had the Spirit of God as their guide and director. So before Peter bade the lame man rise up he fixed his eyes steadily upon him. This steadfast gaze derived from the special prompting of the Spirit. This is why he speaks with such confident assurance of the miracle that is to take place. Furthermore by these words he wished to awaken the lame man to receive the grace of God; yet the man himself was looking for nothing but alms.

6. *Silver and gold.* Peter excuses himself as not possessing the kind of aid which the lame man was seeking. He thereby confesses that he would willingly relieve his poverty if he were able to do so, even as every one of us ought to consider what the Lord has given to him, that he may therewith help his neighbour. For God desires whatever wealth He has given to each man to be a means and an instrument for practising charity. So Peter says that he gives what he possesses. At first indeed this was an illusory promise; for Peter to speak of his poverty after he had raised the lame man to a rare sense of expectation was like mocking a gaping crow; but he comforts him immediately, so that the value of the miracle may be heightened by the contrast. It is a shocking impiety by which the Pope, at his appointment, perverts this passage by a grotesque and ludicrous pantomime. There are two cells of stone in one of which he sits; the people beg an alms, and he, using these words of Peter, sows crosses in the air with his fingers. He passes into the next cell where he has bags full of money. Then his angels acclaim him, 'He hath dispersed, he hath given to the poor' (Ps. 112.9). I quote this so that all men may see that Satan plainly is lord in that place where they so openly mock the sacred Word of God. But, to come back to the previous sentence, it is clear enough that Peter was guided by a sure revelation when he claimed to have the gifts of healing.

In the name of Jesus. He says that it is the work and blessing of

Christ which has restored to the cripple the use of his feet, for *name* is taken for authority and power. We must not dream that there is any magic virtue in the sound of the word, as the Jews foolishly allege about the name Jehovah. In brief, Peter desired to testify that he was only the minister, but that the Author of the miracle was Christ. For it was his duty and concern to see that Christ should be made known to the world and that His name should be sanctified. But why does he give Christ the description, *of Nazareth*? I leave to every man his own verdict: mine is, that, as Christ was so called in contempt, Peter meant deliberately to express that that Jesus of Nazareth whom they had crucified, whose name was despised and without glory among the Jews and was to most of them detestable, was nevertheless the Messiah promised by God, and that all power was given Him of the Father; as Paul says, that he preaches Christ, and Him crucified (I Cor. 2.2).

Rise up and walk. This might have seemed to be absurd. The cripple could readily have objected, Why have you not first given me legs and feet? For it is mockery to bid a man without feet to walk. But he believed Peter's words, and he who was at first so slow now embraces the gift of God with an eager and joyful mind. This makes plain both the efficacy of the Word and the fruit of faith. The efficacy of the Word is twofold: first that the cripple is so moved by it that he obeys at once without delay, and then that it gives strength to his dead members and makes a new man of him. And faith has her reward, for he did not in vain obey the command to rise. So we see how God works through His Word, both by giving success to the preaching of it so that it pierces the hearts of men, and also by giving from His own hand those things which are there promised. Moreover He does not allow faith to be in vain, but it truly gains possession of all the blessings which it looks for and which are offered to it through the Word. We must remember what I have already said, that in this history we have a universal type of our spiritual restoration; namely, that as the Word, laid hold of by faith, restored the cripple to health, so the Lord by His Word pierces our souls, to the end that He may restore them too. First of all, He speaks by the mouth of men and urges us to the obedience of faith; thereafter, He moves our hearts inwardly by His Spirit, that the Word may take living root within us; finally, He stretches forth His hand, and by every means completes His work in us. We gather from Matthew that miracles are to be dealt with in this way.

9. *And all the people saw.* He now begins to declare the fruit of the miracle, whereby the lame man testified his gratitude by praising God, and all the people were seized with wonder. The fruit here is twofold. The man who was healed acknowledges and confesses the

goodness of God; on the other hand, the people are moved, the report is spread abroad, and many come to behold. And whereas Luke says that they were filled with astonishment, he indicates only the first stage, which was followed by still fuller progress. It was important that they should go forward from there, because their marvelling was of no value in itself, serving rather to amaze them than to lead them to God.

Therefore the fact that the people were smitten with astonishment served as a kind of foundation for the building that was to come. If we pass over the works of God with contempt, we shall never be able to profit from them. Indeed this passage bears witness to the effect in themselves of miracles upon men, namely, a confused astonishment. For although the Lord calls us directly to Himself by showing in the miracle His power and goodness, yet such is the weakness of our nature that we stumble or faint while yet on the way to Him, until we receive the assistance that doctrine provides.

Let us therefore learn reverently to consider the works of God, that our wonder at them may serve as an entrance for doctrine. When doctrine is cold and unprofitable to us, God is thereby justly punishing us for our ingratitude in despising the glory of His works. Again, because we do not possess insight enough to discern as much as we ought in the works of God by themselves, let us learn, if we would attain to the mark, to join with it the help provided by doctrine. In brief, the one is not to be separated from the other. Experience is rich in evidence of this. For it is this fault that has caused the world to abuse miracles so shamefully.

The Papists constantly cast up to us their miracles. Though we should grant for the sake of argument that the boasts they make are true, their error would yet be great in wresting them to a false conclusion, obscuring thereby the Name of God and polluting the pure truth of the Gospel with their invention. For whence comes a cult of the saints, so widespread, superstitious, and impious, but through the abuse of miracles? For when any miracle is wrought men must be moved. But because they are deaf to the Word and do not mark God's design, Satan craftily finds an opportunity for superstition out of our own stupidity. To give an example: I acknowledge the power of God in a miracle. If it was wrought by Peter, Satan will at once suggest to me, 'Do you not see that this is a divine man? Then you owe him divine honour.' Now the same thing would have befallen the Jews in their amazement unless Peter's sermon had recalled them into the right way. But in Popery where no one condemned the superstition, an admiration of men that was beyond reason easily gained the upper hand. So we must the more earnestly seek for medicine out of the Word, that when we are transported by miracles doctrine may direct us to the proper end.

11. *In the porch.* There was probably a porch built on the site where Solomon's porch once stood and took its name from that. For the old temple had been destroyed but Zerubbabel and Ezra had imitated its form so far as they could. Afterwards Herod restored it even more magnificently, but the money that he spent in vain had not blotted out the memory of Solomon in the hearts of the people. Luke names it as a very popular spot where people often gathered.

And when Peter saw it, he answered unto the people, Ye men of Israel, why marvel ye at this man? or why fasten ye your eyes on us, as though by our own power or godliness we had made him to walk? The God of Abraham, and of Isaac, and of Jacob, the God of our fathers, hath glorified His Servant Jesus; whom ye delivered up, and denied before the face of Pilate, when he had determined to release him. But ye denied the Holy and Righteous One, and asked for a murderer to be granted unto you, and killed the Prince of life; whom God raised from the dead; whereof we are witnesses. And by faith in his name hath his name made this man strong, whom ye behold and know: yea, the faith which is through him hath given him this perfect soundness in the presence of you all. (12-16)

12. *Men of Israel.* He begins his sermon by rebuking the people. Yet he does not simply rebuke them because they wonder; for that was altogether profitable and worthy of praise; but because they wickedly ascribed to men the praise which is due to the work of God. It is as if he should say, 'You do wrong in fixing your attention upon us, when you ought rather to turn your eyes upon God and Christ.' Such astonishment then is reprehensible as it fixes our attention upon men. We must notice that he condemns respect being given to men: 'as though,' he says, 'by our own power or godliness', we had done this. So we are at fault and in error if we ascribe to the godliness or virtue of men that which belongs to God and Christ. All men agree concerning power that it comes from God alone, but when they have in a word admitted this, they do not cease to rob God of His right, and adorn His creatures with what they have taken from Him. Thus we see the Papists locating the power of God in the saints; they even enclose His divine presence in a stone or a stump of wood, as soon as the image is consecrated to Barbara or Chrysogonus. Yet even supposing they do not offend in that first aspect, they foolishly imagine that they have done their duty towards God, when they leave Him

the power, but ascribe the miracles to the godliness of the saints. For why do they run to them, when they want to obtain wet weather or fair weather or relief from illness, unless they imagine that the saints have by their godliness earned this right and privilege to be granted them by God? This is a childish evasion when, admitting that God is the Author of the power, they thank the piety of the saints for the benefits they have received. Whatever excuses they make, we must hold to the general condemnation by Peter of those who, in the event of miracles, so look to men as to imagine that their holiness is the cause of them. This is the first part of the sermon, in which superstition is reproved. We should note the manner and sequence of his teaching, for, because there is nothing to which men are more inclined than to slip away from God to His creatures, it is very important to prevent this error in good time. And if the people were forbidden to look to the apostles, the Spirit still more draws us back from the invocation of every petty saint.

13, 14. *The God of Abraham.* He now offers the cure, in calling them back to Christ, and the substance of it is this, that the purpose of God in the miracles which He works through the apostles is to set forth the glory of His Christ. It follows from this that all those who exalt Peter, or anyone else, act improperly, since all men must decrease, and Christ alone have the pre-eminence (John 3.30). In this there comes to light a clear distinction between Christ and the apostles. In the first place He is the Author, they are merely the ministers; secondly, the lawful object is that He alone should have the glory, but where glory is concerned no account is to be taken of men. It is certain that those who glorify in miracles any others but Christ, are flatly opposed to the intention of God.

He mentions the God of Abraham, Isaac, and Jacob with the object of witnessing to the people that nothing is farther from his mind than to direct them away from the former worship of the true God which they had received from their fathers. Moreover, God had taken this title to Himself, to distinguish Himself by some indication from idols. For we do not comprehend God in His essence, which is invisible and infinite. He therefore uses such means as are appropriate to us (*rationem ergo nobis congruam attemperat*) to lead us to the knowledge of Himself. Now the Turks boast that they worship God, who is the Creator of heaven and earth, but before they may approach heaven, they vanish away. To keep His people from vague and false inventions, God keeps them within His own covenant. So when He calls Himself the God of Abraham, He is teaching them briefly what Moses expounded at greater length (Deut. 30.12): 'Say not, who shall ascend into heaven? who shall go down into the depth? or who shall sail over the seas? The word is nigh,' etc. Furthermore, as among the Jews the name of the holy fathers was in high esteem, Peter tacitly reminds them that without the only begotten Son of God they were no better than other men. And in this day it is God's will to be known by a clearer indication yet, when He calls Himself the Father of Jesus Christ.

Let us now return to Peter. He says that he is bringing in no new religion such as would draw the people away from the Law and the Prophets. For God had forbidden them to listen to anyone who tried to do this (Deut. 13.3). Just as Paul teaches that in the spiritual building a single foundation must be maintained, because, as soon as we depart even a little from Christ, nothing but ruin can ensue. Hereby also we may easily discern in what sense he calls God the God of the fathers. He does not take it for a general maxim that we must continue whatever form of worship the fathers practised, even as the Papists make the foolish boast of following the worship practised by the fathers. Peter expressly names Abraham, Isaac and Jacob, from whom true religion proceeded and was handed down from God. He thereby shows us that all the fathers are not to be models for us, for many of them fell away from the first standards; but the honour of imitation should be given only to the children of God, and others are to be repudiated. This also is the constant teaching of the prophets: 'Walk not in the ways of your fathers,' etc. (Ezek. 20.16).

Whom ye have delivered. He mingles with doctrine a severe rebuke, as was required by the events. For it was impossible to bring them truly to God, unless they were first brought to the knowledge of their sins. Nor does he touch upon them lightly, but solemnly points out to them the shocking nature of the offence which they had committed. This is the point of the contrast, that they delivered to death One whom Pilate desired to set free; again, that they spared a murderer, and put to death the Prince of Life; and that they rejected the Just and Holy One. Men must be so smitten that they recognize their guilt and earnestly flee to the remedy of pardon. Peter used a like vehemence also in his first sermon. Afterwards he says that God raised Him up, by which they are to know that, in putting Christ to death, they made war against God; though Peter had his eye upon a higher outcome, namely that their cruelty in no way impaired the glory of Christ, because God nonetheless restored Him to life. When he says that he and his associates were witnesses of the resurrection, he means that they saw it with their eyes. The reference therefore is not only to the office of the apostolate, but to the fact that they saw Christ with their eyes after He was risen from the dead. I admit nonetheless that the other reference is also covered by these words, because it is likely that Peter makes mention of the function committed to him, that his authority might thereby be the greater.

16. *By faith in His name.* When he says *by faith in His name*, and, *His name*, and again, *the faith which is through Him*, such repetition is a token of a fervent affection, for because he was wholly devoted to setting forth the glory of Christ he repeatedly stresses His glory. For we see how Paul, however often he applies himself to preaching the grace of Christ, is never satisfied that he has said enough. And indeed, the nature of men is so wicked that Christ cannot be so highly extolled as to leave His glory unassailed. Let us remember therefore that Peter enlarges so freely upon his theme to ensure that we are founded upon Christ. The expression, 'His name by faith in His name hath made this man strong', points to both the cause and the manner of the healing. It was the power of Christ that healed the cripple, but operative through faith. The other expression, 'The faith which is through Him', means that our faith cannot attain to God unless it is grounded in Christ, and so that our faith looks to Christ and leans upon Him; he thus shows that there is no true faith in God except by this means.

Furthermore, just as he pointed out previously that he and the other apostles were witnesses of the life of Christ, so now he shows that this life was attested to the Jews by a sign, which was the consequence of that life; for they see the crippled healed, in whom they have a signal evidence of the divine power of Christ. And whereas in this last clause he makes faith the cause of his cure he charges them obliquely with ingratitude, if they do not give faith its rightful honour. And although faith may be referred as much to the man who was healed as to the apostles, we need not be too much concerned about this, because the power of the Gospel is set forth by synecdoche.

And now, brethren, I wot that in ignorance ye did it, as did also your rulers. But the things which God foreshewed by the mouth of all the prophets, that His Christ should suffer, he thus fulfilled. Repent ye therefore, and turn again, that your sins may be blotted out, that so there may come seasons of refreshing from the presence of the Lord; and that he may send the Christ who hath been appointed for you, even Jesus: whom the heaven must receive until the times of restoration of all things, whereof God spake by the mouth of his holy prophets which have been since the world began. (17-21)

17. In view of the danger that they should be cast down by despair and reject his doctrine, he encourages them. Our sermons must be so tempered as to profit the hearers. For unless there be some hope of pardon left, dread of punishment hardens men's heart in ob-

stinacy. The words of David are true, that we fear the Lord when we feel that He is favourable to us and able to be appeased (Ps. 130.4). In this way Peter extenuates the sins of his people because of their ignorance. For they could not have supported the awareness of this if they had knowingly and deliberately denied the Son of God and delivered Him to be slain. He has no intention of flattering them, when he says they did it through ignorance; he simply softens the harshness of his words lest they should be overwhelmed and swallowed up by His death. Again, we are not to take the words to mean that the people sinned simply through ignorance, for hypocrisy underlay this, but in so far as wickedness or ignorance was dominant, the action is attributed to the one or the other. Peter's meaning is therefore that they did it rather through error and blind zeal than through deliberate wickedness. It may be asked, whether a man who has sinned knowingly and deliberately is to despair or not. I reply that reference is not made here to every kind of sin but to the denial of Christ and the extinguishing, so far as any man can, of the grace of God. Anyone wishing to know more of this, may learn of it from I Tim. 1.13.

As did also your rulers. This seems at first to be an unfair comparison, for the scribes and priests were the victims of a fearful madness and overflowed with wickedness and treachery, whereas the people were urged on by a perverse zeal for the Law. Again, the people were incensed against Christ, in so far as their leaders urged them on. I would say in reply that they were not all of one mind: no doubt many of them were like Paul, who has such as they in mind when he writes in a certain passage of the rulers of this world, that if they had known the wisdom of God, they would never have crucified the Lord of glory. Therefore he is not speaking of rulers in general, but if any of them can be restored he invites them to repent.

18. *And God.* From this it is clearly seen to what end he speaks of ignorance. For when he says that God accomplished what He had foretold, he charges them with their responsibility in the death of Christ in such a way as to turn it to their salvation. Ignorance, he says, made you guilty, yet God has brought to pass what He determined, that Christ should redeem you by His death. It is most wonderful to consider and meditate that in the marvellous purpose of God our evil deeds are turned to a different end. Yet this does not in any way excuse us. For we go as far as we can in destroying ourselves by our sins; but that conversion of which I have spoken is a notable work of God's mercy, which we must extol with humility. The Jews did all they could to extinguish all hope of life through the person of Christ; and yet that death gave life to them as to the whole world. It is well to remember also what we saw elsewhere, lest any false and absurd

opinion should insinuate itself to the effect that Christ was exposed to the will of wicked men, that God stands as the supreme author by whose will His only begotten Son suffered. 'Repent.' We must observe that in calling them to repentance, he makes plain that there is a remission of sins prepared for them in the presence of God. For as I said a short while ago, no man can be stirred up to repentance unless salvation is set before him. The man who despairs of forgiveness and is as good as given over already to destruction has no qualms about rushing headlong against God. This is why the Papists are not able to issue the doctrine of repentance. They babble a great deal on the subject; but because they overthrow the assurance of grace they cannot hope to persuade their disciples to the study of repentance. I admit that they also babble a little regarding forgiveness of sins, but because they leave men's souls in suspense and fear and by various falsehoods drive them into a labyrinth, the corruption of this part of their teaching subverts the other part also.

That so there may come. If we follow Erasmus and the earlier translator, this sentence is elliptic, and, expressed in full would read: 'When the time of refreshing shall come you also may enjoy this refreshing; when Christ shall come to judge the world, you may find in Him a Redeemer and not a Judge.' But since Beza well translates it, 'after there shall come', it is better to adopt the less-forced rendering, provided we understand it thus: that our sins are forgiven with the day of final judgment in view, because unless we are cited to appear before the judgment seat of God we are not greatly concerned to propitiate Him. First of all, we must observe that the day of judgment is set squarely before them, to heighten the effect of the previous exhortation. For there is no more effective goad to us than the warning that we shall one day give account. For so long as our senses have their whole concern within this world, they are oppressed, as it were, by a kind of lethargy. Therefore the message of the last judgment must sound as a trumpet to cite us to appear before the judgment seat of God. For then at last we are truly awakened, and begin to think about a new life. Similarly, when Paul is preaching at Athens, he says that God now wills all men to repent; because he has appointed a day wherein He will judge the world (Acts 17.30, 31). In short, Christ, who when He teaches us through the Gospel acts as a master, has been appointed by the Father as our Judge, and will come in His own time. Therefore we are to obey His teaching in good time, so that in that day we may gather the fruits of our faith.

But some may object that Peter does not speak in these terms of the Last Day. For the words, *A time of refreshing*, are not such as to create fear. My reply is that the faithful have a twofold stimulus to encourage them when they hear tell of the last judgment. For in this world the advantages of faith are not evident; indeed it is those who despise God who seem rather to prosper while the lives of the godly are full of countless miseries. Therefore our hearts would often be dismayed, if we did not recall that the day of rest will come, which will cool the fever of our troubles and bring an end to our miseries. The other stimulus that I mention is that the fearful judgment of God shakes us out of our pleasures and sloth. So Peter in this passage combines threats and promises partly to win the Jews to Christ, partly to prick them with fear. This is a common practice in the Scriptures, since it speaks both to the reprobate and to the elect, representing the day of the Lord at one time as dreadful and fearful and at another time as pleasant and desirable. Peter therefore, in putting the Jews in hope of pardon, rightly presents the day of Christ to them as a day of joy, so that they may desire it.

20. *And that He may send Him.* He expressly names Christ as the Judge, to let them know that contempt of the Gospel will not go unpunished. For surely Christ must be the One to punish that. At the same time this fact brings wonderful comfort to the faithful, when they know that the verdict regarding their salvation will be in the control of Him who now promises and offers it. He adds that He who is to come is the one who is now preached to them, to take away every excuse of ignorance. It is as if he should say: 'Christ is preached to you now, before He comes to judge the world, so that those who now embrace Him may in that day receive the fruit of their faith, while others who refuse Him may receive the punishment of their unbelief.' There are two readings found in the Greek. Some manuscripts have *προκεκηρυγμένον*, i.e. preached before: others read *προκεχειρισμένον*, i.e. shown, or set before their eyes. But the sense is the same in both cases, that in the teaching of the Gospel Christ is not offered to them in vain, because He shall be sent by the Father a second time to be a Judge, armed to execute vengeance, unless they receive Him now as their Redeemer.

21. *Whom the heavens must receive.* Because men's senses invariably tend to the material and earthly vision of God and Christ, the Jews might think that while Christ was preached as having been raised from the dead it was not revealed where He was. Peter anticipates this by saying that He is in heaven. It follows that they must raise their minds on high to seek Christ with the eyes of faith, although in respect of distance He is infinitely far removed from them, and although He dwells outwith the world in the heavenly glory. Yet this is an ambiguous expression, because we can as well understand that Christ is received or comprehended by the heavens as that He Himself compre-

hends the heavens. Let us therefore not press the word since it is of uncertain meaning; but let us content ourselves with that which is certain, that we must seek for Christ nowhere else but in heaven, while we await the final restoration of all things; for He will be far removed from us until our minds can transcend this world.

Until the times of restoration. Christ by His death has already restored all things, as far as the power to achieve this and the cause of it are concerned; but the effect of it is not yet fully seen, because that restoration is still in process of completion, and so too our redemption, forasmuch as we still groan under the burden of servitude. For as the Kingdom of Christ is only begun, and the perfection of it is deferred until the last day, so the benefits that are annexed to it are now only partly evident. If therefore at the present time we see much confusion in the world, let us lift up our hearts and be revived by the hope that Christ shall one day come and restore all things. Meanwhile, if we see the remains of sin hanging about us, if we are beset on all sides with miseries of many kinds, if the world is full of destruction, let us not so bewail our miseries that we be not sustained by the hope of restoration. This is the reason why Christ does not immediately appear, because the warfare of the Church is not yet complete, the season for which, being appointed by God, is not ours to anticipate.

Whereof He spake. I do not interpret this of the special times alone; I refer it to the whole period, so that the sense is, that whatever he had said before regarding the Kingdom of Christ is witnessed to by all the prophets. Indeed it is no small testimony to the truth of the Gospel that, from the time when God began to manifest Himself to the world, He always set Christ before men; from the time that he began to speak to the fathers, this was the fundamental doctrine that He laid down. By the same argument Paul commends the Gospel, both at the beginning of his epistle to the Romans and at the end, as being no new doctrine but something promised from the earliest days. This is antiquity indeed, designed to win credence for doctrine, when God Himself is the Author of it and the holy prophets the witnesses, and an unbroken course of time confirms the testimony. This confirmation was especially necessary for the Jews who had been brought up in the doctrine of the Law, and for whom it was not proper to admit anything which did not agree with it. Therefore Peter bids them recognize only what the prophets testified of Christ.

Moses indeed said, A prophet shall the Lord God raise up unto you from among your brethren, like unto me; to him shall ye hearken in all things whatsoever he shall speak unto you. And it shall be, that every soul, which shall not hearken to that prophet, shall be utterly destroyed from among the people. Yea and all the prophets from Samuel and them that followed after, as many as have spoken, they also told of these days. (22-24)

22. By this argument he proves that he is not urging them to revolt from Moses, because it is a part of the Law to learn from and obey this supreme teacher. It may be questioned why Peter thought fit to quote this testimony rather than others, since there were many more striking passages available; but he did it because at this point he is dealing with the authority of the teaching, and this was a fair method of bringing the Jews to be disciples of Christ. For he would have preached in vain on other matters, unless they had been persuaded that his teaching was to be received with reverence. Peter's object therefore is to make them hear Christ gladly, as the Teacher appointed for them by God.

But another question of much greater difficulty arises at this point, namely that Peter applies to the person of Christ what Moses spoke generally of the prophets. For although he uses the word *prophet* in the singular, yet the context clearly indicates that he is not speaking of one only but uses the word in the most general sense. For after Moses has forbidden the people to give themselves to the superstitions of the Gentiles by turning aside to wizards and soothsayers, he at once shows them a remedy whereby they may avoid all such vanity; namely, if they depend wholly upon the Word of God alone. By this means he promises that God will take care always to provide prophets to teach them aright. As if he should say, God will never allow you to be destitute of prophets from whom you may learn whatever will be advantageous for you to know. And Moses says expressly, *of thy brethren*, so that the Jews may know that the oracles of God are to be sought nowhere else, since God has appointed for them teachers from the race of Abraham. He adds further, *like unto me*, to let them know they were not to hear God only at one time or by the voice of one man; but as God continues to teach us through the unbroken line of the ages, so we must go on in obedience to the Word. Therefore as the Jews were accustomed to reverence Moses, he claims the same honour for the prophets. I know that many would restrict this to Christ. They seize upon the word where Moses testifies that the prophet shall be like himself, whereas it is written that there arose none like unto Moses. I admit that in both passages there is the same indication of similarity, but in a different sense. For in the second passage, as can clearly be seen, likeness or equality is expressed. They also seize on another point, that the prophet to whom like a herald Moses bears witness shall far excel him (Deut.

18.15). But this objection has no greater force than the other, because Moses is simply concerned to ensure that the Word of God will be believed, whoever the bearer of it may be.

There is no reason then for us to incur the mockery of the Jews by using violence to twist the words of Moses, as though he spoke of Christ alone at this point. Nevertheless we must examine whether Peter is justified in quoting the testimony, whose authority ought to give us a sound basis for our position. I maintain that there is nothing in Peter's sermon which is not wholly appropriate. For he saw what all men ought to admit, that this testimony applies to the other prophets, and yet in such a way as principally to commend Christ, not only because He is the Chief of all the prophets but because all the earlier prophecies were directed towards Him, and because God at the end spoke absolutely by His Mouth. For God spoke in diverse manners and at sundry times in the past unto our fathers by the prophets, but has finally in these last days completed His revelation in His only begotten Son (Heb. 1.1-2). Therefore it came to pass that for many ages before His coming they were without prophets, as we may clearly gather from the words of Malachi, who, after bidding the people be mindful of the Law, passes on at once to John the Baptist and to Christ, as if to say that the prophecies have now come to an end until the final revelation comes (Mal. 4.4-6): in accordance with the words, 'The Law and the prophets prophesied until John; after that the Kingdom of God is preached' (Matt. 11.13). This was so commonly accepted among the people that the woman of Samaria could say, expressing the view widely held, 'We know that Messiah shall come, who will teach us all things' (John 4.25). Therefore we know that after the return of the people all the prophets ceased, that by reason of the period of silence when there was an interval in revelation they might be made more attentive to hear Christ. Peter therefore did not distort this passage, or misuse it through ignorance, but he took as a principle the teaching that was accepted by all: that God had promised to teach His people, in the early stages through the mediation of prophets, but at the end principally through Christ, at whose hands they were to look for the full and perfect manifestation of all things. This is the purpose of the notable testimony with which the Father commended him, 'Hear him' (Matt. 17.5).

23. *Every soul.* The authority of all the prophets, but especially of Christ, is here established by the gravity of the punishment of the rebellious. And rightly so, for since there is nothing which God accounts more precious than His Word, he cannot allow it to be despised with impunity. If any man therefore rejected the law of Moses, he was adjudged worthy of death. Moses had regard to this

when he said, 'He shall be put away from among the people.' For God had adopted the race of Abraham for Himself, upon the condition that their highest blessing should consist in being counted in that number; as it is said in the Psalm, 'Blessed is the people whose God is the Lord' (33.12), and in another passage, 'Blessed is the nation whom the Lord hath chosen to be His inheritance.' From this there is no doubt that He declares that whosoever shall refuse to hear Christ shall be blotted out of the Book of Life. For he does not deserve to be counted within the Church, who refuses to have as his Master Him by whom alone God teaches us, and by whom He will have us to hear Himself. That man severs himself from the Body, who refuses to be subject to the Head.

24. *And all.* His statement that all the prophets with one consent send their disciples to Christ bears out more clearly my words, that the commendation of the Gospel is contained within the testimony of Moses, and so that the final cessation of prophecy is especially noted. Now this serves to confirm the certainty of the Gospel, that through a long succession of ages all the prophets so order the manner of their teaching that they testify with one voice that men are to look for some better and more perfect thing. Therefore, whoever will believe Moses and the prophets must submit himself to the doctrine of Christ (John 5.47), apart from which all that they taught is lame and incomplete.

Ye are the sons of the prophets, and of the covenant which God made with your fathers, saying unto Abraham, And in thy seed shall all the families of the earth be blessed. Unto you first God, having raised up his Servant, sent him to bless you, in turning away every one of you from your iniquities. (25-26)

25. *Ye are the sons.* He signifies that the grace of the covenant which God made with their fathers was destined particularly for them. Just as he has urged them to obey the Gospel by inspiring them with fear of punishment, so now he encourages them again to receive the grace of God offered them in Christ. We may see thereby that God omits nothing whereby He may bring us to Himself. It is the duty of a wise minister both to goad onward those who are lazy and sluggish, and to lead gently those who are prepared to be taught. We must carefully note the course of this teaching, whereby Peter shows that the Gospel is destined for the Jews. For it is not enough to have the mercy of God preached to us in general terms, unless we also know that it is offered to us by the definite ordinance of God. It is for this reason that Paul is so insistent upon emphasizing the calling of the Gentiles (Rom. 15.18; Eph. 3.3-4): because if a man thought that the

Gospel had been scattered broadcast and had come to him by accident, his faith would be unsure—indeed there would be an uncertain opinion in place of faith. Therefore, that we may have secure faith in the promise of salvation, this application, if I may so term it, is necessary, that God does not fling out vague utterances which remain suspended in the air but that He directs his Word to us by His determinate counsel. Peter tells the Jews that it is in this manner that Christ is promised to them, to the end that they may the more confidently embrace Him. How does he prove this? Because they are the children of the prophets and of the covenant. He calls them children of the prophets, for they were descended from the same nation and were therefore heirs of the covenant which applied to the whole body of the people. His argument is that God made His covenant with our fathers, and therefore we who are their descendants are included within it.

The foolish subtleties of the Anabaptists are thereby refuted, who interpret the sons of Abraham allegorically, as though God had had no regard to his race when He said, 'I will be the God of thy seed' (Gen. 17.7). Certainly Peter is not here speaking about the shadows of the Law, but he affirms that this is applicable within the Kingdom of Christ, that God's adoption extends to the children as well as the fathers, and thus the grace of salvation may be extended to those who are not yet born. I grant that many who are the children of the faithful according to the flesh are counted bastards and not legitimate (Rom. 9.7), because by their unbelief they banish themselves from the family of the holy. But this in no way prevents God from calling and admitting the seed of the godly into the fellowship of His grace, nor common election, though not effectual in all, from opening a door for special election, even as Paul set forth in Rom. 11.23, where the answer to this question must be sought.

And in thy seed. He establishes that the covenant was made with the fathers, because God said to Abraham, 'In thy seed shall all nations be blessed.' But if we accept Paul's interpretation this testimony does not affect the present case. Paul teaches that this seed is Christ. If the blessing is promised through Christ to the entire human race what connexion has this with a special privilege for one family? Then again, Peter himself seems shortly afterwards to subscribe to the exposition of Paul, when he says that Christ was sent, in whom the Jews may be blessed. For this could not be, unless Christ were that blessed seed. I reply that in his reference to Christ Paul does not take his stand upon the word 'seed' but has a wider concern, namely, that the seed cannot be one, unless it is made one in Christ as the Head. For Ishmael and Isaac, though both sons of Abraham, do not constitute one seed, because they were divided into two peoples. Therefore although many are estranged from the family of Abraham who derive from him, according to the flesh, Moses yet points to a single definite body, when he promises the blessing to the seed of Abraham. Now where is this unity to be found, save only in Christ as the head? In this sense Paul understands the word *seed* of Christ, even though it is a collective noun; for if He is deserted, the posterity of Abraham will be as members torn asunder; they will have nothing to show in themselves but will be scattered and dispersed. Peter agrees with this doctrine, when he extends the blessing to all the people, and yet seeks the source of it in Christ.

Furthermore, since the Jews leave no stone unturned to extort this testimony from us, godly readers must arm themselves against their arguments; and all the more, because Christian writers have been too slack at this point, as I pointed out in commenting on Gal. 3.16. In the first place, regarding the word *seed*, they have no right to babble on that Paul is in error in restricting it to Christ, for he does not do so simply and exclusively, but in the sense that I have indicated. In this point, I confess, our interpreters, both Greek and Latin, have erred. Let us see what is the significance of the saying, that the Gentiles shall be blessed in the seed of Abraham. They think that one cause is being mentioned, namely, that through that seed the Gentiles are to be blessed. The Jews make much play with this, because everywhere in Scripture this phrase refers to an example or simile; as, conversely, to be cursed in Sodom, or in Israel, or in another people is to use them as a notable example of a curse. I reply that this is a doubtful expression and to be understood in a variety of ways according to the context of the passages—a fact which the Jews basely and craftily conceal. For they assemble many passages in which they show that a comparison is made; as if the meaning were, 'The Gentiles desire to be blessed like the seed of Abraham.' But in other passages where Scripture records, 'They shall bless themselves in the living God', as Jer. 4.2, Isa. 65.16; and again, 'To bless in the name of the Lord' (Deut. 10.8), and in other similar passages, it is surely evident that there is a cause expressed. Therefore I maintain that this form of speech must be taken in accordance with the context.

And now that I have shown that the seed of Abraham is only to be found in Christ it remains for us to consider the nature of the office of Christ. From this it will appear beyond question that He is not given as a bare example, but that the blessing is truly promised in Him, because without Him we are all accursed. Yet one difficulty remains. For while both expressions, *they shall be blessed in thee*, and, *in thy seed*, are used with the same sense, Abraham was no more than a type or mirror of the blessing. My reply is that in the person of Abraham there is also shown forth that body which depends on, and is knit together in, the one head.

All the families. The Jews expound these words crudely, to the effect that all nations shall desire to be blessed like the seed of Abraham. But we expound it in a different sense—that they shall be ingrafted into the one society. For the name of Abraham points to a day when God shall gather all the nations to Himself. When the prophets too desire to express the meaning of these words they always foretell that the inheritance of salvation shall be shared by the Gentiles. Hence we see that the covenant of God, which at that time belonged to the Jews alone, is not only common to all men but is made expressly with ourselves. We could not otherwise conceive that hope of salvation which from the Gospel is assured to us. Let us then not allow this promise to be wrested from us, which is a solemn proclamation by which the Lord makes us His heirs together with the fathers. Peter had this in mind too, when he said presently that Christ was sent first to the Jews; for he indicates that the Gentiles also have their place, even though it be secondary.

26. *He hath raised up his Son.* He gathers from the words of Moses that the Christ is now revealed. The words might seem to have no such meaning, yet his reasoning is correct, that the blessing could not otherwise come to pass unless it had its source in the Messiah. For we must always remember that all mankind is accursed, but that a singular remedy is promised to us which is provided through Christ alone. He therefore is the only source and fount of blessing. But if Christ came with the purpose of blessing the Jews first, and thereafter ourselves, He has undoubtedly fulfilled His duty; and we shall experience in ourselves the power and effect of this work, unless we are hindered by our unbelief.

Under the Law it was part of the priestly office to bless the people; and lest this should be only an empty ceremony, there was added a promise, which we find in Num. 6.27. Now what was foreshadowed in the former priesthood was truly performed in Christ. On this we have spoken at greater length on Heb. 7.16. I do not like Erasmus' translation; for he says, *when He had raised Him up*, as if he spoke of something done long ago. But Peter means rather that Christ when He was shown to be the Author of the blessing was raised from the dead, and that the fact that this took place recently and suddenly ought to affect them the more. For the Scriptures commonly refer thus, as in the last passage, to Moses, of whom Peter is speaking. To raise up a prophet is to furnish him with the gifts necessary for the fulfilling of his office, and to promote him as it were to the rank of prophetic honour. Christ was raised up when He performed the duty laid upon Him by the Father, yet this happens daily when through the Gospel He is offered, that He may have first place amongst us. We have noted that the adverb *first* points to the right of the first begotten, for it was right that Christ should begin with the Jews and afterwards pass to the Gentiles.

In turning away every one of you. He again commends the doctrine of repentance, that we may learn to include in the blessing of Christ newness of life; even as when Isaiah, in promising that the Redeemer shall come to Zion, adds the reservation, 'As many in Jacob as shall turn from their iniquities' (59.20). For Christ does not do away with the sins of the faithful to the end that they should thereby grant liberty to themselves to sin; but He makes them at that moment new men. And yet we must carefully distinguish these two benefits that are linked together, so that the basis of the Gospel may remain, namely, that we are reconciled to God by free pardon. I know that other men turn it differently, but this is the true meaning of Luke; for these are his very words, 'In turning every one from his iniquities.'

CHAPTER FOUR

And as they spake unto the people, the priests and the captain of the temple and the Sadducees came upon them, being sore troubled because they taught the people, and proclaimed in Jesus the resurrection from the dead. And they laid hands on them, and put them in ward unto the morrow: for it was now eventide. But many of them that heard the word believed; and the number of the men came to be about five thousand. (1-4)

Three things are to be chiefly noted in this narration. First, that as soon as the truth of the Gospel comes to light, Satan sets himself in opposition to it by every means in his power, and uses every endeavour to crush it in its earliest beginnings. Secondly, that God furnishes His children with unconquerable fortitude, that they may stand firm and unmoved against all the devices of Satan and may not yield to the violence of the wicked. Finally, we must note the outcome, that however completely the enemy may appear to be dominant and in control of events, leaving no stone unturned to blot out the Name of Christ, and however much on the other hand the ministers of sound doctrine be as sheep in the mouths of wolves, God none the less spreads abroad the Kingdom of His Son, keeps alive the light of His Gospel, and looks to the safety of His children. So when the Gospel begins to be taught but meets with various movements arising in opposition and finds its course hindered in many ways, there is no cause for the minds of the godly to faint or fear as though what happened was strange; they should rather remember that these are the normal endeavours of Satan. We ought therefore to consider well, before it comes to pass, that Satan will surely pour forth his own attacks whenever Christ appears in the open with His teaching. Let us also recall that the constancy of the apostles is given us as an example, lest we be overcome, whether by dangers or threats or fears, and withdraw from that profession of faith which the Lord requires of us. Moreover, let us comfort ourselves with the assurance that we need not doubt that the Lord will give success at the last, when we have done our duty faithfully.

1. *And as they spake.* This shows how watchful the wicked are, since they are prepared at an instant to stop the mouth of the servants of Christ. Evidently they came together in haste as though there were a fire to be put out. Luke shows this, when he says that the governor

of the temple came also, and adds that they were grievously put out because the apostles were teaching. So they came upon the scene, not by chance but of set purpose, to restrain the apostles by their authority. They had indeed justification in law. For it was the duty of priests to restrain the audacity of such as rashly intruded, and at the same time to keep the people obedient to the Law and the Prophets, and to prevent all new doctrines. Therefore when they heard unknown men who had no public authority preaching to the people in the temple, it seems that they applied themselves, as required by their office and by the command of God, to dealing with the situation. At first glance indeed there seems to be nothing in this action worthy of censure, but the outcome shows that their design was wicked and their disposition ungodly.

Again, it was difficult for the apostles to escape being branded with censure in that, being private individuals without honour, they claimed for themselves public authority. And this they did, because in times of disorder much has to be attempted contrary to accepted custom, and especially when religion and the worship of God require to be defended and those in authority bar every road and oppose God by abusing the office to which He has appointed them. This is the ignominy which the faithful champions of Christ have to swallow under the Papacy. For a thousand summers will pass before any reformation and improvement will come to maturity among them. So Luke takes his stand upon this point, when he says that they were grieved and troubled because the resurrection was preached in the name of Christ. For it follows from this that they hated the doctrine before they knew what it was. He mentions the Sadducees expressly as those who were more zealous in this cause. For they were generally associated with the priests, but because the resurrection was at issue they set themselves in opposition more than the rest. It was indeed a sign of monstrous confusion among the Jews that so profane a sect could have such authority. For what godliness could remain when the immortality of the soul could be counted, without censure, as a fable? Yet so it is that men must rush headlong in this way when once they allow the pure doctrine of God to lapse among them. We must with all diligence beware of every turning aside to evil, lest such a ruinous fall should speedily follow.

Some think that the *captain of the temple* was chosen from among the priests, but I rather believe that he was some officer of the Roman army. For the place was fortified both naturally and artificially. Again Herod had built there a tower which was called Antonia. So it is likely that he had put a garrison there and that the Roman captain was in control of the temple to ensure that if the Jews stirred up a tumult they could find no refuge there; this we may gather from Josephus. It agrees well that the enemies of Christ implored the help of the secular power under the pretext of putting down a tumult. Meanwhile they seek favour at the hands of the Romans, as though they were anxious to maintain the rights of their empire.

4. *And many of them.* The apostles are shut up in prison but the effect of their preaching spreads far and wide and has free course. Thus too, Paul boasts in triumph that the Word of God is not bound with him (II Tim. 2.9). Here we see that Satan and the wicked have freedom given them to rage against the children of God, yet by all their machinations they cannot prevent God from advancing the Kingdom of His Son, or Christ from gathering together His sheep, or a few men unarmed and with no warlike resources from revealing more power, by their words alone, than is possessed by the whole world in its raging against them. This is no ordinary work of God, that one sermon should produce such abundant and plentiful fruit; and yet it is still more remarkable that the dangers of the present time do not terrify the faithful from taking up the cross of Christ as the accompaniment of faith. This was a hard beginning for novices. By the effectiveness of this teaching Christ showed that He was alive more clearly than if He had offered His body to be handled and to be seen by the eyes of men. Where it is said that the number of those who believed increased to about five thousand, I take this to refer not to those who were newly added, but to the number of the whole Church.

And it came to pass on the morrow, that their rulers and elders and scribes were gathered together in Jerusalem; and Annas the high priest was there, and Caiaphas, and John, and Alexander, and as many as were of the kindred of the high priest. And when they had set them in the midst, they inquired, By what power, or in what name, have ye done this? Then Peter, filled with the Holy Ghost, said unto them, Ye rulers of the people, and elders, if we this day are examined concerning a good deed done to an impotent man, by what means this man is made whole; be it known unto you all, and to all the people of Israel, that in the name of Jesus Christ of Nazareth, whom ye crucified, whom God raised from the dead, even in him doth this man stand here before you whole. He is the stone which was set at nought of you the builders, which was made the head of the corner. And in none other is there salvation: for neither is there any other name under heaven, that is given among men, wherein we must be saved. (5-12)

5. It is worth noting in this place, that the wicked overlook no act

of cunning to blot out the Gospel and the name of Christ, and yet their hopes remain unfulfilled, because God frustrates their counsels. They meet together in an assembly where the control of tyranny is such that wilfulness has the appearance of law and liberty is banished, and truth can appear to have been rightly condemned. But the Lord brings upon them sudden fear so that they dare not do what is in their power and what they most desire. Again, whatever the apostles bring in defence of their case shall remain shut up within prison walls where there is none to support them; and so there is no place for truth. Yet we see how the Lord brings their counsel to nought; for they stand still through the pressure of fear of the people, and they bridle their fury to avoid envious hostility. It is strange that Luke here makes Annas the high priest, since it is clear from Josephus that this office was not taken from Caiaphas until Vitellius entered Jerusalem to take command after Pilate had been ordered to Rome. All agree that the Lord was crucified in the eighteenth year of Tiberius. And the reign of Tiberius continued for four more years. Not less than three years must have passed after the death of Christ before Pilate was removed from the office of pro-consul. For Tiberius was dead when he came to Rome. So Caiaphas was still high priest for three years after the death of Christ. It is likely therefore that the events narrated here by Luke did not happen immediately after the resurrection of Christ; although not even in this way will the whole difficulty be solved. For Josephus reports that Jonathan was appointed in place of Caiaphas; yet because this Jonathan was the son of Annas it is not unlikely that the son was called by the father's name; Caiaphas also had two names, being also known as Joseph.

7. *By what power.* They still give the appearance of having zeal for God. For they profess to be concerned that the honour due to God should not be given to another. *Name* here indicates authority. In a word, they act as if they were notable defenders of the glory of God. Meanwhile they are remarkably insistent in their questioning, whereby they seek to bring the apostles to make denial by constant questioning on a matter which is evident to all, and to wring out of them by fear a statement at variance with what they had confessed. But God brings their craft and guile to nought, and makes them hear what they have no desire for.

8. *Peter, filled with the Holy Ghost.* It is with good reason that Luke expressly adds these words, that we may know that Peter did not make such a superb utterance of himself. Surely, he who had been frightened by the voice of a mere woman and had denied Christ would have collapsed utterly before such an assembly at the mere sight of such pomp, unless he had been upheld by the power of the

Spirit. He had great need of prudence and fortitude. In both of these he so excelled that his reply was truly divine. He was quite another man than what he had been before. Now this profits us in two ways, for this commendation carries much weight in introducing the doctrine which is presently to follow, when it is said to have come forth from the Holy Spirit. Also, we are taught to seek from the Lord when we make profession of our faith the Spirit of fortitude and prudence to direct our hearts and minds and spirits. The fulness of the Spirit denotes a full and exceptional measure.

9. *If we today*. There is no doubt that Peter here charges the priests and the scribes with tyranny, because they examine them unfairly concerning a benefit that is worthy of commendation, as though he and his companion had committed some heinous offence. 'If', he says, 'we are accused because we have conferred health upon a sick man': Peter is here more concerned with their wicked attitude of mind than with the precise terms of the charge. For if, under the guise of a miracle, the apostles had sought to draw the people away from the true and sincere worship of God, they would rightly have been summoned to answer for themselves, since religion far excels all the good things of this present life. But since the accusers wickedly and without cause create an offence out of what they should have held in honour, Peter, supported by his confidence in this, begins by rebuking them lightly in a mocking preface because they sit as judges to condemn good deeds. However he merely touches on this in passing on to the more weighty matter.

10. *Be it known unto you*. Peter could, as I have said, have turned aside to various subterfuges, if he had been unwilling to embark upon the cause, but because the miracle was wrought to the end that the name of Christ might be glorified, he soon comes round to this. For he knew that he was the minister of this supreme power of God that he might have a seal to confirm his teaching. In the process the wicked are obliged to hear what they would have chosen to have hidden and buried. All that they achieved by all their machinations was to have Peter declare to their very face what they objected to when it was spoken to others. In the first place he attributes the miracle to Christ. Secondly, because it seemed absurd and incredible that a dead man should be endowed with divine power, he testifies that Christ is alive because God raised Him from the dead even when they had crucified Him. Thus the miracle gives him the opportunity to preach the resurrection of Christ. By this testimony Peter intended to prove that He was the true Messiah. He reminds them that they crucified Him, not simply to upbraid them and bring them to acknowledge their faults, but also that they may understand that they have striven

in vain against God and may thereby desist from their mad folly with its disastrous and ill-fated outcome.

11. *He is the stone.* He confirms by the testimony of Scripture that it is no new thing that the prelates of the Church who exult in their glorious titles and occupy the chief place in the temple of God have yet wickedly rejected Christ. Therefore he quotes the passage in Ps. 118.22, where David complains that he is rejected by the leaders of the people and yet boasts that he was chosen by God to have the chief place. Moreover, by a common metaphor, he compares the Church, or the state of the Kingdom, to a building. He calls those who hold the reins of government the master builders, and he names himself the principal stone on which the whole weight of the building rests. That is what is meant by *the head of the corner*. Therefore this is David's consolation, that no matter how thoroughly he has been rejected by the captains, so that they would not leave him even the lowest station, yet their godless and wicked endeavours did not hinder him from being raised by God to the highest degree of honour. But in David there was foreshadowed what God intended to express most fully in the Messiah. Peter was therefore quite in order in citing this passage in his speech to the Jews as a prediction of Christ, since they were well aware that it properly referred to him. Now we know Peter's object in quoting the Psalm; namely, lest the elders and priests should be so puffed up beyond reason on account of their honour that they should take to themselves authority and power to allow or disallow whatever they pleased. For it is evident that the stone that was rejected by the master builders is placed by the hand of God in the most important position to support the whole house.

Furthermore, this happens not once only but is of necessity fulfilled every day; it ought at least to seem no strange or unlikely thing if today also the master builders reject Christ. By this the empty boasting of the Pope is plainly refuted, who makes his boast of a bare title, that he may usurp whatever belongs to Christ. Should we allow to the Pope and his horned creatures what they demand, namely, to be ordinary pastors of the Church, they could not rise any higher in the end than to be called, with Annas and Caiaphas, master builders. It is evident what is the value of this title which they regard as sufficient for mingling together heaven and earth. Now let us briefly gather from this passage some things worth noting. As the leaders of the Church are called master builders, the name itself reminds them of their duty. Let them give themselves therefore wholly to the building of the temple of God. And since all men do not do their duty faithfully, let them observe what is the correct method of building aright, which is to keep to Christ as the Foundation. Next, let them not mix straw or stubble in the building, but let them complete the whole building from pure doctrine, as Paul teaches in I Cor. 3.12. The fact that God is said to have extolled Christ who had been rejected by the builders ought to encourage us when we see the very pastors of the Church, or those at least who have the most exalted offices, wickedly rebel against Christ to cast Him forth and banish Him. For we may safely ignore the unreal objections which they raise against us, and we need not hesitate to grant Christ the honour which God gives to Him. But though He is patient and turns a blind eye to them, He yet laughs from on high at the boldness of His enemies while they fret and fume upon earth. Furthermore though their conspiracies be strong and well equipped and furnished, we must yet always assure ourselves that Christ's honour will remain secure. And let it follow as the fruit of this confidence, that we be valiant and fearless in maintaining the Kingdom of Christ, of which God affirms that He Himself will be its invincible Champion. We have already spoken of Peter's constancy, in that one simple man, in face of such hostile judges, and with only one companion in danger, showed no sign of fear, but freely confessed in that violent gathering what he knew would be received with great indignation. From his severe rebuke of their crimes we are to learn a rule of speech for the occasions when we have to deal with the open enemies of the truth. For we must beware of two faults in this connexion. The first is that we do not appear to flatter by keeping silence or turning a blind eye, for silence by which the truth should be betrayed would be disloyal. The second is that we are not puffed up with impudence or undue indignation, as men's tempers are liable to break out in the heat of contention. Let us therefore show gravity, yet not more than is reasonable. Let us rebuke freely, and yet stop short of the passion of abuse. We see how Peter stayed within these limits. For at the beginning he addresses them in honourable terms, yet when he comes to the point at issue, he attacks them sharply, for such shameful wickedness as theirs could not be passed over in silence. Those who follow this example will have not Peter only, but also the Spirit of God as their guide.

12. *And in none other is there salvation.* He passes from the particular to the more general, from bodily advantage to the health of the whole. Surely Christ had offered this single indication of His grace so that He might be recognized to be the only Author of life. Amid the various blessings of God we must take note of this—that He is the source of salvation. By this sentence Peter meant to prick the priests, by declaring that there is salvation in none other than in Christ, whom they sought to obliterate. It is as if he were saying that they were doubly damned who not only rejected the salvation offered them by God

but sought to bring it to nought, denying the effect and advantage of it to the whole people. And although he seems to be addressing men who are deaf, he yet preaches of the grace of Christ, if perchance some can endure to hear it: and if not, that by this testimony they may be made the more inexcusable.

For neither is there any other name. He adds an explanation of the previous sentence. In Christ alone, he says, is salvation, for God has so decreed it. For by *name* he means the cause or means, as if he had said, 'Since salvation is in God's power only, He will not have us partakers of it by any other way than that we seek it from Christ alone.' The words, *under heaven*, are commonly taken as applying to created beings, as meaning that in all creation there is given to Christ the power and authority to save. Yet I rather think that this was inserted because men cannot ascend to heaven to attain to God. Since we are therefore so far from the Kingdom of God, it is necessary that God should not only invite us to Himself but should reach out His hand and offer salvation to us so that we may enjoy it. Peter teaches us here that this is what God has done in Christ, who came down to earth to bring salvation with Him. This does not disagree with the doctrine that Christ has ascended above all heavens (Eph. 4.10). For He took our flesh upon Him once, that He might be an everlasting pledge of our adoption. He has reconciled the Father to us for ever by the sacrifice of His death; by His resurrection He has purchased for us eternal life. And now also He is present with us, that He may make us partakers of the fruit of eternal redemption. But in the present passage we are dealing with the revelation of our salvation, which we know to have been so revealed in Christ, that we need no longer say, 'Who shall ascend into heaven?' (Rom. 10.6). If this doctrine were deeply imprinted on the minds of all men, many controversies concerning the causes of salvation, by which the Church is so troubled, would be settled. The Papists admit with us that salvation is of God alone, but they coin a multitude of ways whereby it is to be attained. They dare not altogether deny that salvation is conferred upon us by Christ, but they create so many additional details that they leave to Him scarcely a hundredth part of salvation. But salvation was intended to be looked for solely in Him; for Peter clearly excludes every other means and ascribes full and perfect salvation, and not only part of it, to Christ alone. So they are far from holding this doctrine.

Now when they beheld the boldness of Peter and John, and had perceived that they were unlearned and ignorant men, they marvelled; and they took knowledge of them, that they had been with Jesus. And seeing the man which was healed standing with them, they could say nothing against it. But when they had commanded them to go aside out of the council, they conferred among themselves, saying, What shall we do to these men? for that indeed a notable miracle hath been wrought through them, is manifest to all that dwell in Jerusalem; and we cannot deny it. But that it spread no further among the people, let us threaten them, that they speak henceforth to no man in this name. And they called them, and charged them not to speak at all nor teach in the name of Jesus. (13-18)

13. Here we may see an evil conscience; for being destitute of right and reason they break out into open tyranny, the odium of which they had sought to avoid. First then he declares that they were convicted in spirit, to make evident that like the giants of old they warred wittingly and of their free choice against God. For they see a manifest work of God in the man who was healed, and yet they wickedly set themselves against Him. Inasmuch as they know that Peter and John were unlearned and ignorant men, they acknowledge that there was something more than human in their boldness; therefore they are despite themselves compelled to wonder. Nevertheless they break out into such shamelessness that they do not fear to seek some tyrannous means of oppressing the truth. When they admit that it is an evident sign, they thereby admit themselves guilty of an evil conscience. When they say that it is known to all men, they show that they are careless of God and have respect to men only. For they show their want of shame in that they would have had no qualms in turning their backs upon anything that savoured of denial. When they ask what they shall do, they betray their stubborn wickedness. For they would surely have submitted themselves to God, had a devilish fury not carried them away to another end. This is the spirit of giddiness and madness, whereby God intoxicates His enemies. So too, when they hope shortly afterwards to succeed by threats in preventing any word of what has happened going farther, could anything be more foolish? Simply by putting two simple men to silence, will the arm of the Lord be broken?

17. *Let us straitly threaten them.* Here we may see the deadly evil of power divorced from the fear of God. For when religion does not exercise the authority that it ought to have, the more sacred the position that a man holds, the more presumptuously he rages. That is why we ought always to take care that the wicked are not exalted to the government of the Church. And those who are called to this function ought to behave themselves reverently and modestly lest they appear to have been armed for the causing of hurt. But if

it happen that they abuse their office, the Spirit makes plain there as in a mirror that whatever they order and decree ought to be regarded as void. The authority of pastors in particular has fixed limits which they are not to overstep. If they venture to do so, we may lawfully refuse to obey them; for to do so would be the height of wickedness, as now follows.

But Peter and John answered and said unto them, Whether it be right in the sight of God to hearken unto you rather than unto God, judge ye: for we cannot but speak the things which we saw and heard. And they, when they had further threatened them, let them go, finding nothing how they might punish them, because of the people; for all men glorified God for that which was done. For the man was more than forty years old, on whom this miracle of healing was wrought. And being let go, they came to their own company, and reported all that the chief priests and the elders had said unto them. (19-23)

19. *Whether it be right.* Let us remember to whom they make this answer. For this council did undoubtedly represent the Church; yet, because they abuse their authority, the apostles say they are not to be obeyed. And, as it often happens when there is no doubt about the case, they use the verdict to reprove their adversaries. Furthermore, it is worth noting that they set against their decrees the authority of God—which would be inappropriate were it not that those who in other respects were ordinary pastors of the Church were at the same time enemies of God. The apostles further make clear that obedience offered to evil and unfaithful pastors, even though they exercise lawful authority in the Church, is contrary to God. The Pope lightly disposes of this question by pronouncing that all the sayings it has pleased him to babble forth are divine oracles. The danger of any opposition is thereby removed. Yet the bishops can claim no more for themselves today than God formerly assigned to the order of priests. It is therefore puerile trifling for them to allege that no command can possibly proceed from them without being agreeable to the will of God. The facts rather clearly show that conflict is simply avoided by their dispensing with and tramping underfoot the doctrine of Christ and allowing their vain and unbridled lust to wander at will.

Whatever title then men may hold, they are to be listened to only on the condition that they do not lead us away from obeying God. So we must examine all their traditions by the rule of the Word of God. We must obey princes and others who are in authority, but only in so far as they do not deny to God His rightful authority as the supreme King, Father, and Lord. If such limits are to be observed in civil government, they ought to be of still greater importance in the spiritual government of the Church. Lest they should think in their usual manner that their authority is being minimized since God is being exalted above them, Peter turns them aside from such complacent thoughts by warning them that this matter must be settled at the judgment-seat of God. He says plainly, *in the presence of God*; for however men may be blinded, God will never suffer any man to be preferred before Him. And surely the Spirit put this answer into the mouth of the apostles, not only to repress the savagery of their enemies, but that He might also teach us where our duty lies, whenever men become so proud that they shake off the yoke of God and desire to lay their own yoke upon us. At such times let us recall the sacred authority of God, which blows away the vain smoke of all human excellency.

20. *For we cannot.* Much that is learnt by seeing and hearing may, and indeed should, be kept silent about, when peace may be procured thereby. It is discourteous and shows a malicious obstinacy to raise a commotion about unnecessary matters: but the apostles are not speaking in general terms when they say that they cannot but speak. For the Gospel of Christ is now in question, wherein consist both the glory of God and the salvation of men. For this to be suppressed through the prohibitions of men is a crime, both unseemly and impious; for God commands that His Gospel be preached, and the more since they knew they were chosen to be witnesses and preachers of Christ and that God had opened their mouths. Whoever therefore bids them be silent is seeking to the best of his power to make the grace of God of no effect and to destroy the salvation of men. Woe to us for our cowardice, if such a godless prohibition should stop our mouths. Now let all men see what confession God requires of them, lest, when they keep silence out of consideration for men, they hear a dreadful voice proceed out of the mouth of Christ condemning their faithlessness. In particular let not those who are called to the office of teaching (*ad docendi munus*) be terrified by any threats of men or by any form of authority, but let them freely execute that office which they know to have been laid upon them by God. 'Woe be unto me', says Paul, 'if I preach not the Gospel, because the duty has been entrusted to me' (I Cor. 9.16). And we must set this commandment of God not only against the tyrannous commands of men but against every obstacle that Satan often sets up in order to break off or impede the course of the Gospel. For we have need of a strong buckler to ward off such sore assaults, which are experienced by every minister of Christ. But whatever may befall, here is a wall of brass—that the preaching of the Gospel is pleasing to God, and therefore must not be suppressed on any account.

21. *And they, when they had further threatened them.* Here is the outcome of sedition—that the wicked do not cease to breathe out fury but are yet bridled by the hidden power of God so that they have no means of doing harm. How does it happen that they content themselves with threats, and do not assault them bodily, except that they are chained and bound by the power of God? Not that fear of God has any weight with them, for it is regard for the populace that holds them back; yet, though they do not know it, God is binding them with His bonds. Luke commends to us the providence of God in preserving His children; though it is hidden from the wicked, we are to observe it with the eyes of faith. Further, the wonderful counsel of God is shown in this, that the glory of Christ is furthered by those who are His most deadly enemies. For the assembling of the priests does not take place without being widely known. All men await expectantly some remarkable event; the apostles are acquitted, and go out free men. So the enemy are not only defeated, but against their will confirm the Gospel. Yet we must again observe that while the faithful gain the victory it is always under the humiliation of the Cross.

They are threatened again not to teach henceforth in the name of Christ, So they conquer, and yet are triumphant only under the reproach of the Cross. By the words, 'All men glorified God', Luke notes a second time the effect of the miracle, although it may be that they did not all reach fully to the goal. For the man who is touched by a sense of the power of God, and yet does not come to Christ or have his faith established by the miracle, stops halfway. But it was something, though not all, that the power of God was acknowledged in the healing of the man so that the enemy were put to shame and ceased from the fury of their attacks and gave ground a little.

23. *And being let go.* We shall see presently why they recounted to the other disciples what had befallen them, namely, that they might thereafter be emboldened and encouraged by the grace of God, and further that they might arm themselves with prayer against the savage threatenings of their foes. This is essential for the children of God—to encourage one another, and to join in godly fellowship so that under the banner of Christ they may vanquish the common enemy. Let them consider what dangers overhang them, to be the more ready to face them even when they see the enemy pressing hard upon them. Let them not be dismayed at facing a new conflict from time to time but remain confident in being ever invincible through the same power of God whereby they won the victory before. It is likely, though Luke does not expressly say so, that the apostles were satisfied with the answer they had previously made and so did not contend again

with these furious men; yet they were not so forgetful of their former constancy as to submit servilely to their ungodly decree.

And they, when they heard it, lifted up their voice to God with one accord, and said, O Lord, thou that didst make the heaven and the earth and the sea, and all that in them is: who by the Holy Ghost, by the mouth of our father David thy servant, didst say, Why did the Gentiles rage, and the peoples imagine vain things? The kings of the earth set themselves in array, and the rulers were gathered together, against the Lord, and against his Anointed: for of a truth in this city against thy holy Servant Jesus, whom thou didst anoint, both Herod and Pontius Pilate, with the Gentiles and the peoples of Israel, were gathered together, to do whatsoever thy hand and thy counsel foreordained to come to pass. And now, Lord, look upon their threatenings: and grant unto thy servants to speak thy word with all boldness, while thou stretchest forth thy hand to heal; and that signs and wonders may be done through the name of thy holy Servant Jesus. And when they had prayed, the place was shaken wherein they were gathered together; and they were all filled with the Holy Ghost, and they spake the word of God with boldness. (24-31)

We learn from this example what our duty is when our enemies imperiously threaten us. For we ought not to laugh carelessly in time of danger, but the fear of danger ought rather to drive us to crave the help of God; this is a remedy to set us on our feet, lest being terrified by threats we abandon our duty. Here are two lessons to derive from this narrative: when the disciples of Christ hear that their enemies are pressing hard and threateningly upon them, they do not jest as stupid and unimaginative men would do, but being touched with fear they fly to seek help at the hands of God; yet, further, they are not dismayed and do not collapse into such terror as might divert them from their duty, but through prayer to God they seek after a constancy that will not be overthrown.

24. *Thou art God that madest.* Though this is a general description of the power of God, it is to be referred to the present situation. For their acknowledgment of the power of God in the creation of the whole world is with a view to its application for their present advantage. So too the prophets often set forth His power to outweigh the fear that troubles us when we see the power of our enemies; they couple with it the promise, and regard these two as the foundation upon which they find boldness to pray with assurance. And surely our prayers are what they should be, and acceptable to God, when we rest upon His promises and His power and pray with a sure confidence that we shall obtain what we ask. We cannot have any confidence

unless God invites us to come to Him and promises that He is ready to help us, and unless we for our part acknowledge that He has the power to help us. Let the faithful therefore give themselves to this twofold meditation as often as they set themselves to pray. We learn here too how we ought to regard the creation of the world—so that we may know that all things are subject to God and ruled by His will, and that, when the whole world has attempted all that it can, nothing shall come to pass but what He has decreed, and may understand how monstrous is the arrogance of the wicked, as though the clay should rebel against the potter. For in general the faithful understand that, whatever dangers hang over them, God can deal with these in ways without number, since He holds all things in His hand and is able to make every part of heaven and earth obey Him who is their Creator.

25. *Who by the mouth of David.* They come now to the second section—that they ask nothing but what God has promised to perform. His will is allied to His power, so that they may have full assurance of receiving what they ask. As the Kingdom of Christ is in question, they refer to the promise of God whereby He undertakes to defend it. So the whole world's endeavours to overthrow it will be in vain. Their godliness and the sincerity of their zeal are shown by their concern, not so much for their personal safety as for the advancement of the Kingdom of Christ.

25. *Why did the Gentiles rage?* We must admit that David is speaking about himself. After he was chosen by God to be king and was anointed by Samuel, he had the greatest difficulty in taking possession of his kingdom because of the opposition of enemies in every quarter. We know how the rulers and the people conspired together with Saul and his family, and how afterwards the Philistines and other foes from without were so contemptuous of the new king that they vied with one another in making war upon him. It is not without cause that he complains that the kings rage and take counsel together and the people make their various plans. Yet because he knows that God is the supporter of his kingdom, he mocks their foolish enterprises and affirms their vanity. Yet because his kingdom was established to be an image of the Kingdom of Christ, David does not remain in the shadow but grasps the solid form; indeed, the Holy Spirit, as the apostles here remind us, reproves the absurd folly of the world which dares to invade the Kingdom of Christ which God had established as much in the person of David as of Christ Himself. It is a wonderful comfort to hear that when we go to war under the banner of Christ God is on our side. We may be assured that, even when all men, high and low, wickedly conspire together against this Kingdom, they will

not prevail. For what is the whole world compared with God? But of this we must first of all be certain—that God will maintain for ever the Kingdom of His Son, of which He is Himself the Author; we may thus set His inviolable decree against the temerity of men and, trusting in the help of His hand, may with confidence treat lightly all the preparations of men, formidable though they may be. He is diligent in assessing the resources of the enemy—he says there is no end to their devices—and he reckons up their counsels, in case we should be dismayed thereby. The teaching of the Psalm that Christ's Kingdom will endure, in spite of its enemies, is an indication that there will be many adversaries who will try to overthrow it. He refers on the one hand to the kings raging and on the other to the people creating tumult, showing thereby that every section will be hostile to it. Nor is this to be wondered at, since there is nothing more opposed to the flesh than the spiritual sword of the Gospel, wherewith Christ slays us that He may bring us to His obedience. We must therefore understand that the Kingdom of Christ will never be at peace in the world, lest we be dismayed as at something unusual when we are required to fight.

26. *Against the Lord, and His Christ.* The Spirit here teaches us that all who refuse to submit to Christ are making war against God. They often do not consider this; and yet it is the case that, as it is God's will to reign in the person of His Son alone, we reject His Lordship as often as we rebel against Christ. As the Lord Himself says in John's Gospel, 'He that honoureth not the Son, honoureth not the Father' (5.23). Let the hypocrites then profess a thousand times that nothing is further from their intention than to make war against God, they will yet find that God is their declared enemy unless they embrace Christ with His Gospel. This doctrine is to be applied in two ways: it arms us against all the terrors of the flesh, since we need not be afraid that those who withstand the Gospel will win the victory over God, and, in the second place, it cautions us against despising godly doctrine and advancing ourselves against God to our own destruction.

27. *In this city were gathered together.* They declare that this prophecy was confirmed by the event, so that it may be the more certainly believed. The meaning is: Thou, Lord, hast spoken it, and we have indeed experienced it to be true. They call to mind the events that took place some four years before. It is right that we should in the same way apply the outcome of what had been foretold to the confirmation of our faith. It might seem, though, that the outcome was far different from what is set forth in the Psalm; for the raging of the enemy was far from being in vain, and their assaults were of such effect that they put Christ to death; moreover their subsequent violence

was furious and dreadful. The faithful meet this difficulty by saying that their enemies could do no more than God had decreed. However much the wicked thought Christ to have been destroyed by death and sang their empty songs of triumph, the faithful are aware that their raging was all in vain. It may be asked why they are described as *the Gentiles and the peoples of Israel*, when they were one body. I think the reference is to the diversity of countries from which the Jews came together to the feast; the meaning is that Jews born in a variety of places were all banded together to assault the kingdom of Christ. Yet their fury was wholly without effect.

Thy holy Son, Jesus. The Greeks use the same word in reference to David that I have translated *servant.* For they sometimes use παῖς in the meaning of *servant* and sometimes of *son.* David is so called, because he was the minister of God, both in ruling the people and in the office of prophet. But the word *Son* is more suited to the person of Christ, though some may prefer to take it that Luke meant to allude to the similarity of Christ to David in the double significance of the word. It is expressly said that God anointed His Son, to make a true parallel with what is recorded in the Psalm. For it was by anointing that God consecrated Him King. Yet we must observe what kind of anointing this was; for we know He was anointed, not with visible oil but with the Holy Spirit.

28. *To do.* I have explained the reason for this statement—that the Kingdom of Christ was so far from being overthrown by that conspiracy that it then began to flourish. Yet there is an important doctrine here, that God so orders all things by His own secret counsel that He brings to pass what He has determined even through the agency of the wicked. It is not that they are ready to do Him such service willingly, but that He turns back their own plans and designs so that there are clearly set forth justice and the highest probity on the one hand, wickedness and iniquity on the other. We have treated of this more fully in chapter 2, but in passing let us observe how we are to regard the providence of God, so that we understand it to be the chief and sole director (*moderatrix*) of all that happens in the world, and that the Devil and all the wicked are bridled and restrained by God so that they may not do us any harm. When they rage most violently, they are not at liberty to do what they choose, but are given only such a loose rein as may serve for our own profit. Those who admit God's foreknowledge but do not agree that all things come to pass in accordance with His will are clearly confuted by these words, that God foreordained to happen those things that came to pass. Indeed Luke is not content with the word *counsel* but adds *hand*—not accurately, indeed, but in order to express more clearly that the outcome

of things is not only governed by the counsel of God but is also ordered by the power of His hand.

29. *And now, Lord.* They do well to apply to themselves what they have cited concerning Christ. For He will not be separated from the Gospel. Whatever trouble befalls His members, He applies to His own Person. They ask God to restrain the cruelty of their adversaries, yet not so much for their own sake that they may live a quiet and untroubled life, as through zeal for the spreading of the Gospel. It was not for them to desire a life to be spent in idleness, having deserted their calling. They add, '*Grant unto Thy servants, O Lord, that they may speak boldly.*' And we must notice the words, that God would *look upon their threatenings.* For as it is His special work to resist the proud and to cast down their haughtiness, it follows that the more insolently they vaunt, the more they undoubtedly provoke the wrath of God against themselves. There can be no question but that, being offended with such indignity, He will take action against it. So it was that Hezekiah, seeking help in his extremity, declared before the Lord the arrogance of Sennacherib and his cruel threatenings (Isa. 37.14 and 17). Let the cruelty and reproaches of our enemies rather stir up in us the desire to pray than discourage us from going forward in the course of our duty.

Grant unto thy servants. When one miracle had caused such anger among their enemies, how is it that these holy men desire to see fresh miracles performed daily? We observe here what I have already remarked on—that they regard the glory of God as of such account that they regard everything else as of little consequence. They are conscious only that through miracles the power of God is displayed. So miracles are always to be desired by the godly although their adversaries may burst forth and the whole of hell break out in fury. The same is true of boldness in speaking. They know that the wicked can abide nothing worse than the free course of the Gospel; yet because they know that that is the doctrine of life, which God desires to have preached whatever may befall, they count that preaching as of greater importance than anything else, because it is acceptable to God. We learn from this that we rightly acknowledge the benefits of God as we ought, when we are thereby encouraged to pray that He will confirm what He has begun. The apostles had shown an example of heroic fortitude: they now pray again that they may be furnished with boldness. So it is that Paul asks the faithful to pray to the Lord that his mouth may be opened (Eph. 6.19), although his voice already sounded in every place. Therefore the more we are aware of being helped by the Lord, we should learn to ask for still greater progress. In particular, since the freedom to confess the

Gospel is a special gift of God, we must constantly pray that it may be continued to us.

31. *And when they had prayed.* Luke declares that God not only heard this prayer but attested it by a visible sign from heaven. The shaking of the place would of itself have profited them little, but it had another effect in letting the faithful know of the presence of God with them. It is nothing else than a token of the presence of God. There follows the fruit, in that they are all filled with the Holy Spirit and endowed with greater boldness. It is this second point that we must regard as the more significant. For in that God declared His power by shaking the place, that was a rare and extraordinary event. But the evidence the event supplied that the disciples had gained their request is a sign of the perpetual benefit of prayer, set before us for an example.

And the multitude of them that believed were of one heart and soul: and not one of them said that aught of the things which he possessed was his own; but they had all things common. And with great power gave the apostles their witness of the resurrection of the Lord Jesus: and great grace was upon them all. For neither was there among them any that lacked: for as many as were possessors of lands or houses sold them, and brought the prices of the things that were sold, and laid them at the apostles' feet: and distribution was made unto each, according as any one had need. And Joseph, who by the apostles was surnamed Barnabas (which is, being interpreted, Son of exhortation), a Levite, a man of Cyprus by race, having a field, sold it, and brought the money, and laid it at the apostles' feet. (32-37)

32. *The multitude.* Three things are commended here: first, that the faithful were all of one mind; second, that there was a mutual sharing of goods; third, that the apostles were forthright and vigorous in proclaiming the resurrection of Christ. He says the multitude *were of one heart*, for this is far better than if a few men shared the same views. Earlier he said that the Church had increased to about five thousand. And now—and this is no easy statement—he says that concord reigned among this great multitude. And yet where faith rules, it so knits the hearts of men that they all desire and reject the same things. Discord springs from the fact that we are not governed by the same Spirit of Christ. It is well known that by the words *heart* and *soul* he means the will. Because the wicked often conspire together to do evil, this concord was holy and laudable in that it existed among the faithful.

And not one of them said. This is the second point, that this love was expressed in outward practice. We shall see presently what form this sharing of possessions took. What is now worth noting in Luke's record is that the root, the inner unity of spirit, came first, and the fruit followed.

Surely we ought to observe the same order, first loving one another with a sincere heart, and thereafter our love showing itself in its application to others. For even external beneficence, if it comes not from the heart, is of no value in the sight of God. We boast in vain of proper affections, unless the evidence of them is seen in outward performance. Moreover Luke points out in passing that they were not of one mind with a view to the private advantage of each, since the rich in bestowing their goods freely had nothing further from their thoughts than their own profit.

33. *And with great power.* This third section refers to doctrine. For Luke indicates that the zeal which the apostles had for preaching the Gospel was so far from being lessened that they were rather endowed with new power. His reference to the resurrection of Christ alone is a synecdoche: for this part is put for the whole Gospel. But Luke mentioned the resurrection alone, because it is the fulfilment of the Gospel, and, secondly, because they had lately engaged in sore conflict regarding it: for the Sadducees, who then were in authority, were much grieved regarding it.

And great grace was. He shows that by helping the poor so bountifully they found favour at the hands of strangers, and that this therefore served greatly for the spreading abroad of their teaching. They were, he says, well liked because they were generous. There is therefore a reason expressed in the words 'Neither was there among them any that lacked.' Yet there is no question that their honesty and self-control, their moderation and patience and their other virtues inclined the mind of many to be well disposed towards them. He proceeds to expound at greater length the form which the sharing of goods, already referred to, took; for the rich sold their lands and houses, to relieve the poverty of those in need.

34. *For as many as were.* Although this could be taken as applying to everyone, it should be regarded as no more than indefinite. It is most likely that there were many who made no inroads upon their possessions; this may be gathered from the context. He goes on to speak of Barnabas, with the evident intention of taking note of one who was more worthy than any other to be remembered. The action taken by many of the disciples in various places is attributed to them all, in accordance with a usage common in Scripture. Furthermore, he does not mean that the faithful sold all that they possessed, but only so far as need required. It is by way of detail that he adds that the rich

did not only relieve the poverty of their brethren from the annual revenue of their lands, but in their liberality spared not even the lands themselves. This could be achieved without their wholly impoverishing themselves, and by incurring only a certain reduction of their revenue. This also we may read into Luke's words, that the object of their doing so was that no one should lack. He further shows that prudence was used, in that distribution was made in accordance with the need of each. The goods were not equally divided, but a reasonable distribution was made, to ensure that no one was burdened with the extremes of poverty. It may be that Barnabas is specifically commended by name, because he sold the only piece of land which he possessed and thereby surpassed all the rest. This points us to the meaning of the words that no one counted anything his own, but that they had all things common. For no one held his possessions privately for himself to be selfishly enjoyed to the neglect of others, but they were prepared, as need required, to share them in common.

And now we must have hearts that are harder than iron if we are not moved by the reading of this narrative. In those days the believers gave abundantly of what was their own; we in our day are content not only jealously to retain what we possess, but callously to rob others. They set forth their own possessions with simplicity and faithfulness; we devise a thousand cunning devices whereby we may acquire everything for ourselves by hook or by crook. They laid down at the apostles' feet; we do not fear, with sacrilegious boldness, to convert to our own use what was offered to God. They sold their own possessions in those days; in our day it is the lust to purchase that reigns supreme. At that time love made each man's own possessions common property for those in need; in our day such is the inhumanity of many, that they begrudge to the poor a common dwelling upon earth, the common use of water, air, and sky.

These things then are written for our shame and reproach. Yet even the poor themselves are to blame for some part of this evil. For since there cannot be such common holding of possessions, unless there is godly agreement under the direction of a single heart and spirit, in many men there is such pride or ingratitude, such sloth or greed or such hypocrisy, that the desire to do well and the ability to do well are alike hindered and extinguished. We must remember the admonition of Paul that we be not weary in well-doing (Gal. 6.9). The drivellings of the Anabaptists and fanatics, who in our own day have made much ado on the basis of this passage, as if there ought to be no personal right to possession among Christians, I refuted earlier, in writing on 2.44. For Luke does not here prescribe a law for all men which they must of necessity follow, in relating the actions of men in whom the Spirit of God was manifest with singular efficacy and power; nor does he speak so generally of all men without exception as to lead us to suppose that no one was regarded as a Christian who did not sell all his possessions.

CHAPTER FIVE

But a certain man named Ananias, with Sapphira his wife, sold a possession, and kept back part of the price, his wife also being privy to it, and brought a certain part, and laid it at the apostles' feet. But Peter said, Ananias, why hath Satan filled thy heart to lie to the Holy Ghost, and to keep back part of the price of the land? Whiles it remained, did it not remain thine own? and after it was sold, was it not in thy power? How is it that thou hast conceived this thing in thy heart? thou hast not lied unto men, but unto God. And Ananias hearing these words fell down and gave up the ghost: and great fear came upon all that heard it. And the young men arose and wrapped him round, and they carried him out and buried him. (1-6)

1. Luke has given us to understand from his accounts so far that the company that had been gathered together in the name of Christ, were more like angels than men. It was an unparalleled act of virtue on the part of the rich to strip themselves of their lands as well as their money for the succouring of the poor. Now, in truth, he shows that Satan had devised a trick to penetrate that holy community, and under cover of such noble virtuousness at that; for in order to insinuate himself he makes use of marvellous shifts of hypocrisy. But of course that is the way Satan attacks the Church of God, when he can get nowhere with open war.

But at this point we must pay particular attention to the intention of the Holy Spirit. For in this story He wished to bring out, first, how pleasing honesty of heart is to God, and what an abomination deceit, crookedness and hypocrisy are to Him; and, secondly, how greatly He approves a pure and holy polity in the Church. For the main point is the punishment which God inflicted on Ananias and his wife. As the seriousness of it terrified them all at that time, so it testifies to us that God cannot abide such perfidy, where we contemptuously sport with Him, by making pretence to a holiness that is non-existent. For if, having weighed all the circumstances, we wish to know the whole truth, it is that Luke condemns Ananias for only one crime, his wishing to deceive God and the Church with a false offering.

But there were many evils lying hidden behind this deceit; (1) contempt of God of whom he does not stand in awe, although God knows of his crookedness; (2) sacrilegious fraudulence because by stealth he holds on to a part of what was acknowledged to be set apart for God; (3) perverse vanity and ambition, because without a thought for the judgment of God he ingratiates himself with men; (4) infidelity, because he would not have set foot on this forbidden way had he not lacked faith in God; (5) the spoiling of a godly and holy plan; and furthermore (6) the actual hypocrisy was a great evil in itself. And to this there had to be added his deliberate and audacious lying.

Even if Ananias had given away half of his land, his deed was a splendid and noteworthy one to all appearances. And there is indeed great virtue in a rich man dividing his goods fairly with the poor; but 'the sacrifices of the wicked are abominations to God' (Prov. 15.8); and where honesty of heart is absent nothing can be pleasing to Him. Thus Christ thinks more of the two coins offered by the widow, than of the huge sums that others draw from their great piles (Luke 21.2). That is why God made Ananias an example of such severe vengeance.

Now let us turn to individual details.

2. *He laid it at the apostles' feet.* See what ambition does. Ananias is ashamed that he is not regarded as one of the best of men. Therefore, greedy for money though he is, he deprives himself of part of his property in order to acquire a good name for himself among men. At the same time it does not enter his head that he is lying and cheating in the sight of God, and that God will punish him for this falsehood. In effect he honours the feet of the apostles more than the eyes of God. Therefore when we are doing what is right we must be all the more careful not to be striving for the approval of onlookers (*theatri plausum*). And Christ truly advises us to some purpose that it is fitting, when we are giving alms, for the left hand not to know what the right is doing (Matt. 6.3).

3. *But Peter said.* How did Peter come to know about Ananias' fraud? Without a doubt it was by the revelation of the Spirit. Luke therefore indicates that the apostles to some extent represented God (*sustinuisse Dei personam*), and acted in His stead. Now if the Spirit of God uses the mouth of a mortal man to deal so summarily with a hypocrite, yet one tricked out in a false show of virtues, how will the spurious stand up to the voice of God Himself, accompanied by the shrill of the trumpet, when they will be brought before His judgment seat? Furthermore Peter points out the horribleness of the crime by saying that Satan has filled Ananias' heart. For there is not a man whose heart is not tormented by the stings of Satan; many temptations come stealthily upon individuals also and make their way right into their minds; but when Satan takes possession of the heart he holds sway over the whole man, as if God had been driven out. The sign

of a reprobate man is this; he is so given over to Satan, that no room is left for the Spirit of God.

What follows about lying can have a twofold meaning, either that he made a false show of having the Spirit, or that he lied against the Spirit. And in fact (the Greek) is literally 'to cheat the Holy Spirit'[1] (*Spiritum mentiri*) but since[2] the Greek word *ψεύδεσθαι* may be joined to a double accusative, and that suits the context better, I am also rather inclined to the view that Ananias is blamed because, in his treachery, he made a mockery of the Holy Spirit. And he confirms this a little later when he accuses him of lying not to men but to God. Therefore we must be very much on our guard that hypocrisy does not dominate in us, for its very nature is that wickedness which wishes to deceive God, and, as it were, to catch a weasel asleep, as the proverb says[3]; and this can only be done by shameful mockery. Accordingly Peter is quite right in saying that where this happens the heart has been possessed by Satan. For who, unless he were devoid of all sense and reason, would dare to be so abusive of God? Peter therefore interrogates him as if it were about a monster, for blindness of that sort is a horrid thing.

4. *Whiles it remained.* The fact that no necessity drove him to sin makes his crime worse. For since it is no proper excuse at all to have been spurred on by some outside influence, how much worse is it to rush into evil of one's own accord, and, as it were, seriously to call down the vengeance of God on oneself? But from this we gather that there was no law binding a man to alienate his goods. For Peter says that Ananias had just as much the liberty and the right to hold on to his land as to keep the money, because in the second part of his sentence the field that was sold is referred to instead of the actual price. Therefore had he held on to what was his own property, he would not have been regarded as any less faithful. Thus it is evident that people who say that the faithful are not allowed to have any property of their own, are quite mad.

Thou hast not lied unto men. Although this sentence is differently constructed, I have no doubt that it confirms the previous one. For hypocrites conceal themselves under so many coverings that they think that they have nothing to do with God. Indeed Peter expressly says so, because Ananias had deceived the Church. But he ought to have considered that 'where two or three are gathered in the name of Christ, He is present, presiding' (Matt. 18.20), and that he should

[1] *ψεύσασθαί σε τὸ Πνεῦμα τὸ Ἅγιον.* Calvin, with Vulg., *ut mentireris Spiritui sancti*. Tr.

[2] Footnote, C.R. text, 'The Greeks frequently understood a preposition'. Tr.

[3] *cornici configere oculos*: 'to put out the eyes of a crow'. Tr.

behave in that assembly as if he were seeing God with his eyes. For since God wishes to bear rule in the Church, if we give any reverence to Him at all, then that sovereignty, which He exercises by His Word, must be scrupulously respected by us. The apostles were certainly men, but not acting on their own (*privati*), because it was by God's commission that they held their offices. Besides, we must note that he who lies to the Holy Spirit lies to God, for the divinity of the Holy Spirit is clearly asserted in this way of speaking. Paul says, in similar vein, 'you are the temples of God, because the Spirit dwells in you' (I Cor. 3.16).

5. *And Ananias hearing these words.* The death of Ananias truly confirms the force of the Word, which Paul magnificently brings out, in saying that 'it is the savour of death unto death to those who are perishing' (II Cor. 2.16). He is speaking indeed of the spiritual death of the soul, but in the body of Ananias there was a visible symbol of that punishment which escapes human eyes. He was not struck down by a sword, by force, or by a hand, but he was deprived of life merely by the hearing of a voice. When we hear this let the threats of the Gospel terrify us, and be quick to humble us, in case we ourselves also experience a similar fate. For what is declared about Christ, 'with the breath of his lips he shall slay the wicked' (Isa. 11.4), applies not only to the head of the wicked, but also to every single member. Since the proper nature of His Word was to save, it must indeed bring death to those who reject the salvation it offers. But if it seems absurd to anyone that the apostle made use of a physical punishment, I make reply, first, that this was an extraordinary affair, and, secondly, that this was one of the gifts of the Spirit, as is plain from I Cor. 12.10. As we shall see later that is why Elymas the sorcerer was struck with blindness by Paul (Acts 13.11). Peter therefore did not go beyond his function, when at the proper time he shot the dart that was given him by the Holy Spirit. But some are of the opinion that the punishment was too cruel, and this is because they weigh Ananias' sin in their own, and not in God's scales, and so regard a very serious crime, which we have already shown to abound in so many evils, as a trivial offence. Others think that this is an incredible thing, because every day they see very many hypocrites get off scot-free, men who make a laughing-stock of God just as much as Ananias, indeed one should rather say that they think so because they themselves are the grossest despisers of God and yet do not suffer punishment for their impiety. But as God poured out visible graces on His Church in the beginning, so that we may know with assurance that He will be present with us by the secret virtue of His Spirit, and, furthermore, showed openly by external signs what we realize inwardly by the experience of faith, so

He has demonstrated by the visible punishment of two persons, how horrible a judgment awaits all hypocrites, who have held Him and the Church in derision.

And great fear came. It was God's purpose to strike the rest with fear by the punishment of one person, so that they might conscientiously abstain from all deceit. And what Luke says about their being afraid applies also to us. For God wished to give a general warning to all generations at that particular time, that all may learn to be sincere in their dealings with Him. However the punishment of this wretch ought to have encouraged the godly to be more liberal afterwards in setting apart their goods for God and the poor; because they could gather how precious alms were in the sight of God, when the profaning of them had been punished so severely.

And it was about the space of three hours after, when his wife, not knowing what was done, came in. And Peter answered unto her, Tell me whether ye sold the land for so much. And she said, Yea, for so much. But Peter said unto her, How is it that ye have agreed together to tempt the Spirit of the Lord? behold, the feet of them which have buried thy husband are at the door, and they shall carry thee out. And she fell down immediately at his feet, and gave up the ghost: and the young men came in and found her dead, and they carried her out and buried her by her husband. And great fear came upon the whole church, and upon all that heard these things. (7-11)

7. There is no more to say about the punishment which God inflicted on Sapphira, except that it adds greater force to the example. Moreover it happened by the certain providence of God that the Church saw, separately, the treacherous intention and the stubborn wickedness of each of them. Since they were equally responsible we could have been informed about them at the same time, but it was more appropriate and beneficial for the edification of the Church that each should quite plainly disclose his own impiety. For, although it does often happen that way, the sight of her husband was not the cause of Sapphira's pretending, so that her offence could be put down to shame, but, acting on her own accord, with no pressure put on her from any outside source, she appears no better than her husband. Also, they were on a level in wickedly lying, since she is aware from Peter's interrogation, that their fraud has been found out.

8. *Tell me.* We learn that God does not break out in punishment on a sudden impulse, but first holds a proper investigation, lest He might be taking vengeance, except in the case of the obstinate and those who cut themselves off from pardon. For since Sapphira knew that the business had been kept secret, she ought to have been struck

with consternation by Peter's questioning, just as if she had been summoned to appear before the judgment-seat of God. Time is given to her to come to her senses, indeed this is like a quiet invitation to repentance. But by going heedlessly on she shows that she is incurable, and this because she has no terror of God.

But from this we are taught that we must take great pains to bring back sinners to the way. For the Spirit of God possesses this moderation; but when obstinacy and headstrong contempt of God are added to the crime, then it is already high time for punishment. Therefore those who are displeased with the excessive severity of God, are arrogating far too much to themselves. It is rather for us to reflect upon how one day we shall come to stand before His judgment-seat. Yet, if we mean to deceive Him without being punished for it, then we are despising His sacred majesty too much.

Furthermore, all those circumstances which I have detailed above give abundant proof that Ananias and Sapphira did not deserve just one death. For, first, hypocrisy is in itself extremely abominable to God; and secondly, because their intention to lie to God is born of the highest contempt. Impiety is added to their impudence, because they do not reverence Christ, who presides in the assembly of those to whom they belong; and, again, because it means nothing to them to deny their manifest wickedness to God, simply in order to avoid shame and disgrace among men, with whom they had determined to make a good show of themselves. Their persistent denial of their sin, as it were, crowns everything (*veluti summus cumulus*). Now I have already said why it ought not to seem absurd that innumerable hypocrites daily deceive God and the Church just as much as these two, but yet are not punished with death. Since God is the only Judge of the world it is for Him to punish individuals by His own decision, and whenever and however He pleases. Accordingly we have no right to prescribe a particular method of punishment to Him. But in the bodily punishment of these two, there has been set before us, as in a mirror, the gravity of the spiritual judgment which is still hidden. For if we think over what it means to be cast into the eternal fire, we shall not consider it the worst of evils to fall dead before the eyes of men. See I Cor. 10.5.

9. *To tempt the Spirit.* He uses other words to point out exactly what he said before, that they were impiously and contemptuously making a mockery of God. But he said that they tempted the Spirit because they had heedlessly devised their fraud as if the Spirit of God was not the Searcher (*cognitor*) of hearts. For when they became mutual accomplices in their crime, they were far too careless in laying their plans with each other, as if God had been shut out. For Scripture

says that God is tempted, when either His authority is taken away from Him, or His omniscience is slighted. Furthermore he means the Spirit, who was ruling in the Church through the apostles. For when Christ says, 'When the Spirit comes He will judge the world' (John 16.8) the only kind of jurisdiction in His mind is the one that He exercises through the ministry of the Church.

11. *And fear came.* Again he repeats that the punishment of one person was a warning for all. But here he explicitly describes a two-fold fear. He says that the Church was afraid, because believers never fear God so perfectly that they do not benefit still further by being warned by His judgments. Therefore God is so often calling us back by fear from the allurements and licence of sinning, when we read of all the punishments that were inflicted on the ungodly long ago, and actually see them laid upon them every day. For the flesh must be continually held in check in this way, because one bridle would scarcely be enough for this purpose. There was fear of another kind among the outsiders; not such as won them over to whole-hearted worship of God, but yet forced them to give glory to God.

And by the hands of the apostles were many signs and wonders wrought among the people; and they were all with one accord in Solomon's porch. But of the rest durst no man join himself to them: howbeit the people magnified them; and believers were the more added to the Lord, multitudes both of men and women; insomuch that they even carried out the sick into the streets, and laid them on beds and couches, that, as Peter came by, at the least his shadow might overshadow some one of them. And there also came together the multitude from the cities round about Jerusalem, bringing sick folk, and them that were vexed with unclean spirits: and they were healed every one. (12-16)

12. He returns to miracles of a different kind which are more in line with the Gospel, viz. those by which Christ bears witness not only to His power but also to His goodness, so that He may attract men to Himself by the delightfulness of His grace. For He came to save, and not to condemn, the world (John 3.17). Therefore when the sick are healed and others are set free from demons, those blessings which are bestowed on their bodies represent the spiritual grace of Christ, and therefore are derived from His natural function (*ex genuino officio*), if I may put it like that. That terrible sign which was performed in the case of Ananias and Sapphira was, so to speak, accidental. Luke narrates that the Church increased by miracles, because they are hand-maidens to faith (*fidei subserviunt*), as we have said, by preparing some and confirming others. So proof is given once more, as I have

pointed out elsewhere, that miracles must never be separated from the Word.

Luke indicates the great number of signs by reporting that the sick were everywhere brought out into the public street, in order to receive healing. For God meant this to illustrate the Gospel of His Son, especially at the beginning, so that it might have been made quite clear to the Jews that there is now present that renewal of all things which had been so often promised, and on which they had set all their hopes, according to their own admission. It is well enough known that couches were small beds on which the ancients used to take their mid-day siesta. Because they were rather easy to carry outside, people laid the sick on them.

And they were all with one accord. This shows that they were accustomed to meet together at certain hours, not only for the sake of prayers and teaching, but in order to win others for the Lord, as opportunity was given. Of course every man lived in his own house, but they used to have their meetings in this particular place, for indeed the body of the Church can continue in no other way. For if everyone wished to teach himself and pray privately, all on his own, and there were no common meetings, then no matter how well the Church has been organized, it will inevitably collapse and soon fall into ruins. He says that they were unanimous, to let us know that they all respected that arrangement, and that there was no refractory individual who neglected the public assembly by keeping within his own four walls. In this way they gave an example not only of propriety but also of determination. For they met under the threat of danger, seeing that this place was so well-frequented. Thus their unanimous agreement to run a risk deserved all the greater praise.

13. *But none of the rest.* A second result of the miracles was that unbelievers were so convinced by the remarkable power of God that they do not dare to make light of the apostles; on the contrary they are forced to give honour to the Church. Yet their avoiding God and His people because they are terrorized by miracles could look absurd. To that I reply that they were prevented from making an approach by their own guilt (*culpa*), for there is no doubt that God invites us to come to Him by miracles. Therefore whoever do not come to the point of eagerly embracing the grace of God, which shines out in the miracles, are kept back by a bad conscience.

Nevertheless in this instance there is some fruit, because God wrests some fear out of them; although Luke does not put this down to miracles alone, but rather includes everything which could make for increasing the dignity of the Church. For all things were so arranged[1]

[1] *composita erant*; French: *toutes choses estoyent tellement disposees.* Tr.

that a certain divine majesty should shine among them (*illic*); for the faithful[1] were as different from others as angels are from men. For in holy discipline and sincere cultivation of piety there lies a certain secret dignity (σεμνότης), which restrains the wicked even against their will. But today we are ignorant of the nature of it; indeed the truth is that we make ourselves, and the Church along with us, contemptible by our worldly licence and evil living. And even the punishment of Ananias and his wife was of considerable value in terrifying the ungodly, keeping them from rashly bursting in on the company of those men, where God had shown Himself so stern in His punishment. Yet we must take note that he is not referring here to men who were of the worst sort, but to those who were undecided. Certainly there were at this time in Jerusalem a great many who remained quite untouched by any regard either for signs or for the angelic sanctity of godly men. Luke therefore means moderate men, in whom there lay concealed some seed of the fear of God. Today we see some like that, whom the vanity of the world, it is true, keeps back from assuming the yoke of Christ, but because they detect something divine in our teaching, they scruple to regard it lightly. At the same time, however, it is apparent how Satan holds back with deadly chains all who lack the Spirit of Christ, so that, not only are they afraid to see to their own interests, but they deliberately avoid the remedies offered for their salvation. They see and approve those things that are holy and beneficial, and yet they are carried off to worse things, or lie still in their filth.

15. *The shadow of Peter as he came.* The Papists are deceiving by the wrong use they make of this, not only to get support for false miracles, which they say take place at the tombs of martyrs, but to vaunt their relics to us. 'Why', they say, 'did Peter's shadow have more power for healing, than his grave, or his robe, or even the touching of his bones will have?' I reply that it ought not to be immediately imagined that the true state of affairs is that Luke is narrating something done by ignorant men, unacquainted with the pure faith. However, a surer refutation lies to hand. For the apostles were endowed with this virtue just because they were ministers of the Gospel. They therefore used this gift in so far as it made a difference in promoting the faith of the Gospel; and indeed God put forth His power in their shadows just as much as in their mouths. The miracles, about which the Papists prate have so little relation to these, as to be, rather, right at the opposite pole. For the purpose of their miracles is to let the world be led away from Christ in order to desert to the saints.

[1] With French, *les fideles*. Tr.

But the high priest rose up, and all they that were with him (which is the sect of the Sadducees), and they were filled with jealousy, and laid hands on the apostles, and put them in public ward. But an angel of the Lord by night opened the prison doors, and brought them out, and said, Go ye, and stand and speak in the temple to the people all the words of this Life. And when they heard this, they entered into the temple about daybreak, and taught. But the high priest came, and they that were with him, and called the council together, and all the senate of the children of Israel, and sent to the prison-house to have them brought. But the officers that came found them not in the prison; and they returned, and told, saying, The prison-house we found shut in all safety, and the keepers standing at the doors; but when we had opened, we found no man within. Now when the captain of the temple and the chief priests heard these words, they were much perplexed concerning them whereunto this would grow. And there came one and told them, Behold, the men whom ye put in the prison are in the temple standing and teaching the people. Then went the captain with the officers, and brought them, but without violence; for they feared the people, lest they should be stoned. (17-26)

Luke has already informed us that the Church had been increased in numbers, that it had been magnificently equipped with various gifts, that it excelled in miracles, and in short that the rule of Christ was flourishing there in every way. He now begins to tell that, because of those things, the anger of the ungodly was kindled afresh, to rage even worse than ever. We gather from this how Satan drives them on with a blind fury when the remarkable power of God strikes no terror into them, so that they are the more audacious and violent in the way they rush on, and drive themselves, as if they were going to turn heaven itself upside down. Great blindness such as this, being a horrible punishment by God, ought to be a warning to all, to waste no time in submitting themselves to God. Otherwise they too may be swept along by a spirit of dizziness, only to be broken in pieces by the very hand of God that they are pushing against. Meanwhile let us realize that God wills to load His Church with spiritual blessings so that He may nevertheless permit it to be harassed by the ungodly. We ought therefore to be always ready to do battle, for our situation today is similar to theirs. In particular the acknowledgment of the gifts of God, by which He bears witness to His presence with us, ought to give us courage so as not to be frightened by the fury and boldness of the wicked. For it is no small comfort to know that God is with us.

They that were with him. He means those who were more closely connected to the high priest, whose advice he was accustomed to follow, and whom he had, so to speak, picked out of the whole class, not for judicial purposes indeed, but for their love and zeal for his party; for at that time they were struggling shamelessly among themselves like bitter enemies. Furthermore Luke again repeats that it was the Sadducees who at that time had the power over everything in their hands, so that we may know that the whole government of the Church then had been wrecked by terrible devastation, because a sect like this was able to dominate. But God plainly allowed the synagogue to be immersed in this extreme infamy, after He had separated His Church from it, so that there might be all the less excuse for those who spurned the Gospel and remained among dregs like that. Besides, what drove on those swine, who were unaffected by any anxiety for the life to come, except naked ambition and a desire to cling on to the mastery which they had seized?

They were filled with zeal. I preferred to keep the Greek word (ζήλου; *zelo*), (especially since it is common enough otherwise), rather than translate 'emulation' (*aemulationem*). For he is speaking in a general way of the perverse and violent force which sweeps hypocrites along and inflames them to defend their superstitions. From this it is plain what value the zeal of men has in God's eyes, and what praise it deserves, when it is not controlled by reason and prudence; in other words when the Spirit of God is not its guide.

Today we see men roused by a diabolical fury, men wishing to be regarded devout in comparison with others, going about in a savage passion to shed innocent blood. But all the same let us note that it is not a question here of thoughtless zeal, such as many of the Jews had, according to Paul, but rather we are to understand a fervid and unbridled attack. For however much the wicked know they are wrong in themselves because they deliberately resist godliness, yet they deceive themselves with a misleading sort of zeal, that it is right to oppose innovations. So today almost all the Papists boast of themselves simply on the basis of their zeal (*solo zeli nomine*), when they are, nevertheless, zealots for their belly. But granting the truth of what they allege, how can this excuse the burning cruelty to which their blindness drives them, as if it is the highest of virtues to give free rein to their passion to take vengeance on anything that displeases them? But the first thing to do is this: to discriminate between what is good and bad, so that nothing may be rejected (*improbetur*) in a rash moment.

19. *But an angel of the Lord.* The Lord brought the apostles out of prison, not because He wished to deliver them from the hand of their enemies for ever, for later on He allowed them to be brought back again, and be beaten with rods. But by this miracle He meant

to demonstrate that they were in His hand and care for the defence of faith in His Gospel; partly in order that the Church might find fresh encouragement from the event, and partly to leave the ungodly without any excuse. For that reason we must not always hope, not even are we to desire, that God may deliver us from death; but the proper thing for us is to be content that our life is protected by His hand, as needs be. His making use of an angel for this purpose is in accordance with His normal practice, for it is testified throughout Scripture that angels are the ministers of His kindness towards us. And that is no empty speculation. For it is a helpful support for our weakness to know not only that God cares for us, but also that the heavenly spirits are watchful for our safety. In short it is no ordinary pledge of God's love towards us that the noblest creatures of all are appointed to look after our safety. Moreover the angel opened the prison by night because he did not wish the ungodly actually to see him perform the miracle, although he did intend that people should know about it after it had taken place.

20. *Speak in the temple.* The purpose of their deliverance is that they may continue to make strenuous efforts to preach the Gospel, and challenge their enemies courageously, even to the point of meeting death bravely. For, finally, when their course was run and the hand of God was inactive,[1] they were dragged off to death. But at this particular time the Lord opens the prison for them so that they may be free to carry out their duty. That deserves attention because we see very many people who, if they escape from some persecution, keep their mouths shut afterwards, as if they had no further obligation towards God; others find a way out for themselves by denying Christ. But the Lord sets His people free, not that they might abandon the course that they began, but rather that they may show more ardour in the future. The apostles, indeed, could have objected: 'It is better to keep quiet for a time, seeing that we shall not be able to utter one word without danger. We are now held captive because of one meeting; will the fury of our enemies not be much more inflamed after this, if they see us persisting?' But because they knew that they must live and die to the Lord (Rom. 14.8) they do not reject His commandment. Therefore we always ought to be concerned about the duties which God imposes upon us. We will often meet many things to dishearten us, unless we are content with the simple command of God and carry out our duty, leaving the issue to Him.

The words of this Life. The Gospel is splendidly described here as lifegiving doctrine, bringing salvation to men. For in it 'the righteousness of God is laid open to us' (Rom. 1.17), and Christ offers Himself

[1] *quiscente Dei manu*, and French, 'the hand of God resting itself'. Tr.

to us with the sacrifice of His death, with the Spirit of regeneration, with the earnest of our adoption by God. And this is said expressly to the apostles so that they may the more boldly enter into all sorts of struggles on behalf of the Gospel, when they hear that they are ministers of eternal salvation.

The demonstrative, *this*, is added to make it all the more certain, as if the angel were pointing out the life with his finger; just as we certainly do not have to go far afield to find it, when we have the Word in our mouth and in our heart. Somebody may perhaps prefer to understand 'the words of this Life' as being used by hypallage instead of 'these words'. I do not reject that view; but yet the former sense seems better to me, for there was a new revelation of Christ, in which life was present for them.

21. *But the high priest came.* The chief priest now calls together the whole council in case he could not be equal to the responsibility were he to pass over others by giving[1] official standing to his own sect. Fear therefore drives him to convoke the total number. However they maintain the form of law sedulously and exactly. The elders, who had the government in their hands, are called, that nothing may be done but by the decision and authority of the council. From such a beginning, who would not have hoped for a moderate finding? And they certainly make whatever pretext they can in order not to appear to be suppressing the truth by force or tyranny. But when they hear that the apostles are teaching in the temple, whatever way they learn that they did not come out of prison by some act of human deception but by a miracle, they do not stop carrying out their purpose. And this reveals not only their impious behaviour and contempt of God, but also horrible madness. Therefore plausible displays of justice do not hide hypocrites in such a way that they do not bring their own wickedness into the open in the end. Certainly they ought to gather from all the circumstances that the prison was opened by the work of God; yet they do not hesitate to rage openly against God.

These things are also suitable for our time. We know how proudly the Papists boast of that axiom of theirs that lawful councils must be obeyed because they represent the Church. Moreover what they call, and wish to be regarded as, lawful, are those councils where in external form everything is complete. But now, the one to which Luke is referring here was like that, although we know, however, that it was assembled to extinguish the name of Christ. For no matter how much the priests at that time stealthily reached office (*honorem*) by fraud, or canvassing, or other evil tricks, or even forced their way to it by bribery and murder of each other, yet the office (*dignitatem*)

[1] Reading *deferens* with Tholuck, for C.R.'s *deserens*. Tr.

of the priesthood itself was still continuing in existence, for the Christ had not yet been revealed. There was a representation of the Church in the assembly of the elders; but yet where the truth of God is not sought the whole outward appearance is nothing but a mere mask. Therefore, it is in vain for the Papists to try to hide their abominations under the shelter of this shield. Because it is not enough for those who bear rule in the Church to gather together, unless it is done in the name of Christ. Otherwise, since it is a normal artifice of Satan's to disguise himself as 'an angel of light' (II Cor. 11.14), we shall be giving to him under the title of the Church the most suitable hiding-place that he can wish for.

26. *He brought them without force.* We have said something before about the captain of the temple (on 4.1). For I do not think it likely that the Jews were allowed to set anyone they liked over the temple, but that it was decided by the governor of the province who should be in charge of it. But he says that they were brought without force, that is, they were not dragged with violence, for fear of starting an uproar. Thus while they neither fear nor reverence God they are afraid of men. The discretion of the apostles shows itself in this, that while they are surrounded by a great number of men, yet they allow themselves to be led away by the officials, so that they might not be the cause of a tumult.

And when they had brought them, they set them before the council. And the high priest asked them, saying, We straitly charged you not to teach in this name; and behold, ye have filled Jerusalem with your teaching, and intend to bring this man's blood upon us. (27-28)

28. The chief priest charges the apostles with two offences. For since they did not comply with the decision of the council, he accuses them of contumacy. In the second part of his statement he reveals a bad conscience, or at least shows that he is acting in his own interests rather than dealing with a public matter in a court of law. For he complains that the apostles wish to transfer the odium of the death of Christ to the priests and scribes. Look therefore what consumes them, fear of the avenging and punishment of a wicked murder. To start with he makes a pretext of their teaching, indeed, but we may gather from his final words that it is not their teaching that he is so anxious about. But in the meantime he does accuse the apostles of sedition, for he takes it for granted that Christ had been justly put to death. However the chief point of the accusation is that they were disobedient to the order of the priests. It was a capital offence not to obey the chief priest; how much more so to spurn the whole order? But on the other hand the chief priest does not consider what his

responsibility ought to be to God and to the Church; he abuses his power like a tyrant, as if that power were independent of all laws. Today the Pope deals with us in the same way. For when he arrogates[1] unbridled supreme power to himself he has no hesitation about condemning us as schismatics, as soon as he sees his decrees repudiated by us. For he seizes on this sentence, 'He that rejecteth you, rejecteth me' (Luke 10.16); and from that draws the conclusion that we are rebels against God. But if he is to be heard as the ambassador of Christ, he must speak with the words of Christ (*ex Christi ore*). Now, since he openly plays the minister of Satan, he borrows authority from the name of Christ without shame and without excuse. And even the form of speech which the chief priest uses is proof how spiritual tyrants usurp for themselves a power that is unrestricted and is not subject to the Word of God, and freely and heedlessly venture on anything they like. He says, 'We have strictly commanded you.' And what gives rise to such peremptory firmness except their belief that whatever they ordered must be followed out without question?

But Peter and the apostles answered and said, We must obey God rather than men. The God of our fathers raised up Jesus, whom ye slew, hanging him on a tree. Him did God exalt with his right hand to be a Prince and a Saviour, for to give repentance to Israel, and remission of sins. And we are witnesses of these things; and so is the Holy Ghost, whom God hath given to them that obey him. But they, when they heard this, were cut to the heart, and were minded to slay them. (29-33)

29. This is the main point of the defence, that men must, indeed are bound to, put God before men. 'God commands us to bear witness to Christ, therefore it is in vain for you to order us to be silent.' But I have explained in chapter 4.19 when this sentence, 'God must be obeyed rather than men' is relevant. God sets men over us with power in such a way that He keeps His own authority unimpaired. Therefore we must do the will of those who rule over us to the extent that the authority of God is not violated. When the use of power is legitimate, the comparison between God and man is inopportune. If a faithful pastor orders or forbids from the Word of God there will be no purpose in inflexible men objecting that God must be obeyed; for God intends to be heard by means of men; indeed man is nothing else but an instrument of God. If a magistrate is carrying out his function properly, then anyone setting him in contrast with God will be inverting things, seeing that the magistrate is not out of step with God. Rather, the opposite rule will then hold good, in order to obey

[1] Reading *arroget* with Tholuck for C.R.'s *abroget*. Tr.

God we must submit to his ministers, just as happens in the case of parents and masters.

But as soon as governors lead us away from obedience to God, seeing that they enter into conflict with God impiously and boldly, they must be put in their place, so that God and His authority may stand supreme. Then all the fumes of their offices will vanish. For God does not think men worthy of titles of honour in order that they may obscure His own glory. Therefore if a father, who is not content with his own station, tries to take from God the highest honour as Father, then he is a man and nothing else. If a king or a prince or a magistrate extols himself so much that he minimizes the honour and authority of God, he is nothing but a man. The same thoughts must also hold true of pastors. For anyone who goes beyond his function, because he sets himself against God, must be stripped of the title of his office, in case he may strike a pose and deceive. The office of a pastor is honourable, the authority of the Church great, but yet not so as to detract from the power of God and the headship of Christ. From this we can easily infer that the boasting of the Pope is ridiculous, for at the same time as he is treading the whole dominion of Christ under his feet, and openly rising against God, he is yet wishing to hide under the name of God.

30. *The God of our fathers.* They move on to their explanation (*hypothesis*)[1] to show that they had not rashly dismissed the priests' instructions as of no consequence. For as I have already said there is no room for the comparison of God and men except when there is some sort of opposition. They therefore prove that they are forced by fear of God to repudiate the commandment of the priests, for the reason that the very thing they forbid, God commands. In the first place therefore they say that Christ has been *raised up* by God, as Scripture usually puts it. For this phrase occurs everywhere; prophets and judges or other ministers, whom God determined to use for some great work, were *raised up* by Him. This means that any pre-eminence of nature is yet a weak thing, unless God equips with special gifts those on whom He lays some extraordinary or distinguished task.

They are perhaps also alluding to that famous word of Moses, which Peter quotes in his first sermon (Deut. 18.15; Acts 3.22). They expressly refer to the 'God of the fathers' as the Author, so that they make it clear that they are not bringing in a new kind of religion, or forcing some new God on the people. For they had to put an end to the false accusation, with which they knew they were being burdened, that they were trying to lead the people away from the Law and the

[1] French: 'They pass on to the special circumstances which affect their situation to show etc.'

Prophets. Not that they approve everything about the worship they received from their forefathers, as for instance unenlightened men (*profani*) are content to harp on the one theme that the fathers taught in a certain way, and they are doing nothing that is out of step with the custom and practice of their ancestors. But here the apostles mean the fathers with whom God had made His covenant, who had followed the right and pure doctrine, who had embraced the promise of salvation with true faith, who, finally, derived their origin from the heavenly Father, and who, through the only-begotten Son, were sons of God along with their descendants.

Whom you. In this clause the apostles cogently argue that those who were wishing the chief honour to be reserved for themselves as the protectors of the Church, are clearly enemies of God. It follows from this that they do not deserve even the least authority. However at the same time they anticipate any objection, a sign of confidence, when spontaneously and freely they commend the very thing that those men thought a matter of shame, viz. that it does not appear that the glory of Christ is in any way diminished because He suffered an ignominious death on the cross. It might have been put like this: 'You have killed Him indeed, and your cruelty was not satisfied with a simple or ordinary death, for He was hanged on a tree. But death was not able to put an end to His power, and the unjust dishonour inflicted on Him by you could not destroy His honour. The calling of God therefore remains firm and sure.' Therefore as the apostles cast in the teeth of the priests the crime committed by them, and their wickedness, so they anticipate by way of a concession, describing the kind of infamous death inflicted on Christ, in case the perpetrators of the crime might exult as if they had gained the victory.

31. *Him God raised . . . to be a Prince.* Therefore the apostles mean that whatever the ungodly have contrived, it does not prevent Christ fulfilling the function imposed on Him by the Father. *The right hand of God* here stands for His power. We do not have the same metaphor as we had earlier, in chapter 2, and which often occurs elsewhere, where Christ is said to have been lifted up to the right hand of the Father. But the meaning here is that Christ, who had been killed by the hand of men, has been raised on high by the power of God to rule over angels and men. And it seems to be silently opposed to all the machinations of Satan and the world. As if he said, 'Those contrivances will have no success, because they will never climb so high as to impede the hand of God, by which He has already been powerfully at work in His only-begotten Son; and He will never cease to be so.' However the purpose is added at the same time, that He might be a Leader and *Saviour.* For whenever God gave the hope of salvation

to the people, He was accustomed to promise a prince or a king by whose hand He would restore all things to wholeness. The apostles testify that this sovereignty has been given to Christ. However they describe His function more clearly with the other term. The main thing is that Christ has been placed on the highest level of honour, that He may govern the people of God, and not only that, but that He may perform the role of a saving Leader or the Author of salvation.

To give repentance. Here they show the way in which Christ reigns for the salvation of the people, viz. when He brings His own to repentance, and reconciles them to God by the forgiveness of sins. Moreover we know that the whole substance of the Gospel is contained in these two statements. For that reason the apostles are not only standing here in the defence of their own case, but are giving a splendid account of the office of Christ, so that, if at all possible, they might win even some of the dangerous enemies of the faith.

Now we have already said what the word *repentance* means (on 2.38), viz. that it is an inward turning round of man to God, which reveals itself afterwards in outward works. For Christ imparts the Spirit of regeneration to us in order that He may renew us within, and that a new life may then follow the renewal of mind and heart. For if the function of giving repentance belongs to Christ, it follows that it is not something that has been put in the power of man. And since it is truly something of a wonderful reformation, which makes us new creatures, restores the image of God in us, transfers us from the slavery of sin to the obedience of righteousness, men will no more be able to convert themselves than to create themselves.

Repentance is indeed a voluntary conversion, but what is the source of this willingness except that God changes our heart, making a heart of flesh out of a heart of stone, one that is pliable out of one that is hard and stiff, and, finally, one that is upright out of one that is crooked? And this happens when Christ regenerates us by His Spirit. Of course this is not the gift of a single moment, but one that must be increased daily all through life, until at last we draw near to God completely; and that will only take place when we have put off our flesh.

It is certainly the beginning of repentance when a man who was previously alienated from God renounces himself and the world and begins a new life. But because we have only started out on the way and are far from the goal we must constantly press on. We obtain both these things by the help of Christ. For as He begins repentance in us, so He also gives us perseverance. This is indeed an inestimable grace, but it would be of little use to us if it was not linked to the forgiveness of sins. For at first Christ finds that we are enemies of God, and also defects always stick to us, causing separation between us and Him, so that He may have every right to be hostile rather than gracious to us. And yet righteousness depends on God not imputing our sins to us. Therefore this latter grace must never be separated from the former. On the contrary the Gospel will be mutilated and corrupted if it does not consist of these two parts, i.e. unless men are taught that they are reconciled to God through Christ by the free imputation of righteousness, and that they are fashioned again in newness of life by the Spirit of regeneration. So that is our understanding, in brief, of how salvation must be laid hold of in Christ.

32. *And we are His witnesses.* After they have testified that their doctrine was obtained from God, they now move on to the other aspect, that they only speak because God has commanded them to do so, in case they might appear to be undertaking something rashly. For this was also an indispensable factor in their defence, as it is for all ministers of the Gospel, that they openly intimate that they are preaching in public only what they have received from God; and, secondly, that they have been called to do this, so that they cannot avoid the necessity of teaching, without being rebels against God.

Luke here puts 'words' (*ῥήματα, verba*) for 'things' (*rebus*) in accordance with the Hebrew usage. Although if anyone wishes to take it as referring to the speech itself, I do not object. The point is that when witnesses are brought forward by God, it is not right for them to turn their backs on Him, but they must make known what He orders.

And the Holy Spirit besides. They confirm their calling by what followed. For it was, so to speak, a sign of approval of their teaching, when God gave the gift of the Holy Spirit to believers. For indeed it was quite plain from this that the faith of the Gospel is approved by Him and even gratifying to Him. When they say, 'to those who obey Him' I take it as referring to Christ. It might have been put like this: 'Those who believe in Christ are handsomely rewarded by God for their obedience.' Therefore God wishes Christ to be obeyed; and so even our ministry pleases Him in that respect. However it can be asked, 'Since we obtain faith by the revelation of the Holy Spirit, how is He said here to be given after faith?' My reply is that what is meant are the gifts of tongues, prophecy, interpretation, healings, and similar things, by which God was enriching His Church at that time; as Paul also says, when he asks the Galatians if 'they received the Spirit by the law or by the hearing of faith' (Gal. 3.2). So the illumination of the Spirit precedes faith, seeing that it is the cause of faith; but afterwards other graces follow to benefit us, in accordance with that word, 'To him who has, it will be given' (Matt. 13.12). And if we wish to be continually enriched with new gifts of the Spirit, let us lay bare the bosom of faith to God. But today our unbelief brings us a far different reward, because the majority, destitute of the Spirit of God, neither see nor understand anything.

33. *They were cut to the heart.* The priests ought to have been deeply moved, even if their hearts were of iron, but they give vent to their rage. We gather from this that it does not matter what arguments are used, they have not the slightest effect on the reprobate to turn them to obedience to God. For if God does not speak within, the outward teaching will be able to beat upon the ears and nothing else. The apostles had it in their power to defeat and silence their enemies, but their wild nature was not subdued and corrected so that they rave all the more like madmen. At the same time, however, we must note the effectiveness of the Word, because even if it does not change the reprobate for the better, yet it penetrates into their hearts to stir their consciences; for their fury springs from the fact that they feel that they are being pressed by their judge. They would gladly ridicule the whole of the Gospel as if they are doing something important, so that they can reckon it as nothing. But a certain hidden majesty belongs to it which violently brings their frivolities to nothing. It is particularly true that their madness is apparent when they are summoned by the blast of the trumpet to the judgment-seat of God.

But there stood up one in the council, a Pharisee, named Gamaliel, a doctor of the law, had in honour of all the people, and commanded to put the men forth a little while. And he said unto them, Ye men of Israel, take heed to yourselves as touching these men, what ye are about to do. For before these days rose up Theudas, giving himself out to be somebody; to whom a number of men, about four hundred, joined themselves: who was slain; and all, as many as obeyed him, were dispersed, and came to nought. After this man rose up Judas of Galilee in the days of the enrolment, and drew away some of the people after him: he also perished; and all, as many as obeyed him, were scattered abroad. And now I say unto you, Refrain from these men, and let them alone: for if this counsel or this work be of men, it will be overthrown: but if it is of God, ye will not be able to overthrow them; lest haply ye be found even to be fighting against God. (34-39)

34. Luke now narrates how the Lord dissipated that madness of the ungodly. When they were intending to put the apostles to death, Gamaliel interposes to put an end to that mad consultation. Furthermore, Luke takes note of his circumstances so that we may understand how one man had so much influence over many. He says that he was a Pharisee, a sect that was held in the highest regard, as we know. He informs us that he was held in honour by the people; but also that the

authorities feared the people. That is why they do not dare cross his opinion. God does this sort of thing frequently, arresting the violence of His enemies by setting before them sudden and unexpected causes of terror. Further, Gamaliel orders the apostles to withdraw in case his words might make them bolder still. For it is unlikely that he spoke in this way because he approved the teaching of the Gospel or wished to plead in its defence. But because he sees all the others are incensed with madness, he, being a gentle and moderate man, tempers their excess with a moderate speech.

However, if anyone weighs everything properly, his opinion is not what one might expect from a man of prudence. Indeed I do know that it is regarded as an oracle by many, but that they are mistaken in their judgment is plain enough even from the fact that, if this happened, men must punish nobody, and, further, all crime must go uncorrected. Yes, and there must be rejected all the protections of life, life which it is not in our power to extend even for a moment.

Both the things that he says are certainly true, that all the efforts of men cannot do away with what is 'of God', but on the other hand whatever is 'of men' has not got such strength that it can endure. But it is wrong to infer from that that in the meantime it is a case of doing nothing. Rather, we must see what God is commanding us; for of course He does wish us to hold crimes in check. For this purpose He has set up magistrates, and armed them with the sword. For this purpose He has set elders over His Church, to force the refractory to order; and they are not to allow sin to be freely indulged in and to rage with impunity. Therefore it is wrong to infer that we must do nothing, because God is sufficient in Himself for removing evils. However his whole advice is like that. Gamaliel warns the scribes and elders not to wage war against God. Yet he speaks as if there were doubt about the matter. From that it is evident that he is already fundamentally unsure, seeing that he continues to waver as to the merits of the case, not daring to make up his mind, whether it is good or bad, but only directing that it be deferred for a time, until the situation clarify itself better.

To sum up, Gamaliel draws the wrong conclusion from correct premises; because he wrongly adapts what ought to apply to faith only, to outward function and method of acting. Let this be our logic, on the other hand. What is 'of God' is bound to stand, even if the whole world is against Him. Therefore, faith, which is sustained by the eternal truth of God, ought to remain unshaken against any assaults whatever of Satan and men. Even if heaven falls our salvation is secure for God is its Author and Protector. Because God guards the Kingdom of Christ no force will ever be able to overthrow it. Because the teaching of the Gospel has its foundation in God, no matter how men may fight against it or shake it, yet will it remain secure. Again, no matter how active the ungodly may be, leaving no stone unturned to bring the Church into ruins, no matter how they wage furious war against Christ and His Church, yet they will not prevail, because it is God's property to blast the purposes of men; and in this way He brings punishment on their temerity. We see that both statements are properly applied to faith. But nevertheless it is not the case that the servants of Christ ought to be less diligent in defending the truth; there is no reason why they should allow the Church to fall in ruins because of their sloth; there is no cause why they should sit back and connive at the wickedness of those who try to turn everything upside down.

36. *Theudas arose.* If Josephus is regarded as trustworthy, Gamaliel is making an alteration to the true course of events here. For the former reports that Judas Gaulanites, who was born in the town of Gamala, when Quirinius or Cyrenius was Governor, caused a disturbance with his followers to prevent a census being taken; that Theudas however made boast of himself as a prophet of God, when Cuspius Fadus was Governor. But Fadus had been sent to Judaea by Claudius Caesar. The former story is recounted in *Antiquities* Book 18; but the latter is in Book 20. But I think that when Luke says, 'after this man Judas appeared', he is not indicating a chronological order, where this man came second, but since Gamaliel brings forward two similar examples, he could substitute the one for the other without respect for time. Therefore the preposition *post*[1] means as much as 'over and above' or 'besides'.

Moreover, the examples with which Gamaliel supports his opinion do not even adequately fit the present case. For they did not immediately resist Judas, with the result that the sedition that he instigated gave rise to many disasters, and finally was put down by force of arms. Theudas would have done even far more harm, had he not been quickly overthrown by the efforts of Cuspius Fadus. But Gamaliel is mindful only of this, that things turn out badly for men, when they push themselves without regard to consequences; and that is brought about by the just punishment of God. But because the ungodly priests refuse to hear God's good advice, it serves them right to be deprived of their wits with worthless arguments by a man vacillating in different directions because of a foolish perplexity. Furthermore we may deduce from reckoning up the time that at least twelve years had passed from the death of Christ before the beating of the apostles. For to the five years remaining of the rule of

[1] v. 37. *Post hunc surrexit Judas Galilaeus.*

Tiberius, three and a half must be added in which Caligula reigned. Fadus was not sent to Judaea by Claudius before the second or third year of his reign. Gamaliel is not recalling the event as if it happened only yesterday or the day before. Consequently we arrive at that space of time, which I mentioned. That is why the firmness of the apostles was the more outstanding; for when they received such a harsh reward for the troubles they had long endured, yet they do not break down, and they do not cease to persist in the way they had been going.

To be someone great. Some manuscripts have, 'saying that he is somebody'; but the meaning is the same. For he was boasting that he was a prophet who could make the Jordan dry, to provide a crossing for his men. At the same time we see how far Gamaliel is from a right understanding, for he compares the holy ministers of Christ to impostors and robbers; although he does tone down his words afterwards, and, while inclining to the more favourable view, leaves it undecided whether they have undertaken this business with God as its author. Yet he speaks with doubt, because he thinks only of doing nothing, with no call for further investigation. The only thing that must be approved in his speech is that he discourages the ungodly from impious audacity, for there is nothing to be feared more than opposing God.

And to him they agreed: and when they had called the apostles unto them, they beat them and charged them not to speak in the name of Jesus, and let them go. They therefore departed from the presence of the council, rejoicing that they were counted worthy to suffer dishonour for the Name. And every day, in the temple and at home, they ceased not to teach and to preach Jesus as the Christ. (40–42)

40. *They beat them and charged them.* He says that Gamaliel's advice was accepted; yet the apostles are scourged and forbidden to teach. From this we infer how great the fury of their enemies had been, for though they are now appeased, or at least quietened down, yet they do behave in such an intemperate fashion. At the same time it is also obvious how unfortunate are the results of those indefinite counsels, in which attention is given only to men, with the truth of God neglected. Gamaliel certainly procures the sparing of the lives of the apostles; but nevertheless in the persons of those same men reproach is inflicted on the Son of God. The truth of the Gospel is buried in an eternal silence, as far as their enemies are concerned. Certainly God does marvellously propagate His Word in this way; yet that advice does not cease to be bad. And we must note this for the reason that today very many think that they do no small service

to God if they only spare the lives of those who run into danger on account of the teaching of the Gospel, or turn enemies, who might otherwise be out for blood, into ways of gentleness. Meanwhile they are not afraid to drive them to abjuring Christ infamously; but the confession of Christ is far more precious in the eyes of God than the life of all men. But what should become of those who dismiss a concern for piety and wish to redeem themselves with God by the duty of humane conduct?

41. *They therefore went . . . rejoicing.* It must not be thought that the apostles were so stolid as not to feel ashamed, and even to suffer from a sense that they had been wronged; for they had not discarded nature completely. But when they thought over the cause, joy got the upper hand. So the faithful ought to be affected in a twofold way, as often as they suffer persecution for the sake of the Gospel; although they are certainly afflicted by the bitterness of their punishment, yet they may rise above this sadness with spiritual joy. For they would have beaten a hasty retreat, if ardour born from joy had not given them new strength. There is no doubt that death would also have been just as sweet and pleasant to Peter, even although the Lord declares that it will be a bitter thing for him. Let us therefore learn that we must wrestle with affliction and anxiety, in order that we may gladly continue to encounter the Cross (*ad obeundam crucem*) and carry it when it is laid upon us.

Because they were counted worthy. This could appear absurd at first sight, because Luke gives honour to what was a disgrace. But this is caused by the dissimilarity between God and the world, since something that is thought to be shameful in the highest degree by men, stands out in great dignity and glory in the eyes of God and His angels. We know that the kind of death that Christ endured, was the most ignominious of all, and yet He wrought the noblest Triumph on the Cross; so when we are being conformed to Him (cf. Phil. 3.10, Rom. 8.29), we can worthily boast that being objects of shame in the eyes of the world is in fact a mark of pre-eminence. So Paul speaks openly of the marks of Christ (Gal. 6.17).

For attention ought to be paid here to the grounds of our union with the Son of God, who not only absorbs the shame of the world with His glory, but converts reproaches, infamies and derision into the highest honour. Thus it is not to be wondered at that there are so few who are courageous and quick to bear the cross, seeing that we are nearly all overwhelmed by the mind of the flesh; indeed hardly one in a hundred understands that the ignominy of Christ is superior to all the triumphs of the world, and this is the only ground for comfort. For that reason we must think about this sentence more earnestly, that at the present time we are being conformed to the sufferings of Christ so that we may be partakers and partners of His glory (cf. Rom. 8.17; I Pet. 4.13).

42. *They ceased not.* Along with their joy there also went steadfastness. For is not the cause of persecution weakening us and taking the heart out of us, the fact that nobody lifts himself to Christ, to take into his heart now, in advance, the fruit of victory, and to be stirred up to endurance? But he who considers himself blessed when he suffers for Christ's sake, will never be a deserter, however hard may be the battles that have to be fought. Therefore the apostles were, in a way, armed with lashes to hasten undaunted to death. Alas therefore for our delicate ways! for having got through the smallest persecution, we at once hand over the torch to others, as if we were veteran soldiers already.

CHAPTER SIX

Now in these days, when the number of the disciples was multiplying, there arose a murmuring of the Grecian Jews against the Hebrews, because their widows were neglected in the daily ministration. And the twelve called the multitude of the disciples unto them, and said, It is not fit that we should forsake the word of God, and serve tables. Look ye out therefore, brethren, from among you seven men of good report, full of the Spirit and of wisdom, whom we may appoint over this business. But we will continue stedfastly in prayer, and in the ministry of the word. And the saying pleased the whole multitude: and they chose Stephen, a man full of faith and of the Holy Spirit, and Philip, and Prochorus, and Nicanor, and Timon and Parmenas, and Nicolas a proselyte of Antioch: whom they set before the apostles: and when they had prayed, they laid their hands on them. (1-6)

1. Luke is telling us here about the creation of deacons, dealing first with the occasion, secondly with the deliberation involved, and finally with the rite used. Nevertheless he does say that this was the remedy adopted to silence the grumbling that had arisen among the disciples; as the common proverb says, 'Bad customs give rise to good laws.' But it could appear an extraordinary thing, since this is such an honourable and necessary office in the Church, why it never entered the heads of the apostles from the beginning to appoint deacons on their own responsibility, and why the Spirit had not given them advice along these lines, when they now accept it as if under pressure. But in fact what did happen was a better way at that time, and also is more beneficial to us today as an example. If the apostles had spoken about the electing of deacons before any necessity demanded it, they would have found the people less disposed to it; they themselves would have given the appearance of avoiding irksome labour; many would not have been so generous in handing gifts over to other men. It was therefore necessary for the faithful to be convinced by experience, learning that they could not do without deacons, and this really because of their own fault, so that they would be glad to choose them.

Now we learn from this story, first of all, that the Church cannot be formed all at once in such a way that nothing remains to be corrected; and that an edifice of such a massive size cannot be finished on the first day so that nothing needs to be added to make it perfect.

Furthermore we learn that there is no institution of God so sacred and praiseworthy that it is the case that it is not corrupted or rendered less useful by the fault of men. We are amazed that things are never so well ordered in the world that some evil is not mixed up with things that are good; but the corruption of our nature (*ingenii*) is the cause of this. It was without any doubt a divine ordering of things, that Luke described earlier, when the goods of all were set apart as sacred to God, and shared out in common; when the apostles, being so to speak the stewards of God and the poor, had charge of the alms. But a little later grumbling springs up to throw that very arrangement into disorder. Here there appears that corruption of men which I mentioned, and which does not allow us to make use of our blessings. At the same time we must observe the artifice of Satan who is constantly engaged on depriving us of the use of God's gifts, and makes it his business that that use may not remain pure and whole, but that it is mixed up with other things that cause inconvenience, and may come to be despised, then loathed, and finally wiped out. The apostles by their own example indeed have taught us that we must not yield to Satan's stratagems of that sort. Displeased at the grumbling, they do not decide that they must put an end to a service which they knew to be pleasing to God, but they think out a remedy to remove the complaint, and leave what is of God. This is surely the right way of doing things. For whatever causes of offence Satan may raise up day by day, we must take great care that he does not drive out institutions that are beneficial to us in some other way.

The number was multiplying. There is nothing to be desired more than that God may increase His Church, and add as many as possible to His people from every quarter; but the corruption of our nature prevents anything prospering in every respect. For, from the additions made to the Church many troublesome things take their rise. For there is the difficulty that a few hypocrites stealthily creep into the crowd, and their wickedness is not discovered at once, but only when they have corrupted part of the flock with their infection. There are also many ungodly, forward and dissolute people who worm their way in on a false pretext of repentance. And not to mention innumerable other things, it is never so easy to get agreement among people, but their opinions vary as their customs differ, so that one and the same thing scarcely pleases all alike. This scandal causes many to wish to choose a few people for themselves instead of the Church, to despise the multitude or even to hate it. But no trouble, no dislike, ought to be so great that the increase of the Church does not always lie close to our hearts, that we do not take pains to propagate it, that we do not cherish, as much as we can, unity with the whole body.

A murmuring of the Greeks. It is evident from this that people who find in the difference of race and country an occasion for disagreement were not fully regenerate by the Spirit of God. For in Christ there is neither Jew nor Greek (Gal. 3.28), and therefore this rivalry smacks of the flesh and the world. That is why we must be the more careful that nothing of the sort ever takes us by surprise. Another fault follows, for they show their indignation by complaining. Moreover it is not certain whether the complaint was justified. For when Luke says that the Greeks murmured, because consideration was not being given to their widows, he is reporting not something that actually did take place, but what they supposed happened. But since the apostles would prefer the Jewish widows, because they were better known, it may be that the Greeks thought, wrongly, that their women were being despised as foreigners. And that does seem more likely. Also, the word *ministration* (*ministerium*) can be explained in two ways, actively or passively. For we know that widows were chosen for the diaconate of the Church at the beginning. However I myself am of the opinion that the Greeks were complaining because less generous provision was being given to their widows. So 'the ministration' will be that daily distribution which it was their custom to make.

2. *The twelve called the multitude.* It is a mark of tolerance and equanimity that the apostles are not more annoyed. It is a mark of prudence and godly concern that they quickly nip the evil in the bud, and do not put off finding a remedy for it. For after every dissension and rivalry has gathered strength it becomes a wound that is difficult to heal.

It is clear from this assembly that the Church was governed with order and reasonableness (*ordine et ratione*), so that while authority was in the hands of the apostles, yet they let the people know what was in their minds. It must also be observed that *disciples* is used for 'believers' or 'Christians'. In their case must be fulfilled that word of Isaiah's, 'They are all taught by God' (Isa. 54.13, cf. John 6.45); and also the word of Jeremiah's, 'They will all know God from the least to the greatest' (Jer. 31.34).

It is not fit. The Greek is οὐκ ἀρεστόν. By this word the Greeks mean sometimes what is superior to other things and what is preferred as better, sometimes what is determined. I rather think that the apostles are announcing what may be advantageous rather than simply what they have decreed. But if it is not beneficial for them to be involved in this administration, they now appear to be acknowledging some fault in their previous management of it. And it is certainly true that experience is the father of wisdom. So there will be nothing absurd were we to say that after the apostles find by experience that that task does not suit them, they ask the Church to be relieved of it. But if there was any blame it ought to have been put down to necessity rather than to them. For they had not been eager to snatch at this burden, but since another method did not present itself they preferred to be excessively burdened rather than that the poor be neglected. But when they say that it is not equitable that they should forsake the Word of God and busy themselves in looking after the poor, they mean that they are unable to cope with maintaining both burdens, so that they must necessarily give up one or the other. For it is just as if they said, 'If you wish to enjoy our ministry in the preaching of the Gospel, free us from the care of the poor, because we are not able to bear the strain of both tasks.' But it does appear that this is not a timely remark of theirs, because they had not previously abandoned the office of teaching, although they had been in charge of the alms. I reply that since the administration had been combined, they were so involved that they could not give such undivided attention to teaching as it deserved. They therefore decline the task which takes them away from an unrestricted and total concern for teaching. Yet we are not to understand that they gave up entirely a regard for the poor, but that they sought relief so that they could turn their attention to their own task.

At the same time they are showing that the ministry of the Word is so demanding that it occupies a man entirely, and does not allow him to be free for other occupations. And if that had been properly considered the conduct of affairs (*ratio*) in the Church would have been apportioned quite differently. Under the pretext of deaconship the Papal bishops devoured riches in abundance. At the same time they involved themselves in various occupations, with which they would scarcely cope if each one had ten heads. Yet their wickedness is such that they deny that the Church can exist unless it is plunged into this abyss, and they continually boast that they are the successors of the apostles, when nothing more to the contrary is plain to see. Indeed they took good care not to be involved with 'serving tables' and be forced to give up the pleasures of their own tables (*delicias*). For whoever is solicitous about his own table claims that he has nothing to do with others.

But passing those things over let us apply this sentence to our own benefit. We know what a holy thing it is to look after the poor. Therefore when the apostles put the preaching of the Gospel first we infer from that that no obedience is more pleasing to God than this. At the same time however the difficulty is pointed out, when they say that they are not equal to those two offices. We are certainly not superior in any way to them, hence let anyone who has been called to teaching apply himself wholly to 'making the most of his Sparta' (as the proverb has it). For there is nothing easier than for us to fall into sluggishness. Further, the flesh supplies plausible pretexts in abundance so that those who involve themselves with extraneous affairs do not immediately perceive that they are being taken away from their proper task. Therefore so that ministers may urge themselves on, let them frequently remind themselves of this sentence, in which the apostles testify that they must give up the care of the poor, since they have been called to the office of teaching. Therefore what excuse will there be for worldly occupations, even taken up for private gain, when something has to be given up that is otherwise considered a not unimportant part of the worship of God?

3. *Look ye out therefore brethren.* We now ascertain the purpose for which deacons were created. The term itself is certainly a general one, yet it is properly taken for the stewards of the poor. It is apparent from that how wantonly the Papists make fools of God and men, for the only duty that they assign to their deacons is the handling of the paten and chalice. There is surely no need of a long argument to prove that they have nothing in common or in agreement with the apostles. But if readers wish to find out more about this matter, they will be at liberty to make inquiry from my *Institute* (4.3.9).

In regard to the present passage, in the first place choice is permitted to the Church. For it is a tyrannous thing if any single individual appoints ministers by his own authority. Therefore the appropriate method is for those who are to enter on any public office in the Church to be elected by common votes. On the other hand the apostles lay down what sort of men ought to be chosen, viz. men of proved trustworthiness, endowed with wisdom and other gifts of the Spirit. And this is the middle way between tyranny and disorderly licence, for it means that nothing indeed may be done except by the consent and approval of the people; but on the other hand that the pastors may rule with their authority like a bridle to hold in check the impulses of the people, to prevent their enthusiasm running away with them. At the same time it is worth while noting that the principle is imposed on the faithful so that they may appoint only somebody who is suitable. For we do God no small injury if we accept in fortuitous fashion anyone at all to govern His household. Therefore the greatest scrupulousness must be employed so that nobody may be chosen for a sacred function in the Church, unless he has proved himself. The number *seven* was appropriate to the need at the moment, so nobody need think that anything mysterious lies hidden under it. I interpret Luke's words that they were *full of the Spirit and of wisdom* as follows. It is necessary for them to be provided not only with other graces of the Spirit, but also certainly with wisdom, for without it that task cannot be properly carried out. They may thus be on their guard not only against the impostures and frauds of those who are far too inclined to begging, and suck up what was needed for the brethren who were in extreme poverty, but also against the calumnies of those who are constantly making disparaging remarks, even if there is no occasion for doing so. For as well as being full of difficulties that office is also exposed to unjustified complaints.

4. *But we shall devote ourselves to prayer.* Again they point out that other things will give them more than enough to keep them busy all their lives long. An old saying, which was once used in worship (*in sacris*) fits in very well with this, 'This do'. Therefore they use the verb προσκαρτερῆσαι, which means, as it were, to be attached to something, and to be busy. It is not the case therefore that pastors are to think they have discharged their obligation if they have spent some time each day in teaching. Another endeavour, another ardour, another assiduity are all required, so that they can properly pride themselves that they are exerting themselves in that task of teaching. They add prayer, not because they are the only ones who ought to pray (for that is a practice common to all the godly), but because, compared with others, they have special reasons for praying. Indeed there is nobody who ought not to be concerned about the general welfare of the Church; therefore ought not the pastor to strive all the more anxiously for it, when those duties are expressly enjoined on him? Thus Moses certainly urged others to pray, but he himself led the way like a standard-bearer. And it is not for nothing that Paul makes mention of his own prayers so often. Finally, we ought to bear in mind always that we shall throw away our labour in ploughing, sowing and watering, unless the increase comes from heaven (I Cor. 3.7). It will therefore not be enough to carry out the task of teaching strenuously if at the same time blessing is not being sought from the Lord, so that the work may not be useless and unfruitful. From this it is evident that it is not for nothing that zeal for prayer is commended to the ministers of the Word.

5. *Stephen, full of faith.* Luke does not separate faith from the Spirit as if faith itself were not also a gift of the Spirit; but by 'the Spirit' he means other gifts with which Stephen was endowed. Such are zeal, prudence, readiness to do good, brotherly love, diligence, the integrity of a good conscience. He then mentions one example in particular. He therefore means that Stephen especially excelled in faith, and after that in other virtues, so that it might be perfectly obvious that he abounds in the grace of the Spirit. He does not praise the

others in that way, because without any doubt they did not match up to him. No! and the writers of old tell us with great unanimity that this Nicolas, who was one of the seven, is the one mentioned by John in the Apocalypse (2.15), as the founder of a scandalous and shameful sect, since he wished women to be prostitutes. Accordingly it is fitting that we should not be in a state of torpor when electing ministers of the Church, for if the hypocrisy of men also deceives those who take the utmost care to be on their guard, what may happen to those who are unconcerned and negligent? At the same time if, after proper attention has been given, it does happen that we are deceived nevertheless, let us not be unduly perturbed, seeing that Luke tells us that even the apostles were liable to this evil. Somebody is asking, 'What then was the use of exhortation, and of prayer, when the actual result showed that the election was not wholly directed by the Spirit of God?' I reply that it is a great matter that the Spirit directed their judgments in choosing six men; that He allowed the Church to err in the seventh ought not to appear a senseless thing. For it is right for us to be humbled in various ways; partly that the evil and the ungodly may vex us; partly that warned by their example we may learn to examine ourselves within, lest there may be any hidden pockets of deceit in us; partly that we may be more careful about discerning, and be perpetually on guard, as it were, so that fraudulent and treacherous men may not surround us. It may even be that the ministry of Nicolas was useful for a time, and that he fell into that monstrous error afterwards. But if he fell like that from such an honourable position, then the higher each one of us has been raised, let him submit himself to God with modesty and fear.

6. *Having prayed they laid their hands on them.* The laying on of hands was a solemn symbol of consecration under the Law. The apostles now place their hands on the deacons for this purpose, that they may know that they are being dedicated (*offerri*) to God. Because the ceremony was empty in itself however, there is added at the same time a prayer, in which the faithful commend to God the ministers whom they are presenting to Him. This is certainly ascribed to the apostles, for the whole of the people did not lay their hands on the deacons, but when the apostles said prayers on behalf of the Church the others added theirs. We gather from this that the laying on of hands is a rite consistent with order and dignity, seeing that it was used by the apostles; not of course that it has any efficacy or virtue in itself, but its power and effect depend solely on the Spirit of God. That must be the general opinion about all ceremonies.

And the word of God increased; and the number of the disciples multi-

plied in Jerusalem exceedingly; and a great company of the priests were obedient to the faith. And Stephen, full of grace and power, wrought great wonders and signs among the people. But there arose certain of them that were of the synagogue called the synagogue of the Libertines, and of the Cyrenians, and of the Alexandrians, and of them of Cilicia and Asia, disputing with Stephen. And they were not able to withstand the wisdom and the Spirit by which he spake. (7-10)

7. Luke again tells about increases to the Church, the better to illustrate the grace and power of God in its continual advancement. Certainly the sudden raising up of the Church, in a moment as it were, was already a remarkable work of God's. But just as much admiration should deservedly be given to this, that He furthers the work begun by Him in spite of so many obstacles, and that the number is increased of the very people, whom the world works so hard to cut down, even to the point of destroying the whole stock. When he says that 'the Word of God grew', the meaning is that it was propagated further. The Word of God is said to grow in a twofold way, either when new disciples are added to its obedience, or in proportion as each one of us makes progress in it. Luke is dealing here with the former kind of growth; for he explains himself immediately after by speaking of 'the number of the disciples'. Nevertheless he confines this increase of faith to a single city. For even if it is credible that disciples were scattered in other places also, yet the only place where there was a definite body was Jerusalem.

And a great company. Since, properly speaking, our faith is obedient to the teaching of the Gospel, Luke is using metonymy in saying that they 'were obedient to the faith'. For he takes the word *faith* for the Word of God, and the actual profession of Christianity. He expressly picks out the priests, because they were usually hostile; and for that reason the conversion of only some, never mind many of them, was all the more wonderful a work of God. For at the beginning they were raging against Christ Himself, scoffing and saying, 'Have any of the rulers believed in Him? But this crowd who do not know the law are accursed' (John 7.48f).

8. *And Stephen.* Luke here refers to a new struggle for the Church. From that it is evident that the glory of the Gospel has always been joined with the cross and various vexations. But the point is that the Church was attacked in the person of one man. And so what happened was that their enemies took greater courage, and, soaked with innocent blood, vented their rage more cruelly than usual; for before this they had gone no further than prison and beatings.

But so that we may know that the name of Christ was glorified in the life as well as in the death of Stephen Luke begins by saying that he was 'full of faith[1] and power'. He means by that that his faith was outstanding, and that he excelled in the power to do miracles. For it must not be imagined that his faith was perfect because he is said to be 'full of faith', but it is not an uncommon expression in Scripture to call those, who have been endowed with the gifts of God in abundance, *full* of those gifts. Without any question I take *power* as the ability to perform miracles. *Faith* embraces not only the gift of understanding, but also the eagerness of zeal. Since his name was famous because of his pre-eminence in this way, the result was that the crowd of the ungodly turned on him in one fell swoop so to speak. For just as the power and grace of the Spirit come on the scene and show themselves, it usually happens at the same time that the fury of Satan is aroused. But it will be obvious from the context that Stephen was unremitting and undaunted in spreading the teaching of the Gospel, but Luke says nothing about this at the moment, being content to have praised his faith, which could not have lain idle and at rest.

9. *But there arose certain.* This was the beginning of persecution, because, after the unbelievers had tried in vain to set themselves in opposition to Christ by disputing, when they discover their first attempt at it brings no result, they have recourse to calumnies and disturbances, and finally they break out into violence and even go as far as slaughter. Therefore Luke means by the verb, *rising*, that those, of whom he is speaking, attacked the teaching of the Gospel by speech; that they did not drag Stephen to trial at once, but first fell upon him with opposing arguments.

He points out, moreover, that they were foreigners, who were in Judaea either for the sake of business or out of a desire for learning. Accordingly he recalls that some were from Cyrene, others from Alexandria, others from Cilicia, and still others from Asia. He says that they all belonged to the synagogue of the Libertines. It is probable that freedmen of the citizens of Rome had caused a synagogue to be built at their own expense, to be specially for the Jews who were in the habit of coming frequently to Jerusalem from the provinces. Therefore those who had been prompted to do that by the grace of God, and ought to have been so much more eager to embrace Christ, are the first to oppose Him and rouse the fury of others, as if by the call of a trumpet. And Luke will show in many later passages that the Jews of the provinces were especially hostile to sound doctrine, and were most virulent in promoting disturbances. He mentions many so that the victory of the truth may be all the clearer, when many,

[1] So Calvin, and A.V.; Vulg.: *plenus gratia et fortitudine*; Greek, πλήρης χαρίτος καὶ δυνάμεως; cf. R.S.V., N.E.B. Tr.

drawn from various regions, give up, having been outdone by one man, for there is no doubt that they were forced with shame to fall silent.

His faith and miracles had already brought favour and standing to Stephen. He now replies to the disputers in such a way that he appears far superior. He does not put down as separate things, *the wisdom and the Spirit*, for which, he says, Stephen's adversaries were no match. Therefore interpret those words like this: they were not able to withstand the wisdom with which the Spirit of God supplied him. For Luke wished to bring out that on both sides they were not fighting as mere men, but that the reason why the enemies of the Gospel were broken was that they were fighting with the Spirit of God, who was speaking through the mouth of Stephen.

As far as we are concerned, since Christ has promised the same Spirit to all His servants, only let us fight for the truth conscientiously, and let us ask for a mouth and wisdom from Him, and we shall be sufficiently equipped for speaking, so that neither the shrewdness nor the garrulity of our enemies may ever put us to shame. Thus the Spirit was just as effectual in our own time in the mouth of the martyrs who were dragged off to the torture of fire; and He still produces the same activity every day, so that, uneducated though men might be, they might astonish the chief theologians of the Papacy with their voice alone, as if it were a thunderbolt.

Then they suborned men, which said, We have heard him speak blasphemous words against Moses, and against God. And they stirred up the people, and the elders, and the scribes, and came upon him, and seized him, and brought him into the council, and set up false witnesses, which said, This man ceaseth not to speak words against this holy place, and the law: for we have heard him say, that this Jesus of Nazareth shall destroy this place, and shall change the customs which Moses delivered unto us. And all that sat in the council, fastening their eyes on him, saw his face as it had been the face of an angel. (11-15)

11. Having been overthrown by the power of the Spirit they gave up disputation, but they bring forward false witnesses to crush him with calumnies. It is evident from that that they were fighting with a bad conscience. For what is more shameful than their basing the defence of their case upon lies? A man may well be culpable in other respects, yet he must not be put down on false testimonies. But hypocrites nonchalantly indulge in that under the cover of their zeal. We are aware that today the Papists knowingly corrupt plain passages of Scripture, when they wish to twist the evidence falsely against us.

I think that it is mainly through ignorance that they offend. But not one of them will be found who does not permit himself to distort both the meaning and the words of Scripture, in order to bring odium on our teaching; they even fabricate monstrous calumnies against us from the pulpit (*pro suggestu*). If you are to ask those Rabbis whether it is right for a man to be slandered, they will certainly say that generally speaking it is not, but when it comes to us, good zeal excuses them, because they think that nothing is unlawful that can bring trouble to us and our cause. Therefore they delude themselves with lies, perfidy and dog-like impudence. Hypocrisy like that also blinded those whom Luke reports here as having taken advantage of false witnesses to destroy Stephen. For when Satan asserts his sway not only does he incite the reprobate to cruelty, but also blinds their eyes so that they think they are at liberty to do anything they like. We are specially taught by this example how dangerous a pretext good zeal may be, if it is not controlled by the Spirit of God; for it always breaks out into furious frenzy, and at the same time is a marvellous disguise to cover all sorts of crimes.

14. *We have heard*. It will be quite evident from Stephen's defence that he never spoke about Moses or the temple except with respect. And yet this charge was not brought against him for nothing; for he had taught the abrogation of the Law. But in that connexion the witnesses are false, and suborned to tell lies, because they deliberately distort what had been well and graciously (*pie*) said. Similarly Christ was forced to vindicate Himself, that He had not come to destroy the Law, because, when He had spoken publicly about the abrogating of ceremonies, the ungodly took it in another way, as if He wished to abolish the whole Law. His enemies also wrongly twisted what He had said about His own body, to refer to the temple at Jerusalem. Why! was the objection not brought against Paul that he was teaching that 'evil must be done so that good may come out of it' (Rom. 3.8)?

Therefore there is no reason for us to wonder today that the godly, proper, and useful things we teach are spitefully laid hold of in an adverse and corrupted sense. No indeed! So we must be quite clear that the teaching of the Gospel can never be handled in such a cautious and moderate way that it is not subject to misrepresentations. For Satan, who is the father of lies, always devotes himself to his business. Again, because many things are out of line with the reasoning of the flesh, there is nothing that men are more inclined to do than to give a hearing to calumnies, which falsify the genuine and sound meaning of the teaching. Indeed this ill-will of Satan's and these devices ought to make us more cautious and more attentive so that we do not miss anything said that is a distortion, or is not quite proper and correct, with which they may be armed to fight against us. For we must take care to deny flatly to the ungodly the opportunity for which they long. But if we do see the teaching, that we have properly and dutifully set forth, corrupted, disfigured and torn to pieces by twisted misrepresentations, there is no reason for us to be sorry that we started, or why we should be more hesitant afterwards. For it is not fair that we should be safe and immune from the poisonous bites of Satan, when even the Son of God could not avoid them. At the same time it is our responsibility to dissipate and do away with the lies with which the truth of God is embarrassed, as we realize that Christ protects the teaching of the Gospel from unjust ignominy. Only let us be so prepared in mind and purpose that that particular baseness may not hinder us in our course.

Since we teach that men are so corrupted that they are complete slaves to sin and evil desires, our enemies make out from that the misrepresentation that we deny that men sin of their own accord, but are driven to evil from some other source, so that they bear no blame. They even make the accusation that we destroy the desire to do good. Because we deny that the works of the saints are meritorious because of an intrinsic worth, since they always have some sprinkling of imperfection, they quibble that we are taking away the difference between good men and bad. Because we say that the righteousness of man is placed in the grace of God alone, and that godly souls can find rest nowhere else but in the death of Christ, they object that in this way control of the flesh is relaxed, so that there is no further use for the Law. When we defend His honour for Christ, which they themselves distribute here and there as it suits them, cut up in a thousand pieces like a hunted animal, they wrongly suppose that we are enemies of holy things. They make the false statement that we seek the licence of the flesh instead of the liberty of the Spirit. When we are trying to restore the Holy Supper of Christ to its pure and proper use, they impudently shout that it is being overthrown and destroyed by us. There are also others who, like the Academic philosophers, throw everything aside. Because what we teach from Scripture about the secret predestination of God does not please them, they odiously complain that we make God a tyrant, who amuses Himself by destroying innocent men, seeing that He has already abandoned people not yet born to eternal death; and such things as can be said in this vein; whereas, however, it has been made abundantly clear to them that we think about God with reverence, and only speak what He teaches out of His own mouth. It is certainly unpleasant and hard to submit to such ill-will; yet we must not give up the defence of a good cause on that account. For the truth of God is a precious thing and ought to be so to us; although to the reprobate it may be 'the savour of death unto death' (II Cor. 2.16).

But I now return to the accusation against Stephen, the principal point of which is that he blasphemed against God and Moses. Rightly do they affront God and Moses in common, because Moses had nothing in his teaching that was his own, or apart from God. They are proving that he spoke insolently about the temple and the Law. Furthermore they consider the blasphemy to consist in this, that he said that an end had been imposed on the temple and ceremonies with the coming of Christ. It is not credible that Stephen spoke in the way that they report, but they spitefully twist his good and devout statements to add colour to their false accounts. But even if they had left the words unchanged, so far from Stephen causing damage to the temple and the Law however, he could not do better honour to them with genuine praises. The Jews were in the habit of thinking that it is all over with the honour of the temple, if its shadowy state were not to endure for ever; and that the Law is ineffectual and of no importance if its ceremonies were not to flourish for ever (cf. Heb. 8.5, 10.1). But the great value of the temple and the usefulness of the ceremonies consist rather in their being ascribed to Christ, as to their original pattern. Therefore whatever excuse there may be for the accusation, nevertheless it is unjust and perverse. Finally, although there may be a question of fact, viz. if a state of affairs, such as his adversaries charge him with, actually holds, yet what is involved is properly a question as to its nature (*status qualitatis*). For they are accusing Stephen that he taught that the form of the worship of God must be changed, and they interpret this as blasphemy against God and Moses. Therefore the dispute is a matter of principle (*de iure*), as we say, rather than of fact. For the question is whether a man is harming and dishonouring God and Moses, when he suggests that the visible temple is an image of a more excellent sanctuary in which the fulness of God dwells, and teaches that the shadows of the Law are temporary?

This Jesus of Nazareth. They speak of Christ with contempt in this way, as if the memory of Him was detestable. At the same time it can be inferred from their calumnies that in abrogating the Law Stephen set the reality (*corpus*) over against the shadows, and the substance over against the forms. For if ceremonies are abolished by Christ, their true nature is spiritual. The Jews were wishing them to last for ever, and thought that they consisted of nothing but what was solid, carnal, earthly and plain to see. In a word, if the ceremonies had been continually in use, they would be fleeting and vanishing; because they would have nothing except an outward appearance, so nothing substantial would underlie them. Therefore their true perpetuity consists in their being abrogated by the coming of Christ; because from then on it follows that their virtue and purpose are established in Christ.

He will change the institutions. There is no doubt that Stephen understood this of the ceremonial part only. But as men usually give their devotion to external displays, those men take what was said to mean that Stephen would reduce the whole Law to nothing. The chief commandments of the Law were certainly about the spiritual worship of God, faith, righteousness, and judgment; but because those men esteem external rites more highly, they call those rites which are laid down for the sacrifices, the institutions of Moses *par excellence.* This has been in human nature since the beginning of the world, and will be right to the end. For instance, today the Papists acknowledge no worship of God except in their masquerades (*larvis*). Yet they do differ a great deal from the Jews, because, instead of the institutions of God, they follow nothing but the frivolous inventions of men.

15. *When they had contemplated him.* It is usual in courts of justice for eyes to be turned on the defendant when his defence is awaited. Now Luke says that Stephen appeared like an angel. But this is not said of his face in normal circumstances, but rather of his expression at the moment. For while the faces of the accused usually grow pale, while they stammer in their speech, and show other signs of trepidation, Luke is telling us that there was nothing like that in Stephen, but rather that a certain majesty shone out in him. For Scripture is sometimes in the habit of borrowing an analogy from the angels in this sense; as I Sam. 29.9, and II Sam. 14.17 and 19.27.

CHAPTER SEVEN

And the high priest said, Are these things so? And he said, Brethren and fathers, hearken, The God of glory appeared unto our father Abraham, when he was in Mesopotamia, before he dwelt in Haran, and said unto him, Get thee out of thy land, and from thy kindred, and come into the land which I shall shew thee. Then came he out of the land of the Chaldaeans, and dwelt in Haran: and from thence, when his father was dead, God removed him into this land, wherein ye now dwell. (1-4)

1. Up to now some semblance of fairness is apparent in the high priest and the council, and yet there is the most unfair prejudice in his words. For he does not ask what grounds Stephen had for teaching in this way; and does not admit him to the defence that the law provides although the defence was the chief thing, but briefly inquires whether Stephen used those words, whatever they may mean. Similarly today the Papists do not venture to inquire about the nature of a doctrine, or whether it can be proved out of the Scriptures, but all they ask is whether anyone has dared to murmur against their superstitions, so that as soon as they convict him they may give him up to the flames.

Further, Stephen's reply could appear at first glance absurd and unsuitable. First of all he starts at the very beginning; then he weaves a narrative of many words, in which almost no mention is made of the present situation. Now, there is no worse fault than wandering from the subject in a flow of words. But anyone who will look more closely will easily perceive that in this long speech there is nothing superfluous, and that Stephen is speaking to the point, as the situation demands. He has been accused of being an apostate who tried to overthrow religion and the worship of God. Therefore he sedulously insists that he is still holding to the same God as their fathers had always worshipped. So he turns aside the charge of impious defection. On the other hand he shows that his enemies are driven on by nothing less than zeal for the Law. For they were pretending that they had nothing in mind but the increase of the glory of God. He therefore tears away this false boasting of theirs. But since they were always having the fathers on their lips, and were full of pride about the glory of their nation, Stephen also shows that these give them no cause for pride; on the contrary the faults of the fathers were so many and so great that they ought to be ashamed and humbled.

Now we come to the main question and the heart of the matter. Since it was a question of the temple and ceremonies he clearly reminds them that their fathers were elected by God to be His peculiar people, before a temple was standing and Moses was born. And the first part of the speech, when looked at more closely, has this end in view. In the second part, he tells them that all the external rites, which God gave them by the hand of Moses, were fashioned according to a heavenly pattern. From that it follows that the ceremonial law is related to some end other than itself, and that those who disregard the truth and stick to signs, are acting foolishly and indeed wrongly. If readers will refer the whole of Stephen's speech to those two principal points, they will find nothing in it that does not fit the situation very well, as I shall briefly repeat again at the close.[1] In the meantime that account of the purpose (*scopum*) of the whole speech will not prevent us from being able to examine details, which will repay attention.

2. *Men, brethren and fathers*. Although Stephen was well aware that those who were sitting on the Council were the sworn enemies of the Gospel, yet, because the orderly government of the people was still in their hands, and they presided over the Church which God had not yet rejected, he does not therefore hesitate, for the sake of propriety, to call them 'fathers'. Indeed he does not curry favour for himself as a flatterer, but gives this honour to the order and government that God had instituted, until authority would be taken away from them with a change of system. At the same time, nevertheless, respect for the position which they occupy, does not stand in his way, or stop him from speaking. And that goes to show how ridiculous the Papists are, who wish to have us tied to false titles, that are bad and indeed empty, so that we may be forced to subscribe to their opinions, no matter how ungodly.

The God of glory. In this introduction he bears witness that he is not departing in the slightest from the fathers and the true religion that they followed. For the whole of religion, the worship of God, the teaching of the Law, all the prophets were dependent upon that covenant, which God had forged with Abraham. Therefore when Stephen acknowledges that God had appeared to Abraham he is including the Law and the Prophets, which flow from that first revelation as from a fountain. He also calls Him the *God of glory* so that he may distinguish Him, who alone is worthy of glory, from false and fictitious gods.

When he was in Mesopotamia. It is well known that this name is

[1] See on v. 51ff, p. 211.

given to the region which lies between the two rivers, the Tigris and the Euphrates. But he says, *before he dwelt in Haran*, because Abraham, having been warned by an oracle, migrated from Chaldea to Haran. This was a town in Mesopotamia, made famous by the defeat of Crassus and a Roman army, although Pliny assigned it to Arabia. And it is no wonder that Chaldea is described here under the name of Mesopotamia, because, although the region embraced by the Euphrates and the Tigris is, strictly speaking, 'the land between the two rivers', the geographers, nevertheless, commonly give this name to Assyria and Chaldea.

The point is that Abraham acted on God's certain command and left his native land; and so the genuine goodness of God preceded him, inasmuch as he sought out what was offered to him when he was at home on the other side. See the last chapter of Joshua (28.2f).

But now Moses' narrative appears to differ from this one to some extent. For having narrated at the end of the eleventh chapter (Gen. 11.31) that Abraham left home and changed his country, he adds at the beginning of the twelfth chapter that God spoke to Abraham. There is a simple solution, for Moses is not relating, in this latter passage, something that happened after Abraham's departure; but so that no one might suppose that Abraham left home in a rash moment to wander in foreign countries, as fickle and unthinking men are sometimes in the habit of doing, he brings out the reason for his departure, namely that he had been commanded by God to migrate to another place. And the words of the oracle imply this. For if he had been a sojourner in a foreign land, God could not have directed him to migrate from his native soil, leaving his kinsmen and his father's house. We see, therefore, that this verse agrees very well with the words of Moses. For after Moses related that this journey was not undertaken out of human light-heartedness, but by the command of God, he later adds what he had previously omitted, and this is a common Hebrew way of putting things.

3. *Get thee out of thy land.* As if it was not bitter enough to be an exile from his native land, God heaps words on words to increase the torment in Abraham's mind. And not only did this aim at putting his faith to the test, but also that other factor, that God does not give him any account of the land in which he is to dwell, but for some time keeps him in suspense and doubt. The obedience of Abraham was all the more praiseworthy because the pleasantness of his native land does not keep him back from departing willingly into what looked like exile, and because he does not hesitate to follow God, although there is no certain residence in view, but he is under orders to be a wanderer for a time. Because the description of the land

is kept back from him, it is close to being deception (*frustratione*).

Moreover, we learn daily from our own experience how beneficial it was for Abraham to be disciplined in such rudimentary things.[1] For many are driven by a pious zeal to undertake great things, but when their ardour has cooled, they soon think better of it, and would gladly turn back on their path. Therefore to prevent Abraham falling out exhausted in the middle of his journey by the memory of the things that he has left behind, God puts his mind thoroughly to the test, right from the start, so that he may not undertake anything lightly or unadvisedly. The parable that Christ puts before us about the building of the tower (Luke 14.28) fits in with this. For He teaches that we must first count the cost, so that we may not be forced with shame to leave the building unfinished. But even if it was Abraham's particular situation to be ordered to depart from his native land and travel to a distant country, and to be led around in all directions by God, there is yet a figurative description of the calling of all of us in these same words. We are not all plainly ordered to leave our native land, but we are ordered to deny ourselves; we are not ordered to go forth from our father's house, but we are ordered to bid farewell to our own will and to the desires of our flesh. Finally, if father and mother, wife and children, keep us back from following God, they must all be given up (cf. Matt. 16.24f, 10.37 and parallels). Abraham is given the simple commandment to move, but we are enjoined to do the same thing in certain conditions. For if we may not be allowed to serve God in any particular place, then we must choose exile rather than remain dispirited and inactive in a nest. Therefore let the example of Abraham always be before our eyes. He is the father of the faithful (Rom. 4.16, 17), and was tried in every way; yet he forgets his native land, his own people, and himself, in order to yield himself completely to God. If we wish to be considered the sons of God, we ought not to be different in quality from him.

Which I shall show thee. We must take note of what was touched on before, that Abraham is being kept in suspense, so that his patience may be put to the test. And that ought to be brought to bear on our own experience also, so that we may learn to depend wholly on the Word of God. And the chief exercise of faith is certainly trusting in God, even when we see nothing. Indeed God will often show us a land in which He grants us our abode, but yet, because we are strangers in the world, we have no fixed and permanent settlement anywhere. Finally, as Paul says in Col. 3.3, our life is hidden; and being like dead

[1] *talibus rudimentis imbui.* French: 'to be instructed by such rudiments and such an apprenticeship'. Tr.

men we hope for a security (*salutem*) that is hidden in heaven. Therefore as far as our everlasting habitation is concerned, when God bids us to be sojourners, He is making us depend on His bare promise. To prevent deferment like that discouraging us, we must adhere to a general rule of faith, that we must go on whither God calls, even although He does not yet show us what He is promising.

4. *Then came he out.* The ready response of his faith is praised in these words. For once he was called, he wastes no time, but makes haste, and gets the upper hand of his feelings to bring them under the direction of God. But it is not certain why he remained at Haran. However it is possible that the weakness of his father caused him to delay, for we read that he died there a little later on; or he did not venture to carry on further until the Lord made the way plain. To me it is more likely that he was kept there for a little time by the fatigue and illness of his father, because Stephen expressly states that he was taken from there after the death of his father.

And he gave him none inheritance in it, no, not so much as to set his foot on: and he promised that he would give it to him in possession, and to his seed after him, when as yet he had no child. And God spake on this wise, that his seed should sojourn in a strange land, and that they should bring them into bondage, and entreat them evil, four hundred years. And the nation to which they shall be in bondage will I judge, said God: and after that shall they come forth, and serve me in this place. And he gave him the covenant of circumcision: and so Abraham begat Isaac, and circumcised him the eighth day; and Isaac begat Jacob, and Jacob the twelve patriarchs. (5-8)

5. Three things must be noted here.

First, God tried the patience of His servant, because He had him brought out of his native land, to live as a sojourner in the land of Canaan. For Abraham did not possess a foot's length, apart from what he bought as a sepulchre for himself. But anything that is not concerned with the needs of this present life is not considered a possession. Then, since that particular field was bought for a sum of money, Stephen is right in saying that the Lord gave Abraham nothing. For what Abraham was expecting from the promise could not be acquired by money or any other human means.

In the second place we must observe that while God does not yet show the actual thing to Abraham, He nevertheless sustained him by His Word. And it strengthens us when God promises that what we do not as yet possess is stored up for us. Therefore when the thing itself, viz. the possession of the land, was non-existent, Abraham had the promise of God by way of support, and content with that alone, he desired nothing more in the land of Canaan than a wanderer's insecure lodging.

Since ἐπαγγέλλεσθαι simply means 'to promise' (*promittere*) I saw no reason to translate it here, with Erasmus, 'that God promised again' (*repromisisse*). For I take it adversatively, 'although He had promised', so that an appearance of deception (*species frustrationis*) might be noted incidentally; unless someone perhaps pleases to apply it to the promises that are repeated rather often; but I leave that open.

In the third place we must note that the promise was of such a kind that it was not far removed from mere mockery. God promised the land to Abraham's seed, when he himself was eighty years old, when his wife was barren, and he had no hope of begetting children. This seems to be silly in the extreme. For why does He not rather promise that He will give seed to him? But this was a remarkable trial of faith, because Abraham asked no question, and did not make persistent argument, but calmly and obediently embraced what he heard from God's lips. Let us therefore bear in mind that God encourages and comforts His servant with His Word in that way, although He is not only deferring the delivery of the actual thing, but also He can appear, in a certain sense, to be mocking him; just as He also deals in some degree with us. For although He calls us to be heirs of the world,[1] He often allows us to go without even a slender standard of living, and helps that we need. But He does this deliberately, so that He may bring the wisdom of the flesh to nothing, when otherwise we do not give proper respect to His Word.

6. *Thy seed shall be a stranger.* Stephen reminds the Jews how wretched and shameful the condition of their fathers was in Egypt, and shows that their oppressive slavery did not happen by chance, because it was predicted long before by an oracle of God. But this account ought to have had the effect, partly of taming their fierce spirits and training them in self-control, partly of commending the grace of God to them, because God had always been caring for that nation. For it is an extraordinary blessing that the people are marvellously restored, as if from death to life. At the same time the Jews are forcibly reminded that the Church of God has been elsewhere than in the land in which they were living, and that the patriarchs were chosen to be a peculiar people, and were protected by the faithfulness and guardianship of God before a temple was standing, or the external rites of the Law were instituted.

Those points belong to the general theme of the speech. But a

[1] *mundi haeredes.* Calvin obviously means 'heirs of the world', but this is a mis-application of Jas. 2.5, quoted by Tholuck, but not by C.R. French also reads, 'heirs of the world'. Tr.

useful warning can be drawn from this. Slavery in itself is a hard and bitter thing, but when the masters are cruel into the bargain, it seems to be an intolerable thing. Accordingly this godly man's feelings must have been deeply hurt when he heard that his descendants would be slaves, and would be treated shamefully and cruelly. In addition it was no trifling vexation that the situations appeared contradictory, inheritance of the land of Canaan, which had already been promised, and slavery in a foreign land. For who would not have supposed that God had, as it were, forgotten His previous word, when he warns Abraham of the miserable slavery of his descendants? He began by saying that He would give the land to his seed. But his seed did not exist as yet; on the contrary, the hope of children was now destroyed. But when does He promise that at last He will give it? After his death. Immediately after, we read that that seed will be taken away to another place to serve foreigners. And for how long? For four hundred years. Does He not seem in this way to be withdrawing His hand, so that He may not carry out what He has promised?

Let us realize that this has not been done on one occasion only, for God often deals with us like that, so that He may appear to be contradicting Himself. He even speaks in such a way that He may appear to be retracting what He had promised. It is therefore not unlikely that the flesh will conclude that He is self-contradictory, but faith knows that the words of God agree very well with each other and with His works. And it is God's purpose to show His promises from far off, as if a great space intervened, in order to extend farther the view of our faith. Therefore it is our duty to press on and strive towards the salvation held out to us, through innumerable digressions, through various obstacles, through a great distance, through the midst of abysses, and finally through death itself. Moreover when we observe that the people chosen by God were slaves to the Egyptians, and were inhumanly ill-treated, we ought not to be discouraged if the same condition befalls us today. For it is not a new thing or an unusual thing for the Church of God to lie oppressed under tyranny, and, so to speak, to be trodden under the feet of the ungodly.

7. *The nation to which they shall be in bondage.* This judgment is connected with the liberation of the people. For God takes vengeance on the tyranny and cruelty of the Egyptians for the sake of the people whom He took into His protection, to show Himself as the Deliverer of the Church. In the same way, as often as we are unjustly afflicted by the ungodly, let us remember that God is the Judge of the world, who will not allow any injuries to go unpunished. And let each one reflect within himself, 'Since I am in the guardianship of God, the Judge of the world, whose property it is to take vengeance concerning

injuries, those who are now troubling me will not escape His hand.' There is a similar passage in Deut. 32.35, where God announces that vengeance belongs to Him. From that Paul concludes in Rom. 12.19 that we must 'give place unto wrath'. He might have put it like this: 'The fact that God promises that He will be the avenger, ought to have the effect of correcting impatience and restraining bad feelings; for the man who avenges himself takes away from God His function of doing this.' However let us keep in mind what I have said, that God is moved by a special concern to avenge the injuries of His own, as we read in the Psalm, 'Touch not mine anointed ones, and do my prophets no harm' (105.15).

After that shall they come forth and serve me. Redemption was therefore at a time prior to the temple and the worship of the Law. From that it follows that the grace of God was not bound to ceremonies. At the same time Stephen indicates the purpose for which they were delivered, viz. that God chose a special people and a special place for the pure worship of His name. Again we gather from that that we must observe and ponder what He demands and approves. Other nations were also disposed to worship God, but because the rites were degenerate and corrupt everywhere, God separates the Jews from the rest, and assigns a place to them where He may be worshipped sincerely and properly. But this verse warns us that the blessings of God must be regarded as having this as their object, that men might yield themselves totally to Him. Now, since God has distributed the treasures of His grace throughout the whole world, no matter what countries we live in, we ought to take pains to honour His holiness (*sanctificemus*) by offering Him pure and holy worship.

8. *He gave him the covenant.* When he acknowledges that circumcision is a divine covenant, he abundantly clears himself of the false accusation that had been made against him. But at the same time he shows that the Jews are in the wrong, if they place the origin of their salvation in the external symbol. For if Abraham was called, and the land and redemption were promised to his seed before he was circumcised, it is plain enough that the glory of the whole race does not depend on circumcision. And Paul uses the same argument in the fourth chapter of Rom. (v. 11). For since Abraham obtained righteousness and was pleasing to God when he was uncircumcised, he infers from that that circumcision is not the cause of righteousness. We see therefore that Stephen weaves no doubtful or irrelevant story, because it had a very great bearing on his case, that the Jews might remember how they had been adopted by God along with their fathers. And it is likely that both aspects were clearly brought out by Stephen, that even if circumcision was given by God, to be a sign of His grace, yet

adoption preceded it in order and in time. Finally, it is not necessary to discuss further the meaning and nature of circumcision here. Let us note only this, that God first of all promises to Abraham the things that He later confirms by circumcision, so that we may realize that, unless signs are preceded by the Word, they are empty and worthless. Let us also take note that a useful doctrine is contained in the word *covenant*, viz. that God makes a covenant with us in the sacraments, to make known His love towards us. Now if that is true, first, they are not only signs of outward profession before men, but they also have the effect of confirming inward faith in the sight of God; secondly, they are not empty forms, because God, who is true, represents nothing in them that He does not perform.

And the patriarchs, moved with jealousy against Joseph, sold him into Egypt: and God was with him, and delivered him out of all his afflictions, and gave him favour and wisdom before Pharaoh king of Egypt; and he made him governor over Egypt and all his house. Now there came a famine over all Egypt and Canaan, and great affliction: and our fathers found no sustenance. But when Jacob heard that there was corn in Egypt, he sent forth our fathers the first time. And at the second time Joseph was made known to his brethren; and Joseph's race became manifest unto Pharaoh. And Joseph sent, and called to him Jacob his father, and all his kindred, threescore and fifteen souls. And Jacob went down into Egypt; and he died, himself, and our fathers; and they were carried over unto Shechem, and laid in the tomb that Abraham bought for a price in silver of the sons of Hamor in Shechem. (9–16)

9. There now follows the most shameful act of the nation of Israel, their wicked and nefarious conspiring to put an end to their innocent brother. Cruelty of this sort is unnatural. And the Jews could not make the excuse that it was the private crime of a few men, for the disgrace extends to the whole of the people, since all the patriarchs, with the single exception of Benjamin, defiled themselves at the same time with that treachery. Therefore the fact that Stephen gives them the dignity of an honourable title underlines the dishonour of the nation all the more. They were proud to extol their fathers. He shows what sort of men the chief ones among them were, fratricides, out and out. For, apart from the fact that slavery was a kind of death, we know what they were plotting at first, and then how Joseph endured cruel tortures, of all of which his brothers were guilty. From this it is clear that God was kind and generous to them, one might say despite themselves, when they were fighting against Him. For the very person, who was going to be the means of their deliverance, they want to destroy and put out of the way. Therefore it is

nobody's fault but their own that they renounce all the blessings of God. Similarly he will tell later that Moses was rejected, when he was brought forward by God as a redeemer. Therefore there is no cause for the Jews to take pride in the superiority of their race. But all that is left for them to do is to assert, in shame and confusion, that whatever they are, they owe to the mercy of God alone, and to consider that the Law was given for the sake of illustrating that.

God was with him. God was not with him in such a way that He always made His power plain in helping him. For it is no trivial thing when Ps. 105.18 asserts 'the iron passed through his soul'. He certainly ought to have been pierced by enormous grief, when he had no one to help him; and he also suffered the disgrace of being put in chains and being punished by an infamous man at the same time. But God is often in the habit of being near His own in such a way that He is hidden for the time being. Moreover, we ought to be bearing in mind continually that Joseph was not set free because he had called on God in the temple but far away in Egypt.

10. Stephen adds the way that God gave him favour in Pharaoh's eyes. Indeed God could have rescued him in some other way, but He had a further end in view, that Joseph, as governor of the kingdom, would receive his father and his whole family. Now, in these two words, *favour* and *wisdom*, there is hypallage. For the wisdom with which Joseph was endowed was the cause of his favour; although I do grant that both were separate benefits. For even although Joseph was a faithful interpreter of dreams and was rich in divine wisdom, yet he would never have been elevated by the proud tyrant into such a high place of honour, if God had not moved the heart of Pharaoh to a certain unwonted love. But yet careful consideration must be given to that ordering of things by which God procured favour for him. Wisdom means not only a gift of prophecy in interpreting dreams, but prudence in the giving of advice, for Moses uses both.[1] But what Stephen says about one man here, is to be extended to all. For whatever skill men may have ought to be regarded, not as a measure of inequality, but among the gifts of God, His special gifts indeed. And He it is who lets a successful outcome follow, as He pleases, so that His gifts may serve the purpose for which it seemed good to Him to confer them. Therefore even if Joseph is set over the kingdom of Egypt by Pharaoh, yet, properly speaking, he is raised to that position of honour by nothing but the hand of God.

11. *Now there came a famine.* It is apparent from this that Joseph's deliverance was a blessing in which the whole of Jacob's family shared. For when the famine was going to come, Joseph was sent in

[1] Gen. 41.33, 39. See the original, נָבוֹן וְחָכָם. Tr.

advance in good time, to have in hand the provision of food for the hungry; and he himself also recognizes God's wonderful purpose in that connexion (Gen. 45.5-8). In due course the free goodness of God shines out more clearly in the person of Joseph, when he is appointed the nourisher of the very brothers of his, who had sold him for money and driven him far from home, and kept on thinking that he had been completely obliterated from the face of the earth. He puts food into the mouths of those who had put him into a pit, depriving him of the air that they all breathed. In short he nourishes and cherishes the life of the men who had not hesitated to take life from him. To come back to the present, Stephen reminds the Jews that the patriarchs were forced to get out of that land which had been given to them for an inheritance, and that they died in another land. Therefore since they were sojourners in that land, in the end they live in exile far away from it.

14. In saying that Jacob came into Egypt with seventy-five people, Stephen does not agree with Moses, whose reckoning is only seventy. Jerome considers that Luke has not given an exact account of what Stephen said, but took this number from the Septuagint translation of Moses' account (Gen. 46.27), either because, being a proselyte, he did not know Hebrew, or because he wished to concede this to the Gentiles, among whom that was the accepted reading. Furthermore it is not certain whether the Greek translators put down that number on purpose, or whether later on it crept in by error. And the latter was of course easy, since the Greeks are in the habit of indicating numbers by letters. In the Twenty-sixth Book of *The City of God* Augustine thinks that Joseph's grandchildren and great-grandchildren are included, and so the word 'descent'[1] means to him the whole of that time in which Jacob lived. But that conjecture cannot be countenanced in any circumstances. For many other children were born in the meantime to the other patriarchs as well. It certainly seems very likely to me that the Septuagint translators correctly translated what Moses had written. For it is not possible to say that their minds were wandering, seeing that Deut. 10 (v. 22), where that particular number is repeated, agrees with Moses, considering that in Jerome's day at least that verse was being read without any controversy; for those copies which are printed today have it different.[2] Therefore I conclude that this discrepancy arose by an error on the part of copyists. But this was not such an important matter that Luke should have confused the Gentiles over it, when they were used to the Greek reading. And it is possible that he himself did write down the true number, but

[1] *descensus*, i.e. 'went down into Egypt'.

[2] Some LXX manuscripts of Deuteronomy have 75. Tr.

somebody erroneously changed it from that verse of Moses. For we know that the New Testament was handled by those who were ignorant of Hebrew, but were thoroughly conversant with Greek. Therefore, to make the words of Stephen agree with the verse in Moses' account, it is probable that that wrong number in the Greek version of Genesis was transferred to this place also. If anyone is to persist in disputing about this, let us allow him a superiority of wisdom. Let us remember that it is not for nothing that Paul forbids us to be troubled and curious about genealogies (Titus 3.9).

Finally, such a small number is mentioned on purpose so that the power of God may be plainer in so great an increase of the race, an increase which did not take a very long time to appear. For such a little band of men could not grow, by human means of procreation and within two hundred and fifty years, into that immense multitude, which is reported in Exodus. It suits us better to ponder that miracle which the Spirit commends to us, than to be troubled and anxious about a single letter, by which the number is altered. Other questions, more difficult of solution indeed, arise out of the rest of the context.

16. Stephen says that the patriarchs were carried over to the land of Canaan after they died. But Moses only mentions the bones of Joseph (Exod. 13.19). And in Joshua 24 (v. 32) it is observed that the bones of Joseph were buried, but no mention is made of the others. A few make the reply that Moses names only Joseph for the sake of honour, seeing that he had given express instructions about his bones; and we do not read of that being done by the others. And in writing about the travels of Paula, Jerome certainly says that when she journeyed through Shechem she saw there the sepulchres of the twelve patriarchs; but in another place he mentions only Joseph's grave. And it is possible that cenotaphs (*κενοτάφια*) were erected for the others. I have no definite statement to make, except that either there is synecdoche here, or Luke has reported this not so much from Moses as from ancient tradition (*fama*), as the Jews long ago used to have many things handed down, as it were, from their fathers. But when he goes on to say that they were buried in the sepulchre which Abraham had bought from the sons of Hamor, it is obvious that an error has been made in the name Abraham. For Abraham bought a double cave, to bury his wife, from Ephraim the Hittite (Gen. 23.9), but Joseph was buried elsewhere, namely in the field which his father Jacob had bought from the sons of Hamor for a hundred lambs.[1] This verse must be amended accordingly.

But as the time of the promise drew nigh, which God vouchsafed unto

[1] So LXX of Gen. 33.19 and Josh. 24.32. Tr.

Abraham, the people grew and multiplied in Egypt, till there arose another king over Egypt, which knew not Joseph. The same dealt subtilly with our race, and evil entreated our fathers, that they should cast out their babes to the end they might not live. (17-19)

17. Stephen moves on to the deliverance of the people, the prelude to which was that numerous offspring, which had increased beyond normal proportion in a short space of time. He therefore assumes that the increasing of the people is a unique gift of God, so that we may know that it did not happen by ordinary means or by the normal natural order. Indeed, on the other hand, God seems to be taking hope away from the Jews seeing that Pharaoh afflicts them in a tyrannous way, and every day their slavery becomes more grievous. But when they are ordered to expose the male infants it seems that the annihilation of the whole race is drawing near. Another sign of redemption is given when Moses comes on the scene, but because he is soon afterwards rejected and is forced to flee into exile, there is nothing left but mere despair. The point is that God remembered His promise and increased the people in time, so that He might perform what He had sworn to Abraham; but the Jews, as they were ungrateful and perverse, repudiated the grace of God, so that it was their own fault that they closed the door on themselves. Furthermore we must note the providence of God here, when He tempers (*temperat*) the course and vicissitudes of the times, so that His moment of opportunity may always suit His acts. But men, whose needs cause them to make disorderly haste, cannot hope patiently and keep quiet until God shows His hand, simply because they do not pay attention to that tempering (*temperamentum*) of which I have been speaking. Finally, so that God may exercise the faith of His own, as often as He shines forth with glad signs of His grace, He sets over against them other things which suddenly cut off the hope of salvation. For who would not have said of the Hebrews, that it was absolutely all up with them, when the king's edict delivers all the male children to death? Accordingly it is all the more necessary for us to meditate on the teaching that God kills and brings to life again, He brings down to the depths and brings back again.

19. *He dealt craftily.* The Vulgate has translated it 'to circumvent' (*circumvenire*), and this is quite good. For Stephen means that the king of Egypt was cunningly thinking up fresh artifices and indirect pretexts to keep imposing still heavier tasks on the people. Almost all tyrants behave like that, for no matter how unjustly they abuse their people, they are exceedingly ingenious in inventing excuses. And there is no doubt that Pharaoh made wrong use of what looked

perfectly correct on the surface, that it was not equitable for the Jews, sojourners that they were, to have free hospitality in his kingdom, and to be free from responsibilities when they were enjoying great privileges. So he insidiously turned them from free men into cheap slaves. When Stephen says that Joseph was not known to this tyrant, it makes plain how the memory of benefits is a fleeting thing among men. For even if ingratitude is universally detested, no fault is commoner.

So that they may not be increased. Erasmus does not translate this properly in my opinion. For ζωογονεῖσθαι means more than 'so that their babies should not live'. For the word is derived from the fact that the life of a people always persists and survives in their offspring. Moreover Stephen does not enumerate all the aspects of their bad treatment, but posits this example of extreme cruelty, and it is easy to infer from that how close the whole seed of Abraham was to destruction. For Pharaoh seemed to have slain all of them at the same time by that cruel edict, as if by a single stroke of the sword. But such violent barbarity illustrates all the more the unexpected and unbelievable power of God, because, having wrestled against Him with all the means at his disposal, Pharaoh achieves nothing in the end.

> *At which season Moses was born, and was exceeding fair; and he was nourished three months in his father's house: and when he was cast out, Pharaoh's daughter took him up, and nourished him for her own son. And Moses was instructed in all the wisdom of the Egyptians; and he was mighty in his words and works. But when he was well-nigh forty years old, it came into his heart to visit his brethren the children of Israel. And seeing one of them suffer wrong, he defended him, and avenged him that was oppressed, smiting the Egyptian: and he supposed that his brethren understood how that God by his hand was giving them deliverance; but they understood not. And the day following he appeared unto them as they strove, and would have set them at one again, saying, Sirs, ye are brethren; why do ye wrong one to another? But he that did his neighbour wrong thrust him away, saying, Who made thee a ruler and a judge over us? Wouldest thou kill me, as thou killedst the Egyptian yesterday? And Moses fled at this saying, and became a sojourner in the land of Midian, where he begat two sons.* (20–29)

20. It is not for nothing that Stephen notes the circumstances of the time. Moses was born when the king had ordered all the male children to be exposed to death. Therefore the agent of redemption appears to be dead before his birth. But when there is no human help or advice available then it is that God has the greatest opportunity for

doing something. And it is also perfectly plain how God makes His power perfect in men's weakness (II Cor. 12.9). Moses is preserved for three months, but out of regard for their own lives, his parents are forced to cast him out on the river. Only they put him into a small chest so that he might not perish quickly. When Pharaoh's daughter takes him out, he escapes death it is true, but only to go over to an alien nation and be cut off from the children of Israel. And what is more, he was going to be a most troublesome enemy to his people one day, if God had not kept a hold on his mind. Forty years go by before he shows any sign of brotherly friendliness.

22. When Luke is reporting that he was *instructed in all the wisdom* of Egypt, he is indeed commending it as a mark of excellence. But all the same it could have happened, as it very often does, that he would become swelled-headed with the knowledge of secular sciences, and despise the ordinary people. Yet because God determined to redeem His people, in the meantime He prepares the mind of Moses, as much as everything else, for the accomplishment of His work. Here the carnal mind might protest, 'Why does God close His eyes to the hardships of the people that went on so long? Why does He allow Pharaoh to grow daily more fierce and cruel? Why does He not allow Moses to come to maturity among his own people? Why does He, in a sense, abduct him from the children of Israel to be adopted by the king's daughter? Why does He wish him to remain among princely pleasures until he is forty, and not rather take him away from them?' But the actual outcome is so astonishing that we are forced to acknowledge that all these things were controlled by an extraordinary purpose and arrangement, in order to illustrate the glory of God.

As I have said Luke speaks of the teaching of the Egyptians here by way of commendation, but I do not wish that to be understood as if there was nothing defective about it. Astronomy is a useful and deservedly praiseworthy science, since it gives close study to the wonderful work of God in the stars, not only in the position, and such clearly distinct variety that they have, but also in their movement, power and secret functions. The Egyptians gave a great deal of attention to this science, but not being content with the simple order of nature, like the Chaldeans they also wandered about in many foolish and futile speculations. It is not certain if Moses was instructed in these superstitions or not. However, whatever the situation was, we see how sincerely, devoid of worldly wisdom indeed (*rudi Minerva*), he shows that what makes for piety is to be studied within the fabric of the universe (*in mundi fabrica*). Certainly there is remarkable modesty about a man who, though he could argue acutely with learned and sharp-witted men about the secrets of nature, not only cuts out the loftier subtleties of speech, but comes down to the ordinary capacity of everyone, even the humblest, and speaks to uneducated people in ordinary language about things they understand from their own experience. When Justin speaks about Moses, he makes him a magician (*magum*) who, with tricks and magic arts, made a crossing for the people through the Red Sea. So Satan attempted not only to overthrow the power of God, but also to sully it with the mark of infamy. But we know that Moses did not vie with wizards in magic arts, but only carried out what God had enjoined on him.

The Egyptians also used to have a theology of secret rites (*mysticam theologiam*) which introduced a pretext for their foolish and crazy inventions, and their unnatural abominations, as if they wished to prove that they had justification for acting like madmen. The Papists are like that when they are play-acting in their Mass and other meaningless rites, and yet invent mysteries to persuade people that there is nothing in them but what is of God. Indeed the rank and file of the priests do not mount right to that height, but those of them who wish to be regarded as more perspicacious miss out no rite, no matter how childish or theatrical, for which they do not invent some spiritual mystery. A most senseless farrago exists in that connexion, which they call 'The Rationale of the Divine Offices'. But since only those connected with sacrifices practised such mad things among themselves, it is unlikely that Moses occupied himself with them, seeing that he had a royal education, but that he was instructed in noble arts.

He was mighty in his words. For the Hebrews this expression means a double pre-eminence, when a person who is rich in ability and learning is also at the same time fitted to accomplish outstanding things. Therefore Stephen understands that Moses was equipped with rare gifts so that all recognized that he was a quite extraordinary man. But since he was regarded so highly, the Israelites had all the less hope that he would be the minister of their redemption.

23. *When the time of forty years was fulfilled.* Many conclude from this that Moses was never without some thought for his own people; but the words of Stephen tend rather to the opposite view, viz. that at long last the Spirit of God aroused his mind, as from sleep, to go and visit the brethren whom he had long neglected. It is indeed very likely that he was not unaware of his origin, since he bore the mark of it in his flesh, and since rumour of it floated about the royal court, for the king's daughter could not have adopted him without the suspicion of scandal, if it was not made known where he came from. Yet for a long time he did not have enough courage to dare to make an open show of his love for his kindred. It contributes greatly to the

increase of the glory of God that for a long time Moses sits idle in the king's court ignorant of his calling, and that later he is suddenly called by the Lord, contrary to the hope of all and that of himself. Therefore this new concern for his brethren, which stole into his mind, took its rise from the new and unaccustomed influence of the Spirit.

24. *When he saw a certain man.* This sight did not present itself to Moses by chance, but when God had appointed him the redeemer for His people, He intended to produce this sign, and, as it were, this prelude by the hand of Moses. For Stephen plainly brings out that he did not set about this in a thoughtless way, but, that, conscious of his calling, he did what was fitting for the vindicator of the people to do. For if God had not roused him he had no right to kill a man, no matter how harmful or criminal he might be. A man is doing a godly and praiseworthy thing when he sets himself against the wicked, restrains their violence, and protects good men from their injuries; but it is not for a private person to arrogate vengeance to himself. Therefore Moses had no right to kill the Egyptian until the Lord had put the sword into his hand by virtue of the right of his calling. But this heroic greatness of character was the work of the Holy Spirit, because God puts forth His power effectively in those whom He appoints to do great things, to make them equal to their task. To sum up, Stephen understands that Moses was already at that time shown to the people as the agent of redemption, since the day was approaching in accordance with the covenant made with Abraham; but that the people had lost all hope.

26. *And the day following he appeared.* Stephen now shows that God's grace was not merely neglected by the fathers, but that it was also spitefully rejected. For although the evil deed, which he describes, originated in only one man, yet he rightly assigns the blame to them all. For if they would have been pleasing to God, all of them, together, ought to have restrained his impudence. But they are all silent, and allow the good deed that Moses had done for them to be cast in his teeth; and they do all they can to expose to the greatest possible danger the man whom they ought to have protected by putting their own heads in the noose.

The tenor of the speech is that it was the fault of nobody but the people themselves that they did not experience relief sooner. It often occurs again and again that the perversity of men causes delay to God. He certainly is prepared to bring opportune help to His own people, but we keep His hand away from us by obstacles of all kinds, and afterwards we make unjust complaints about His slowness. Furthermore this ingratitude shows too much disrespect for God, and too much cruelty towards Moses. For thanks ought to have been given to God because He had given them such a trustworthy defender in the king's court. Moses ought to have been honoured with all their love and respect. But he gains a very poor and very unjust reward, insults and threats. Finally, it is right to put down to the treachery of the people the fact that the deed was reported to the king. Therefore, just as happened later on, when the land of Canaan was already in sight, the people barred their entrance to it by their own fault, so now, when they repudiate the grace of God in the person of one man, they put off for forty years the time of their redemption. For although God had determined what He would do, yet the blame for the delay is rightly laid at the door of those who impede, and cause trouble for, Moses in his office.

Men, ye are brethren. There is certainly a general agreement among men that they ought to practise courtesy among themselves, and keep from injuring each other in every way; but it is rather a shameful and intolerable matter when those who are hurting each other are men joined together by a closer bond. Therefore Moses not only puts forward a general reason for calling them back to fair dealing when their minds were bent on doing harm, but he also mentions their kinship and blood relations here in order to mitigate their ferocity. Yet it was all to no avail; for the man who had done injury to his neighbour repulses him with impudence and threats. And it is normal for a bad conscience to drive men into a rage, and the poorer a man's case is, the bolder and more ferocious is his bearing. But what pretext has the man with a bad case for so insolently rounding on Moses? He says that Moses is no judge. But Moses had not reproached him by virtue of his authority, but had merely admonished them equally in a friendly way. Or is a judge the only person with the duty of warning us when we do wrong? But it is a fault common to all inflexible and stubborn people to admit no admonitions, except when they are compelled to do so by force and authority; yes, and they are like delirious patients who assault their doctors in a fury. That is why we must take more pains to curb our passions, so that we may not similarly rush in a blind fury against those who wish to cure our faults. We are also warned by this example that it is not possible for the servants of God to carry out their duty among men who behave so badly, without constantly suffering many injuries, enduring many affronts, running into dangers, and, above all, hearing evil things about themselves when they do well. But they must swallow the indignity of those evils, so that they may not be the cause of their ceasing to do what they know the Lord has committed to their charge, and is accordingly pleasing to Him. Moses is burdened here with the cruel and false charge that he is usurping the legal authority of a ruler for himself; and in this way he is threatened with the charge of committing treason. Secondly, the infamous reproach is made against him that he inflicted punishment on the Egyptian. Both of these were extremely offensive. From that we may conclude just how the mind of the holy man was struck with consternation by the dangerous attack (*tentatione*). But when we see that he was not subdued by exile or any other evil, to the point of repenting of acting rightly, we may also learn from his example to keep our courage firm and unconquerable against all similar stratagems of Satan.

And when forty years were fulfilled, an angel appeared to him in the wilderness of mount Sinai, in a flame of fire in a bush. And when Moses saw it, he wondered at the sight: and as he drew near to behold, there came a voice of the Lord, I am the God of thy fathers, the God of Abraham, and of Isaac, and of Jacob. And Moses trembled, and durst not behold. And the Lord said unto him, Loose the shoes from thy feet: for the place whereon thou standest is holy ground. I have surely seen the affliction of my people which is in Egypt, and have heard their groaning, and I am come down to deliver them: and now come, I will send thee into Egypt. (30–34)

30. *When forty years were completed.* As Moses was no fool, it is easy for any one of us to infer how many things could have come into his mind to weaken his faith in his call. Satan has insidious tricks, and we ourselves, who have a distinct natural tendency towards mistrust, give an easy entrance to whatever doubts steal upon us concerning the Word of God. It was a hard exchange to be driven out from the pleasures of a palace and a life of splendour to take up the humble and wearisome task of keeping sheep. And in particular, since all the time he was banished in the wilderness Moses was aware that a long period of time was slipping away, what other conclusion could he come to, indeed, but that God's promise to him was an empty mockery? Since he was already eighty years old when he was engaged in looking after his father-in-law's flock, when would he have hoped that his services would be used in liberating the people? It is beneficial to keep thinking about these struggles of godly men, until they are thoroughly imprinted in our memory, so that our spirits may not fail, if at any time the Lord keeps us in a state of suspense longer than we should wish. Again, Moses gives a remarkable example of restraint, for in all the intervening time he causes no trouble, he stirs up no tumults, and does not push himself in any way to seize a position of pre-eminence, as trouble-makers are in the habit of doing. But he devotes himself to his shepherd's task as if he had never been called to

any greater office. But while he waits quietly like this, the Lord appears to him in due time.

An angel of the Lord appeared to him. The first question is 'Who was the angel?', and the second, 'Why did he allow himself to be seen under such a guise?' For after Luke has called him an *angel*, he then introduces him as saying, *I am the God of Abraham, etc.* Some answer that as God sometimes attributes and communicates to His ministers things which belong especially to Himself, so there is nothing absurd about His name being applied to them. But since this angel openly states that he is the eternal God, whose existence is in Himself, and in whom all things subsist, it is necessary to restrict this description to the essence of God; for in no way is it appropriate to the angels. It might be more correct to say that because the angel speaks in the name of God, he assumes His part (*personam*), as if he were repeating His commandments, word for word, yes, as if from the mouth of God. It is also quite common for the prophets to speak like that. But since Luke says afterwards that this was the same angel by whose auspices and leading Moses liberated the people, and Paul asserts in I Cor. 10.4 that Christ was that very guide, there is no cause now for us to wonder that the angel takes to himself what belongs to God alone.

Let us therefore establish in the first place that right from the beginning God made no communication with men except by Christ. For there is no relationship between God and us unless the Mediator be present to procure His favour for us. So this verse gives a shining testimony to the eternal divinity of Christ, and teaches that He is of the same essence with the Father. Moreover He is called an angel not only because He always had angels as attendants and aides, so to speak, but because that redemption of the people foreshadowed the redemption of us all, for the accomplishment of which Christ had to be sent by the Father, to assume the form of a slave with our flesh. It is indeed certain that God has never appeared to men just as He is, but under some form which would suit their ability to understand. Yet, as I have said, another reason for Christ to be given this name, is that, having been appointed the minister of men's salvation by the eternal purpose of the Father, He appears to Moses, with that end in view. And there is no contradiction between this teaching and what is to be found in Heb. 2.16, that Christ never took to Himself angels but the seed of Abraham. For even if He did assume the form of an angel temporarily yet He never took the nature of angels to Himself, since we know that in fact He was made man.

It remains to say something about the burning bush. It is a commonplace that God accommodates signs to realities by some sort of analogy (*similitudine quadam rebus signa aptare*), and this is quite a common procedure (*ratio*) with the sacraments. Moreover nothing more suitable could have been shown to Moses for strengthening his faith in the present undertaking. He was well aware of the state in which he had left his own people. For even although their numbers were enormous, yet they were not unlike a bush. For the denser a bush is, and the thicker it is with masses of branches, the more liable it is to catch fire, with the flames raging all over it. Similarly, the Israelite nation was a weak company, exposed to injuries of all kinds; and the multitude, unfit for war though it was, and crippled by its own bulk as it were, had inflamed the ferocity of Pharaoh merely by the success and prosperity of increasing. Therefore the people who are oppressed by a fearful tyranny are like so much firewood that is completely smothered in flames, with nothing to prevent it being reduced to ashes, unless the Lord is established in the midst of it. But although an unaccustomed fire of persecution was blazing at that time, yet because the Church of God in the world is never entirely immune and free from afflictions, its perennial condition is depicted here to a certain degree. For what else are we but fuel for the flames? It is true that innumerable firebrands of Satan are constantly hovering about, to set fire to our souls as well as our bodies, but with wonderful and extraordinary kindness the Lord delivers and protects us from being consumed. It is therefore necessary for the fire to blaze, that it may burn us in this life. But because the Lord dwells in our midst He will see to it that no afflictions will cause us harm, as it is put in Ps. 46.5.

31. *He wondered at the vision.* Let us realize that God was accustomed to dealing with the fathers like this, so that they might acknowledge His majesty with certainty. For He meant there to be a clear distinction between the visions which He showed, and the illusions of Satan. And this certainty is more than necessary. For in what other way would the oracles of God, in which the covenant of eternal life is contained, be guaranteed? Therefore since the only true support of faith is to have God the source of it, it is necessary for Him to make it perfectly clear that it is He Himself who is speaking. Again since Satan is always on the prowl, worming his way in with marvellous stratagems, since he has so many ways of deceiving, and in particular of course laying false claim to the name of God, we must be unremittingly on our guard against his mockeries. We see that in the past he has deceived all the nations and also the Papists. For all the superstitious monstrosities and erroneous ravings which existed in the past, and still hold sway today under the Papacy had their origins in fantasies, apparitions, and false revelations. Yes and even the Anabaptists have their illusions. Therefore the only remedy is for God to

distinguish the visions that He grants, with certain characteristics. For we are beyond the danger of going wrong only when He discloses His majesty to us. It is because of this that the mind of Moses is struck with astonishment; he then comes near to have a closer look; when he has drawn nearer the Lord touches him with a livelier awareness of His presence so that he becomes greatly terrified. I certainly admit that there is not one of these things that Satan does not emulate, but he does so defectively, like an ape. And the Lord not only manifests Himself with such signs, but comes to the aid of our dullness, and opens our eyes at the same time, so that we may not be just dreaming. Finally, the Holy Spirit engraves marks and symbols of the divine presence in our hearts, so that no doubt may remain.

32. *I am the God of thy fathers.* Now we see why the vision was presented to Moses—so that its authority would rest in the Word of God. For bare visions would be of little use without the addition of teaching. But it is added not as the inferior part, but as the cause or end of all visions.

Now there is a twofold reason for His calling Himself the God of Abraham, Isaac and Jacob. Since the majesty of God is infinite, if we wish to grasp it, what happens rather is that it swallows up our thoughts; if we try to mount up to it, we vanish away. He therefore clothes and adorns Himself with titles under which He can be grasped by us. But we must observe that God chooses titles for Himself, by which He may call us back to the Word. For He is called the God of Abraham, Isaac and Jacob, because He entrusted to them the doctrine of salvation by which He would become known to the world. Even so, God did have especial regard for the present situation when He spoke to Moses in this way. For this vision, and the hope of liberating the people, and the mandate He was about to give to Moses, were all dependent on that covenant that He had once made with the fathers. Thus the suspicion of something new is taken away, and the mind of Moses is lifted up to hope for the redemption which was founded on the ancient promise of God. Therefore this statement can be interpreted as if God had said, 'I who once promised your fathers that your salvation would be my concern, I who took the descendants of Abraham into my protection, by a covenant of grace (*gratuito foedere*), yes, and I who have already fixed this as the time for ending the slavery of your people, I now appear to you to keep faith with what I have said.' Similarly today so that they may be steadfast and enduring for us, all the promises of God ought to rest on this foundation, that God has adopted us in Christ and He has promised that He will be our Father and our God.

Finally, with the fullest justification Christ infers from this verse that the godly survive death (Matt. 22.32). For if the whole man perishes in death, the word *I am the God of Abraham* is senseless. Let us suppose that Rome is no longer in existence; will the man who will call himself a Roman consul not be a laughing-stock? For relation demands this, that the members are counterparts of each other. Another reason must also be observed, that since God has life and death in His control, He undoubtedly preserves alive those to whom He wishes to be a Father, and those whom He reckons among His children. Therefore although Abraham, Isaac and Jacob perished in the flesh, yet in the spirit they are living with God.

And Moses trembled. It could seem absurd for a voice full of encouragement to terrify rather than gladden Moses. But it was beneficial for Moses to be terrified like this by the presence of God, so that he would compose himself for a greater reverence. And of course it is not only the voice of God that strikes his mind with consternation, but His majesty, the sign of which he was seeing in the burning bush. And what is extraordinary about a man trembling at the sight of God? But let us especially remember that in this way minds are prepared for fear and reverence, as it is put in Exod. 20.22, 'You have seen the signs, you have heard the sound of the trumpet, that you may learn to fear God.'[1] But someone will object, 'Why does Moses tremble and not venture to take a look, when he did not hesitate to approach before?' I reply, the nearer we approach to God, the stronger His glory shines, so are we rightly affected by a greater fear. Finally, God causes Moses to tremble for no other reason than to make him yield to Himself. And this fear was by no means an unsuitable preparation for greater confidence. The words that follow, 'Take off your shoes', also serve that purpose. For he is warned by this symbol to receive the commands of God with reverence, and in every way to give Him the glory that is His due.

33. *For the place whereon.* By speaking like this about the place God wished to lift up the mind of Moses as if to heaven, so that he might not let it dwell on anything earthly. Now if Moses had to be prodded by so many goads to forget the earth, and give his attention to God, must we not be dug into, as it were, since we are a hundred times slower?

Be that as it may, someone may ask, 'How did the place acquire this holiness? For until that day it was no holier than any other place.' I reply that this honour is applied not to the place but to the presence of God, and the holiness of the place is commended for the sake of men. For if the presence of God sanctifies the earth, is it reasonable that it should be seen by men with an even greater force?

[1] So Calvin; but this is rather the sense of vv. 18-20. Tr.

However we must also note that the place was honoured in this way temporarily, since by no means did God fix His glory there; just as Jacob erected an altar to God in Bethel when God had given an indication of His presence there. When his descendants imitated the same thing, the worship was corrupted.

Finally the place is called holy for the sake of Moses alone, so that he may the better compose himself to the fear of God and to the discipline of obeying Him. Nowadays since God shows Himself present in Christ everywhere, and not in obscure forms, but in the clearest light and in solid truth, not only ought we to remove the shoes from our feet, but also strip ourselves bare.

34. *In seeing I have seen.* God now promises that He will be the Liberator of the people, so that He may appoint Moses His minister all over again, seeing that such a long period of time had intervened since the earlier promise.[1] For God is said to see our misfortunes, when He is concerned for us and is solicitous about our welfare; just as, on the other hand, He is said to close His eyes and turn His back when He seems to be regardless of our circumstances. We understand His coming down in the same way. For there is no need for God to move Himself in order to bring us help, for His hand is extended throughout heaven and earth. But this is said for our understanding. For when He had not alleviated the affliction of the people, it might have seemed that He was far away and busy about something else in heaven. He now declares that the Israelites will realize that He is near to them. It all amounts to this that, having been made more certain about God's will, Moses may have no hesitation about following Him as his Guide, and may devote himself with more confidence to the redemption of the people, which he knows is God's work.

It must also be observed that God mentions that He heard their *groaning*. For although He does care for those who are wretched and unjustly oppressed, yet it is particularly when we lay our sighs and complaints on His bosom, that He is moved to compassion. However, as often happens elsewhere, this word can be taken for the blind and confused complaints, which are not directed to God.

This Moses whom they refused, saying, Who made thee a ruler and a judge? him hath God sent to be both a ruler and a deliverer with the hand of the angel which appeared to him in the bush. This man led them forth, having wrought wonders and signs in Egypt, and in the Red Sea, and in the wilderness forty years. This is that Moses, which said unto the children of Israel, A prophet shall God raise up unto you from among your brethren, like unto me. (35-37)

[1] Reading *promissio* with Tholuck, for C.R.'s *obiectio*. Tr.

35, 36. Stephen is missing many things out, because he is hastening to this conclusion, that the Jews may understand that the fathers were not redeemed because their piety had made them deserving of it, but because this blessing was bestowed on them when they did not deserve it, and, secondly, that out of those beginnings something even more perfect was to be hoped for. When Moses had been ordained by God as their vindicator and redeemer and was already prepared for it to some extent, they had barred the way to him. Therefore God is now delivering them, one might say, in spite of themselves. What is added about miracles and wonders serves as much to commend the grace of God as to make the call of Moses clear. It is certainly wonderful that God deigns to put forth His power with many different signs for the sake of such an ungrateful people. But at the same time he is procuring authority for His servant. Therefore, because the Jews do not defer to him afterwards, now trying to drive him away with insults, now being scornful, sometimes wrangling with him, at other times clamouring against him, and yet again rising against him in rebellion, in that way they are making more obvious both their ill-will and their irreverent contempt of the grace of God. Their unworthy behaviour was always on the increase, so that God had to contend with such a perverse and stiff-necked people with wonderful patience.

A prince and a redeemer. The antitheses, which magnify their offence, must be understood. They would have submitted to Moses if a tyrant had appointed him their judge; but since he was appointed by God, to be a redeemer at that, they despise and reject him in their pride. So they were impious in spurning his authority, and they were ungrateful in turning grace aside.

Now, when such an honourable description is bestowed on Moses, it does not mean that God surrenders to men an honour due to Himself, in such a way as to take anything away from His own authority. For Moses is called *redeemer* in no other sense than that he was a minister of God, and in this way the glory of the whole undertaking remains entirely in the hands of God alone. Let us therefore learn that as often as men are honoured with God's titles, God is not stripped of His own honour; but because the work is carried out by their agency, they are commended in this way. What Stephen is saying amounts to this, that this responsibility was entrusted to Moses at the hand of the angel. For in this way Moses is made subject to Christ, so that under His guidance and auspices he may show his obedience to God. For *hand* is to be taken here, not in the sense of serving, but of pre-eminence. That is why God made use of the services of Moses in such a way that the power of Christ might be conspicuous above him. Similarly even today He is the chief Governor (*moderator*) in accomplishing the salvation of the Church. Yes, and He employs men as His ministers in such a way that the power and the accomplishment depend on Him alone.

37. *A prophet shall God raise up unto you.* There is no doubt that Stephen wishes to prove by these words that Christ is the end of the Law, although he does not say so in so many words. And indeed, as I have already said, Luke is not giving us here a word for word account of everything that Stephen said at that time, but it is sufficient for him to note the main points. Furthermore, I have already said in the third chapter that this testimony is properly applied to Christ, but in such a way that it is also appropriate to the other prophets. For after Moses had forbidden the people to be driven about this way and that by the vicious superstitions of the heathen, he shows what exactly ought to be coming after. 'For', he says, 'there is no reason for you to desire magicians or soothsayers, for God will never deprive you of prophets to teach you faithfully.' It is now certain, indeed, that the ministry of the prophets was a temporary one, like that of the Law; until Christ brought the full perfection of wisdom to the world. Therefore Stephen's speech brings out that when Moses places another teacher before them and commends him, he is not keeping the people devoted to himself alone. The prophets were indeed interpreters of the Law, and the whole of their teaching was like a supplement to the things that had been introduced by Moses. But at the same time, when it was well-known that teaching of a more perfect kind had to be brought in by Christ, since He was going to put an end to all prophecies, it follows that He is established in the chief place. And the principal magisterial office (*praecipuum magisterium*) if I may put it like that, is claimed for Him, so that there may be no doubt about the trustworthiness (*fides*) of the Gospel.

We now understand why Stephen included Moses' testimony, viz. that he (Moses) may show that the Jews, who kept making bombastic boasts about him being the only teacher for them, treat him with as much contempt and disrespect when he is dead, as long ago they had repudiated him wickedly and impudently when he was alive. For whoever has confidence in Moses will not refuse to be a disciple of Christ, whose herald Moses was. For the other things connected with this subject see the third chapter (on v. 22).

This is he that was in the church in the wilderness with the angel which spake to him in the mount Sinai, and with our fathers: who received living oracles to give unto us: to whom our fathers would not be obedient, but thrust him from them, and turned back in their hearts unto Egypt, saying unto Aaron, Make us gods which shall go before us: for as for this Moses, which led us forth out of the land of Egypt, we wot not what is become of him. And they made a calf in those days, and brought a sacrifice unto the idol, and rejoiced in the works of their hands. (38-41)

38. Stephen goes on with his account of the perverseness of the people, who, stimulated as they were by so many blessings from God, yet never ceased to reject Him with a bad grace. If they had been disobedient and not grateful enough to God before, at least such a wonderful deliverance ought to have called them back to a healthier frame of mind, but it shows that they were always true to their character. Certainly it was reasonable for so many miracles not only to stick in their minds, but also to remain before their eyes. But in fact they forgot everything and hastily took flight to the superstitions of Egypt. Their cruel slavery, from which they had escaped by crossing the sea, was fresh in their minds, but they preferred the tyrants, who had ill-treated them worse than inhumanly, to their redeemer. Therefore their desperate impiety reached a climax, because their contumacy could not be broken and overcome by so many blessings of God, but in fact they always reverted to type. Stephen's statement that Moses was with them in the desert at that time, adds to the great heinousness of their offence. For, setting aside the fact that the rare and inestimable goodness of God is apparent here in putting up with them, they leave themselves without excuse, when, hemmed in on all sides by so many difficulties, limited by so many exigencies, having Moses as the leader of their pilgrimage and the faithful guardian of their life, nevertheless they perfidiously defect from God Himself. In short they appear to have been like wild animals, whom God could not keep under control with so many chains. Therefore, seeing that Moses did not cease to rule them under the leadership and protection of the angel throughout the wilderness period, it is easy to gather from this particular incident of the time, how obstinate and incurable their perversity was; as it was indeed due to their unnatural contumacy that they were not humbled by so many misfortunes and by the very sight of death.

He says that Moses was with the angel and with the fathers. But his relation to each was entirely different. For he was with the fathers to show that he was their leader appointed by God's mandate; he was with the angel as a minister. It follows from that that injury was not done to a private individual but to the direction of God, when reverence for both did not prevent the people from rushing into infamous treachery. I have already spoken about the angel. But the participle λαλοῦντος is ambiguous. For it can be understood either of the first vision by which Moses was called to redeem the people, or of the conversation which God had with Moses after the crossing of the Red Sea. But since Christ has made known in both ways that He is the Author of redemption, it does not matter very much which you choose; indeed there is nothing to prevent you stretching to both. For He who had begun to speak to Moses at the first, to send him into Egypt, afterwards maintained the tenor of what He said, until the task would be completed.

Who received living oracles (*oracula*). Erasmus has translated it as 'living word' (*sermonem*),[1] but those who are familiar with Greek will acknowledge that I have given a truer rendering of the word used by Stephen (λόγια). For the word 'oracles' has greater majesty about it than 'word'. I am speaking only about the word (*voce*),[2] for I know that whatever comes out of the mouth of God is an oracle. Moreover he gains authority for Moses' teaching by these words, because he made known to the people nothing but what originated from God. It follows from that that the Jews were rebels, not so much against Moses himself, but against God in the person of Moses, and in this way their hard-hearted and high-handed behaviour is all the more laid bare. Now the method that generally establishes teaching is when men teach nothing but what is commanded them by God. For who, may I ask, will dare put himself before Moses, for the Spirit pronounces that credence ought to have been given to him as of right, for the simple reason that he faithfully expounded to the people the teaching that he received from God?

But it is asked, 'Why does he call the Law a living word (*sermonem*)?' For this phrase does not seem to agree with Paul's words that the Law is the 'ministration of death' (II Cor. 3.7), and 'worketh wrath' (Rom. 4.15), and is 'the power of sin' (I Cor. 15.56).[3] If you take 'living word' (*sermonem*) to mean one that is effectual, and which cannot be invalidated by the contempt of men, there is nothing to contradict about that; but I myself take it as used in an active sense for 'life-giving'. For since the Law is the perfect rule for leading a godly and holy life, and makes plain the righteousness of God, it is justifiably regarded as the teaching of life and salvation. In line with this is that solemn attestation of Moses, when he calls heaven and earth to witness, that he has set the way of life and death before the people (Deut. 30.19). God complains in similar vein in Ezek. chapter 20 that His good Law has been violated, His good commandments about which He had said, 'He who shall do these things, shall live in them' (Ezek. 20.13 *et al.*, Lev. 18.5, cf. Luke 10.28). The Law therefore holds life

[1] French: 'la parole vive'. [2] French: 'mot'.
[3] Only the first reference is given by Calvin. Tr.

in itself. But if anyone prefers to interpret *living* as full of efficacy and power, I shall not offer much resistance. But its description as the 'ministration of death' is something that is accidental to it on account of men's corrupt nature. For the Law does not create sin, but finds it in us. The Law offers life; but because of our corruption we ourselves can receive nothing but death from it. It is therefore death-bearing only with regard to men.

Nevertheless in this verse Stephen had something deeper in mind; for he is not speaking about the bare commandments, but he is embracing the whole of Moses' teaching, in which the promises of grace are included, and indeed Christ Himself, the only life and salvation of men. We must remember the kind of men with whom Stephen had to deal. For they were preposterously zealous for the Law, and cleaved only to the dead and death-bearing letter; and at the same time they were even raging against Stephen because in the Law he was seeking for the Christ who is indeed its very soul (*anima*). Therefore while lightly touching on their perverse ignorance in an indirect way, he is pointing out that hidden in the Law there is something greater and more excellent than they had realized up to now. For, as they were carnal, content with the outward appearance, they were looking for nothing spiritual in it, and what is more they would not allow it to be shown to them.

To give unto us. This is capable of removing the calumny of which he had been falsely accused. For since he submits himself to the yoke of the Law, and openly confesses that he is one of Moses' disciples, he is far from discrediting him among others. On the contrary he turns back the charge brought against himself on the authors of the misrepresentation. For the charge that the fathers had not been willing to obey the Law was one that, to a certain extent, brought reproach on all the people in common. Yet at the same time he warns them that Moses was appointed a prophet, not merely for his own generation, but so that even when he was dead his authority might persist among later generations. For it is not right that God's teaching should be extinguished or removed along with His ministers. For is there anything more contradictory than that the very thing that confers immortality on us should itself die? So today we must consider that, just as the prophets and apostles actually spoke to the men of their own day, so they wrote down for us, and their teaching is perpetually vigorous, because it ascribes the authorship to God rather than to human ministers. At the same time he is warning that if any reject the utterance intended for them, they are rejecting the purpose of God.

39. *They thrust him from them and turned back.* He says that Moses

was rejected by the fathers, and, at the same time, points out the reason why they preferred to devote themselves to the superstitions of Egypt. But it was a horrible thing and worse than blind madness to long eagerly for the customs and practices of Egypt, where they had recently suffered so severely. He says that *they turned back in their hearts to Egypt*, not because they desired to return there, but because they turned back their minds to those corruptions, no trace of which ought to have been lingering in their memory, except with the greatest abomination and aversion. It is indeed true that there was once a movement among the Jews to return, but Stephen does not mention that episode now. Moreover he underlines their contumacy when he says that they *turned back*. For having entered on the right way under God's leadership and guidance they suddenly rush off in another direction, like a refractory horse, impatient of its rider, wilfully running back on its tracks.

40. *Make us gods.* Although the Jews took retrograde steps in different ways Stephen chooses here an example of their foul and detestable treachery, more memorable than any other, namely, the occasion when they fashioned a calf for themselves, which they were to worship instead of God. For one can imagine nothing more scandalous than this ingratitude. They acknowledge that they have been redeemed from Egypt, and make no secret of the fact that it was done by the grace of God and the work of Moses, yet at the same time they coolly reject the Author of such a great blessing along with His minister. And on what pretext? They allege that they do not know what has happened to Moses. But they are not unaware that he is on the mountain. With their own eyes they had followed him up there, until God took him to Himself in the cloud that confronted them. Besides they know that Moses is absent for the sake of their own well-being, for he had promised to return in due course, and bring them the Law he received from God. He ordered them to wait quietly only for a little time. Within a short time and with no justification they are suddenly raising outrageous commotions, but to tinge or adorn their madness with a show of reason, they want gods present on the scene with them, as if indeed God had given them no sign of His presence up to now. But every day His glory was plain to be seen in the cloud and the fiery pillar. Therefore we see how they rush into idolatry with a malicious contempt for God, so that I may say no more meanwhile about how disgraceful and wicked their ingratitude was, seeing that in such a short space of time they lost sight of miracles, when the memory of them should have been celebrated right to the end of the world. Therefore it is abundantly evident from this one defection how headstrong and intractable a people they

were. We must also take into account the fact that it helped Stephen's case to refer to this rather than the other instances of rebellion. For the people openly overthrow the worship of God, repudiate the teaching of the Law, and bring in a foreign and profane religion.

Apart from that, this is a remarkable verse because it shows the fount from which superstitions of every kind have flowed from the beginning, especially what was in fact the primary reason for the making of idols, namely, that man, who is carnal, wishes, nevertheless, to have God present in a way that the flesh can grasp. That is why men of all generations have had such a passion for fashioning idols. Yet God certainly does accommodate Himself to our ignorance to this extent, that He allows us to see Himself after a fashion under figures. For under the Law there were very many symbols to testify to His presence; and today He comes down to us by means of baptism, and the Supper, and even in the external preaching of the Word.

But men sin here in a double way First, not content with the means appointed by God (*ordinatis a Deo mediis*), they boldly seek new things for themselves. At present it is no small fault that men, knowing no limit (*nullum modum tenentes*), are always itching for new inventions, and so they do not hesitate to jump over the bounds that God has set. But there can be no true image of God except such as He Himself has ordained. Therefore whatever things are contrived contrary to His Word[1] by the will of men are false and counterfeit. Secondly, there follows another fault, just as intolerable; as the human mind conceives nothing about God except what is solid and earthly, so it transfers all signs of the divine presence into the same materialism (*crassitiem*). Not only does man so mistakenly find pleasure in idols made by himself, but he also corrupts and spoils whatever God has instituted, twisting it to serve a contrary purpose. God does indeed come down to us, as I have said, but for this purpose, that He might lift us up into heaven. But we who are attached to the earth, wish to have Him similarly on the earth. In this way His heavenly glory is disfigured, and Israel's words, *Make us gods* are entirely fulfilled. For the man who is not worshipping God in a spiritual way is creating a new deity for himself. And yet, if you give closer consideration to the whole thing, the Israelites do not wish to have God (*Deum*) created with great pains by themselves, but on the contrary they think that they have the true and eternal God under the image of the golden calf. For they earnestly present themselves for the sacrifice that has been agreed upon, and they unanimously approve of what Aaron says, that these are the gods by which they have been led out of Egypt. But the Lord pays no attention to those frivolous fancies, but complains

[1] Reading *praeter ipsius verbum* with Tholuck instead of C.R.'s *ipsum*. Tr.

that foreign gods are substituted for Him as soon as men turn away, even a very little, from His Word.

41. *And they made a calf.* Why this particular image was more pleasing to them than others, it is easy to gather from the preceding verses. For although Egypt was swarming with innumerable idols, yet it is well known that the greatest honour was given to the ox. But what gave rise to their desire for an idol, except that 'they were turning back in their hearts to Egypt' as Stephen already said? But we must note the part of his speech where he says that *they brought a sacrifice to the idol.* Aaron decrees that the people should assemble to worship God, and they all gather together. They therefore demonstrate that they have nothing less in mind than to cheat God of His worship, to transfer it to the calf. One should rather say that they intended to worship God in the image of the calf; but because they departed from the true God in making an idol, everything else that follows after is regarded as being given to the idol, in view of the fact that God has disapproved of all irregular cults. For it is not right for devotion, that He has not commanded, to be offered to Him; and because He has expressly forbidden that a visible likeness be erected to Himself, whatever is attempted afterwards in its honour is sacrilege.

They rejoiced over the works. This verse is taken from Isaiah, one should rather say from the prophets, who similarly reproach the Jews for having taken delight in the things they have made. And it is certainly a strange madness when men arrogate to themselves anything that is God's prerogative (*in rebus divinis*). I understand the *rejoicing* to be that ceremonial religious dancing of which Moses gives an account in Exod. chapter 32. However Stephen is censuring a common fault, under which idolaters labour. For while men have no right to enter on anything in religion except what God has prescribed, yet they heedlessly make up what they like, and, setting God's Word aside, choose the works of their own hands. But yet Stephen is showing that when they give pleasure to themselves in this licence, they are giving all the more displeasure to God. Therefore if we wish our worship to be approved, we must abstain from the works of our own hands, or, in other words, from our own inventions. For whatever men devise by themselves is nothing else but sacrilege and profanation. Indeed it is proper to use such terms of an idol by way of reproach, as if it were a thing of no value, for on no condition are men allowed to fabricate God (*Deum*).

But God turned, and gave them up to serve the host of heaven; as it is written in the book of the prophets,

Did ye offer unto me slain beasts and sacrifices
Forty years in the wilderness, O house of Israel?
And ye took up the tabernacle of Moloch,
And the star of the god Rephan,
The figures which ye made to worship them:
And I will carry you away beyond Babylon. (42-43)

Stephen is teaching here that the Jews were never done sinning, but repeatedly wandered further in their perverse errors, so that that first lapse was like the entry into a labyrinth for them. But he ascribes it to the just punishment of God that their madness increased from that time, so that instead of just one idol they summoned up innumerable idols for themselves. This example warns us to give careful attention to following the rule of God, because as soon as we have turned away from it even in the slightest direction, we are inevitably swept hither and thither by various madnesses, entangled in a great many superstitions, and pitched up to the neck into a vast cesspool of errors. Now God justly imposes this punishment on men who refused to obey His Word. Stephen therefore says that God 'was turned round' and this expression amounts to saying that 'He turns His back'. For one might say that He had His eyes fixed on the people, when He showed His unique care in guiding them. Now He is displeased at their defection and turns His face in another direction.

From this we may gather, at the same time, that we can follow the right way only when the Lord is watching over us to direct us, but as soon as His face is averted we are dragged away into errors. Indeed the Israelites had already been abandoned by God on the occasion when they fashioned the calf, but Stephen wished to point out the severity of the punishment, as though he had said that they were then driven into a completely reprobate state of mind (cf. Rom. 1.28). And Paul similarly teaches that those, who did not give glory to God, when He had manifested Himself to them, are given up to blindness and stupefaction and to disgraceful lusts (Rom. 1.21ff). It happened as a result of this, that, from the time religion began to be corrupted, abominations without number took the place of a few superstitions, and gross monstrosities of idolatry took the place of trifling corruptions. For seeing that men had neglected the light kindled for them, they were deprived of their senses altogether by the just judgment of God, so that in their judgments they were no better than brute beasts. Idolatry is a fertile thing indeed, since from one false god a hundred are produced, and from a single superstition a thousand swarm. But such senselessness on men's part is due to the fact that God is avenging Himself by handing them over to Satan; because, from the time He undertook to rule over us, His role remains unaltered, but He is torn away from us by our heedless and fickle nature.

Did ye offer unto me slain beasts and sacrifices? This verse is taken from the prophet Amos (5.25). The utterance used by Stephen shows that all the prophecies were collected into a single corpus. But after Amos has inveighed against the idolatry and various crimes of the people, he adds to them that it is no new evil for the Jews to be rebels against God, because already in the very wilderness the fathers had departed from true godliness. Moreover, He denies that beasts had been offered to Him, not because there were no sacrifices at all in the wilderness, but because God was refusing their corrupt worship. Similarly in Isaiah He expostulates with the people for not honouring Him with any sacrifices, saying, 'You did not call upon me, Jacob; you have not honoured me with your sacrifices; and I have not burdened you with an offering or incense. You have not bought me sweet cane and you have not sated me with the fat of animals. But you have been a burden to me in your sins, and you have wearied me with your iniquities' (Isa. 43.22-24). The Jews were certainly doing everything of that sort every day, but God does not accept any response from the ungodly, or approve of it; in short he detests anything that is defiled by adventitious mixtures. Amos is speaking as yet in this way about the fathers. What is immediately annexed, can be referred to them, or to their descendants.

43. *And ye took up the tabernacle of Moloch.* Some take the copula in place of an adversative particle, as though he were saying, 'But on the contrary you have shown honour to an idol.' But it could also be understood in a causative sense, like this, 'You have not offered sacrifices to me, because you have erected a tabernacle to Moloch.' But I myself interpret it a little differently, viz. that for the sake of greater emphasis God first makes complaint against the fathers, and then goes on to say that their descendants went further in their involvement in superstitions, since they summoned up a variety of new idols for themselves. It is as if the prophet spoke like this in the name of God, 'If I may go over again from the earliest of times how your race has behaved towards Me, O House of Jacob, already in the very wilderness your fathers began to corrupt and subvert the worship commanded by Me, but you, you have surpassed them in ungodliness for you have brought in a countless horde of gods.' And this sequence squares better with Stephen's purpose. For, as has already been said, he wishes to prove that, after the Israelites fell away into strange and degenerate rites, there was no end to their sinning, but, struck with blindness by God, they repeatedly polluted themselves with new idolatries until they reached the pitch of impiety. Therefore in the

testimony of the prophet Stephen gains fitting confirmation for this judgment, that the Jews, descended from ungodly and disobedient fathers as they were, yet never ceased to get rapidly worse.

Finally, the words of the prophet are a little different; however, the meaning is the same. It is probable that Stephen, who was speaking with Jews, actually repeated word for word, in their own language, what the prophet said; while Luke, who was writing in Greek, followed the Greek version. The prophet says, 'You have honoured Siccuth[1] your king, and Chiun your image, the star of your gods.' The Greek translation made a common noun out of a proper one, because of the affinity of the word סִכּוּת, which means a 'tent'. But I do not know where he got that word 'Remphan' (*sic*) except that it could have been that that name was more generally used at that time.

And the figures which ye made. The word 'image', which the prophet uses, in itself means nothing with which to find fault. For the word *τύπος*, 'figure', is taken in a good sense by the Greeks. Again, all the ceremonies which God has instituted are called *τύποι*, 'figures'. Nevertheless, the prophet expressly condemns the *τύπους*, 'figures', fabricated by the Jews. Why is that, except that God does not wish to be worshipped under a visible and external form? If anyone objects that stars are mentioned here, I admit that is true, but I insist only on this, that even if the prophet does grant a respectable name to the idols, he is yet sharp and severe in his condemnation of corrupt worship.

In this way the silly and childish sophistry of the Papists is refuted. Because they deny that the images and statues which they worship are idols, they say that the worship, in which they act like madmen, is *εἰκονοδουλεία*, the service of images, but not *εἰδωλοδουλεία*, the service of idols. Since they make a laughing-stock of God with their sophistry, there is nobody endowed with plain common-sense who does not see that such absurdities make them laughable in the extreme. For although I am raising no dispute with them about the word, it is certain that the word *τύπος* has a more respectable air about it than *εἰκών*. But *τύποι*, 'figures', which men fabricate for themselves, are plainly condemned here, not only *πρὸς τὴν λατρείαν*, for service, but also *πρὸς τὴν προσκύνησιν* i.e. for adoration of any kind. Therefore that distinction, in which the Papists think that they have a crafty means of escape, falls to the ground.

Beyond Babylon. The prophet says 'Damascus'; and the Greek version agrees. Therefore it is possible that the name *Babylon* slipped in here by mistake; although it makes no difference in the end. The

[1] Reading 'Siccuth' with Tholuck, for C.R's 'Succuth'. Hebrew is 'Siccuth' as R.V.: סִכּוּת מַלְכְּכֶם. LXX: *τὴν σκηνὴν τοῦ Μολόχ*. The Hebrew also reads 'images' and 'god'. Tr.

Israelites were to be carried away to Babylon; but because they were in the habit of thinking that there was sure and impregnable protection for themselves in the kingdom of Syria, whose capital was Damascus, the prophet therefore declares that Damascus will not be able to prevent God driving them farther away. He might have put it like this: 'As long as you have Damascus confronting your enemies, you think that you are particularly well protected, but God will transfer you farther away, viz. into Assyria and Chaldea.'

Our fathers had the tabernacle of the testimony in the wilderness, even as he appointed who spake unto Moses, that he should make it according to the figure that he had seen. Which also our fathers, in their turn, brought in with Joshua when they entered on the possession of the nations, which God thrust out before the face of our fathers, unto the days of David; who found favour in the sight of God, and asked to find a habitation for the God of Jacob. But Solomon built him a house. Howbeit the Most High dwelleth not in houses made with hands; as saith the prophet,

The heaven is my throne,
And the earth the footstool of my feet:
What manner of house will ye build me? saith the Lord:
Or what is the place of my rest?
Did not my hand make all these things? (44-50)

44. *The tabernacle of testimony.* Stephen is pointing out here that God cannot be blamed because the Jews corrupted themselves with many different superstitions, as if He allowed them to wander about unbridled. For he says that God gave instructions about what kind of worship He wished from them. It follows from that that they were involved in so many errors for no other reason than that they were not willing to follow the form laid down by God. However he reproached them on a double count, first, not being content with God's directions alone they heedlessly devised strange cults for themselves, and, secondly, they did not have the right object in view in the temple as well as in the ceremonies instituted by God. For while those things ought to have been means for exercising them in spiritual worship, because of their material outlook they grasped only what was earthly and carnal, or, in other words, the shadow instead of the very substance. We see therefore that it is because of their presumption that the Jews are first of all censured, because they were not content with the simple Word of God and were dragged along in the wake of their own inventions. We see that rebuke falls, in the second place, on their perversion and abuse of the true and sincere worship, because they pursued the flesh instead of the spirit.

He says that they ***had the tabernacle of testimony.*** Therefore they were driven to sinning only by their own wantonness and heedlessness. For seeing that they were thoroughly instructed as to what the true way of worshipping God was they were deprived of the excuse of ignorance. This deserves our attention. For when God makes known His will to us He puts a bridle on us, so to speak, so that if we turn aside in this direction or that after accepting His will, we become doubly guilty; because the servant who knows His master's will and does not do it will be beaten more severely (Luke 12.47). This is the primary mark by which the Holy Spirit distinguishes all degenerate and corrupt cults from true and sincere worship. Of course it is, and to put it in a nutshell, the basic difference between proper worship and idolatry is that the godly undertake nothing except what is in conformity with the Word of God; but others think that they are entitled to do anything that suits themselves, and so they have their own will in place of a law, when the fact is that God approves only what He Himself has prescribed.

The word *testimony* also relates to this. The Hebrew word מוֹעֵד (*moed*) means an appointed place and time, or an assembly of men; but the method of its employment in the writings of Moses shows another basis for the name. For in Moses' writings God repeats quite often, 'I shall meet with you there' (e.g. Exod. 29.42, 43; 30.6, 36). Therefore the *tabernacle* was consecrated by the covenant and the Word of the Lord, and His voice was continually resounding there, so that it was different from all common places.

According to the forms that he had seen. This is to be referred to the second characteristic that I touched on. For it is possible for a man to use only the ceremonies that God has enjoined, and yet worship God in the wrong way. For God wastes no time on external rites except in so far as they are symbols of the heavenly truth. So He wished the structure of the ancient tabernacle to be completed after the heavenly archetype, so that the Jews might realize that they must not remain attached to external figures. Further, anyone so desiring may find out from my Commentaries on the Epistle to the Hebrews (8.5) the meaning of that *figure* (*typum*) which is mentioned by Moses in Exod. 25.40. Here Stephen is only briefly warning that the worship which God demanded from the Jews was spiritual, but that they interpreted it badly and perversely, because of their carnal stupidity. Therefore, as I have said, no worship is approved by God except what is based on His commandment; so let us learn here that for the proper use of the commandment the presence of spiritual truth is necessary. Similar to this incontrovertible fact was the question, which, we said, turned on the point whether the shadows ought to yield to the substance or not.

In saying that Moses saw a figure (*formam*) the Spirit of God means that we are not allowed to invent figures on our own authority, but that all our senses must be turned intently on the figure shown by God, so that the whole of religion may be regulated according to it. The word *figure* (*typus*) means here the principal pattern, because it is nothing else but spiritual truth.

45. *Which they brought in.* The stubbornness of the people is shown up all the more by the fact that, when the tabernacle remained with them, and they carried it everywhere on the march, yet they could not be kept within the bounds of God's testimony, but with treacherous light-heartedness went over to strange and profane rites, declaring that God was surely dwelling in their midst, when they were so far removed from Him, and were driving Him out of the inheritance, which He had given to them. Add to this that God was honouring the tabernacle with a variety of miracles, for its value was confirmed by the victories by which the Jews got the possession, as is plain from several parts of the sacred history. Therefore they must have been very intractable when they were repeatedly in the habit of recoiling from a way of worship that was approved in so many ways.

Until the days of David. Even although the ark of the Lord had its resting-place in Shiloh for a long time, yet it had no settled abode until the reign of David. For men were forbidden to erect a place for it; but it was to be set up in that place which the Lord had shown, as Moses mentions quite frequently. Indeed, after David had received it from his enemies, he himself did not dare to bring it into the threshing-floor of Araunah, until the Lord made known to him by an angel from heaven that that was the place which He had chosen (II Sam. 24.16). But Stephen quite rightly thinks of it as an extraordinary favour of God that David was shown the place in which the Israelites should afterwards worship God. So in the Ps. (122.1) he rejoices as if over another unusual event, 'I was glad when they said unto me, "Into the house of the Lord shall we go, in thy courts, O Jerusalem, shall our feet be standing." ' The offices of priest and king were united. Therefore the establishing (*statione*) of the ark demonstrates the stability of David's rule. That is why he is said to have been so anxious in his desire for this that he bound himself with a solemn vow, that he would not dwell in his own house first, that he would give no sleep to his eyes, or rest to his eyelids, until he knew of a place for the Lord and a tabernacle for the God of Jacob (Ps. 132.3f). Furthermore, the place was shown to David, but it was Solomon who was allowed to build the temple (I Kings 5.5).

47. *Solomon built.* Stephen seems to be giving an indirect rebuke to Solomon here, as if he did not give consideration to God's nature

in building the temple; yet that work was not undertaken without God's commandment. A promise was also added in which God testified that He would be present in it with His people. I reply that when Stephen denies that God dwells in temples 'made with hands' that is not being directed against Solomon, who knew quite well that God is to be sought in heaven, and that men's minds must be lifted up there by faith. He also said this clearly in the preface to the solemn prayer which he made, 'Heavens of heavens cannot contain Thee, and how much less this house' (I Kings 8.27). But he is finding fault with the stupidity of the people, who made wrong use of the temple, as if it had God tied to it. And this comes out more clearly in the testimony of Isaiah which he added at the same time (Isa. 66.1f). 'God', he says, 'wished a temple to be built for Himself by Solomon, but those who thought that He was shut up, so to speak, in a building of that sort, were greatly mistaken; just as He complains through His prophet that the people are treating Him in the wrong way when they imagine Him to be confined to a place.'

Finally, the prophet inveighs against the Jews, not only because they worshipped God in a superstitious way, thinking that His divinity was fixed to the temple; but also because they measured Him against their own way of looking at things, and thought that, after they had performed their sacrifices and their outward show, He was reconciled, and even indebted to them. It has been a fairly common error in all generations for men to think that cold ceremonies are abundantly sufficient for the worship of God. The reason is that they imagine that God is like them, when they are carnal and devoted to the world. Therefore, in order to shake them out of this stupidity, God proclaims that He fills all things.

49. When He says that heaven is His throne and describes the earth as a footstool for His feet, these statements ought not to be taken as if He had a body, or can be divided into parts, like men; but because He is boundless He denies that He is contained in any spatial limits (*ullis locorum spatiis*). Therefore those who measure God and His worship by the standard of their own nature are mistaken. But because the prophet is dealing with hypocrites he is not simply discussing the essence of God, but is teaching in a general way that He is very different from men, and is not affected as they are, by the vain splendour of this world.

Here again that question is raised, 'Why does the prophet say that God has no resting-place in the world, when the Spirit nevertheless plainly presents a different side elsewhere, in Ps. 132.14, "This is my resting-place for ever"? Yes, and Isaiah honours the Church with this same description, that it is the glorious resting-place of God, referring of course to the temple.' My answer is that when long ago God instituted signs of His presence in the temple and the sacrifices He did not do so in order to tie down Himself and His power to those things. Therefore the Israelites were in the wrong when they fixed their attention on the symbols, and fabricated an earthly God for themselves. Also in the wrong were those who assumed for themselves the licence to sin on this pretext, as if bare ceremonies gave them a ready and easy way of appeasing God. This is the way that the world habitually trifles with God.

When God testifies that He will be present to His people by external symbols, so that He may dwell in their midst, He is inviting them above, so that they may seek Him in a spiritual way. Hypocrites involved in the world wish, rather, to drag God out of heaven; and since they have nothing except bare figures, they are filled with obtuse confidence and unconcernedly indulge in sins. So in our day those in the Papacy fancifully shut up Christ in the bread and wine. Then, having done with playing at worship towards their idol, they carry their heads high with pride, as if an angelic sanctity possessed them. These two faults must be carefully noted. The first is that men superstitiously create a worldly and carnal God for themselves, a God who comes down to them so that they may remain firmly bound to the earth and not aspire to heaven. Secondly they dream that God is appeased with worthless services. The result of these is that they are infatuated by visible signs, and then, neglecting godliness, make a great commotion to put God in their debt with a childish method and things of no value.

Now we know what the prophet means when he says that God has no resting-place anywhere in the world. Indeed He had intended the temple to be a sign and pledge of His presence, but to the godly, who would ascend to heaven in heart, and would worship Him spiritually with pure faith. But He has no resting-place among the superstitious who, with their stupid things, made by themselves, bind Him to the elements of the world, or foolishly set up an earthly cult for Him; and He has none among the hypocrites who are swollen with a drunken confidence, as if they have acquitted themselves very well towards God, after they have amused themselves among absurdities. In a word, the promise accepted by faith brings it about that God listens to us, and gives out His power in the sacraments, as if He were present; but if we do not reach up to Him in faith, He will not be present for us. From this it is easy to conclude that, when He dwells in the midst of His people, He is neither fixed to the earth, nor contained in any place, seeing that they seek Him spiritually in heaven.

50. *Did not my hand?* The prophet reminds us in these words that

God has no need of gold, or the precious ornaments of the temple, or the sacrifices. The consequence is that the true worship of Him does not consist in ceremonies. For none of those things which we offer to Him does He desire for His own sake, but only that He may discipline us in the pursuit of godliness; this theme is dealt with at greater length in Ps. 50. For although it is foolish and abominable to wish to feed God with sacrifices, yet if hypocrites were not immersed in that, they would not value their play-things so highly, seeing that anything that is divergent from spiritual worship is distasteful in God's sight. Let us therefore realize that it is we who are sought after by God, and not our possessions, for we obtain them only by His favour (*precario ab eo*). And at the same time it is plain from this how far apart true religion is from the carnal creations of men.

Ye stiffnecked and uncircumcised in heart and ears, ye do always resist the Holy Ghost: as your fathers did, so do ye. Which of the prophets did not your fathers persecute? and they killed them which shewed before of the coming of the Righteous One; of whom ye have now become betrayers and murderers; ye who received the law as it was ordained by angels, and kept it not. (51-53)

51. Since Stephen does not expressly reply to the points of the accusation, I willingly agree with those who think that he would have said much more if his speech had not been violently broken off by an uproar. For we know what the assembly, who were judging him, were like; and accordingly it is not to be wondered at if they forced him into silence with their clamour and shouts of rage. And we also see that he deliberately used long insinuations in order to calm them down, as if they were wild beasts. But it is probable that their fury was inflamed at the moment when he pointed out that the Law was very badly corrupted by them, the temple was polluted by their superstitions, and there was nothing that they had that was unspoiled, because they clung to bare figures and did not worship God in a spiritual way, and this in turn, because they did not trace the ceremonies back to the heavenly pattern. Finally, even if Stephen did not take up his case just straight away, but tried to soothe their fierce minds by degrees, yet his arguments were appropriate for clearing him of the charge that had been laid against him.

As I have said, the two main points of the investigation were (1) that Stephen had been abusive of God and the temple, and (2) that he had tried to abrogate the Law. In order to remove those calumnies Stephen begins with the call of Abraham and shows that the Jews are superior to the Gentiles, not by nature, not by any right of their own, not by the merits of their works, but by the gratuitous privilege that God had adopted them in the person of Abraham. Similarly it helps his case that the covenant of salvation was concluded with Abraham before there were a temple, ceremonies and even circumcision itself. The Jews prided themselves in these things so much that they said that there was no worship of God and no holiness without them. After that he told how wonderful and many-sided the goodness of God was towards the descendants of Abraham, and how, in turn, the people wickedly and perversely repulsed the grace of God as much as they could. From that it is established that it cannot be put down to their own merits that they are regarded as God's people, but because, on His own accord, God chose them for Himself in their unworthiness, and did not cease to bestow His benefits on them in their ingratitude. Their proud and lofty spirits could have been tamed and reduced to humility in this way, so that, with the breath of vainglory squeezed out of them, they might come to the Mediator. In the third place he explained that in the bringing of the Law and the redeeming of the people the angel was in charge, and that while Moses discharged his own ministry he also said that other prophets would come after him, and of these one must however be pre-eminently the greatest, one who would put an end to all prophecies and predictions and bring about a genuine fulfilment. The implication of all that is that those men, who are repudiating the kind of teaching, promised and praised in the Law, along with the author of it, are nothing less than disciples of Moses. In the last place he shows that the whole of the ancient worship, which had been prescribed by Moses, must not be appraised on its own, but rather ought to be referred to another object, because it was formed in accordance with the heavenly archetype; but yet that the Jews were always perverse interpreters of the Law, because they grasped nothing except what was carnal and earthly. It follows from this that no harm can be done to the temple and the Law, when Christ is openly established as the end and truth of both.

Finally, because the state of the case turned on the particular point that the worship of God does not properly consist in sacrifices and other things, and all rites do nothing else but foreshadow Christ, Stephen's intention was to insist very strongly on this point, if the Jews would have let him. But when he comes to the heart of the matter, because they are inflamed with fury and cannot bear to hear any more, there is no application of all that he had said to the case in hand. And for an epilogue he is forced to add a sharp rebuke, saying that they are *stiffnecked*. We see that he is suddenly burning with a holy zeal against them, but because he realized that he was pouring out his words on deaf ears with no success, he breaks off the thread of his teaching. Now this is a metaphor taken from horses or oxen, which Moses often uses, when he wishes to say that his people are stubborn and disobedient to God, and even untamable (Exod. 32.9, 33.3, 5).

The subsequent reproach had more force among them. For circumcision to them was a veil to cover all their faults. Therefore when he calls them *uncircumcised in heart* he means not only that they are rebels against God, and intractable, but even in that symbol, in which they prided themselves, they are found to be treacherous and breakers of the covenant; and so the very thing, that they were boasting about for their own glory, he most suitably casts back at them to shame them. For it amounts to his saying that they have defiled the covenant of the Lord, so that their circumcision was ineffectual and commonplace. Now this way of speaking is taken from the Law and the Prophets. For as God instituted the symbol so He wished the Jews to realize why they were circumcised, viz. so that they might circumcise their hearts and the whole of their corrupt minds to the Lord, as we read, 'And now circumcise your hearts to the Lord' (Deut. 10.16; Jer. 4.4). Accordingly, 'literal circumcision', as Paul calls it, is an empty thing, and a valueless veil (*larva*) in God's sight (Rom. 2.29). Similarly today, since spiritual washing is the truth of our baptism, we must be anxious in case the objection might rightly be made against us, that we are not really participating in baptism, because our flesh and soul are stained with filthy things.

You do always resist. To begin with Stephen had thought the men, against whom he inveighs so vehemently, fit to be called fathers and brethren. Accordingly as long as there was the hope that they could be moved to clemency, not only did he deal with them amicably, but he also addressed them with respect. But now when he perceives their desperate inflexibility, not only does he give them no further honour, but, so that he might have nothing in common with them, he takes them to task as if they were the offspring of another race. He says, 'You are like your fathers, who were always rebels against the Spirit of God.' And he himself was also descended from the same fathers, but in order to unite himself with Christ, he forgets about his origin, as if it was something accursed. Yet he does not put them all in the same bundle, as they say, but he is addressing this particular crowd.

Finally, they are said to be resisting the Spirit, when they stubbornly reject what He says by the prophets. And here it is not a question of the secret, inward revelations, which God breathes into everyone, but of His outward ministry. And we must pay particular attention to that. He wishes to remove every appearance of an excuse from the

Jews. Therefore he casts it in their teeth that it was not out of ignorance that they rebelled against God, but, as it were, seriously and intentionally. It is evident from that how highly God values His Word, and how reverently He wishes us to receive it. Therefore so that we may not wage war on God like the giants, let us quietly learn to listen to the ministers by whose lips He teaches us.

52. *Which of the prophets.* Since they ought not to be taking responsibility for the offence of their fathers, Stephen appears to be unfair in including this among the crimes of the people whom he is addressing. But he has good reasons for doing so. In the first place, because they were proudly boasting that they were the sacred posterity of Abraham, it was worth his while to tell them how useless a thing that really was. It is as if Stephen said that there is no reason why they should be boasting of their origin, when they are the descendants of wicked men who murdered the prophets. So, briefly and indirectly, he touches on what is set out more clearly in the writings of the prophets, that they are not the sons of the prophets, but degenerate and illegitimate offspring, the seed of Canaan, etc. The same sort of thing can be said about the Papists today, when they boastfully exalt their fathers.

Again, he says that their resistance to the truth is no new thing for them, but they have this bad streak as a kind of inheritance from their fathers, and this statement has the effect of amplifying what he has said. Moreover it was necessary for the disguise (*larvam*) of the Church to be stripped off them in this way, the very thing with which they were charging Stephen. For the teaching of the Gospel was severely prejudiced by their boasting that they were the Church of God, and their arrogating this title to themselves because of a long succession. Stephen therefore presents the other side, and proves that their fathers, no less than themselves, raved against the prophets with irreverent contempt and hatred of sound doctrine. Lastly, it is the constant custom of Scripture to unite the sons with the fathers in guilt, when they have committed the same crime. And the famous word of Christ is relevant to that, 'Fill up the measure of your fathers, until the righteous blood comes upon you, from Abel unto Zachariah' (Matt. 23.32, 35).

Who have foretold. From this we gather that all the prophets were eager to direct their nation to Christ, as He is the end of the Law. It would take too long to list all the prophecies which foretold the coming of Christ. Let it suffice with the general principle that the prophets had the common task of promising salvation by the grace of Christ.

The name, the *Righteous One*, is given to Christ here, not only to bring out His innocence, but also on account of what He effects, for it is His property to establish righteousness in the world. However Stephen convincingly argues in this verse that the Jews were extremely undeserving of the benefit of redemption, because already in the past the fathers not only rejected what had been made known to them by the prophets, but also cruelly slaughtered the messengers of God, but in fact their sons endeavoured to destroy the Author of righteousness and salvation, who was offered to them. By this comparison Christ is making us know that the infamous plotting of His enemies is the culminating point of all their ungodly acts.

53. *You who received the Law.* The fury burning in them against Stephen they were calling 'zeal for the Law' as if he himself were a deserter and apostate from the Law, and were driving others into similar defection. Although he intended to put an end to this false accusation, he did not complete his answer. For they did not give him a hearing, and it was futile to pour out words on deaf ears. He is therefore content to put an end to their false pretext in a word or two. He says, 'It is evident that you are lying when you allege that you are zealous of the Law, which you never stop transgressing and violating.' And just as he reproached them with the treacherous murder of the Righteous One in the preceding verse, so now he charges them with defection from the Law. Someone will say that it makes not the slightest difference to Stephen's case that the Jews transgress the Law. But, as we have said, Stephen is rebuking them in such a way, not because his defence turns on this point, but that they may not preen themselves with deceitful boasting. For hypocrites must be handled in this way, when they wish to give the appearance of being the keenest vindicators of God's glory, but in reality have no qualms about despising Him. Here there is also a telling antistrophe, that although they had made the pretence of submitting to the Law, that had been entrusted to them, yet they scorned it in their insolence.

In the dispositions of angels (*In dispositionibus*). Literally, it is 'into the dispositions' (*in dispositiones*), but it comes to the same thing. Furthermore we need look for no other interpreter of this phrase than Paul, who teaches that the Law was 'disposed' or 'ordained by angels' (Gal. 3.19). In that verse he uses the participle (διαταγείς) from which the noun is derived (διαταγή). But he understands that the angels were God's intermediaries, and His witnesses in the promulgating of the Law, so that its authority might be firmly established. Therefore, since God summoned the angels to be, as it were, solemn witnesses of His giving the Law to the Jews, the same angels are to be the witnesses of their treachery. And Stephen mentions the angels, so that, before their eyes, he might condemn the Jews as transgressors of the Law. We may surmise from this what will happen to those who despise the Gospel, something so far superior to the Law that somehow it obscures its glory, as Paul teaches in II Cor. 3 (7ff).

Now when they heard these things, they were cut to the heart, and they gnashed on him with their teeth. But he, being full of the Holy Ghost, looked up stedfastly into heaven, and saw the glory of God, and Jesus standing on the right hand of God, and said, Behold, I see the heavens opened, and the Son of man standing on the right hand of God. But they cried out with a loud voice, and stopped their ears, and rushed upon him with one accord; and they cast him out of the city, and stoned him: (54-58)

54. *Hearing these things.* At the beginning the proceedings had some appearance of justice, but in the end the judges cannot contain their anger. His speech is first broken off by a murmuring and rustling of disagreement. Then they break into a tumult of hostile shouts, so that no voice may penetrate their ears. After that they drag the holy man off to death.

Now Luke gives a very fine description of what great power Satan has in driving on the adversaries of the Word. When he says that 'they were broken apart within' he means that they were not simply burning with anger, but were stirred up by frenzy. And that fury breaks out into *gnashing of teeth,* like a violent fire into flame. All the reprobate, over whom Satan rules, are of necessity affected in this way, when they hear the Word of God. And the nature of the Gospel is to drive to madness hypocrites, who could previously have presented a mild appearance, just like a drunkard who is suddenly roused up when he is trying to get to sleep. Therefore Simeon ascribes to Christ as His own, the property 'to disclose the thoughts of many hearts' (Luke 2.35). Yet this ought not to be attributed to the doctrine of salvation, for it has been intended rather to serve the purpose of subduing the minds of men and then changing them to obedience to God. But the truth is that, when men's minds are in Satan's grip, if they are being pressed by the Word, impiety is bound to break out. This is therefore an accidental evil (*accidentale malum*). Nevertheless we are warned by these examples that we must not entertain the hope that the Word of God will call everybody back to soundness of mind; and this teaching is very necessary to maintain our perseverance. Those who carry the burden of teaching cannot perform it and carry it through faithfully, without bringing themselves into a sharp clash with those who despise God. Now, since impious men who make light of the majesty of God, are never lacking, it is frequently necessary to have recourse to vehemence like Stephen's. For we have no right to close our eyes to it, when God's honour is being taken away from Him. But what will the outcome of that be? Their impiety will be the more inflamed; and so we shall appear to be pouring oil upon the flames, as the saying goes. But whatever the result may be, yet we must not spare the ungodly, but we must powerfully suppress them, even if they are bound to spew out all the furies of hell. And it is certain that those, who wish the ears of the ungodly to be soothed with pleasing things, have not so much an eye for success, as that they are soft because of fear of danger. But as for ourselves, even if the result may not always correspond to our wishes, let us realize that firmness in declaring the teaching of godliness is a sweet-smelling sacrifice to God.

55. *Since he was filled by the Spirit.* No words can express how great were the straits into which the servant of Christ was forced when he saw himself ringed about on all sides by raving enemies, and the excellence of his case shattered partly by calumnies and ill-will, partly by violence and mad shouting; when grim faces were threatening him on all sides; when he himself was being dragged off to a fearful and horrible kind of death, and there was nowhere any sign of help or alleviation. Accordingly when he was deserted in this way, with no man to help him, he turns to God. In the first place we must note this, that when Stephen reached the ultimate point of despairing of everything, with death alone staring him in the face, he turned himself away from the sight of men and the world, and promptly turned his gaze to God, the Arbiter of life and death. In the second place, we must add, at the same time, that his hopes were not dashed, because Christ appeared to him at once. However Luke means that he was now armed with the unconquerable power of the Spirit, so that nothing would block his vision of the heavens. Therefore Stephen does look towards heaven, with the result that, trusting to a vision of Christ, he composes himself, and in dying triumphs in a splendid victory over death. But as for ourselves, since we are bound too much to the earth, it is no wonder if Christ does not show Himself to us. As a result our courage fails, not only in the face of death, but also at every faint rumour of danger, and even at the rustle of a falling leaf. And it serves us right; for where is our courage but in Christ? But we disregard heaven, just as if the only help available for us is in the world. Moreover the only way that this fault in us, who are naturally bent to the earth, can be corrected, is if the Spirit of God lifts us up on high. Therefore the reason Luke gives for Stephen having turned his eyes to heaven, is that he was full of the Spirit. With Him as our Guide and Leader we ought also to ascend in spirit (*animis*) into heaven, as often as we are beset by misfortunes. And certainly until He shines upon us, our eyes are by no means so sharp-sighted as to

reach to heaven. No! the fact is the eyes of the flesh are too dull to search for heaven!

He saw the glory of God. Luke points out, as I have said, that, when Stephen raised his eyes to heaven, Christ appeared to him at once. But he reminds us previously that he was given other than earthly eyes, so that by their penetrating sight he may fly up all the way to the glory of God. From this we can derive the general encouragement that God will be no less present to us, if we leave the world behind and strain after Him with all our mental powers (*sensus*). It is not the case that He may appear to us by means of an outward vision, as He did to Stephen, but He will reveal Himself within us, so that we may really be aware (*sentiamus*) of His presence. And this way of 'seeing' ought to be enough for us, since by His power and grace God not only shows that He is near us, but also proves that He dwells within us.

56. *Behold I see the heavens.* God wished not only to show regard for His servant privately, but also to inflame and torment His enemies, in the way, for example, that Stephen courageously provokes them by openly declaring that a miracle was granted to him. But someone asks how the heavens were opened. As far as I am concerned I consider that nothing was altered in the nature of the heavens, but a new sharpness of vision was given to Stephen, to penetrate past every obstacle right to the invisible glory of the Kingdom of Heaven. For even if we grant that there was some rending of heaven, yet the eye of man would never transcend to such a height. Again, the glory of God was visible to Stephen alone. For to the ungodly who were standing in that place, not only was such a spectacle hidden, but being inwardly blind they were not perceiving the open light of truth. Therefore he says that the heavens are open to himself, in the sense that nothing impedes him from the sight of the glory of God. From that it follows that the miracle was produced not in the heavens but rather in his eyes. That is why there is no need for us to give much discussion to physical vision; because it is certain that Christ did not appear to him in the natural order, or by natural means, but in a new and unique way. And, pray, what colours did the glory of God have, to strike the eyes of flesh in a natural way? Therefore the right course is to conclude that there is nothing in this vision but what is divine. Moreover, it is worth while noting that the glory of God did not appear to Stephen in the fulness of its constituent nature (*in solidum qualis erat*), but only as much as the capacity of man could bear. For that immensity cannot be comprehended by the measure of a created being.

The Son of man standing. He sees Christ reigning in that flesh in which he had suffered humiliation (*exinanitus*), as victory certainly lodged in this one Man. There is therefore nothing pointless about

Christ appearing to him. And on this account he also calls Him the *Son of Man*. It is as if he had said, 'That Man who, you think, was destroyed by death, I see in possession of the sovereignty of the heavens. Hiss, therefore, as much as you like, there is no reason for me to hesitate to fight for Him even to the point of blood, for He will be the Defender both of His own cause, and my safety.'

Yet the question is raised, why he saw Him *standing*, when He is said, elsewhere, to be seated. Augustine, being sometimes more sharp than reasonable, says that He sits as a Judge, but on this occasion He stood as an Advocate. I really think that even if those phrases are different, yet they both mean the same thing. For neither sitting nor standing describes the position of the body of Christ; but this refers to His power and sovereignty. For where shall we set up a tribunal for Him, on which He may sit at the right hand of the Father, when God fills all things in such a way that no place (*nullus locus*) ought to be devised for His right hand? Therefore there is a metaphor in the entire context, when Christ is said to stand or sit at the right hand of the Father. And the meaning is simply that all power has been given to Christ, so that in the flesh, in which He had been humiliated, He might reign in place of His Father, and be second to Him.

Finally, although this power is diffused through heaven and earth yet some people wrongly imagine that Christ is everywhere in His human nature. For the fact that He is confined to a certain place (*certo loco continetur*) does not prevent Him putting out His power through the whole world. Accordingly if we desire to be aware of His presence by the efficacy of His grace, we must seek Him in heaven; as for example He revealed Himself to Stephen from there. Some also make the ridiculous contention from this verse that He drew near to Stephen so that He could be seen by him. For I have said that by the power of the Spirit Stephen's eyes were so lifted up by faith that no spatial distances might break off their sharpness of vision. Indeed I think, properly speaking, that, philosophically, there is no place (*nullum locum*) above the heavens. But it is enough for me that it is perverse madness to place Christ anywhere than in heaven, and above the elements of the world.

57. *Crying with a loud voice*. One might explain this as a show of zeal, in the way that vanity nearly always drives hypocrites to boil over in an excess of passion, as, for example, Caiaphas responded to Christ's word, 'After this you will see the Son of man etc.' (Mark 15.62f), by tearing his clothes as a sign of indignation, as if this were an intolerable blasphemy. Another explanation is that the preaching of the glory of Christ annoyed them so intensely that they simply had to explode with frenzy. I am rather inclined to take the second view.

For afterwards Luke says that they were seized as if by a violent impulse, as men, who cannot keep a grip on themselves, are in the habit of making rushes at things, suddenly and wildly.

58. *They stoned.* God established this kind of punishment in the Law for false prophets, for example in Deut. 13. But God also defines there who is to be included in their number, viz. the man who tried to lead the people away to foreign gods. Therefore the stoning of Stephen was unjust and heinous because he was condemned on a false charge. Thus Christ's martyrs must submit to the same punishment as criminals. It is the cause alone that distinguishes between them. But this distinction counts for so much in the eyes of God and His angels that the abuses suffered by the martyrs surpass in merit all the glories of the world.

But here it can be asked how the Jews were allowed to stone Stephen when they had been deprived of authority. For in Christ's case they make the reply, 'It is not lawful for us to put any man to death' (John 18.31). My answer to that is that they did this with the force of a rebellion. But it is possible that the governor did not punish this outrage, because he tolerated many things in secret among a people that were turbulent and almost ungovernable, lest he might bring down on himself the odium from which the name of Christ was suffering. Especially are we aware that the Roman governors were accustomed to wink deliberately at the internal quarrels of that nation, so that when both sides had exhausted themselves they would then be more quickly subdued.

And the witnesses laid down their garments at the feet of a young man named Saul. And they stoned Stephen, calling upon the Lord, and saying, Lord Jesus, receive my spirit. And he kneeled down, and cried with a loud voice, Lord, lay not this sin to their charge. And when he had said this, he fell asleep. And Saul was consenting unto his death. (58-8.1 R.V.; Calvin 58-61)

58. *But the witnesses.* Luke means that some appearance of justice was nevertheless preserved in that uproar. The commandment that the first stones should be cast by the witnesses had not been made without good reason, because many who are held back by conscientious scruples from murder to be done by their own hands, have otherwise little fear of cutting innocent throats with their perjuring tongues. But at the same time we gather how blind and savage the impiety of those witnesses was, for having already slain with their tongues they did not hesitate to lay bloody hands as well on this innocent man.

In saying that his clothes were laid at the feet of Saul, he is showing that Saul did not owe it to himself, that, having been thrown into a reprobate mind, he did not perish with the others. For who would not consider as beyond hope a man who was already staining his youth with an initiation of that sort? And his age is not mentioned to extneuate his offence, after the fashion of certain ignorant men who labour on his behalf; for he had already reached that age, when ignorance could no longer be pled as an excuse. And a little later Luke will record that he was sent by the high priest to persecute believers. He had therefore left boyhood behind, and so now he could be included among the men. Why is mention therefore made of his youth? So that each may think again about himself, and how much harm he would have done to the Church, if Christ had not held him in check in good time. And so a rather noteworthy example of both the power and the grace of God shines out in the fact that in a moment He tamed a wild beast when he was at his fiercest, and raised a wretched murderer to honour, when, because of his crime, he had already been plunged almost into hell.

59. *Crying out*. Because he had already wasted enough words on men, he rightly turns to God, and arms himself with prayer to carry the whole issue through to the end. Although we must of necessity have recourse to God's assistance every single moment in the whole course of our warfare, there is greatest need to call upon God in the final conflict, the hardest of all. Luke again brings out how they were really possessed by a heedless fury, because, when they saw the servant of Christ humbly praying, there was nevertheless no abating of their ferocity.

Apart from that a prayer of Stephen composed of two parts is recorded here. In the first part, where he commends his spirit to Christ, he shows the firmness of his faith. In the second where he prays for his enemies he bears witness to his love (*caritatem*) for men. Since the complete perfection of our religion lies in these two directions we have, in the death of Stephen, a rare example of a man dying in a godly and holy way. We can well believe that he used many other words, but they all amounted to this.

Lord Jesus. I have already said that this prayer bore witness to his confidence. And his courage was certainly tremendous, because, seeing the stones, by which he is soon to be buried, already flying about, and hearing cruel curses and insults flung at his head from every direction, he yet rests securely on the grace of Christ. So clearly, the Lord sometimes wishes His servants to be reduced to nothing, as it were, so that their salvation may be all the more marvellous. Let us explain this salvation, not by the mind of the flesh, but by faith. And we see that Stephen does not give himself up to an opinion of the flesh, but, on the contrary, even in the face of annihilation itself, he is confident that he will be saved, and he faces death calmly. For there is little doubt that he was carrying this imprinted on his mind, that 'our life is hid with Christ in God' (Col. 3.3). Therefore, not being anxious about his body any longer, he is content to have placed his soul in the hands of Christ. For he could not have prayed from the heart in the way he did, unless he had forgotten about this present life, and had completely cast aside all concern about it.

As long as we remain in the world, because we are always being set upon by a thousand deaths, it is right for us to commend our spirit into the hands of God every day along with David (Ps. 31.5), so that God may clearly snatch our lives out of all dangers. But when we are called to certain death, we must have recourse to this prayer, that Christ may receive our spirit. For He Himself committed His own spirit into the hands of the Father expressly so that He may keep ours for ever (Luke 23.46). It is an inestimable comfort to know that when our souls leave our bodies they do not wander about haphazardly, but are taken into Christ's safe protection, if only we place them in His hands. This confidence ought to teach us to face death calmly; yes! and what is more, everyone who commits his soul to Christ with a serious attitude of trust must, at the same time, necessarily resign himself to a total obedience to His will.

Finally, this verse clearly testifies that the soul of man is not a vanishing breath, according to the ravings of some madmen, but that it is an essential spirit, and survives this life. Moreover, we are taught from this, that it is right and proper for us to call upon Christ, since all power has been given to Him by the Father, so that all men may give themselves into His protection (*fidem*).

60. *He kneeled down and cried.* This is the second part of his prayer, in which Stephen links his love of men to his faith in Christ. And it is certain that if we desire to be added to those finding salvation in Christ, we ought to adopt this attitude. Stephen is praying for his enemies, mortal enemies indeed; and at the most critical moment, when their cruelty could have roused him to desire revenge, he makes quite clear the kind of good-will he bears towards all the others. We know that Christ enjoins us all to do what Luke tells us Stephen did, but because there is hardly anything more difficult than to forgive injuries so as to wish well to those who want us out of the way, we therefore ought to keep Stephen before our eyes as an example. He certainly *cries with a loud voice*; but he lets out nothing in the presence of men but what God Himself may testify to as being said sincerely and from the heart. Yet he does raise his voice so as not to neglect anything to mitigate the ferocity of his enemies. No result appeared immediately, yet it is certain that he did not pray in vain; and Paul

is clear proof that this sin was not laid against them all. Indeed I shall not say along with Augustine that, if Stephen had not prayed, the Church would have had no Paul, for that is putting it too strongly. All I say is that it is certain, from the fact that God forgave Paul, that Stephen's prayer was not ineffectual.

The question arises how Stephen prays for those whom he had recently said to be rebels against the Holy Spirit, in view of the fact that this appears to be the sin against the Holy Spirit, for which forgiveness is for ever denied. The reply is easy, that what actually applies indiscriminately to many people, is said universally about everybody. Therefore he did not say that the body of the people was rebellious, in such a way that there were no exceptions. Then, I have pointed out above what kind of resistance he condemned there. For it does not follow at once that those who resist Him for a time, are sinning against the Holy Spirit. When he prays God not to *lay this sin to their charge* he means that the guilt may not remain in them.

When he had said this, he fell asleep. This is added so that we may know that he uttered these words as he was breathing his last. That is one proof of his wonderful steadfastness; for the word *sleep* also brings out the peaceful character of his death. Because he uttered this prayer when he was already dying, he was not moved to do so by the hope of procuring his own pardon, thus making him so very anxious to appease his enemies, but only by the hope that they would come to their senses again.

When the word 'sleeping' is used in Scripture for death, it ought to be taken as referring to the body, in case anyone might make the ridiculous assumption, with the uninstructed, that the souls sleep as well.

CHAPTER EIGHT

And there arose on that day a great persecution against the church which was in Jerusalem; and they were all scattered abroad throughout the regions of Judaea and Samaria, except the apostles. And devout men buried Stephen, and made great lamentation over him. But Saul laid waste the church, entering into every house, and haling men and women committed them to prison. They therefore that were scattered abroad went about preaching the word. (1-4)

In this narrative the condition of the godly in this world is first of all shown to us, viz. that they are like sheep destined for the slaughter, as the Psalm puts it (44.22), and especially when the Lord gives freedom of rein to His enemies, so that they can execute the cruelty conceived in their minds. Then we are made to see the effect that persecutions have, viz. that they do not so much break off the progress of the Gospel, but rather become aids in its advancement, according to God's wonderful purpose. For example it was plainly a miracle that the dispersion, which Luke mentions, gathered into the unity of the faith many who had previously been alienated from God. Now let us consider each point in turn.

1. *On that day.* A start was made with Stephen. After that, when their fury had been aroused, it broke out indiscriminately on everybody. For, just like wild beasts, once they have tasted blood the ungodly are more eager than ever in their desire for it, and they are more and more carried away by their murders. For Satan, the father of all cruelty, first deprives them of a sense of humane conduct, once they have been stained by innocent blood, and then raises an insatiable thirst for it in them. That is the source of those violent impulses to cruel slaughter, with the result that once begun they do not cease on their own accord. In addition when the power has been put into their hands to hurt men with impunity, their audacity increases with their very success, so that they rush on all the more uncontrolled. Luke is also indicating that by saying that the persecution was great. Certainly the Church was by no means quiet before, and was not immune from annoyance by the ungodly, but the Lord was sparing His people for a time, so that they might have some respite, but now they began to be harder pressed.

These things must also be applied to our own time. If the fury of our enemies ever seems to be, as it were, lulled to sleep, so that its flames do not leap out far, let us realize that the Lord is having regard to our weakness; but at the same time do not let us suppose that hostilities are over for us for ever, but let us be prepared to face stronger attacks, as suddenly and as often as they may burst upon us. Let us also remember that, if ever the constancy of one man incites the reprobate to cruelty, the blame for the wrong is unjustly put on him. For Luke is not branding Stephen with disgrace when he records that he was the occasion of the Church being troubled more severely than usual, but rather he regards him as praiseworthy, because as the fighter for the standard, he inspired the rest by his example to fight bravely.

When he calls it *the Church at Jerusalem* he does not mean there were also churches in other places, but he is making a transition for himself to the events that followed after that. For when this was the only body of believers in the world, it was broken in pieces by flight; but immediately more churches sprang up from the mutilated and scattered members. So the Body of Christ was spread far and wide, whereas it had previously been shut up within the walls of Jerusalem.

They were all scattered abroad. It is certain that they were not all scattered. But Scripture uses the universal term for our expressions 'far and wide' or 'everywhere'. The point is that danger did not exist just for a certain few, because the cruelty of their enemies raged through the whole Church. Many often flee in different directions at the slightest rumour, because they are faint-hearted; but there is quite a different reason for the flight of the people here. For they do not make a bid for flight rashly and in consternation, but because they were seeing that the fury of the ungodly could not be brought to an end in any other way.

Now he says, not only that they were scattered throughout different places in Judaea, but that they came right into *Samaria*. So the *middle wall*, that was separating the Jews from the Gentiles, began to be demolished (Eph. 2.14). For the conversion of Samaria was like the firstfruits of the calling of the Gentiles. For although circumcision was common to them and the people of God, yet we know that there was a great difference between them. And that was not without good reason, since Christ states that in Samaria there was nothing but a counterfeit worship of God, because it was only a pale imitation. God therefore opened a door for the Gospel at this time, so that when the sceptre of Christ was banished from Jerusalem it might reach even to the Gentiles. He does not include the apostles in this number, not because they were beyond common danger, but because it is the duty of the good pastor to intercept raiding wolves for the safety of the flock.

But it can be asked why, since they had the commandment to

spread the Gospel throughout the world, they remained at Jerusalem, even when they were being driven out of it by force of arms? I reply that, since Christ commanded them to begin from Jerusalem, they stayed there until they might know with certainty that He was their Guide, bringing them out elsewhere by His hand. And we see how timidly they proceeded with the publishing of the Gospel, and this was not because they were shrinking from the task laid upon them, but because they were bewildered by the newness and unfamiliarity of it. Therefore when they see that the Gospel is resisted so powerfully at Jerusalem, they do not venture to transfer themselves elsewhere, until they have broken through that first great mass of difficulties. They are certainly not looking to their own ease, or safety, or convenience by staying there, for they maintain a burdensome charge, they are being continually involved in many different crises, they are harassed by the greatest vexations; accordingly there is no doubt of their intention to carry out their roles. And especially is it a clear proof of undaunted steadfastness that they remain when all the rest are taking flight. If anyone objects that they could have divided and apportioned provinces among themselves, so that they would not all be at work in the one place, I reply that Jerusalem alone provided work enough for them all. To sum up, Luke mentions it as a praiseworthy thing that they did not follow the others into voluntary exile in order to avoid persecution.

But yet he does not condemn the flight of those who did not have the same responsibility (*quorum liberior fuit conditio*). For the apostles were reflecting upon what was peculiar to their calling, viz. to stick to their post when wolves were attacking the sheepfold. Tertullian and those like him were far too severe in making no exception to their denial of the right to flee from fear of persecution. Augustine is better, in permitting flight so long as churches are not surrendered to their enemies because of the desertion of their pastors. That is certainly a very good compromise, because he is neither being too indulgent to the timidity of the flesh, nor rashly rushing to their death, those who have a chance of saving their lives. Anyone who cares may read the 180th Epistle to Honoratus.

To return to the apostles, if they had been dispersed by fear of persecution right at the very beginning, who would not have rightly said that they were hirelings? How harmful and disgraceful would the desertion of their post have been at that moment? Would it not have a great effect in breaking everybody's spirit? How much damage would the example of it have caused to posterity? Indeed it will sometimes happen that a pastor may also be permitted to flee; that is, if he alone is being attacked, and if there is no fear of the church being scattered because of his absence. But if the struggle involves him and the flock in common, he is deserting his office treacherously, if he does not hold on right to the bitter end. There is greater freedom for private individuals.

2. *They took care of Stephen.* Luke shows that the minds of godly men were not so prostrated in the heat of persecutions as not to burn with zeal for devoting themselves to the duties of godliness. Burial seems to be a matter of trifling consequence; but rather than neglect it they run the risk of their lives with open eyes. But just as the circumstances of the time bear witness to their brave contempt of death, so, on the other hand, we also gather from them that they really had a strong and necessary reason for being so anxious about this matter. For it was of the greatest importance for exercising their faith, that the body of the holy martyr, in whom Christ had achieved a splendid triumph for the glory of His Gospel, should not be left lying in the open, exposed to wild beasts. For they could not truly live to Christ, if they were not prepared to be included in the fellowship of death along with Stephen. Therefore their zeal in burying the martyr was practice for them in the invincible steadfastness that comes from openly professing their faith. So they were not busy with something that was useless, in order to provoke their opponents with unconsidered zeal. Nevertheless there is little doubt that the general reason, which ought to be valid among the godly always and everywhere, also carried weight with them. For the rite of burial looks to the resurrection hope, since God ordained it for this purpose from the beginning of the world. Accordingly it was always regarded as a monstrous barbarity to leave bodies unburied deliberately. Unenlightened men did not know why they should consider the right of burial to be such a sacred thing; but to us the purpose is certainly not unknown, viz. that those still living may know that bodies are committed to the earth as to a prison, until they are raised up from it. It is evident from that, that this ceremony is of value to the living rather than to the dead. And yet it is also part of our human nature to bestow due honour on the bodies, to which we know blessed immortality has been promised.

They made great lamentation. Luke is also commending the profession of their godliness and faith in their lamentation. For a sad and unfortunate event has the effect on very many people of making them abandon causes that had previously given them pleasure. On the contrary those men show by their mourning, that they are not terrorized by the death of Stephen so as not to persist in giving their backing to the cause; at the same time they are reflecting how great a loss the Church of God sustained in the death of one man.

Now that mad philosophy must be repudiated which requires men to be utterly impassive (*stupidos*) in order to be wise. The Stoics of long ago must have been devoid of common-sense for they used to keep all feelings away from a man. Today there are certain fanatics who would gladly introduce the same mad ideas into the Church. And yet while they demand a heart of iron from others, there is none softer or more effeminate than they. They cannot bear a single tear in others; but if a thing turns out for them differently from their desires, there is no limit to their wailing. In this way God punishes their conceitedness in fun, if I may put it so, since He makes it a laughing-stock even for boys. Let us indeed know that the feelings, which God has placed in human nature, are in themselves no more corrupt than the Author Himself; but that they must be appraised first in relation to the occasion, and secondly as to whether they preserve the limit of moderation. Certainly the man who denies that we must rejoice in the gifts of God is more like a stock or stone than a man. Therefore sorrow will be no less permitted when they are taken away. And not to pass beyond the present verse, Paul does not altogether forbid believers to mourn when one of their number is taken from them by death (I Thess. 4.13), but he wishes a difference to exist between them and unbelievers; because hope ought to be a comfort to them, and a remedy for impatience. For the actual origin of death is quite rightly a cause of sorrow to us, but because we know that life is restored in Christ, we have what is sufficient to allay our grief. Similarly, when we lament that the Church is bereft of remarkable and outstanding men, there are good grounds for sorrow; but such consolation as may correct excess must be sought.

3. *But Saul.* Two things are to be noted here; how great the savagery of their enemies was; and how wonderful the goodness of God was in honouring Paul by making a pastor out of such a cruel wolf. For that passion for destruction, with which he was seething, seemed to cut off all hope. His later conversion was therefore all the more remarkable. And there is no doubt that, after he had been plotting along with other ungodly men for the death of Stephen, the penalty inflicted on him by God was that he should be the leader in the campaign of cruelty. For God often punishes sins more severely in the elect than in the reprobate.

4. *They therefore that were scattered.* Luke also recounts here that it happened by the incredible providence of God that the dispersion of believers led many into the unity of the faith. This is God's normal way of bringing light out of darkness, and life out of death. For the sound of the Gospel, which was being heard only in one place, is now resounding everywhere. At the same time we are warned by this

example that we must not give in to persecutions, but that we must rather discipline ourselves to bravery. For when the faithful flee from Jerusalem they are not broken by exile and the distresses of the moment, or by any fear of the future, so that they degenerate into cowardice or inactivity, but they are just as keen to proclaim Christ, as if they had never gone through any trouble. Yes, and Luke seems to indicate that they led a wandering life, with frequent changes of lodgings. Therefore if we wish to be counted as brethren of these men, let us eagerly urge ourselves on, so that no bitterness of the Cross or fear may discourage us from continuing to make open confession of our faith, and so that we may never grow weary of promoting the teaching of Christ. For it is absurd that exile and flights, which are the first things to experience in martyrdom, should make us dumb and lifeless.

And Philip went down to the city of Samaria, and proclaimed unto them the Christ. And the multitudes gave heed with one accord unto the things that were spoken by Philip, when they heard, and saw the signs which he did. For from many of those which had unclean spirits, they came out, crying with a loud voice: and many that were palsied, and that were lame, were healed. And there was much joy in that city.

But there was a certain man, Simon by name, which beforetime in the city used sorcery, and amazed the people of Samaria, giving out that himself was some great one: to whom they all gave heed, from the least to the greatest, saying, This man is that power of God which is called Great. And they gave heed to him, because that of long time he had amazed them with his sorceries. But when they believed Philip preaching good tidings concerning the kingdom of God and the name of Jesus Christ, they were baptized, both men and women. And Simon also himself believed: and being baptized, he continued with Philip; and beholding signs and great miracles wrought, he was amazed. (5-13)

5. Luke has said that they were preaching the Word of God everywhere, but he now makes special mention of Philip, not only because his preaching was more effectual and fruitful than that of the others, but also because memorable events (*historiae*) followed, which he will add next.

He puts the *city of Samaria* for the city, Samaria, which was destroyed by Hyrcanus, and having been restored by Herod, was called Sebaste. Reference should be made to Josephus, *Antiquities*, Books 13 and 15.

When he says that Christ was *proclaimed* by Philip, he means that the whole substance of the Gospel is comprehended in Christ. The other expression which he employs a little later on (v. 12) is more complete indeed, yet it means the same thing. He unites the Kingdom of God with the name of Christ. But because it is through Christ that we obtain the blessing that God reigns in us, and that we lead a heavenly life, having been renewed in spiritual righteousness, and having died to the world, therefore the preaching of Christ also embraces this function within itself. But it amounts to this, that Christ restores a ruined world by His grace, and that happens when He reconciles us to the Father, and, secondly, that, when He regenerates us by His Spirit, and Satan has been put to flight, the Kingdom of God is set up in us. Further, since he previously reported that the apostles did not set foot outside Jerusalem, it is probable that it is one of the seven deacons, whose daughters also used to prophesy, who is being described here. (Cf. Acts 21.9.)

6. *And they gave heed.* Luke records how the Samaritans embraced the teaching of Philip. For he says that they heard, and that rather whetted their appetite. Another stimulus was added from miracles; so that finally their attention followed. This is the proper progress to faith. For how would those, who reject teaching they have not yet heard, ever come to faith, when it is born from hearing? (cf. Rom. 10.14). Therefore the fact that they showed themselves willing to hear was the first step towards respect and attention. And so it is no wonder if faith is so rare, almost non-existent indeed, in the world today. For how many deign to listen to God speaking? So what happens is that the majority reject the truth of which they know nothing, and which they have not had even the slightest taste. Finally, as hearing is the beginning of faith (*fidei exordium est auditus*), so it would not be sufficient in itself, if the majesty of the teaching (*doctrinae maiestas*) did not influence our souls at the same time. And certainly everyone who reflects upon the fact that he has to do with God, cannot possibly be contemptuous when he hears Him speaking. And the teaching itself that is contained in His Word acquires authority for itself; so attention will spring spontaneously from hearing (*sponte ex auditu*). As far as the miracles are concerned we know that they have a twofold use, to prepare us to hear the Gospel, and to confirm us in believing it.

The adverb 'unanimously' (*unanimiter*), can be joined just as well to hearing as to attention. I myself prefer the latter, that they were unanimously attentive. Now Luke commends the force and effectiveness of the preaching in the fact that a great number of men was suddenly made to listen seriously with common consent.

7. *Unclean spirits.* He briefly mentions a few kinds, so that we might know by what type of miracles the Samaritans were induced to ascribe authority to Philip. The cry, which the unclean spirits gave out, was a sign of their opposition. Therefore it was of no small value

in demonstrating the power of Christ, that he restrained the devils by his authority, stubbornly resisting though they were.

8. The *joy* which he mentions is a fruit of faith. For when we realize that God is gracious to us, there can be no other possible result, but that our hearts are transported with joy incomparable, joy such as surpasses all understanding (Phil. 4.7).

9. *A certain man, Simon by name.* This was such an obstacle, that it could appear as if the way was barred for the Gospel among the Samaritans. For the minds of all were bewitched by Simon's tricks; and this bemusing had increased in strength because of a long lapse of time already. Moreover experience does teach just how difficult it is to strip men's minds of error, which has taken root over a long period of time, and to call back those who have already become set in their ways, to soundness of mind. Superstition was making them more obstinate in their error, because they were regarding Simon, not only as if he were a prophet of God, but as if he were the Spirit Himself.

10, 11. For the description *Great Power* had this tendency, that no matter how divine anything might be in itself (*alioqui*), this 'greatness' would eclipse it and render it worthless. Therefore the power of Christ shines out more clearly in the fact that Philip broke through this obstacle. But Luke amplifies this, when he says that they were all *amazed, from the least to the greatest.* For since men of all classes were being deluded, and, in particular, because this was no ordinary imposture, pray what access was there for the Gospel? For wonderment took possession of their wits. But as well as it being evident from this how powerful the truth is, at the same time an example of perseverance is also set before us in Philip. For although he does not see a way, he yet undertakes the Lord's work with unbroken spirit, looking for such success as He wishes to give. And all that we have to do is to attempt undauntingly whatever God commands us, even when it seems that our efforts will be ineffectual. Moreover let us realize that such bewitchment by Satan as befell the Samaritans is the common punishment for faithlessness. All men, it is true, are not misled by the tricks of magicians, for there are not Simons everywhere to deceive people with such impostures; but, as I understand it, it is no extraordinary or unusual thing if Satan makes fools of people in various ways in the dark, for all who are not controlled by the Light of God are liable to become the prey of all errors. Besides, when Luke says that all of them, without distinction, were carried away, we are warned that neither sharpness of wits, nor whatever reason or wisdom we have, is enough to guard against the subtlety of Satan. And we certainly see how those, whom the world regarded as preeminently acute, were involved in silly and stupid errors.

The Great Power of God. Satan therefore had abused the name of God to deceive, and far from being of value as an excuse, that is the most pestilential kind of deception. It has already been said that Simon arrogated to himself the title of God's peculiar power, so that he might suppress all that was divine elsewhere, just as the sun dims all the stars by its own light. This was an impious and infamous profanation of the name of God. But we read of nothing done here, that is not done daily still. For there is nothing easier to men than to transfer to Satan what belongs to God. A pretence is made of religion indeed; but what benefit did the Samaritans get from this pretext? Therefore we are blessed when God discloses His power to us in Christ, and shows that it must not be sought elsewhere, and when He uncovers the frauds and impostures of Satan, which are to be shunned, so that He may retain us in His own control.

12. *When they had believed.* As I have said it is a miracle that men who were utterly deprived of their senses by Simon's illusions listened to Philip, that men, who were dull and stupid, became sharers of the heavenly wisdom. In this way they were brought out of hell into heaven, so to speak. The fact that baptism came after faith is in accordance with Christ's institution with regard to strangers (Mark 16.16). For they ought to have been ingrafted into the body of the Church by faith before receiving the sign. But the Anabaptists are being quite absurd in trying to prove from these verses that infants must be kept back from baptism. Men and women could not have been baptized without making open confession of their faith; but they were admitted to baptism on this condition, that their families were consecrated to God at the same time. For the covenant is in these terms, 'I will be thy God and the God of thy seed' (Gen. 17.7).

13. *Simon also himself.* The man who had infatuated the whole city with his tricks receives the truth of God along with others. The man who had boasted himself to be the supreme power of God submits himself to Christ. However he was enlightened with knowledge of the Gospel, not so much for the sake of himself alone, as for the sake of the whole nation, so that the stumbling-block, which could have kept back the ignorant, might be removed. And Luke's later statement that he was amazed at the signs, has a bearing on this. For the Lord wished to triumph over the man whom the Samaritans regarded as a demigod, and that does happen when his empty boasting is driven out, and he is forced to glorify the true miracles. For he does not surrender himself to Christ with love (*affectu*) that is sincere and from the heart; otherwise his perverse ambition and his ungodly and common estimate of the gifts of the Spirit would not be breaking out at once. Yet I do not agree with many who think that he only made

a pretence of faith, since he did not believe. Luke clearly asserts that he did believe, and a reason is added, that he was moved with admiration. How therefore does he betray himself as a hypocrite a little later? I reply that there is some middle position between faith and mere pretence. The Epicureans and Lucianists profess that they believe, when they are nevertheless laughing inwardly, when the hope of eternal life is a fairy-tale to them, when, finally, they have no more piety than dogs or pigs. But there are many who, although they have not been regenerated by the Spirit of adoption, and do not yield themselves to God with genuine love from the heart, have yet been conquered by the power of the Word, and not only acknowledge the truth of what is taught, but are touched by fear of God so that they accept the teaching. For they perceive that they must listen to God, who is both the Author of salvation, and the Judge of the world. Therefore they are not making pretence to a non-existent faith in the eyes of men, but they think that they do believe. And this is the temporary faith which Christ mentions in Mark, chapter 4 (Luke 8.13), viz. when the seed of the Word, which has been received in the mind, is yet quickly choked by various worldly cares or bad desires, so that it never comes to maturity, but on the contrary rather degenerates into a useless weed. Therefore Simon's faith was like that. He feels that the teaching of the Gospel is true and is forced by awareness of his conscience to accept it; but the fundamental thing is lacking, i.e. denial of himself. From that it follows that his mind was involved in pretence, which he soon brings out. But let us realize that his hypocrisy in which he deceived himself, was of that sort, and not that gross hypocrisy in which the Epicureans and their like vaunt themselves, because they do not dare to acknowledge their contempt of God.

He was baptized. It is quite plain from Simon's example that the grace, which is figured in baptism, is not conferred on all men indiscriminately when they are baptized. It is a dogma of the Papists that unless anyone presents the obstacle of mortal sin, all men receive the truth and the effect with the signs. So they attribute a magical potency to the sacraments, as if they are beneficial without faith. But as for ourselves, let us realize that whatever the accompanying promises say is offered to us by the Lord in the sacraments, and is not offered uselessly or to no purpose, provided that, directed by faith in Christ, we seek from Him whatever the sacraments promise. But even although the receiving of baptism was of no use to him at that time, yet if conversion followed afterwards, as some conjecture, the benefit was not terminated, or wiped out. For it often happens that, after a long time, the Spirit of God is at last active, so that the sacraments may begin to realize their efficacy.

He clung to Philip. How difficult it is to pick out hypocrites is apparent from the fact that Philip accepted him. And this is a test of our patience. Thus Demas was a companion of Paul's for a time, but later became a treacherous deserter (II Tim. 4.10). In short we cannot avoid this unfortunate experience of wicked and deceitful men sometimes joining themselves to us. And if ever ungodly men cunningly worm their way in on us, proud critics unjustly charge us, as if we were responsible for all their crimes. Nevertheless we must be strictly on our guard against a facility which often brings the stain of disgrace to the Gospel. And whenever we hear of great men having been deceived we ought to be all the more cautious in our own attitude so as not to admit all sorts without selection. He says that he was amazed by the greatness of the signs, so that we may know that that great power, of which he was boasting, was nothing else than hazy illusions. For it is not simple admiration that is referred to here, but ecstasy that transports a man outside of himself.

Now when the apostles which were at Jerusalem heard that Samaria had received the word of God, they sent unto them Peter and John: who, when they were come down, prayed for them, that they might receive the Holy Ghost: for as yet he was fallen upon none of them: only they had been baptized into the name of the Lord Jesus. Then laid they their hands on them, and they received the Holy Ghost. (14-17)

14. Here Luke is describing the progress of the grace of God among the Samaritans, according to His custom of constantly enriching believers with greater gifts of His Spirit. For we must not think that the apostles formed the plan, of which Luke speaks, except by the inspiration of God Himself, who had already begun His work in Samaria by Philip's agency. But He uses His instruments in different ways for different aspects of His work according to His will. By Philip's work He had brought them to faith. He now appoints Peter and John as ministers to confer the Spirit. So He clearly fosters the unity of His Church, when they stretch out their hands to one another, and when He in turn unites not only men, but also whole churches, with each other. He could indeed have completed through Philip the work that He had begun, but so that the Samaritans might learn to cultivate brotherly union with the first church conscientiously, He wished to bind them with this as if with a chain; secondly, He wished to honour with this privilege the apostles, to whom He had given the commandment to publish the Gospel all over the world (Mark 16.15), so that they might all grow closer together into the one faith of the Gospel. And we know that, since the Jews and the Samaritans were for long different from each other in characters and customs, there was, besides,

the danger, when they were so divided, of their tearing Christ apart, or at least of forming a new and separate church for themselves.

At the same time we see how eager the apostles were to be solicitous in helping the brethren. For they do not wait until they are asked, but voluntarily undertake this charge. Certainly the apostles do not do this with distrust, as if they were suspecting Philip of discharging his duties with less skill than was proper; but they offer help to him in his work; and Peter and John come to be not only fellow-labourers but also to give their approval to the labours. Again, Philip does not complain that he is being disparaged in any way because others put the finishing touch to the building that he has begun, but they courteously exert their efforts for each other in common good faith. And without a doubt it is ambition alone that closes the door on holy sharing. We can infer from Luke's statement that Peter was sent by the others, that he did not exercise the supreme power over his colleagues, but was pre-eminent among them in such a way that he was still subject to and obedient to the body.

Who were at Jerusalem. This can have two meanings; either that all the apostles were then at Jerusalem, or that some had been left behind there when the others had departed hither and thither. And I rather favour the latter; for it is probable that they agreed among themselves that some would engage in various embassies as the occasion presented itself, and that the other part would remain at Jerusalem as though at headquarters. It is possible also that after each one had been on his particular expedition for some time, they were in the habit of meeting together there. It is quite certain that the time, during which they were at Jerusalem, was not spent sitting idle, and, secondly, that they were not tied, as it were, to the nest, since Christ had ordered them to travel over the world (Mark 16.15).

15. *They prayed.* There is no doubt that they first carried out the function of teachers, for we know that they were not dumb actors, but Luke passes over in silence what they and Philip had in common, and only mentions the new thing their coming brought to the Samaritans, viz. that now at last the Holy Spirit was bestowed upon them.

16. But a question arises here. For he says that they were only baptized into the name of Christ, and that therefore they were not yet sharers of the Spirit. Now baptism must either be an empty thing, devoid of all power and grace, or it has from the Holy Spirit whatever efficacy it does possess. In baptism we are washed from our sins, but Paul teaches that our washing is the work of the Holy Spirit (Titus 3.5). The water of baptism is the sign of the blood of Christ, but Peter advises that it is the Spirit by whom we are washed in the blood of Christ (I Pet. 1.2). In baptism our old man is crucified, so that we

may be raised up into newness of life (Rom. 6.6). But what is the source of all this except the sanctification of the Spirit? In short, nothing will be left to baptism if it is separated from the Spirit. Therefore it is not to be denied that the Samaritans, who really had put on Christ in baptism, were also clothed with His Spirit.

And certainly Luke is not speaking here about the general grace of the Spirit, by which God regenerates us to be His own sons, but about those special gifts, with which the Lord wished some to be endowed in the first days of the Gospel, for the bestowing of honour on the Kingdom of Christ. It is in this sense that John's words (7.39) ought to be understood, that the Spirit was not yet given to the disciples, since Christ was still active in the world. Not that they were completely without the Spirit for of course they had received from Him both faith and a devout desire to follow Christ; but that they were not yet rich in the extraordinary gifts in which the glory of the Kingdom of Christ later shone more completely. To sum up, since the Samaritans had the Spirit of adoption conferred on them already, the extraordinary graces of the Spirit are added as a culmination. In these God for a time showed to His Church something like the visible presence of His Spirit (*quasi visibilem spiritus sui praesentiam*), in order to establish for ever the authority of His Gospel, and at the same time to testify that the Spirit will always be the Governor and Director of the faithful.

Only they had been baptized. This ought not to be taken as a contemptuous statement about baptism; but Luke understands that all that was given them at that time was the general grace of adoption and regeneration, which is offered to all the godly in baptism. It was indeed an extraordinary thing that the gifts of the Spirit, that would add lustre to the Kingdom of Christ and the glory of the Gospel, were conferred on some of them. For the value of them was that each one would benefit the Church according to the measure of his own ability. We must pay attention to this because, when the Papists wish to extol their fictitious confirmation, they do not hesitate to burst out into this sacrilegious assertion, that those, who have not yet had the laying on of hands, are half-Christians. This is not to be tolerated now, because they have made a permanent principle in the Church, out of what was a temporary sign, as if the Holy Spirit was at their disposal (*illis ad manum*). We know that it is a thoroughly shameful mockery when the testimony and pledge of the grace of God is displayed in vain, without the reality itself; but they themselves are also forced to acknowledge that the Church was furnished with those gifts only for a time. From that it follows that the laying on of hands, which the apostles used, came to an end when the purpose of it was served.

I omit their addition of oil to the laying on of hands; but, as I have already said, it was exceedingly high-handed to impose a perpetual law on the Church, that there should be a general sacrament of something that the apostles used in a special way (Mark 6.13), so that the sign would last forever, after the reality itself was no more. Indeed a detestable blasphemy has been added, because they said that only sins are forgiven by baptism, and that the Spirit of regeneration is bestowed by means of that rotten oil, which they have dared to introduce without the Word of God. Scripture testifies that we put on Christ in baptism, and are ingrafted into His Body, so that our old man is crucified, and we are renewed in righteousness. Those sacrilegious robbers have transferred the spoils taken from baptism to the misleading masquerade of their own sacrament. And this was not the fabrication of one man, but the decree of one Council, about which they babble daily in all their schools.

17. *When they had laid on hands.* The laying on of hands follows prayers, and in this way they show that the grace of the Spirit, which they humbly ask from another, is not part and parcel of the external ceremony. Yet in acknowledging God as the source, they do not neglect the ceremony, which had been entrusted to them by God, and, because they do not employ it casually, the effect is tied to it at the same time. The benefit and efficacy of signs is that God is at work in them, and yet remains the one giver of grace, and the judge, by virtue of His own right, of how it should be dispensed. But let us remember that the laying on of hands was God's instrument, by which He conferred the visible grace of the Spirit on His own at the appropriate time; and that since the Church has in fact been deprived of such gifts this act is merely an empty form.

Now when Simon saw that through the laying on of the apostles' hands the Holy Ghost was given, he offered them money, saying, Give me also this power, that on whomsoever I lay my hands, he may receive the Holy Ghost. But Peter said unto him, Thy silver perish with thee, because thou hast thought to obtain the gift of God with money. Thou hast neither part nor lot in this matter: for thy heart is not right before God. Repent therefore of this thy wickedness, and pray the Lord, if perhaps the thought of thy heart shall be forgiven thee. For I see that thou art in the gall of bitterness and in the bond of iniquity. And Simon answered and said, Pray ye for me to the Lord, that none of the things which ye have spoken come upon me.

They therefore, when they had testified and spoken the word of the Lord, returned to Jerusalem, and preached the gospel to many villages of the Samaritans. (18-25)

18. *Now when Simon saw.* Simon's hypocrisy is laid bare now. Not

that there had been any pretence about his believing before, for having been convicted he surrendered himself to Christ in earnest. Similarly many yield to the Gospel so as not to carry on war with God, but at the same time they remain as they were, when, in fact, denial of ourselves ought to follow true faith. Indeed it is to mix up Christ with Satan, when teaching does not penetrate right to the hidden affections of the heart, but inward impurity lies there as if buried. Therefore God now removes that pretence in Simon, so that by professing the name of Christ he might not further deceive others as well as himself. For ambition, which was hidden, now reveals itself, in his desire to be equal to the apostles. There is one fault already; another certainly is that he supposes that the grace of God is for sale, and wishes to prostitute it for gain. It is apparent from that that here is a worldly man, who has not the slightest inkling of the first principles of true religion, for he is not affected by any concern for the glory of God, and, what is more, he does not consider what it means to be a minister of God. As he had previously made money out of his magic, so he thought that it would be profitable for himself if he were to confer the graces of the Spirit. For there is no doubt that what he was after was riches and glory in the eyes of the world. At the same time he does grave injustice to God, in that he thought that this heavenly power was no different from his magic enchantments. We now know briefly what Simon's sins were, and how many there were; he neither acknowledges nor honours the power of Christ in the gifts of the Spirit; he does not perceive that the apostles were furnished with heavenly power in order to make the glory of Christ clear by their own ministry; his own ambition urges him on and takes possession of him, so that he desires to push God into the background and put himself in the forefront, and to make the world subject to himself; he wishes to buy the Holy Spirit as if a price could be put on Him.

20. *Peter answered.* Peter repulses him sharply here, and not being content with a rebuke, he adds an awful curse, that Simon may perish along with his money. However he does not so much call down destruction on him as declare that the just punishment of God threatens him closely, in order to strike him with terror. In a word he shows what he deserved, because he subjected the Spirit of God to unseemly trafficking. It is as if he said, 'You deserve to perish along with your money, seeing that you inflict such an insult on the Spirit of God.' For it will be easily understood from what follows that Peter desired Simon's salvation rather than his destruction. But as though assuming the role of a judge, he pronounces what punishment Simon's irreverence deserves; and he had to be indicted with such vehemence,

so that he might realize the enormity of his crime. He has the same purpose in view when he consigns his money to destruction. For he means that it was, so to speak, corrupted and polluted by the contagion of the crime, because it had been put to such a nefarious use. And certainly the destruction of the whole world is to be preferred rather than that things, worthless in themselves, should obscure the glory of God.

Finally, when he curses a sacrilegious man like this, he is not looking so much to the person as to what he has done. For we ought to be incensed against men's offences in such a way that we reach after the men themselves with mercy. The sentences of God are like that, for they appoint to destruction adulterers, thieves, drunkards and rogues (I Cor. 6.9, 10; Eph. 5.5). Indeed, in so far as they are men, they do not cut off hope of salvation, but they are made to apply only to their present state, and they declare what kind of end awaits them if they stubbornly persist.

21. *Thou hast neither part.* Some make a different connexion in the speech, that Simon has no share in grace, because he evaluates it by money. But the other reading, which I have followed, is more usual, viz. that that explanation is joined to the phrase before it. And it certainly gives a better connexion to say, 'Your money perish with you, since you suppose that the inestimable gift of the Spirit can be balanced with it.' Where the Vulgate had put, 'in this word',[1] Erasmus has rendered it, more appropriately, 'in this matter'. For Peter means that there is no room in the whole of that administration of theirs for a sacrilegious man who commercializes it in impious fashion.

Furthermore, the Papists and the old theologians have discussed *simony* at length, but what the Papists call simony has nothing to do with what Simon did. Simon wished to buy the grace of the Spirit with money; the Papists apply the evil practice of simony to their vacant livings. Yet I am not saying this by way of extenuating the shameful things that are rampant in the Papacy today in the buying and selling of priestly offices. This offence is now disgraceful enough in itself, because they are carrying on such a trade in the Church of God. But at the same time the proper definition of simony must be insisted on, viz. that it is a wicked trafficking in the gifts of the Spirit, or some other similar thing, when anyone may abuse them for ambition or other corrupt purposes. Nevertheless I do admit that all who aspire by bad means to the government of the Church are imitators of Simon, and we see this being done today on all sides without any shame, as if they had every right to do so; and following this method

[1] i.e. The Gospel. Greek, ἐν τῷ λόγῳ τούτῳ. Vulg., *in sermone isto*. Calvin, with Erasmus, *in ratione hac*. Tr.

there is scarcely a priest to be found in the whole Papacy, who is not openly a simoniac, seeing that no one can break into their midst unless he makes his way in by indirect means. Although we must confess what, to our great shame, children see, that it rages just as freely among some pseudo-evangelicals.

But so that we may be unsullied by Simon's contagion let us remember, first of all, that the gifts of the Spirit are not acquired by money, but are conferred by the pure gratuitous kindness of God, and that for the edification of the Church, i.e. that each may strive to help his brethren according to the limit of his ability; that each one may unassumingly apply the gift, that he has received, for the common benefit of the Church; and that the superiority of no individual may prevent Christ alone standing out above them all.

However, it could appear surprising that Peter excludes Simon from participation in the Spirit, as far as special gifts are concerned, because his *heart is not right before God.* For the perversity of Judas did not prevent him from being strong in the gifts of the Spirit; and the gifts of the Spirit would not have been so spoiled among the Corinthians, if their hearts had been right in the sight of God (I Cor. 14). Therefore the reason given by Peter does not seem to be enough, because many whose hearts are unclean very often excel in the gifts of the Spirit. But, in the first place, there is nothing absurd, if God also gives such graces to men who are unworthy of them. Secondly, Peter is not laying down a general rule here, but, because the sharing of the gifts of the Spirit is a peculiar feature of the Church, he pronounces Simon, who does not belong to Christ, unworthy to share in the same graces with the faithful, as one of the members of God's household. In addition reproach had been cast on those gifts, which he is now denied.

22. *Repent therefore.* In urging him to repent and pray, he is leaving the hope of forgiveness open to him. For the only man who will be moved by any feeling of repentance is the one who is confident that God will deal favourably with him. On the other hand hopelessness will always rush men headlong into presumption. Besides, Scripture teaches that God is only properly invoked by faith. We therefore see that after Peter had cast Simon down with words like fearful thunderbolts, he now raises him up again into the assurance of salvation; and yet Simon's sin was no trivial one. Of course, if it is at all possible, we have to drag men out of hell itself. Accordingly, until even all the vicious give clear evidence of being reprobate, not one of them is to be handled so severely that the forgiveness of sins is not made plain to him at the same time. Yes, indeed, and when dealing with those for whom a sharper rebuke is appropriate because of their hardness and obstinacy, it is nevertheless proper to cast them down with one hand,

so as to lift them up with the other. For the Spirit of God does not permit us to strike down with an anathema.

But Peter seems to be raising fear and doubt in saying *if perhaps* (*si forte*). And the Papists strive to prove from this and similar verses that prayer must be made with anxious and doubtful minds, because men may be rash and assure themselves that their prayers will undoubtedly have a happy outcome for them. But there is a simple solution. For the expression εἰ ἄρα, *if perhaps*, amounts to saying, whether (*si qua*) God may forgive you. Peter certainly uses it, not to leave Simon's mind in perplexity, but the better to urge him on to fervent prayer. For difficulty is itself of no little value for stimulating us, whereas, when a thing seems to be within our grasp, we are far too indifferent and lazy. Therefore Peter does not inspire Simon with terror so as to drive out of his heart the confidence of obtaining forgiveness, or to make him anxious. But he assures him of hope, if he were to ask humbly and from the heart; and he reminds him that forgiveness is difficult because of the seriousness of his offence, only in order to stir up his ardour. For it is necessary for faith to be our guiding light in our approach to God, yes, and to be the source of prayer.

23. *In the gall of bitterness.* Peter again gives a stern rebuke to Simon, and fills him with despair by the judgment of God. For if he had not been forced to examine himself he would never have been seriously converted to God. For there is nothing more fatal for people in confusion than for us to flatter them, or only give a slight scratch to the surface of their skin, when they should be wounded instead. Therefore until the sinner will have experienced genuine sorrow, and distress from a sense of his sin, severity like this must be shown, in order to wound his mind; otherwise a putrid ulcer will be fostered within, and it will gradually destroy the man himself. However we must always preserve that moderation, so that, as far as we can, we are concerned for the salvation of men.

Furthermore, there are two choice metaphors in Peter's statement, one of which seems to be taken from Moses, where he commands us not to have a root producing gall and wormwood (Deut. 29.18). By this expression is meant the inward wickedness of the heart, when the poison of ungodliness has been conceived in it, so that once it is infected by that, it can bring forth nothing but bitterness. *The bond of iniquity* has the same import, viz. when the whole heart is kept tightly in Satan's grasp. For it will often occur that men, who are otherwise pious, may break out into evil deeds, and yet they will remain uncorrupted in their innermost hearts. We know that hypocrisy is innate in human nature, but when the Spirit of God shines, we are not so blind in our sins, as to cherish them within us like a hidden bundle.

Peter therefore means that Simon did not lapse in one respect only, but that the very root of his heart is corrupt and bitter; not only that he fell into Satan's snares in one kind of sin, but that all his senses are held in a tight grip, so that he is totally abandoned to Satan, and, so to speak, the bond-slave of iniquity. At the same time we are warned that the gravity of offences is assessed not so much by the shameful deed that we can see, as by the attitude of the heart.

24. *Simon answered.* We gather from this that he did not so much take Peter's threat to heart, as that he came to realize that his salvation was being sought. And even although Peter was the only one who had spoken, he attributed the speech to them all without distinction, because of their general consent.

Now, the question is raised, what are we to suppose happened to Simon? Scripture takes us no further than conjecture. He yields to reproof, is touched by a sense of sin, fears the judgment of God, and then turns to the mercy of God, and commends himself to the prayers of the Church. Since these are certainly not the minimum signs of repentance, we are therefore entitled to conjecture that he did repent. And yet the Fathers unanimously record that later on he was a serious adversary to Peter, and argued with him for three days at Rome. A written disputation bearing the name of Clement is also extant, but it contains such disgusting ravings that it is a wonder that Christian ears can bear them. Finally, Augustine tells Januarius about a variety of incredible rumours that were going about Rome in his time in that connexion. Accordingly the safest course is to have nothing to do with uncertain opinions imposed on us, and simply to embrace what is recorded in Scripture. What we read about Simon elsewhere can rightly be regarded with suspicion for many reasons.

25. *But when they had testified.* Luke teaches us by these words that Peter and John came, not only to enrich the Samaritans with the gifts of the Spirit, but, by confirming what Philip had taught, to establish them in the faith they had already received. For the word *testifying* amounts to his saying that it was due to their testimony that complete and genuine authority existed for the Word of God, and that the truth was honoured as something properly attested and authentic. However Luke reminds us at the same time that they were faithful witnesses of God, when he adds that they made known the Word of God. The chief feature of the apostles' teaching was that they were faithfully proclaiming what they had learnt from the Lord, and not what they or other people made up.

He says that they did this not only in one city but also in the villages. We therefore see that they were so fired to promote the glory of Christ, that wherever they came they had Him on their lips. So the seed of life began to be scattered from one city throughout the whole region.

But an angel of the Lord spake unto Philip, saying, Arise, and go toward the south unto the way that goeth down from Jerusalem unto Gaza: the same is desert. And he arose and went: and behold, a man of Ethiopia, a eunuch of great authority under Candace, queen of the Ethiopians, who was over all her treasure, who had come to Jerusalem for to worship; and he was returning and sitting in his chariot, and was reading the prophet Isaiah. And the Spirit said unto Philip, Go near, and join thyself to this chariot. And Philip ran to him, and heard him reading Isaiah the prophet, and said, Understandest thou what thou readest? And he said, How can I, except some one shall guide me? And he besought Philip to come up and sit with him. (26-31)

26. *An angel of the Lord.* Luke passes on to a different episode, viz. how the Gospel reached the Ethiopians. For although he reports the conversion of only one man to the faith of Christ, yet because he had great authority and power in the whole kingdom, his faith could breathe its fragrance far and wide. For we know that the Gospel grew from frail beginnings; and the power of the Spirit shone the clearer in the fact that one grain of seed filled a wide region in a short space of time.

In the first place Philip is ordered by the angel to go towards the south; but for what advantage or for what purpose the angel does not reveal. And the Lord is often in the habit of dealing with His own in that way, in order to test their obedience. He shows what He wishes them to do, gives them this or that instruction; but He keeps the outcome concealed and in His own hands. Therefore let us be content with the bare command of God, even if the reason for what He enjoins, or the result of our obedience, is not immediately apparent. For although this is not explicitly stated, yet all the commandments of God contain the tacit promise that, as often as we obey Him, whatever task we undertake can only work out successfully. In addition it ought to be enough for us that our efforts are approved by God, when we undertake nothing rashly and without His command.

If anyone objects that angels do not come down from heaven every day to make plain to us what we have to do, there is an easy answer, that the Word of God gives us an abundance of instruction about what we must do; and whoever inquire of Him and submit themselves to the direction of the Spirit are not destitute of advice. Therefore our own laziness and neglect of prayer are the only things that impede and hinder us from being ready and eager to follow God.

To the way going down to Gaza. There is agreement among all scholars that what is named Azzah (עַזָּה) in Hebrew, is called *Gaza* here. Accordingly Pomponius Mela is mistaken when he says that the name was imposed on the city by Cambyses, king of Persia, because, when he was waging war on the Egyptians, he had his treasure stored up there. It is indeed true that 'gaza' is the Persian word for treasure or wealth; and Luke uses it in this sense a little later,[1] when he says that the eunuch was in charge of Candace's treasure. But because that Hebrew name was in use before the birth of Cambyses, I have no doubt that it was afterwards corrupted, the letter ayin (ע) having been changed into a G,[2] something we are aware of having been done in almost all other instances.

The epithet, *desert*, is added because Alexander the Great laid that old Gaza waste. Those who make Constantine (A.D. 274-323) the builder of the second and new Gaza are refuted by Luke, for, one hundred and fifty years before Constantine, he affirms its existence. But it is possible that he beautified and extended the city that he found already built. Finally all agree that this new city was 'maritime', and about two and a half miles from the old city.

27. *Behold, a man of Ethiopia.* He calls him a man, although he says immediately afterwards that he was a eunuch. But because kings and queens in the East were in the habit of setting eunuchs over their most important affairs, the result was that overseers were called 'eunuchs' indiscriminately, even although they were men.

To go on, now at last the actual event brings home to Philip that he did not submit to God in vain. So anyone who will commit the outcome to God, and will proceed where he commands, will at last learn by experience that whatever is undertaken under His auspices, and by His command, turns out well.

The name, *Candace*, was not the name of one queen only, but just as the name, Caesar, was common to the Roman emperors, so the Ethiopians, according to Pliny, used to call their queens Candaces. It it also relevant to this incident, that the historians recount that it was a kingdom of splendour and wealth, because, from its grandeur and power, it can be all the better gathered just how magnificent were the circumstances and standing of the eunuch. The capital and principal city was Meroe. Secular writers agree with Luke's evidence, for they report that women were accustomed to reign there.

He had come to worship. We gather from this that the name of the true God was widely spread, seeing that He had some worshippers in distant lands. This man must certainly have been openly practising a different way of worship from his own people. For such a great

[1] v. 27. ὃς ἦν ἐπὶ πάσης τῆς γάζης. Tr.

[2] So Tholuck. C.R. has cheth (ח) but this is obviously wrong. Tr.

ruler could not have come to Judaea secretly; and there is no doubt that he brought a great retinue along with him. And indeed it is no wonder that all over the East there were some who were worshipping the true God, because, after the people had been scattered, some fragrance of the pure knowledge of God had been diffused among foreign nations at the same time; and what is more, the exile of the people had been a certain propagation of true piety. And indeed we see that, when the Romans condemned the Jewish religion with cruel edicts, they were yet scarcely able to prevent droves of people transferring to it. These were preludes to the calling of the Gentiles, until Christ, scattering the shadows of the Law by the splendour of His coming, would remove the difference between Jews and Gentiles, and, destroying the dividing wall, would gather together the sons of God everywhere (Eph. 2.4).

The eunuch's coming to Jerusalem in order to worship must not be attributed to superstition. He certainly could have prayed to God in his own country; but this pious man did not wish to neglect the practices which were prescribed to the worshippers of God; and so his intention was not only to nourish his faith privately in the secrecy of his own heart, but also to profess it openly among men. Yet he could not make such a break with his own people without realizing that he would be hateful to many; but the external profession of religion, which he knew God demanded, meant more to him than the esteem of men. Now, if the tiny spark of knowledge of the Law enlightened him to such a great extent, how shameful will it be for us to stifle the full light of the Gospel with perfidious silence? If anyone objects that the sacrifices were abrogated by then, and it was now the time in which God wished to be called upon everywhere, without any distinction as to place, the reply is easy, that those to whom the truth of the Gospel had not yet been revealed were kept in the shadows of the Law without any superstition. For the statement that the Law has been abolished by Christ, as far as ceremonies were concerned, must be understood in this way: where Christ shows Himself openly, those old rites, which were representing Him while He was absent, vanish.

It is credible that the reason why the Lord allowed the eunuch to come to Jerusalem before he sent a teacher to him, was because it was to his advantage still to be prepared by the rudiments of the Law, so that afterwards he would be all the readier and fitter to receive the teaching of the Gospel. But the reason for God not confronting him at Jerusalem with some of the apostles lies in the secrecy of His purpose, unless perhaps he might put greater value on a treasure that is presented to him suddenly, and exceeds his expectations. Or it might have been because it was better for Christ to be set before him after he was removed from the external pomp of the ceremonies, and the sight of the temple, and he sought the way of salvation more freely in peace and quiet.

28. *He was reading Isaiah.* His reading of the prophet shows that the eunuch did not lightly worship a god whom he had conceived for himself according to his own ideas, but the God whom he had come to know from the teaching of the Law. And the proper way to worship God is certainly not to lay hold of bare and empty rites, but to add the Word at the same time; otherwise there will be nothing but haphazardness and confusion. And indeed the form of worship prescribed in the Law does not differ in any other respect from what men make up, except that God shines out in it by His Word. Therefore it is only His disciples who worship God properly, that is, those who have been taught in His school.

But he seems to be wasting his efforts when he reads without any benefit. For he admits that he cannot understand the prophet's meaning unless he is helped by means of some other teacher. I reply, as he was reading the prophet with a desire to learn, so he hoped for some success, and in fact he also realized it. Why then does he say that he cannot understand the passage he is reading? The reason is that he modestly acknowledges his ignorance in the more obscure verses. For there are many things in Isaiah which do not need a long explanation, as when he is inspired about the goodness and power of God, partly to invite men to faith, partly to instruct and encourage them as to a holy life. Therefore nobody will be so raw and ignorant as not to get some benefit out of reading that book, yet perhaps he will hardly understand every tenth verse fully. The eunuch's reading was like that. For since he got such things as were of use for edifying him, even if they were according to his own capacity, his studies were definitely to his advantage. Again, if many things were hidden from him, yet the irksomeness of it did not make him throw the book aside. There is no doubt that this is the way we also must read Scripture; we ought to accept eagerly and with a ready mind those things which are clear, and in which God reveals His mind; but it is proper to pass by those things which are still obscure to us, until a clearer light shines. But if we shall not be wearied by reading, the final result will be that constant use will make us familiar with Scripture.

31. *How can I?* The eunuch is remarkably modest, for not only does he calmly allow himself to be questioned by Philip, a common man, but acknowledges his ignorance, freely and frankly. And there must certainly be very little hope of a man who is swollen-headed with confidence in his own abilities ever proving himself docile.

That is also why the reading of Scripture bears fruit with such a few people today, because scarcely one in a hundred is to be found who gladly submits himself to teaching. For as long as nearly all men feel ashamed by the consciousness of their ignorance (*nescire quod nesciunt*), in his pride each one prefers to nurse his ignorance, rather than appear to be the pupil of other men. Yes, and what is more, the majority superciliously take it upon themselves to instruct others. However, let us remember that the eunuch was so conscious of his ignorance that he was, for all that, one of God's pupils by reading the Scripture. Finally, there is true reverence for Scripture when we acknowledge that there is hidden in it a wisdom which surpasses and escapes all our powers of understanding; yet we do not feel aversion to it for that reason, but, reading diligently, we depend on the revelation of the Spirit, and long for an interpreter to be given to us.

He asked Philip to come up. It is another instance of his modesty, that he sought an interpreter and teacher for himself. He could have rejected Philip out of the haughtiness that is common to the rich; for there was a certain tacit reproach of his ignorance in Philip's words, 'Do you understand what you are reading?' Now, rich men think that they are being insulted, if anyone is rather free in addressing them. They therefore burst out at once in words like, 'What is that to you?', or 'What business have you with me?' But the eunuch quietly entrusts himself to Philip for instruction. We ought to have such an attitude of mind, if we wish to have God as our teacher, whose Spirit rests upon the humble and the quiet (Isa. 66.2).

Now if any of us is diffident about himself, but shows that he is teachable, angels will come down from heaven to teach us, rather than that the Lord allow us to labour in vain. However, following the example of the eunuch, we must make use of all the aids which the Lord sets before us for the understanding of Scripture. Fanatics seek inspirations (ἐνθουσιασμούς) from heaven, and at the same time despise the minister of God, by whose hand they ought to have been ruled. Others, relying on their own penetrating insight, do not deign to hear anybody or to read any commentaries. But God does not wish the aids, which He appoints for us, to be despised, and does not allow contempt of them to go unpunished. And we must keep in mind here, that not only is Scripture given to us, but interpreters and teachers are also added to help us. That is why the Lord chose Philip for the eunuch rather than an angel. For what was the purpose of this roundabout process, where God summons Philip by the voice of an angel, and does not send the angel himself direct, except that He wished us to become accustomed to hearing men? It is certainly no ordinary recommendation of outward preaching, that the voice of God sounds on the lips of men, while the angels keep silence. I shall have more to say about this in chapters 9 and 10.

Now the place of the scripture which he was reading was this,
He was led as a sheep to the slaughter;
And as a lamb before his shearer is dumb,
So he openeth not his mouth:
In his humiliation his judgment was taken away:
His generation who shall declare?
For his life is taken from the earth.
And the eunuch answered Philip, and said, I pray thee, of whom speaketh the prophet this? of himself, or of some other? And Philip opened his mouth, and beginning from this scripture, preached unto him Jesus. (32-35)

32. *The sentence of Scripture.* It is strictly speaking a connected sequence or short passage.

Let us realize that he did not come upon this passage by chance, but it happened by the wonderful providence of God, so that Philip had a theme or basic principle from which the whole substance of Christianity could be suitably drawn out. Therefore, first, matter for thorough instruction is put into his hand by the secret direction of the Spirit, and, secondly, the form is clearly accommodated to the ministry of man.

Now this is a famous prophecy about Christ, one that is memorable above the rest, because in it Isaiah makes the undisguised statement that the way in which the Church will have to be redeemed is this, that the Son of God gains life for men by His death, that He makes Himself a sacrificial victim for the expiation of men's sins, that He is afflicted by the hand of God, and goes down right to hell itself in order to raise us right up into heaven after we have been brought out of destruction. To sum up, this passage clearly discusses how men are reconciled to God, how they obtain righteousness, and how, set free from the tyranny of Satan and the yoke of sin, they reach the Kingdom of God; in a word, the source from which all aspects of salvation are to be sought.

However I shall only expound those things which Luke quotes here, and there are in fact only two sections. In the first he teaches that in order to redeem the Church and restore it to life, Christ must be so crushed that He seems like one to be given up for lost. In the second he asserts that His death will be life-giving, and that out of the depths of hopelessness a unique triumph will emerge. In comparing Christ to a *lamb* that allows itself to be led to the slaughter, and to a *sheep* quietly submitting to shearing, he means that Christ's sacrifice will be voluntary. And the fact that He showed Himself to be obedient was certainly the means of appeasing God. He did indeed speak before Pilate (John 18.34, 36), not in order to save His life however, but rather to offer Himself of His own accord as the sacrificial victim, as He was appointed by the Father, and so call down on Himself the penalty that was waiting for us. The prophet therefore teaches both things, that Christ had of necessity to die to obtain life for us; and that He had to submit to death of His own free will to destroy the wilful disobedience of men by His own obedience. Finally, from this we must derive encouragement to suffer, as Peter does (I Pet. 2.18ff). But that teaching about the faith, which I have touched on, properly has the precedence.

33. *In his humiliation his judgment.*[1] Either the eunuch had a Greek scroll, or Luke has recorded, as he usually does, the reading in use at that time. The prophet says[2] that Christ was taken out of restraint and judgment, and with those words He is celebrating a wonderful victory, which soon followed His degradation. For if He had been overwhelmed by death, nothing could have been hoped for from Him. Therefore, after the prophet has described Him as smitten by the hand of God, and put to death, in order to establish our confidence in Christ, he now ascribes a new role to Him, that He emerges from the abyss of death, the victor, and issues forth from hell itself, the Author of eternal life.

I am well aware that this verse is interpreted in different ways. There are those who understand that He was carried by force from prison to the cross. To others the verb 'to be taken away' (*tolli*) means the same as being reduced to nothing. And the meaning of the Hebrew word לקח (*laqach*) is no less ambiguous than that of the Greek word *αἴρεσθαι*. But if anyone will consider the context more closely he will agree with what I have said, that he is now making a transition from that melancholy and loathsome spectacle, that he had set before us, to the new emergence of unexpected glory. Therefore the Greek translation is not very different in substance from the words of the prophet. For in humiliation or rejection Christ's judgment was taken away (*sublatum est*) just because, when he could have given the appearance of being crushed, the Father defended His cause. In this way 'judgment' will be taken for 'right' as in many other places. But in the Hebrew text it means 'condemnation'. For the prophet says that after Christ has been reduced to extreme straits, like one condemned and desperate, He will be raised up by the hand of the Father. The meaning therefore

[1] Calvin: *in humilitate eius iudicium eius sublatum est.* Greek: *Ἐν τῇ ταπεινώσει ἡ κρίσις αὐτοῦ ἤρθη* agrees with LXX of Isa. 53.8. Tr.

[2] Hebrew of Isa. 53.8: מֵעֹצֶר וּמִמִּשְׁפָּט לֻקָּח. Tr.

is that it was necessary for Christ to be given up to death before the Father would raise Him up into the glory of His kingdom. And this teaching must be carried over to the whole body of the Church, because all the godly must be marvellously raised up by the hand of God, so as not to be devoured by death. But when God appears as the vindicator of His own, not only does He restore them to life, but He procures notable victories for them out of many deaths, just as Christ brought about that glorious victory on the Cross, as the apostle mentions in the second chapter of Colossians.

His generation. After the prophet has celebrated the victorious death of Christ he now goes on to say that His victory will not be for a short time, but one that must extend over the whole range of the years. For the prophet's exclamation implies as much as if he denied that the perpetuity of Christ's Kingdom can be expressed by a human tongue. But interpreters have sadly distorted this verse. The attempt of the Fathers, in their contest with Arius, to prove the eternal generation of the Word of God from this, is in violent disagreement with what the prophet had in mind. Chrysostom's explanation is not one bit nearer the truth, for he applies it to His human generation. And those who think that he is inveighing against the men of that particular generation do not understand the prophet's meaning. Others are better when they take it as said about the Church, except that they are also mistaken about the word 'generation', which for them, means posterity or offspring. But the word דּוֹר (*dor*), which the prophet uses, means, in Hebrew, an age, or the span of human life. Therefore there is no dubiety about the prophet's meaning, that the life of Christ will be for ever, when He has been once and for all delivered from death by the favour of His Father; although this life, which is without end, extends to the whole body of the Church, because He rose again, not to live for Himself, but for His own. Therefore the fruit and effect of that victory, which he made to depend on the Head, he now celebrates in all the members. Accordingly every single believer can receive confidence in eternal life from this verse; and, secondly, the perpetuity of the Church is affirmed in the person of Christ.

Because his life is taken from the earth. It seems a very absurd reason that Christ reigns so magnificently in heaven and in earth, because He was destroyed. For who is to believe that annihilation is the cause of life? But it happened by the wonderful purpose of God that hell was a staircase by which Christ should ascend to heaven, that ignominy was for Him the transition into life, that the glad splendour of salvation emerged from the horror and darkness of the Cross, that blessed immortality flowed from the abyss of death. Because He emptied

Himself the Father therefore exalted Him, so that every knee may be bent before Him (Phil. 2.10). Now we must reflect upon the kind of fellowship we may have with Christ, so that it may not be hard or grievous for anyone to proceed on the same way.

34. *The eunuch said to Philip.* It is evident from this how passionately eager the eunuch was to learn. He wanders about among the many prophecies of Isaiah as if through uncertain labyrinthine ways, and yet he does not grow weary of reading. But while he arrogates nothing to himself, suddenly, and beyond his expectation, he gets further than he could have got, if he had used his own acumen and toiled hard all his life. So, if we are conscious of our ignorance and do not disdain to submit ourselves to learning, the Lord will also present Himself as a teacher to us children. And just as the seed lies hidden for a time under the ground where it has been cast, so the Lord, by the illumination of His Spirit will cause a reading, that is sterile, unfruitful and producing nothing but boredom, to take on the clear light of understanding. Indeed the Lord never keeps the eyes of His own so closed that the way of salvation in Scripture does not lie open to them right from the first moment, and that they do not profit immediately from their reading. But he often allows them to be stuck, and their way to be blocked, as though by a barrier placed there, sometimes to test the endurance of their faith; sometimes to train them in humility after reminding them of their ignorance; now to make them shake off their torpor and to be more attentive; now to kindle the flames of prayer; again, by the very longing for it, to urge them on to a greater love of the truth, and, yet again, the better to commend the superiority of His heavenly wisdom, which is sometimes not valued as it should be. But even if the faithful may not reach the goal of complete knowledge at once, yet they will always realize that their labour is not wasted, provided that they do not close the road for themselves by haughty contempt. Until the time of full revelation arrives, let it be a sufficient rate of progress for us, that a very small taste of knowledge instils in us the fear of God and faith.

35. *Philip, opening his mouth.* In Scripture, *to open the mouth* means to begin a long speech about an important and serious matter. Luke therefore means that Philip began to speak at length (*quasi pleno ore*) about Christ. He says that he began from this prophecy because none portrays Christ more sharply, and because it was conveniently put into his hands at that time. Therefore after Philip showed what the coming of Christ would be like, and what was to be expected from it, he then turned to the reality itself, so that the eunuch might know that that Christ, who had been promised, has now appeared, and so that he might possess His power.

Where we have translated he *preached* Christ (*praedicasse*) Luke has 'proclaimed the Gospel' (*evangelizasse*). The meaning is that he taught about Christ what He Himself made known in His own Gospel, and ordered to be handed on. We gather from that, that when we are made acquainted with Christ, the whole of the Gospel is ours.

And as they went on the way, they came unto a certain water; and the eunuch saith, Behold, here is water; what doth hinder me to be baptized? (And Philip said, If thou believest with all thy heart, thou mayest. And he answered and said, I believe that Jesus Christ is the Son of God.)[1] *And he commanded the chariot to stand still: and they both went down into the water, both Philip and the eunuch; and he baptized him. And when they came up out of the water, the Spirit of the Lord caught away Philip; and the eunuch saw him no more, for he went on his way rejoicing. But Philip was found at Azotus: and passing through he preached the gospel to all the cities, till he came to Caesarea.* (36-40)

36. *What prevents.* The baptism of the eunuch now follows; and we gather from that how much progress he made in a short time, when he freely offers himself in surrender to Christ. For mature faith must have been in some way already in his heart, since he proceeds ardently to outward profession.

I do not accept Chrysostom's comment that he was kept back by modesty from making a direct request for baptism, for that question of his carries more fervour, than if he had simply said to Philip, 'I wish you to baptize me.'

Apart from that we see that Christ had been preached to him in such a way that he knew that baptism is the sign of the new life in him, and therefore he would not neglect it, because it was something added to the Word, and indeed inseparable from it. Therefore just as he has gladly embraced what he has heard about Christ, so he now breaks out into the outward profession of his faith with pious ardour. And it is not enough for him to believe inwardly, before God, without testifying among men that he is a Christian. Many things could have come into his mind, to keep him back from baptism, and not expose himself to the hatred and abuses of his queen and all his people, but he denies that any of these things prevent him from desiring to be numbered among the disciples of Christ. If he progressed as far as that with a few hours of the rudiments, how disgraceful is the tardiness of those who keep within themselves the faith that they have received from five, ten or twenty years of teaching.

37. *If thou believest with all thy heart.* A general rule is to be adopted

[1] v. 37, R.V. margin.

from the fact that the eunuch is not admitted to baptism without professing his faith, viz. that those who have previously been outsiders, should not be received into the Church before they have testified that they believe in Christ. For baptism is, so to speak, the appendix of faith, and therefore subsequent in order. Secondly, if it is given without faith, of which it is the seal, it is an impious and extremely gross profanation. But fanatics stupidly and wrongly attack infant baptism on this pretext. Why was faith bound to precede baptism in the case of the eunuch? It is because those who are to be baptized must be ingrafted into the Church, since Christ distinguishes only the members of the family of the Church with this sign. But as it is certain that adults are ingrafted by faith, so I say that the children of the godly are born sons of the Church, and are numbered among the members of Christ from birth, because God adopts us on the principle that He is also the Father of our children. Therefore even if faith is required in the case of adults, it is wrong to carry this over to children, since the pattern (*ratio*) for them is quite different.

Again, certain great men have made wrong use of this evidence when they wish to prove that faith has no confirmation from baptism. For they used to argue in this way: the eunuch is ordered to bring complete faith to baptism; therefore nothing could be added. But Scripture often takes 'the whole heart' to mean 'sincere' and 'not false'. So there is no reason for us to imagine that those who believe 'with all their heart' believe completely; since it will be possible for faith that is weak and thin to exist in a man whose mind will yet be sound and free of all pretence. That is the proper way to explain David's statement that he loves the Lord with his whole heart. Philip had indeed baptized the Samaritans before, and yet he knew that they were still far from the goal. Therefore the faith of the whole heart is that which has living roots in the heart, and yet desires to increase every day.

I believe that Jesus Christ is the Son of God. As baptism is founded on Christ, and its power and truth are contained in Him, so the eunuch sets Christ alone before himself. For the eunuch was aware before that there is one God, who had made a covenant with Abraham, who had given the Law at the hand of Moses, who had separated one people from the rest of the nations, who had promised Christ, through whom He would be gracious to the world. Now he acknowledges that Jesus is that Redeemer of the world, and the Son of God, and that title briefly embraces everything that Scripture ascribes to Christ. This is the complete faith just mentioned by Philip. It receives Christ both as once promised, and at last revealed, and does so with the earnest desire of the heart, without any pretence, as Paul requires it to be. Everyone who does not already have this as an adult boasts in vain of his baptism as an infant. For Christ initiates infants to Himself for this purpose, that, as soon as their age and ability to understand will allow, they yield themselves to Him as disciples, and having been baptized by His Spirit, they may know, by the discernment of faith, His power, which is represented in baptism.

38. *They went down into the water.* Here we see how the rite of baptism was carried out by the men of long ago: they immersed the whole body in the water. The practice that has now become dominant is for the minister only to sprinkle the body or the head. But the trifling difference in the ceremony ought not to mean so much to us that we split the Church because of it, or throw it into confusion with disputes. Indeed we ought to fight even to the death a hundred times for the ceremony of baptism itself, since it has been delivered to us by Christ, rather than allow it to be taken away from us. But since we have evidence in the symbol of water of new life as well as our washing; since Christ represents His blood to us in the water, as in a mirror, so that we may seek cleansing for ourselves from it; since He teaches that we are recreated by His Spirit, so that we, being dead to sin, may live to righteousness (I Pet. 2.24), it is certain that we have everything that makes for the substance of baptism. That is why, this substance apart, the Church allowed itself freedom from the beginning to have slightly different rites. For some used to immerse three times, while others did it only once. Accordingly there is no call for us to be too particular about things that are not so necessary, provided that adventitious ceremonials do not contaminate the simple institution of Christ.

39. *When they had come up.* Now, in order to bring to a close his narrative about the eunuch, Luke says that Philip was carried away out of his sight. And that was of no little value in confirming him, since he saw that that man had been sent to him by God like an angel, and that he vanished suddenly before he might offer him a reward for his labour; and from that it was easy for him to infer that he had not ingratiated himself to make money out of him, since he had disappeared not a penny the richer. Let the servants of Christ learn from the way that Philip received no reward from the eunuch, to give their services to Him without any payment; or rather let them serve men for nothing so that they may hope for a reward from heaven. Of course the Lord allows ministers of the Gospel to receive wages from those whom they teach (I Cor. 9.9), but at the same time He forbids them to be mercenary and work for the sake of gain (John 10.12). For their aim ought to be to gain men themselves for God.

Rejoicing. Faith and knowledge of God always bring forth this fruit from themselves. For can one imagine a more genuine ground for joy than when the Lord not only opens the treasures of His mercy for us, but pours out His heart on us (if I may put it like that), in giving us Himself in His Son, so that nothing may be lacking to make our happiness complete? Then does the sky begin to be serene, and the earth tranquil; then is conscience set free from the saddening and fearful sense of the wrath of God, is liberated from the tyranny of Satan, emerges from the darkness of death and beholds the light of life. It is therefore customary for the prophets, whenever they are going to speak about the Kingdom of Christ, to incite us to gladness, jubilation, exultation, and triumphal hymns. But because those, whose minds are taken up with the empty joys of the world, cannot lift themselves up to this spiritual joy, let us learn to despise the world and all its allurements, so that Christ may make us truly glad.

40. *He was found at Azotus.* It is known from Joshua chapter 11, that *Azotus* was one of the cities out of which the Anakim could not be driven. It was nearly twenty-five miles (two hundred stadia) from Ascalon. The Hebrews call it Ashdod (אַשְׁדּוֹד). Philip was carried away to that place, then. From there, in normal human fashion, he began to journey on foot, scattering the seed of the Gospel wherever he passed. It was certainly an extraordinary and wonderful activity to spread the fame of the faith as he travelled. Because Luke explicitly states that he preached in every city until he came to *Caesarea*, and makes no mention of his having returned to Samaria, we can probably conjecture from that, that he stayed for a time in Caesarea. However I leave that open.

CHAPTER NINE

But Saul, yet breathing threatening and slaughter against the disciples of the Lord, went unto the high priest, and asked of him letters to Damascus unto the synagogues, that if he found any that were of the Way, whether men or women, he might bring them bound to Jerusalem. And as he journeyed, it came to pass that he drew nigh unto Damascus: and suddenly there shone round about him a light out of heaven: and he fell upon the earth, and heard a voice saying unto him, Saul, Saul, why persecutest thou me? And he said, Who art thou, Lord? And he said, I am Jesus whom thou persecutest. (It is hard for thee to kick against the pricks.[1]) (1-5)

1. *But Saul.* Luke here takes up what is particularly worth telling, the well-known story of Paul's conversion; how the Lord not only brought him under His own control, when he was raging like a wild beast, but immediately made a new and different man of him. But because Luke describes every detail in order, as befits a memorable act of God, it will be better to follow his context, so that anything worth noting will come in its proper place.

When he says that he was still *breathing threatenings and slaughter*, he means that once he had been imbued with innocent blood, he afterwards carried on with the same cruelty, and that he was always a rabid and blood-thirsty enemy of the Church from that unpropitious beginning, which he mentioned in the death of Stephen. For that reason it was all the harder to believe that he could be tamed so suddenly. But God's wonderful hand was openly shown, not only in such a cruel wolf being turned into a sheep, but also in his assuming the character of a shepherd.

2. At the same time Luke makes it clear that he was furnished with arms and power to inflict injuries, when he says that he procured letters from the high priest, so that he might bring, fettered to Jerusalem, all those whom he would find professing Christ. *Women* are mentioned, to make it all the plainer how great his eagerness to shed blood was; for he had no respect for the sex, which even armed enemies are in the habit of sparing in the thick and heat of the battle. He therefore presents to us a wild and ferocious beast, who was not only allowed free rein to act with violence, but was also given in addition the power to destroy and devour godly men, as if a madman

[1] R.V. margin.

had a sword put into his hand. Where I have translated *sect* (*secta*) Luke has *Way* (*via*), which is a common enough metaphor in Scripture. Paul's intention, therefore, was to extinguish the name of Christ, by the cruel destruction of all the faithful.

3. *When he was on his way.* In begging for letters from the priest he was rushing against Christ on his own accord; he is now forced into obedience against his will. It was undoubtedly the extraordinary mercy of God that the man, whose ardour was so great that it was carrying him headlong into destruction, is called back to salvation against the intention of his own mind. From the fact that the Lord allows him to receive letters and to approach the city, we see how well He knows the exact moments and opportune times for doing any particular thing. He could have encountered him earlier, if He had seen fit, in order to release the godly from fear and anxiety; but He gives a clearer demonstration of His mediation in closing the gaping mouth of the wolf only at the very entrance to the sheepfold. We also know that men's stubbornness has a strange way of increasing with the very progress they make, and so the conversion of Paul was the more difficult, because he had now become more obstinate by keeping his fury going.

Shone round about him. Because it was no easy thing to subdue such pride, to break such savage impulses, to calm down such passion, the blind passion of perverted zeal, and finally, to restrain a beast that was unbridled and even worse, Christ had to give some sign of His majesty, by which Paul might realize that he had to deal with God Himself, and not with a mortal man. However there was also the consideration of humbling him, because he did not deserve to be made immediately accustomed by Christ to obedience by the easy yoke of His Spirit, and indeed he was hardly capable of such gentle treatment until his truculence should be violently broken. Certainly men's powers of perception cannot grasp the divine glory of Christ, as it is in itself, but just as God often adopts forms, by which to manifest Himself, so Christ now gave evidence of His divinity to Paul, and, indeed, gave a sign (*specimen*) of His presence which might strike Paul with terror. For although the godly tremble at the sight of God, yet Paul ought to have been greatly terrified in a far different way, when he was aware of the divine power of Christ confronting himself.

4. Luke therefore says that he fell to the earth. For what else can happen to a man when he is overwhelmed by the direct awareness of the glory of God, except to lie in a state of confusion, and be reduced almost to nothing? But this was the beginning of humbling in Paul's case, so that he would be ready to be taught by hearing Christ's voice, which he was scorning when he was proudly sitting bestride his horse.

Saul, Saul. Luke compares the light which fell upon Paul on all sides, to lightning (*fulguri*[1]), although I do not doubt that lightning flashes flew about in the air. But this voice which Christ hurled to crush his pride could well be called a thunderbolt (*fulmen*), because, not only did it throw him down and reduce him to bewilderment, but also finished him completely, so that this man who previously used to be so very pleased with himself, and used to arrogate to himself the right to overthrow the Gospel, was now a nobody in his own eyes.

In this verse Luke uses the Hebrew name, *Saul, Saul*, because he is reporting the words of Christ, who, there is no doubt, addressed him in the way that was common among that people.

5. *Who art thou, Lord?* We now have a tamed Paul, as it were, but he is not a disciple of Christ's yet. The pride in him is corrected, and the ferocity subdued; but he has not reached the degree of sanity where he obeys Christ. All that happens is that the man who was previously shouting blasphemies is ready to carry out instructions. Therefore this is the question of a man who is stunned, bewildered, and confused. For why does he not recognize from such signs of God's presence that it is God who is speaking? Therefore the cry came from a mind in a state of hesitation and anxiety. Christ accordingly presses him closer to repentance. When he answers *I am Jesus* let us remember that this voice called from heaven. Therefore it ought to have pierced through Paul's mind, when he reflected that up to now he has been waging war on God; it ought to have turned him immediately to genuine submission, when he considered that he would not go unpunished in the end, if he continued to rebel against Him, whose hand he could not avoid.

Besides that, this verse contains especially useful teaching, and indeed its value is many-sided. For, in the first place, Christ shows how greatly He values His Gospel, when He announces that it is His cause, from which He does not wish to be separated at all. Therefore He will never be able to abandon its defence any more than He will be able to deny His very self. Secondly, extraordinary consolation comes to the godly because, when they are labouring to bear witness to the Gospel, they hear that the Son of God shares the Cross with them, and that, in a sense, He puts His shoulders underneath to lift part of the load. For it is not for nothing that He says that He suffers along with us (*in persona nostra*), but He wishes us to be really convinced that He is moved by the same common feeling, as if the enemies of the Gospel wounded us through His side. Accordingly Paul himself says that all the persecution, which believers endure today for the defence

[1] Greek: περιήστραψεν αὐτὸν φῶς ἐκ τοῦ οὐρανοῦ. Calvin's text: *circumfulguravit illum fulmen e coelo*. Tr.

of the Gospel, is something lacking in the sufferings of Christ (Col. 1.24). Moreover the purpose of this consolation is not only that we may not find it a burden to suffer along with our Head, but also that we may hope that He, who proclaims from heaven that all our suffering is common to Him and us, will be the one to deliver us from all our misfortunes. Finally, we gather from this what a horrible judgment awaits the persecutors of the Church, who fight against heaven itself like the giants, and brandish their spears, soon to turn back on their own heads; yes indeed, for by troubling heaven they call down the thunderbolt of God's wrath upon themselves. A general warning is also given to us all, so that not one of us may attack Christ by injuring his brother unjustly, but especially so that not one of us resist the truth rashly and in a blind fury, under the pretence of zealousness.

It is hard for thee. This is a proverb taken from oxen and horses, for when they are pricked by goads, all they gain by kicking is to double the hurt, since the goads are driven in deeper. Christ adapts this simile to Himself very appropriately, because, by struggling against Him, when, whether they like it or not, what they need is to be under His control, men will bring double injury upon themselves. Those who willingly submit themselves to Christ, far from feeling any pricking from Him, have a remedy for all wounds ready prepared in Him. But all the ungodly who try to push their poisonous stings into Him, will at last realize that they are asses or oxen exposed to the goads. So for the godly He is a foundation on which to rest, but for the reprobate, who dash against Him, He is a stone that will crush them by its hardness.

Now, although this expression is used about the enemies of the Gospel, yet its warning can be widened to include us, viz. so that we may not think, whenever we have some dealings with God, that we shall accomplish anything by taking the bit between our teeth. But, like quiet horses, let us allow ourselves to be turned and guided by His hand. And if ever He does prick us, let us become readier to respond to His goadings, so that what is described in the psalm may not happen to us, that the jaws of stubborn horses and mules are bound together and held with a tight curb, so that they may not bolt. (Cf. Ps. 32.9.)

Apart from that, in this story we have, so to speak, a universal type of that grace which the Lord puts out every day in calling all of us. Indeed all do not rise up against the Gospel with such great violence, but both pride and rebellion against God are nevertheless innate in all; we are all by nature perverse and cruel. Accordingly when we are converted to God it happens against our nature and by the marvellous and secret power of God. The Papists certainly also ascribe the credit for our conversion to the grace of God, but only partly, because they think that we co-operate. But in fact when the Lord mortifies our flesh, He subdues us in exactly the same way as Paul, and our will is not one whit readier to obey than Paul's was, until, after our pride has been broken, He has made us not only pliable but willing to follow. Therefore the beginning of our conversion is such, that God, without having been called or sought, by His own initiative seeks us who are wandering and going astray; that He changes the inflexible desires of our heart, so that He may keep us open to His teaching.

Furthermore this narrative is of value for confirming Paul's teaching. If Paul had always been one of Christ's disciples, ungodly and impudent men could weaken the authority of the testimony which he gives to His master. If he had shown himself to be good-natured and compliant at the beginning, we should be seeing nothing but what is human; but when a deadly enemy of Christ, a rebel against the Gospel, a man swollen with confidence in his own wisdom, burning with hatred of the true faith, blind with hypocrisy, absolutely determined to destroy the truth, is suddenly and in an unusual way changed into a new man, when the wolf is not only changed into a sheep, but adopts the character of a shepherd, it is just as if Christ were publicly leading out by His hand some angel sent from heaven. For now we are not looking at that Saul of Tarsus, but at a new man created by the Spirit of God, so that He may now speak through his lips as from heaven.

(And he trembling and astonished said, Lord, what dost thou will me to do? And the Lord said to him)[1] *Rise, and enter into the city, and it shall be told thee what thou must do. And the men that journeyed with him stood speechless, hearing the voice, but beholding no man. And Saul arose from the earth; and when his eyes were opened, he saw nothing; and they led him by the hand, and brought him into Damascus. And he was three days without sight, and did neither eat nor drink.* (6-9)

6. There follows the result of that reproof by which we have said that Paul ought to have been roughly shaken so that his hardness might be broken. For he now offers himself as ready to carry out the orders of Him whom He was recently spurning. For when he asks what Christ wishes, he is acknowledging His authority and power. Indeed the reprobate are also frightened by God's threats so that they are forced to reverence Him and submit themselves to His command, but at the same time they do not cease complaining and nursing obstinacy in their hearts. But as God humbled Paul, so he worked

[1] v. 6a, R.V. margin.

effectually in his heart. For it was not due to goodness of nature that Paul submitted himself to God more willingly than Pharaoh. But because Pharaoh was like an anvil, by his hardness he warded off, as if they were hammer blows, the scourges of God, by which he was to be subdued (Exod. 7.13). But Paul's heart suddenly turned from iron to flesh, after a softness, which was not natural to it, was given to it by the Spirit. We also experience the same thing daily in ourselves; He rebukes us by His Word, threatens us, terrifies us, and even adds scourges, and makes us ready for submission in various ways; but yet all these aids will not make anyone produce good fruit unless the Spirit of God softens his heart within.

And the Lord said to him. After Paul had put his iron neck under Christ's yoke he is now directed by His hand. For the Lord does not bring us on to the track so as to abandon us, either at the very starting-point, or in the middle of the course, but leads us on step by step right to the goal. Here Luke is describing for us this continuous sequence in God's direction, for after He had made him ready to listen to Himself, He then undertook his instruction. And it makes no difference that he uses the ministry of a man for this purpose, because the authority and power remain nevertheless in His own hands, even if He completes His work by a man.

However, it could appear absurd that Christ, the eternal Wisdom of God, deals with a disciple, who is now keen to hear, and, as it were, open-mouthed to imbibe teaching, by sending him away in a state of suspense to another for teaching. But I reply that it was not done without good cause. For in this way the Lord wished to test Paul's modesty, when He hands him over to one of His disciples for teaching, as if He does not yet deign to speak to him intimately, but sends him away to His servants, whom he recently despised so proudly, and persecuted so inhumanly. We are also instructed in humility by his example. For if Christ subjected Paul to the instruction of a common disciple, who are we to be reluctant to hear any teacher, provided he has been ordained by Christ, in other words, proves himself in actual fact to be His minister? Let us therefore realize that the sending of Paul to Ananias is done to show honour to the ministry of the Church. It is certainly no ordinary honour, of which God thinks the human race deserving, when He chooses our brethren out of our midst, to be the interpreters of His will, when on the lips of a man, that are naturally profane and given to lies and vanity, He nevertheless makes His sacred oracles to sound forth. But the disgraceful ingratitude of the world rears its head here again, because nobody can bear to hear God speaking through a man's lips. All men would like the angels to fly to them, or that the heaven be immediately rent and the visible glory of God issue forth from there. Since this preposterous curiosity is born from pride and our ungodly contempt of the Word, it opens the door to many fancies, and breaks the bond of mutual agreement among believers. Therefore the Lord not only declares that it pleases Him for us to be taught by men but also He commends and sanctions the order established by Himself. These words, 'He who hears you, hears me' (Luke 10.16) also relate to this, so that Christ may procure proper reverence for His Word.

It shall be told thee. With these words Christ appoints Ananias to act for Him, as far as the office of teaching is concerned, not because He transfers His own authority to him, but because he will be a faithful and sincere minister of the Gospel. Therefore this guiding principle (*moderatio*) must always be preserved, that God alone is heard in Christ, and only Christ Himself, but speaking through His ministers. But we must be on our guard against these two errors, that ministers are not proud on the pretext of such a valuable function, or that their humble circumstances detract from the heavenly wisdom.

7. *But the men.* He now makes a passing reference to Paul's companions, because they were witnesses of the vision. However, this account seems to be somewhat different from Paul's statement which we shall see in the twenty-second chapter. For there he will say that his companions were terrified at the sight of the light, but did not hear the voice. Some people suppose that there is an error, and the negative has been transposed through the ignorance of a copyist. The solution does not appear to be difficult to me, because it is possible that they did indeed hear the sound of the voice, yet did not make out either who was speaking, or what was being said. He says, 'They did not hear the voice of the one speaking with me.' Surely all he means is that the words of Christ were known only to himself. Therefore it does not follow from that that an obscure and unintelligible voice did not fall on the ears of the others. When Luke says in this verse that a voice was heard, and nobody was seen, he does not mean that the voice was produced by a man, but that it was put forth by God. Therefore, so that faith might be established by the miracle, Paul's companions observe the light like lightning, they see Paul thrown to the ground, they hear a voice, though not distinctly, sounding from heaven; at the same time Paul alone is taught what he had to do.

8. *He was raised from the earth.* Luke now adds that he was struck down with such great fear that he could not raise himself up; and not only that, but he was temporarily deprived of his sight, so that he might forget the acuteness that was formerly his. When he says that *when his eyes were opened he saw nothing*, it does not appear to agree with the other statement that follows soon afterwards, that his eyes

were covered as if by scales (v. 18). But yet the meaning of this verse is that this was genuine blindness, and that he was deprived of his sight for that period of three days, because when he opened his eyes, he saw nothing.

9. His assertion that *he did not eat or drink* for three days must be put down as part of the miracle. For even if Orientals endure hunger better than we, yet we do not read of any of them fasting for three days, except those who had no food available, or were driven to it by some stronger force of circumstances. Therefore we gather that Paul was uncommonly frightened because, like one dead, he did not taste food for three days.

Now there was a certain disciple at Damascus, named Ananias; and the Lord said unto him in a vision, Ananias. And he said, Behold, I am here, Lord. And the Lord said unto him, Arise, and go to the street which is called Straight, and inquire in the house of Judas for one named Saul, a man of Tarsus: for behold, he prayeth; and he hath seen (in a vision[1]*) a man named Ananias coming in, and laying his hands on him, that he might receive his sight.* (10-12)

10. We have said before that this man was chosen rather than any of the apostles, so that once Paul had got rid of his swollen-headed arrogance he might learn to listen to those who were of least importance, and might come down from the topmost height to the lowest level.

Now this vision was necessary for Ananias so that he would not decline the task of teaching Paul that was laid upon him. For although he does recognize that he is being called by the Lord, yet he still shrinks from it, or at least makes excuses. Therefore it was necessary for him to have definite confirmation of his calling, and the promise of a successful outcome to his labour, so that he might undertake what the Lord was commanding, eagerly and courageously. Moreover as Christ quickens and confirms Ananias, by appearing to him in a vision, so he prepares Paul for everything, so that he would listen respectfully to Ananias, as if he were an angel come down from heaven. The Lord could have sent Paul to Ananias straight away, and pointed out his house, but this was more suitable for establishing him, since he came to know better how the Lord was concerned about him. And the Lord is commending His grace to us at the same time, because as he met Paul before, so now, without being asked, He stretches out His hand to him again through His minister. Again, on the other hand, we ourselves are also taught by his example to be readier and more anxious to seek out the lost sheep.

[1] R.V. margin. Calvin's text also.

In a vision. Vision here means some sign (*symbolum*) that was placed before his eyes to testify to the presence of God. For the use of visions is duly to confirm the majesty of the Word so that it might obtain credence among men. And God has often used this kind of confirmation in dealing with the prophets, inasmuch as He says that He speaks with His servants by a vision or a dream. He has indeed permitted Satan to cheat unbelievers personally with fallacious appearances (*spectris*). But since Satan's delusions thrive only in the darkness, God illumines the minds of His own, so that they are quite convinced that they are not to be afraid of an imposture. Ananias therefore answers, *I am here, Lord*, knowing that it really was God.

11. *For behold, he is praying*. Luke shows that during those three days Paul was intent on prayer, and perhaps this is one of the reasons why he fasted; although it is certain, as we have already said, that he was suffering hunger for so long, because, so to speak, he had been deprived of sensation, as usually happens to men in an ecstasy. Christ is certainly not speaking about a brief momentary prayer here, but rather indicates that Paul was persisting in this kind of exercise until a quiet and thoroughly composed mind might be granted to him. For apart from other causes of terror, that voice could still have been ringing in his ears, 'Saul, Saul, why are you persecuting me?' And there is no doubt that the anxious anticipation of a full revelation strangely tormented his mind, and the reason why the Lord kept him waiting for three days was that he might fan his ardour for prayer into stronger flames.

12. *He hath seen a man named Ananias*. It is not certain whether Luke is still reporting the words of Christ, or is adding this on his own. Those who take it as due to Luke, are influenced by an apparent absurdity, because it is not likely that Christ used these words. However this could be easily explained, viz. that Christ is encouraging Ananias in this way, 'There is no reason for you to doubt that he will receive you gladly, since he already knows what you are like from a vision. I have also disclosed your name to him, and everything that you are to do with him.' However let the reader have free choice as to which he prefers.

But Ananias answered, Lord, I have heard from many of this man, how much evil he did to thy saints at Jerusalem: and here he hath authority from the chief priests to bind all that call upon thy name. But the Lord said unto him, Go thy way: for he is a chosen vessel unto me, to bear my name before the Gentiles and kings, and the children of Israel: for I will shew him how many things he must suffer for my name's sake. (13-16)

13. *Lord I have heard.* In objecting to the Lord about the danger Ananias is revealing the weakness of his faith. We thus see that the fear of death befalls the saints and the servants of Christ to keep them back from their duty, yes and sometimes to force them into vacillation. Certainly Ananias would gladly turn his steps in another direction, but it is the mark of a good man that he does not yield to depraved fear to the point that he removes himself from obedience to Christ. Therefore it is a sign of remarkable godliness that, even if his dread of death makes him slow to start with, he soon forgets about himself however, and is quickly on the move to the place to which Christ has called him. Nevertheless by these words he is not flatly refusing to do what he is commanded, but quietly makes use of an indirect excuse, 'Lord, what do you mean by sending me to the executioner?' Therefore we may detect a desire to obey mixed with fear.

14. *He has authority to bind.* From these words we conclude that news of the persecution, which Saul was preparing, had been spread far and wide, so that his conversion ought to have been all the more noteworthy. At the same time the Lord allowed His faithful people to be badly tormented so that later on the blessing of such a sudden deliverance would be all the plainer. We must note the expression he uses, that the name of Christ is called upon by the godly. For whether you are to understand that, because they professed to belong to Christ, they therefore gloried in Him, or that they were accustomed to have recourse to His protection, there cannot be invocation without confidence. So in both these ways not only is the divinity of Christ clearly proved, but if the second, which appears to be the more authentic, is accepted, we are taught by the example of the faithful to call upon the name of Christ, after He has been preached to us.

15. *Go thy way, for he is an elect instrument.* The repetition of the order and the added accompaniment of the promise of success remove any doubt that there was. Therefore torpor will have no excuse left to it, if it is never corrected after the application of many goads. We see that sort of thing in a great many cases, for, no matter how insistently the Lord calls to them, not only do they idle their lives away, but also encourage their laziness with any pleasures they can. That is all the more reason for us to note the example of Ananias who cuts short all delays at the second command. If anyone objects that the Lord does not speak in a vision today, I reply that, since the authority of Scripture is more than established for us, God must be heard out of it.

A *vessel of election* (*vas electionis*), or as Erasmus translates it, 'elected instrument' (*organum electum*) is taken for an extraordinary minister. The word *instrument* shows that men can do nothing except in so far as God uses their labour according to His will. For if we are instruments He is strictly speaking the only Doer (*auctor*): the power and the capability of acting are in His hands. But what Christ predicates of Paul here applies to all without distinction. Accordingly no matter how strenuously each one may labour, and no matter how admirably he conducts himself in office, yet there is no cause for him to arrogate a single particle of praise to himself.

Those who philosophize about the word *vessel* (*vas*) are talking nonsense because of their ignorance of Hebrew. Luke has used the genitive case for an epithet, but that is also according to the common Hebrew practice. Furthermore Luke wished to express pre-eminence, as if he had said, 'This man will be no ordinary minister of Christ, but will be gifted with a greatness that will be outstanding in comparison with others.' At the same time we must observe that any excellence there may be depends on the gratuitous favour of God, as Paul himself teaches elsewhere: 'Who is it that sets thee apart, so that thou art plainly excelling above others?' (I Cor. 4.7.) To sum up, Christ declares that Paul has been chosen for great and splendid things.

To bear my name among the Gentiles. The man who previously tried to destroy the name of Christ is now entrusted with carrying it. If one were willing to take *σκεῦος* for *vessel* (*vase*) the metaphor would be maintained here, because a minister of the Gospel fulfils the role of a vessel in making known the name of Christ; but because it means to the Hebrews, rather, any kind of instrument whatever,[1] I simply take 'to bear the name' for 'elevating' or 'extolling' it to His honour. For Christ is, in a sense, placed on His royal throne, when the world is drawn together (*cogitur*) under His rule by the preaching of the Gospel.

16. But because Paul was not likely to do that with a quiet Satan, and a world ready to yield, Luke therefore adds that he would be taught at the same time to bear the cross. The meaning of the words is, 'I shall make him used to undergoing troubles, to bearing reproaches, to enduring all sorts of struggles, so that nothing may deter or detain him from his task.' Indeed, when Christ makes Himself Paul's teacher in this connexion, He is reminding us that the more progress each one has made in His school, the fitter he is to bear the cross. For we struggle against it, and avoid it as the utmost calamity, until He has brought us to a quiet and submissive state of mind.

Finally, this verse shows that nobody is fit to preach the Gospel in a hostile world, unless his mind has been prepared for suffering. Therefore if we are to prove ourselves faithful ministers of Christ, not only must we ask Him for the spirit of knowledge and of wisdom,

[1] Cf. Hebrew כְּלִי. Tr.

but also for the spirit of steadfastness and of courage, so that we may never be broken by desperate suffering, for this is the lot of the godly.

And Ananias departed, and entered into the house; and laying his hands on him said, Brother Saul, the Lord, even Jesus, who appeared unto thee in the way which thou camest, hath sent me, that thou mayest receive thy sight, and be filled with the Holy Ghost. And straightway there fell from his eyes as it were scales, and he received his sight; and he arose and was baptized; and he took food and was strengthened. (17-19)

17. *Laying his hands on him.* We have said elsewhere that it was a solemn, and, as it were, regular, rite among the Jews, to lay on hands whenever they were commending anyone to God. The apostles carried over that custom, taken from the sacrifices, to their own use, either when they were conferring visible graces of the Spirit, or when they were appointing anyone a minister of the Church. The reasons for Ananias now laying his hands on Paul are partly to set him apart (*consecret*) to God, and partly to obtain the gifts of the Spirit for him. But even if no mention is made of teaching here, yet it will be evident from what Paul says afterwards that the task of teaching him was also committed to Ananias, and from his baptism, which is subsequent in order, we gather that he was instructed in the faith. Readers may find out from the last chapter how this ceremony is effectual for the giving of the Spirit. Finally, since Paul received the Spirit at the hand of Ananias, the Papists are being quite ridiculous when they ascribe the laying on of hands to bishops alone.

18. *There fell from his eyes as it were scales.* As has been already said, Paul's blindness had not come about from fear alone or from bewilderment; but in this way he was reminded of his former blindness, so that he might completely strip himself of the confidence with which he used to be swollen. He boasts that he sat for instruction at the feet of Gamaliel (Acts 22.3), and there is no doubt that he took great delight in his own perspicacity, but it was nevertheless mere blindness. Therefore he is deprived of his eyesight for three days, so that he might begin to see with his mind. For all who appear to themselves to be wise must become fools, to be fashioned according to the true pattern of wisdom. For since Christ is the Sun of Righteousness, when we see without Him, we are not seeing at all; and it is also He who opens the eyes of the mind. Both these aspects were shown to Paul, and they are shown to us in his person, for his eyesight is restricted by scales, so that, condemning the whole of his own acuteness as ignorance, he might learn that he needs the new light, which he lacked previously; and he is advised that the true light must not be

sought anywhere else but from Christ, and is not conferred in any other way but by His favour. Moreover the extreme fervour of his desire to learn is apparent from the way that, although weakened by three days of hunger, yet he does not hurry to get food until he has been baptized, because he did not restore his body, until his soul had been invigorated.

And he was certain days with the disciples which were at Damascus. And straightway in the synagogues he proclaimed Jesus, that he is the Son of God. And all that heard him were amazed, and said, Is not this he that in Jerusalem made havock of them which called on this name? and he had come hither for this intent, that he might bring them bound before the chief priests. But Saul increased the more in strength, and confounded the Jews which dwelt at Damascus, proving that this is the Christ.

And when many days were fulfilled, the Jews took counsel together to kill him: but their plot became known to Saul. And they watched the gates also day and night that they might kill him: but his disciples took him by night, and let him down through the wall, lowering him in a basket. (19b-25)

20. Luke now goes on to tell how fruitful Paul's conversion was, viz. that he appeared in public immediately and not only professed himself a disciple of Christ, but also, by boldly defending the Gospel, exposed himself to the hatred and fury of its enemies. Accordingly the man who was recently rushing against Christ in a furious attack, not only submits himself quietly to His control, but like a fighter for the standard strives to the point of extreme danger for the vindication of His glory. Of course it is certain that he had not been shaped so quickly by the agency of Ananias, but when he imbibed the rudiments from the lips of a man, he was raised by God to higher things.

He sums up his preaching briefly when he says that *Christ was the Son of God.* In similar vein he adds a little later that *this was the Christ.* But understand that when Paul was speaking about the true office of the Messiah from the Law and the Prophets, he was teaching at the same time that whatever was promised or was to be expected about the Messiah, has been exhibited in Christ. For that is what the words mean, when he says that he preached that Christ is the Son of God. Among the Jews it was a principle, about which there was no argument, that a Redeemer would be sent by God, who would restore all things to a happy state. Paul teaches that Jesus of Nazareth is this Redeemer; and he cannot do this without driving out of them the gross errors which they had conceived about the earthly kingdom of the Messiah. Therefore it is certain that Paul dealt with how, and for what purpose, Christ had been promised in the Law; but because everything was directed towards this goal, that he might prove that the Son of Mary is the one about whom the Law and the Prophets were bearing witness, for that reason Luke is content with this one word.

21. *All were amazed.* This is added so that we may know that the power of God was recognized. For since Paul's passion against the Gospel was renowned everywhere, they knew of no other cause for such a sudden change than the hand of God. Therefore it is also one result of the miracle that they are all amazed at the man made suddenly new, so that his teaching has a greater effect on their minds. They mention the very circumstances that have the effect of increasing the miracle, that he was raging with savage cruelty, and that he recently came to Damascus in pursuit of his plan.

We must also note the expression *those who call on this name*, for it testifies that the godly professed the name of Christ in such a way that they placed all their assurance of salvation in Him, and it is equivalent to that verse, 'some trust in chariots, and others in horses, but we shall call upon the name of the Lord' (Ps. 20.7). In fact whatever Scripture enjoins about the invocation of God is appropriate for the Person of Christ.

22. *But Saul increased the more in strength.* Here Luke not only commends Paul's vigour and zeal in confessing the faith of Christ, but he also shows that he fought with powerful arguments with which to refute the Jews. He says that he *increased in strength*, that is to say, he was the superior in debate, and his confession had force and telling power combined, undoubtedly because, equipped with the testimonies of Scripture and other aids of the Holy Spirit, he was, so to speak, overpowering all his adversaries. For the word for *confounding* (*turbandi*) which Luke uses, means that, since Paul was pressing them beyond the limit, they were struck with such consternation, that they were out of their minds. The method of confounding is brought out, that Paul proved that Jesus is the Christ. For the meaning is that when the Jews wished to resist the hardest, they were however defeated and in confusion. So Paul proved by experience that his pronouncement is very true, that Scripture is profitable for refuting (II Tim. 3.16). He also gave a demonstration of what he demands of a bishop and a teacher (Titus 1.7), for he was armed with the Word of God, to defend the truth. And Luke is in fact including two things, (1) that Paul was so victorious in debate that he made the Jews collapse; and (2) that their obstinacy was yet not so broken and tamed that they yielded to the truth. This is because their consciences are none the less in revolt within them, and having been driven out of the position of their false opinions they are not submitting themselves to Christ.

What was the source of Paul's victory, except that the Scripture was a sword for him? Accordingly, as often as heretics rise up to fight against the true faith, as often as ungodly men strive to overthrow all piety, as often as the reprobate stubbornly resist, let us remember that we must seek arms from this source. Because the Papists find no weapons in Scripture, and what is more, because they see that the whole of it is unfavourable to them, they take refuge in this miserable asylum, that there must be no argument with heretics, and nothing can be settled with certainty from Scripture. But if Satan himself is subdued by the sword of the Word,[1] why will it not be capable of putting heretics to flight?—not because they will surrender, or stop being troublesome, but because they will lie convicted in themselves. But if we desire to avoid this disturbance let us not instigate any revolts against God, but with a quiet and gentle spirit let us receive the peace which Scripture offers to us.

23. *When very many days.* He says that *very many days* passed, so that we may know the space of time Paul was given in which to do good. For although the Jews resisted him right from the start, yet the Lord did not allow the course that had begun well to be broken off so quickly; so, by His wonderful plan, He hinders the purposes of His enemies, delays their efforts, restrains their ill-will and fury, until he may advance the Gospel. At the same time we see what hatred of the truth does. For when the ungodly see that they are not equal to the fight, they are driven to blood-thirsty frenzy. They would gladly despise the Word of God, if they could, but because they are forced, willy-nilly, into realization of its power, they rush like mad beasts in a blind and headlong attack. The heedless passion of zeal will nearly always boil over into such cruelty, unless men surrender themselves to the rule of the Word of God. This blindness is horrible indeed. For why are they so enraged except that the wound inflicted on their consciences torments them? But in this way God punishes the hypocrisy of those to whom sound religion is hateful, just because they are friends of darkness and avoid the light.

Moreover we see how delighted those perverted zealots are to indulge themselves in anything they like, once Satan has incited them to persecute the truth. For they do not hesitate to enter upon a plan to murder a man, knowing it to be a heinous act, and yet they do it on the pretext of zeal. Similarly today the Papists hold that everything is permissible to them so long as they are extinguishing the teaching of the Gospel. Not only do they boldly attack with the sword, but they are busy with plots, treachery and utterly detestable tricks for our destruction. So that that may not happen to us, we

[1] Reading *verbi gladio* for *verbo gladii* (C.R. and Tholuck). Tr.

must first of all be on our guard not to involve ourselves in the defence of bad causes; secondly to deal satisfactorily with causes which will be good. Now it is probable that they secretly laid an ambush for Paul; that, secondly, when nothing came of that method, they approached the governor of the city, and, thirdly, that guards were posted at the gates of the city, so that they might intercept him somehow or other. For Paul relates that the governor of King Aretas[1] ordered what Luke here attributes to the Jews.

25. *The disciples took him by night.* The question is raised here whether it was lawful for the disciples to save Paul in this way; and also whether it was right for Paul to avoid danger in this fashion. For the laws pronounce the walls of cities to be sacred (*sanctos*), and the gates inviolable (*sanctas*). He therefore ought to have submitted to death rather than allow public order to be disturbed for his sake. I reply that we must consider the purpose for which the laws forbid, with the addition of a penalty (*sanctione interposita*), the violation of the walls. It is so that the cities may not be open to robberies, and that the citizens may be protected from treacherous attacks. Where it is a matter of freeing an innocent man, that reason ceases to hold. It was therefore no less lawful for the faithful to let Paul down in the basket, as it will be lawful for a private individual to leap over a wall, in order to ward off the sudden attack of an enemy. Cicero deals with this latter instance, and explains correctly that even if the law prevents a stranger from approaching close to a wall, yet a man is not committing an offence, when he mounts a wall for the sake of saving a city, because the laws must always be inclined towards equity. Therefore Paul is free from blame, because he escaped in secret, since that would be possible without an uproar of the people. At the same time we see how the Lord is accustomed to humble His own, when Paul is forced to take himself away from the city guards in stealth, if he wishes to escape in safety. He therefore mentions this instance among his weaknesses (II Cor. 11.32). With this initial experience he was quickly made accustomed to bearing the cross.

And when he was come to Jerusalem, he assayed to join himself to the disciples: and they were all afraid of him, not believing that he was a disciple. But Barnabas took him, and brought him to the apostles, and declared unto them how he had seen the Lord in the way, and that he had spoken to him, and how at Damascus he had preached boldly in the name of Jesus. And he was with them going in and going out at Jerusalem, preaching boldly in the name of the Lord: and he spake and

[1] Reading *Aretae regis.* C.R. and Tholuck read *Aretam regium praefectum mandasse*, but this is incorrect. Vide II Cor. 11.32. Tr.

disputed against the Grecian Jews; but they went about to kill him. And when the brethren knew it, they brought him down to Caesarea, and sent him forth to Tarsus. So the church throughout all Judaea and Galilee and Samaria had peace, being edified; and, walking in the fear of the Lord and in the comfort of the Holy Ghost, was multiplied. (26-31)

26. *When Saul was.* Paul, still a recruit, had a rough and difficult initiation, for scarcely having escaped from the hands of his enemies, he is not admitted by the disciples. For it could have appeared that he is to be tossed about, this way and that, as if he were a butt, so that nowhere might he be given a resting-place. He faced the hostility of the whole of his own people because of the name of Christ. He is repudiated by the Christians. Could he not have lost courage and hope, like one cast out of the society of men? In the first place, what is there left for him to do after his rejection, but to abandon the Church? But remembering the life he had led previously he is not surprised that they hold him in horror. He therefore patiently accepts the fact of the brethren keeping him at a distance, because of a justifiable fear. This was a case of genuine conversion, for, whereas he was previously raging with violence, he is now bravely accepting the storms of persecutions. And in the meantime, when he is denied a place among the faithful, he waits quietly until God reconciles them to him. Again, we must pay particular attention to what he is longing for, viz. that he may be counted among the disciples of Christ. That indeed he does not obtain. This is not a matter of ambition holding sway, but he had to be instructed in this way, so that he might think more of the very lowest place among the disciples of Christ, than all the chief offices in corrupt and apostate synagogues. And indeed from this lowliness he attains to the highest level of honour, so that he may be the principal teacher of the Church right to the end of the world. Indeed nobody is fit to teach in the Church, unless he voluntarily humbles himself, to be a fellow-disciple along with others.

27. *Barnabas took hold of him.* The fact that the disciples avoided Paul to such an extent was perhaps due to excessive timidity. Nevertheless the expression is used not of the ordinary people but of the apostles themselves. It is true that their blame is extenuated or lessened by their justified suspicion of a man whom they had found by experience to be such a deadly enemy. And they ought to have been afraid of rashly bringing danger on themselves if they had showed themselves too yielding. Therefore I do not think that a fear conceived on justifiable grounds is to be turned to their blame, or even that any charge is deserved. For if they had been called to give an account of

their faith they would have undauntedly challenged not only Paul, but all the furies of hell. From that we conclude that every kind of fear must not be condemned, but such as forces us to turn aside from our duty.

The report that Luke adds can be referred as much to Barnabas as to Paul. To me it seems however more probable that Paul recounted to the apostles what had happened to him. Yet the speech can suit Barnabas, especially in that part which deals with the boldness of Paul.

28. After that Luke says that Paul was *going in and going out* with the disciples. To the Hebrews this expression means familiar social intercourse, as for example the inhabitants of a city and the citizens are said 'to go in and to go out' of the gates. Therefore once Paul had been commended by the testimony of Barnabas, he began to be regarded as one of the flock, so that he became thoroughly known to the Church. Again, Luke adds that he spoke (*egisse*) *boldly in the name of the Lord*, and with those words he praises his courage in making profession of the Gospel. For among so many obstacles he would never have dared to open his mouth, if his heart had not been endowed with a rare steadfastness. At the same time all are being directed as to what they ought to do, each one according to the measure of his faith, of course. For even if all are not Pauls, yet the faith of Christ ought to engender so much confidence in our minds, that we are not struck completely dumb, when it is necessary to speak.

I take *the name of the Lord* here for profession of the Gospel, in the sense that Paul powerfully defended the cause of Christ.

29. *He was disputing with the Grecians.* Erasmus is correct in noting that those who are called Grecians here are not those born of Greeks, but rather Jews who were at that time scattered across various parts of the world. And they were accustomed to flocking together to Jerusalem from their own provinces to worship. But it can well be believed that Paul had discussions with foreigners and strangers rather than with natives, because the latter would never have tolerated him; nor would it have been wise for him to appear before their eyes. Therefore having been excluded from those who had known him previously, he tried whether there was any hope of progress among men who were ignorant of him. So with indefatigable firmness of mind he fulfilled all the roles of an active soldier.

They wished to kill him. See before us once again fury instead of zeal! And hypocrisy and superstition cannot possibly be anything else but fierce and cruel. The godly must be inflamed with a holy wrath when they see the pure truth of God corrupted by false and spurious doctrines; but in such a way that they moderate their zeal, so that they make no decision without investigating the situation well, and, then, that they try to bring back the wandering to the way. Finally, if they encounter hopeless stubbornness, let them not take the sword into their own hands, however, because they are to know that the Lord has not given them authority to take revenge. Hypocrites are certainly eager to shed blood at once, when they know nothing about the cause; so superstition is blood-thirsty with a blind and precipitate fury. But Paul who was recently racing hither and thither to torment the godly, now cannot set his foot anywhere. In fact this was a far better situation for him, than if he had lorded it everywhere, untroubled and in peace, turning the faithful out of their homes, and almost putting an end to them.

30. His going to *Tarsus* was undoubtedly done for the express purpose of bringing the teaching of the Gospel to that place; because there was the hope that he would have some favour and authority in his native place, where his name had been famous. Nevertheless he was conducted by the brethren to snatch him out of the hands of the plotters.

31. *Therefore the churches.* Luke means that Paul's presence was a serious provocation to the enemies of the Gospel. For why did peace suddenly light upon the Church after his departure, except that the sight of him roused the fury of his enemies? Yet this is not turned into a reproach against him, as if he was a sort of trumpet of war, but Luke rather considers it praiseworthy of him that he drove the ungodly to madness by the mere suggestion of his presence. For Christ wished to triumph in him in such a way that he would bring upon His Church as much trouble as honour.

We are therefore warned by this example that those who inflame the madness of the ungodly more than others, are not to be condemned out of hand. And this warning is of no small value. For as we are too easy-going and love a quiet life for ourselves, so even nowadays we become angry with all the best and most outstanding servants of Christ, if we think that their vehemence is inciting the wicked to do harm. But in this way we are treating the Spirit of God unjustly, for it is the power of His inspiration that kindles the whole of that fire.

Let us realize that the *peace*, which, Luke says, existed in the churches, was not in fact perpetual, but simply that the Lord granted some relief to His servants for a short time. For He makes allowance for our weakness in this way, when He quietens or lessens the whirlwinds and tempests of persecutions, so that by their persistent pressure they may not push us beyond our limits. And this blessing, of the churches at peace, is no ordinary blessing, and is not to be despised.

But Luke adds other things, which are more valuable, viz. that the churches were being *edified*, that they were *walking in the fear of the*

Lord, and that they were filled with the *comfort of the Spirit*. For as we are accustomed in peacetime to abandon ourselves to a riot of luxury, the churches are for the most part more blessed in the midst of the tumults of war, than if they are enjoying the quietest and most pleasant time they could desire. But if the holy conversation and the consolation of the Spirit, by which their situation thrives, are taken away, not only do they lose their happiness, but they are reduced to nothing. Therefore let us learn, not to abuse external peace by being involved in pleasures and idleness, but, the more rest that is given us by our enemies, to make up our minds to make diligent progress in piety, when we get the chance. But if God ever gives free rein to the ungodly to trouble us, let the consolation of the Spirit within be sufficient for us. Finally, both in peace and in war let us always strive with eagerness towards the One who supervises our course (*agonotheten*).

Edification can be taken either for additions, i.e. when the churches increase with a number of believers; or for the progress of those who are already in the flock, i.e. when new gifts are heaped upon them, and they undergo a greater strengthening of their piety. In the first way it bears reference to persons; in the second, to gifts of the Spirit. I gladly accept both aspects, that there were continually being added to the Church those who had previously been outsiders, and that the actual members of the household of the Church were growing in piety and other virtues. Moreover the metaphor of a building is very suitable, because the Church is the temple and house of God, and believers are also, individually, temples. Certainly the two things that follow, viz. that they walked in the fear of the Lord, and that they were filled with the consolation of the Spirit, are parts of that edification (I Tim. 3.15; I Cor. 3.16, 17). Therefore when the churches had peace, they were not drunk with pleasures and earthly joy, but, relying on God's help, they adopted a more confident and bolder attitude in glorifying God.

And it came to pass, as Peter went throughout all parts, he came down also to the saints which dwelt at Lydda. And there he found a certain man named Aeneas, which had kept his bed eight years; for he was palsied. And Peter said unto him, Aeneas, Jesus Christ healeth thee: arise, and make thy bed. And straightway he arose. And all that dwelt at Lydda and in Sharon saw him, and they turned to the Lord. (32-35)

32. Luke tells what additions came to the Church from miracles. And he gives an account of two miracles, that a paralysed man, who had been bed-ridden for eight years, was suddenly healed; and that a woman was raised up from death.

First of all, he says that when Peter was going round 'among all', he came to Lydda. But understand *all*, not as the churches, but as the faithful, because it is the masculine in Greek, although that has little bearing on the meaning. But, when no definite station was assigned to the apostles, it was fitting for them to move about, going wherever opportunity presented itself. Accordingly when every one of them is occupied with different duties, Peter undertook this task. This gives the lie to the foolishness of the Papists in inferring the primacy of Peter from a right of visiting; as if the rest of the apostles, like private individuals, gave themselves up to ease at Jerusalem, when Peter was surveying the churches. Finally, although we may grant that Peter was the principal apostle, as Scripture often makes plain, does it follow from that that he was the leader of the world? But one's wish is that the Bishop of Rome, who is determined to be regarded as Peter's successor, would follow his example and move about to encourage the brethren, and everywhere prove in actual fact that he is the apostle of Christ. Now he, who from his throne oppresses all the churches with a rule that is worse than tyrannous, makes the excuse that Peter took great pains to survey the churches.

33. *Which dwelt at Lydda. Lydda*, which later on was called Diospolis a city renowned for its antiquity, as well as for its many amenities, was situated not far from the Mediterranean Sea. In its vicinity was Joppa, which had a famous, although rocky, harbour. The city itself was built on a high rock, and from it the view was open all the way as far as Jerusalem. Now only the ruins of the ancient city are to be seen there, except that the harbour, which people commonly call Japhet, remains. Assaron (*sic*) here seems to be named by Luke as if it were some town. Jerome reads *Sarona* (*Sharon*) and thinks that reference is being made to the whole of the plain which lay between Caesarea and Joppa. But because Jerome brings forward no reason why he changes the commonly accepted reading, I gladly accept what Luke's text makes plain to me, viz. that it was a neighbouring town. But I am not making an issue of this matter, since I am not collecting, for my own self-esteem, all the things that could make for an empty show, because it will be enough for godly readers to know the things that suit Luke's meaning.

34. *Jesus Christ heal thee* (*sanet*). It is certain that the apostles never undertook to perform miracles, without being already sure about the will of God, on which the result was dependent. For they were not provided with such power of the Spirit that they were free to heal all the sick, but just as Christ imposed a limit on His miracles, so He wished no more to be performed by His apostles than He knew to be beneficial. Therefore Peter did not blurt out these words unthinkingly, because he could have exposed himself to ridicule, unless the will of

God had already been made plain to him. It is possible that he prayed on his own. Certainly the Spirit, who was the Author of all miracles, and who was working by the agency of Peter, also directed his tongue at that moment and stirred his heart with secret inspiration. Finally, Peter shows openly by these words that he is only the agent carrying out the miracle, but that it comes from the power of Christ, so that in this way he may do honour to the name of Christ alone.

Make your bed. The very circumstances increase the glory of the miracle, because this man, who had previously been unable to move a limb, not only recovers the strength to rise, but can also make his own bed. The long duration of the illness points to the same thing, for the paralysis of eight years is not easily cured. For the same reason it is said that he lay on a pallet bed, so that we might realize that he lost the use of all his limbs; for it was a small couch, on which they were accustomed to take a siesta. Aeneas proved the obedience of his faith in the fact that he was so ready to try out his limbs. For although he felt the power restored to him, yet what most stimulated him into getting up was the effective power of the voice.

35. *All saw him.* He means that news of the miracle spread everywhere, and was celebrated in the whole city. For when Scripture mentions *all*, it is not embracing, to a man, the whole of whatever it is describing, but uses 'all' for many, for the majority, or for a crowd of people. The meaning is therefore that, since there was a small number of believers in that place, a church was gathered together from a large part of the populace. In other words, the result of the miracle is described in this concluding sentence, viz. that they embraced Christ and His Gospel. Accordingly all who have been struck with astonishment at the hands of men make wrong use of miracles, when they do not turn their eyes to this goal, that having been informed about the power and grace of Christ they may cleave to Him alone. Therefore the sign of His divine power that Christ gave, was the beginning of, and preparation for, conversion to Himself.

Now there was at Joppa a certain disciple named Tabitha, which by interpretation is called Dorcas: this woman was full of good works and almsdeeds which she did. And it came to pass in those days, that she fell sick, and died: and when they had washed her, they laid her in an upper chamber. And as Lydda was nigh unto Joppa, the disciples, hearing that Peter was there, sent two men unto him, intreating him, Delay not to come on unto us. (36-38)

36. There follows a more remarkable example of the power of Christ, inasmuch as it is obviously more difficult to restore life to a

dead person, than to restore health to a sick man. But Luke first commends Tabitha, on whom the miracle was performed, and does so in a twofold description, viz. that she was a disciple of Christ's, and she gave proof of her faith in good works and alms. Several times already he has used the word *disciple* for a Christian man, and in case we might think that it is suitable for men only, he applies the same word to a woman. But this title warns us that Christianity does not exist without teaching, and that the learning prescribed is of such a kind that the same Christ may be the only Teacher for all. This is the highest commendation, this is the basis of a holy life, this is the root of all virtues, to have learned from the Son of God what is the way to live, and what true life is. The fruits of good works afterwards spring forth from faith. Now I take *good works* to mean the voluntary acts of love by which our neighbours are helped; and Luke instances a particular example of this, in almsgiving. Well-doing is highly commended, because, according to the witness of the Holy Spirit, it contains in itself the whole of a godly and perfect life. We now know what is said in commendation of Tabitha. For reverence towards God, or faith, has first place; then we learn that she was busy helping the brethren, particularly, indeed, in meeting the needs of the poor. For the practice prevailed of using the word *alms* (*eleemosyna*) to mean whatever help is bestowed on the poor and wretched.

Tabitha is a Syrian rather than a Hebrew word, which Luke translated into Greek, so that we might know that it did not match the virtues of a holy woman, and that she was, so to speak, let down in a name that was far from complimentary. For *Dorcas* is a wild she-goat (*caprea*); but the sanctity of her life easily wiped out the stigma of a rather unbecoming name.

37. *It came to pass that she fell sick.* He makes a clear reference to her illness the better to bear testimony to her death, that followed it. For the same reason he says that her body was washed, and placed in an upper room. Therefore those circumstances are effective in procuring faith in the miracle. Proof that they had some hope of restoring her to life is given in the fact that they do not carry her to a tomb immediately, but into the upper part of the house, there to watch over her.

It is probable that the rite of washing, that Luke mentions, was very old. Indeed I have no doubt that it was transmitted from the holy patriarchs, as if by hand, continuously through the generations, so that in death itself some visible representation of the resurrection might lift up the minds of the godly to a good hope. Indeed, since the manifestation of eternal life was not yet so conspicuous, and what is more to the point, since Christ, the pledge and substance of eternal life, was not yet revealed, it was necessary for both the obscurity of teaching, and the absence of Christ Himself to be made good by such helps. Accordingly they used to wash the bodies of the dead, so that at any time they might appear before God's judgment-seat, clean. Finally there was the same reason for washing the dead as for the living. Daily washings were reminders that no person can please God unless he has been cleansed of all his filthiness. So in the custom of burying God intended there to be a sign by which men would be reminded that, on account of the uncleanness contracted in the world, they depart this life defiled. Certainly washing benefited the dead no more than burial did, but it was used for the instruction of the survivors. For since death has the appearance of annihilation, so that it might not extinguish confidence in the resurrection, it was fitting that contrary appearances should be adduced to represent life in death. The Gentiles also appropriated this ceremony for themselves, so that we find Ennius saying, 'A good woman washed and anointed the body of Tarquin.' But their imitation was a perversion in this connexion, as in all ceremonies. Even the Christians were thoughtless in following this example for themselves, as if the observation of a legal form ought to be perpetual. For during the first days of the Gospel, even if the necessity for it was abolished, yet the use of it was allowable until it would fall into disuse with the lapse of time. But today monks emulate Judaism just as the Gentiles did long ago, without discernment and discretion. For bodies are washed among them, so that they submerge Christ in shadows, which were banished into His tomb, and never ought to have been called back into use.

38. *The disciples who had heard.* The washing of the body shows that the disciples were in doubt about what would happen. For in this way they get the body ready for burial. Yet it is a sign of hope that they place it in an upper room, and send to Peter. Moreover they do not cry out against God, and do not make loud complaint that this is an undeserved blow; but they humbly pray for help from the Lord, not because they wish to make Tabitha immortal, but only because they desire her life to be prolonged for a time, so that she may still be of service to the Church.

And Peter arose and went with them. And when he was come, they brought him into the upper chamber: and all the widows stood by him weeping, and shewing the coats and garments which Dorcas made, while she was with them. But Peter put them all forth, and kneeled down, and prayed; and turning to the body, he said, Tabitha, arise. And she opened her eyes; and when she saw Peter, she sat up. And he gave her his hand, and raised her up; and calling the saints and widows, he presented her alive. And it became known throughout all Joppa: and many believed on the Lord. And it came to pass, that he abode many days in Joppa, with one Simon a tanner. (39-43)

39. *And Peter arose.* It is doubtful whether the messengers explained to Peter the reason why they came to fetch him. Yet it is more likely true that they expressly asked him to perform a miracle. But another question arises, whether God's intention was known to him or not. For he would be rash to undertake the journey if he lacked confidence about its success. I reply that even although he did not yet have personal knowledge of what the Lord would do, yet he cannot be blamed for giving way to the request of the brethren. And there were other reasons why he should come, viz. to lighten their sorrow, to strengthen them with godly exhortations, so that they might not be disheartened by the death of one woman and give up, and to establish the Church which was still tender, and, so to speak, an infant. Finally, this one consideration ought to have been enough for him, that by refusing he would have appeared to be haughtily despising the brethren. Yet at the same time it must be recognized that as often as the Lord had decided to put forth His power in some miracle through the apostles, He directed them by the secret influence of His Spirit. I have really not the shadow of a doubt that, even if Peter was not yet assured about the life of Tabitha, he nevertheless felt convinced that God was the Guide and Director of his journey. The result was that, even if he was anxious and uncertain about the outcome, it was not without due consideration that he prepared himself to go.

All the widows weeping. Here Luke notes the reason why Tabitha was raised from the dead, viz. that God felt pity for the poor and yielded to their prayers for the life of the holy woman. Indeed there were also other ends in view. For when she gains a double life, those virtues which Luke has praised before, are honoured in her person; but the chief object is surely that the glory of Christ might be made plain. For God could have kept her alive longer. And he certainly does not alter his purpose, as if he was led to repent when he quickly restored life to her, but because many of the disciples were weak newcomers, who needed to be confirmed, God declares, in the second life of Tabitha, that His Son is the Author of life. Therefore God had such consideration for the poor and widows, that in hastening to help them in their need, he confirmed the faith of His Gospel in their minds. For in this miracle He provided ample material to enable them to progress.

40. *When they were all put out of the room.* When he takes time to pray, he still seems to be in doubt about what will happen. When

he healed Aeneas he immediately broke out with these confident words, 'Aeneas, Jesus Christ heal thee!' But as the Spirit does not always operate in precisely the same way, it is possible that, being well aware of the power of God, he approached the miracle step by step. Yet it seems absurd that he put all the saints out of the upper room, when it was preferable for them to be eye-witnesses. But because the Lord had not yet revealed to him the time for, and the manner of, putting forth His power, he sought solitude, which was more suitable for praying. A different reason for his plan of action, that we do not know about, could also have been obvious to him. The sacred history records that Elisha did the same thing, for, all alone, without even the mother being present, he lies three times on the dead body.[1] For the Spirit of God has His own powerful impulses, and if anyone will wish to measure them according to ordinary, customary human standards, or to judge them by the perception of the flesh, he will be doing wrongly and unjustly. Indeed we must grasp this, that, when Peter seeks solitude as though he were hesitant, he is countering superstition, so that no one may ascribe to his power a work of God, of which he is only the agent. For this man who removes onlookers and witnesses, and has anxious recourse to prayer, is making sufficient acknowledgment that the matter is not under his own control. Therefore in waiting to know what is pleasing to the Lord Peter has confessed that He alone is the Author of the work.

Kneeling in prayer is a sign of humility, and it has a twofold benefit, that all the parts of our bodies are directed to the worship of God, and that the outward exercise of the body helps the weakness of the mind. But as often as we go down on our knees we must see that the inward submission of the heart corresponds to the ceremony, so that it may not be false and ineffectual.

Turning to the body. It also appears to be an unreasonable thing for him to address a corpse that has no sensation. In fact that speaking to the lifeless body was one aspect of the fervour to which the Spirit of God drove Peter. But if anyone really wishes to have a reason, such a manner of speaking brings out God's power in raising the dead more clearly, than if it were said in the third person, 'Let this body be filled with breath again and live.' Accordingly when Ezekiel is representing the liberation of the people under the figure of a resurrection he says, 'O dry bones, hear the word of the Lord' (Ezek. 37.4). And Christ says, 'The time will come when the dead will hear the voice of the Son of God' (John 5.25). For it was truly the very words of Christ, that issued from Peter's mouth, and restored the spirit to

[1] II Kings 4.32 is quoted, but stretching three times refers to Elijah in I Kings 17.21. Tr.

Tabitha's body. The circumstances which follow are put down to make the miracle a certainty.

41. In the end Luke repeats again that she was presented before the eyes of the disciples; and from that we gather that she was raised up for the sake of others rather than for her own sake. Certain fanatics, who imagine that the soul of a man is nothing other than a breath, which vanishes until the Resurrection Day, snatch at this verse as proof of their fanciful notion. They say, 'What benefit was there for the soul of Tabitha, if it had been received into blessed rest, in being called back into the prison-house of the body, where it would labour with difficulty, contending with so many misfortunes?' As if God had no right to have regard for His own glory in death as well as in life; as if the true blessedness of the godly does not consist in living and dying to Him, and, what is more, as if Christ is not a gain to us, in living as much as in dying (Phil. 1.21), when we dedicate ourselves to Him. Therefore there will be no incongruity if the Lord was more concerned about His own glory rather than about Tabitha herself. However, as the advantage of the faithful is always connected to the glory of God, it was a greater blessing to her to have been restored to life, in order to be a more illustrious instrument of the divine goodness and power.

42. *And they believed.* Many results now appear from the miracle. For God comforted the poor; a godly matron, in whose death a great loss was suffered, was restored to the Church; and many are called to faith. For despite the fact that Peter had been the agent of such great power, yet he does not keep the people bound to himself, but rather directs them to Christ.

43. When he says that Peter stayed with a *tanner*, it can be deduced from this the kind of people of which the church at Joppa consisted. For if the leading people of the city had been converted to Christ, one of them would surely have given hospitality to Peter; for it would have been quite inhuman to neglect an apostle of Christ in this way. Accordingly in that city, as everywhere else, the Lord gathered a church for Himself from the ordinary people, in order to overthrow the pride of the flesh. At the same time Peter's politeness shows itself in the way that he does not despise a host of that standing. However he seems to have been a middle-class merchant, rather than one of the lowest class of workmen. For Luke will afterwards record that in his house there were people who waited upon Peter, and from that it appears that he was looked after well and properly.

CHAPTER TEN

Now there was a certain man in Caesarea, Cornelius by name, a centurion of the band called the Italian band, a devout man, and one that feared God with all his house, who gave much alms to the people, and prayed to God alway. He saw in a vision openly, as it were about the ninth hour of the day, an angel of God coming in unto him, and saying to him, Cornelius. And he, fastening his eyes upon him, and being affrighted, said, What is it, Lord? And he said unto him, Thy prayers and thine alms are gone up for a memorial before God. And now send men to Joppa, and fetch one Simon, who is surnamed Peter: he lodgeth with one Simon a tanner, whose house is by the sea side. (He shall tell thee what thou must do.[1]) (1-6)

1. Luke now passes on to a memorable story, viz. that God regarded a man, uncircumcised and a foreigner, worthy of a unique honour before all the Jews; because He both appoints His angel to go to him, and brings Peter to Caesarea for his sake, to ground him in the Gospel.

But in the first place Luke shows what kind of man this Cornelius was, for whose sake an angel descended from heaven, and God spoke to Peter in a vision. He was a centurion of the Italian cohort. A cohort consisted of a thousand foot-soldiers, and a tribune was in command. Then every company of one hundred used to have its own leader. A legion had five cohorts at the most. This particular cohort was called *Italian*, because the Romans often enlisted soldiers from provincials and allies, but they gathered the flower of the armies from Italy. Therefore Cornelius' nationality was Italian. But he was living at Caesarea with his century as the garrison of the city. For the Romans were accustomed to allocate stations in such a way that every well-known city had some troops to put down sudden disturbances.

He was indeed a rare specimen, because he was a soldier whose piety towards God was so great, and whose dealings with men were so honest and considerate. For at that time when the Italians were brought into the provinces for military service, they used to rush in after plunder like starving wolves, they had generally no more religious scruples than wild beasts, and their devotion to integrity was like that of brigands. Accordingly the virtues of Cornelius are all the more deserving of praise, because in the course of military life, which was then very corrupt, he yet worshipped God conscientiously, and lived

[1] R.V. margin, and Calvin's text.

among men without wrong-doing and harm. And his credit is greatly enhanced by the fact that he rejected the superstition in which he had been born and bred, and embraced the pure worship of the true God. For we know how haughty the Italians were in pluming themselves and despising others. Certainly at that time the Jews were so despicable and hateful to all, that because of them genuine religion was held to be disreputable and almost execrable. Because none of these things kept Cornelius back from abandoning his idols and adopting the proper worship of the one God, he must have been endowed with rare and remarkable sincerity. In addition, among the Jews themselves he could scarcely have found anything, by which he might be attracted to the pursuit of piety, because at that time hardly one in a thousand was even slightly imbued with scanty knowledge of the Law. There is no doubt that Cornelius was singularly privileged to fall in with some upright worshipper of God, who was untouched by false doctrines, and expounded the Law to him faithfully and without the addition of any leaven. But in truth because Luke has several remarkable things to say about him, they must be noted one by one.

2. He says that he was *devout and a God-fearer*; and then, that as a good family head he took pains to instruct the family. He praises him, after that, on account of his charitable services, since he was generous to the people all around him, and, finally, because he prayed to God continually. But it amounts to this, that Cornelius excelled in the virtues in which the integrity of the godly consists, so that every aspect of his life was ordered according to the rule which God lays down for us. But because the Law is contained in two tables, in the first place Luke commends the piety of Cornelius, and then he proceeds to the second part, his exercising the duties of charity towards men. This is especially worth while observing, because the way to live correctly is described for us in his person. Accordingly, in ordering life properly, let faith and religion be fundamental, for if these are taken away all the remaining virtues are nothing else but illusions. Luke counts *the fear of God and prayer* as fruits and proofs of piety and the worship of God, and he is quite right. For religion cannot be torn away from the fear and reverence of God, and nobody can be considered godly unless he knows God as both Father and Lord, and yields himself to Him. But let us realize that what is commended here is spontaneous fear, when those who truly think over in their own minds what is due to God, submit themselves to Him gladly and from the heart. Moreover, because a large part of the world adulterates and perverts the worship of God with fictitious nonsense Luke is justified in adding that Cornelius prayed continually. By that he means that not only did he show his piety by external ceremonies,

but he also worshipped God spiritually, whenever he exercised himself in prayer. At the same time the assiduousness of his prayer must also be noted, for from that we gather that he did not go through with the duty of prayer coldly, as is usually done, but that he exerted himself seriously in prayer, as the constant blessings of God invite and prompt us to do, and the power of faith ought to reveal itself in that. Accordingly let each one of us take the example of Cornelius and encourage himself to persevere in prayer.

With all his house. We ought not lightly to pass over this commendation that Cornelius had a church in his household. And certainly, as far as it will depend on him, the true worshipper of God will not allow Him to be banished out of his house. For how preposterous it is for him to insist on his own right of obedience from wife, children, servants, male and female, but yet indifferently allow contempt for God! Of course it will sometimes happen that a godly man has not even his wife falling in with him, but he, who is set over others, must take care by every means that he assumes his own authority from God; and there is nothing more fitting than to dedicate everything that we have, as well as ourselves, to God. Therefore if a godly man has sons who are different from himself, or a wife who is badly behaved, or servants who are worthless and dishonest, let him not turn a blind eye, and let him not allow his house to be defiled by his own sloth. In the case of Cornelius it is not only his earnestness that is commended, but the blessing of God, as a result of which he had his household yielding to him in godliness. And the point must not be omitted that when he established the family in the fear of God it was with contempt of the fear of danger, which threatened him as a result. For the Jewish religion was exceedingly hateful, and a Roman citizen could not adopt a foreign religion, as they used to call it, with impunity. Accordingly, although the sincere profession of the Gospel gets a very bad hearing[1] in the world today, yet it is extremely depraved cowardice if that unjust enmity prevents a man from daring to offer his family to God as his sacrifice according to godly principles.

Doing alms. There is also synecdoche in this phrase. For just as it has been said a little earlier that the worship of God is proved by prayers, so now when mention is made of charity, Luke picks out one example, by which he shows that Cornelius was a generous and beneficent man. For our piety ought to break out to men so that we testify that we do fear God by the practice of kindness and uprightness (*iustitiam*). Since the word *alms* (*eleemosyna*) is properly speaking mercy (*misericordia*), an inner feeling of the heart, it has been transferred to the outward services by which we help the poor. For from this

[1] Reading *auditur* for *audit*. Tr.

source springs genuine and properly disposed kindness, if the hardships of our brethren move us with pity, if, reflecting upon the unity that there is among us, we look after them and care for them just as if they were our own flesh, and are anxious to help them, just as if they were our own members. Of course hypocrites are also generous at times, or at least give a lot, but yet, although they lavish everything, none of the assistance that they will put out on the poor will be worthy of the name *alms*. For that word of Paul's must be kept in mind, 'he who does not have love is nothing, even if he distributes the whole of his substance among the poor' (I Cor. 13.3). Let us therefore learn from this word that our kindness is only finally approved by God, if we help the poor in their need out of sympathy, and we give, as if with open hearts, what the liberality of God supplies in abundance.

When Luke says that he gave alms *to all the people*[1] he is really meaning all the poor round about; for there were a good many rich people and it would have been ridiculous to give to them. Finally, in devoting himself so generously to the Jews, he bore testimony to the sympathy he had with them for their religion. For that reason Luke says a little later that he was pleasing to all the Jews (v. 27).

But if this man, who was inspired by such a frail and rudimentary faith, was such a splendid mirror of uprightness and sanctity, when so many obstacles confronted him, ought we not to be ashamed, we who wish to be considered Christian teachers, and are so very cold in the exercises of piety? If a small spark of faith had such a great effect on him, what ought the full splendour of knowledge be bringing about in us? But as we boast loud-mouthed of Christ, how far removed most of us are from the example of this holy man, so that there is apparent scarcely a tiny shadow of the virtues which he had in abundance. For how great is our sluggishness in prayer? How slow and reluctant are we to undertake services of mercy? Yes, and what is more, not only do meanness and greed keep many back from generously giving away as much as they ought out of their possessions, but they burn with such an insane passion for possessing, they are driven wild by such great cruelty, that they do not hesitate to seize the property of the poor and to devour their very flesh.

3. *He saw in a vision.* Luke puts *vision* for a kind of divine oracle, so that we may know that Cornelius was led to the faith of Christ from heaven. But because men are often deceived by illusions, in order to remove suspicion Luke points out the time, *the ninth hour.* In those days, of course, it was men's custom to divide the day into

[1] Calvin's text: *faciensque eleemosynas toti populo.* Vulg. agrees with Greek: *ποιῶν ἐλεημοσύνας πολλὰς τῷ λαῷ.* Tr.

twelve hours from sunrise to sunset. It follows from that, that it was in the full light of day when the angel appeared, so that the vision could be quite plain. However signs were always added to visions to free the servants of God from the fear of illusions, because, when He appeared through dreams, such marks of certitude were nevertheless firmly and deeply impressed on the minds, as to admit of no doubt.

4. *He gazed at him in terror.* His attentiveness is described by Luke expressly that we may know that this was not an empty figment of the imagination that suddenly and stealthily came on the man, when he was sleepy or doing something else. The terror, by which he was seized, sprang from his awareness of the majesty of God. For as soon as men perceive the presence of God they are bound to be greatly terrified and indeed confounded by fear. But it must be put down to our indolence that His Word strikes no terror into us, because we do not realize or notice that it is God who is speaking. But the godly, to whom God reveals Himself in His Word, tremble when they hear it, as Isaiah says (66.2, 5). Moreover, the sight of God is terrible to men, not in order that they may always lie confounded, and be consumed by fear, but only that they may humbly prepare themselves to reverence Him.

What is it Lord? It is plain enough from this answer that Cornelius' mind was so affected by religion that he knew that he had to deal with God. Accordingly the common translation has erroneously, 'Who art thou, Lord?'[1] And it is probable that what is read there is a false substitution, seeing that in the Greek phrase there is no ambiguity to make a translator go wrong; and all the copies agree in this reading, τί ἐστι. And certainly when Cornelius realizes that it is God who is speaking, he submits himself to obey; just as the reply is nothing else but a command.

Thy prayers and alms. The fact that God appears, as it were, to be deaf if He does not answer our prayers straight away, has led to this way of speaking, that our prayers reach Him, and that He is mindful of them. Moreover the angel attributes the reason why the Lord thinks Cornelius deserving of the full light of the Gospel to this, that He has heard his prayers clearly, and regarded his alms as acceptable. From that we conclude that virtues and good deeds are not, only pleasing to God, but are also honoured by this splendid reward that in gratitude for them He heaps and enriches us with greater gifts, according to that word, 'To him who has it will be given' (Matt. 13.12). There is the similar word, 'Well done, good and faithful servant, thou hast been faithful over a few things, I will

[1] The Sixtus edition of Vulg. has this reading. Tr.

set thee over many things' (Matt. 25.21). For in this way the Lord raises up His own people with a continuous succession of gifts, as if by sure steps, until He leads them right to the top.

But the Papists abuse this verse in two ways. For, taking the fact that God had regard to the prayers and alms of Cornelius so that He endowed him with the faith of the Gospel, they twist it to the preparations made by themselves, as if a man acquires faith by his own diligence and virtue, and anticipates the grace of God by the merits of works. Then they generally infer that good works are so meritorious that the graces of God are lavished on individuals in proportion as they are deserved.

In the first they are making an exceedingly childish error in supposing that the works of Cornelius were acceptable to God before he had been enlightened by faith. And indeed we do not have to look far for proof to refute their ignorance, for he could not obtain anything by prayer without faith preceding, for it alone opens the gate for us to pray. And Augustine makes a shrewd judgment in scoffing at Pelagius, because he said that faith is procured by prayer, before any existed in a man, for Augustine says, 'Who will look for a doctor, except the man who has already been partly cured?' But it is precisely the healthiness of faith that teaches us to knock (*pulsare*). Moreover his fear of God and his piety clearly demonstrate that he was born again of the Spirit. For Ezekiel claims this praise for God alone, that He forms the hearts of men to fear him (36.26).[1] And Isaiah (11.2) says that the Spirit of the fear of the Lord reposes in Christ; so that we may know that He can be found nowhere except in His members. It is therefore extremely foolish to imagine here, in the person of Cornelius, a man who aspires or presses towards eternal life with nature as his guide. Accordingly, their conclusion that we can anticipate the grace of God by meritorious works, is absurd.

As far as the second error is concerned, when they imagine that each one of us is enriched with greater graces in proportion as he has deserved them, that can be refuted with little trouble. First of all we deny that we have any good works which God has not freely bestowed upon us. Secondly, we say that the right use of the gifts of God is also from Him, and that this is a second grace of His, that we are making proper use of His first gifts. In the third place, we deny that we deserve anything by our works, which are always defective and faulty. Good works do indeed gain an increase of faith for us, but not by their own merit, for they cannot be acceptable to God except with forgiveness, which they procure by the help of faith. That is why it is faith alone which establishes their value. In this way Cor-

[1] C.R. footnote rightly corrects to Jer. 32.40. Tr.

nelius obtained fuller knowledge of Christ from his prayers and alms, but his having God well-disposed and favourable to his alms and prayers was already dependent on his faith.

Moreover if the value of works is determined by faith, it is because of indulgence and not merit, that they are approved by God. For seeing that faith finds nothing worthy in us, on account of which we may please God, what is lacking in us is borrowed from Christ. But it is exceedingly perverse that, when the Papists continually have the word 'merit' on their lips, and do not cease to inflate simple people with an empty confidence, they yet contribute nothing by which the efforts of men may be encouraged to well-doing. For they always leave consciences in suspense, and tell men to be in doubt as to whether their works are pleasing to God or not. When such confusion takes possession of their minds are the indolent and slothful not bound to flag? But as for ourselves, even if we take merit away from works, yet when we teach that a reward is in store for them, we are inciting men, with the best and sharpest of spurs, to a concern for living properly. For it is when we have been persuaded that our labour is not in vain, that we at last make ourselves ready and eager to serve God. Now we must put it down to our own ingratitude that we do not see a richer abundance of the gifts of the Spirit today, but rather a withering away of the greater part of them. For just as God crowned the prayers, alms, and sanctity of Cornelius with the precious gem of His Gospel, so when He sees our irreverent and irresponsible abuse of the treasure of His Gospel, He has good cause, after we have been reduced by hunger and want, for finally starving us to death.

However the question can be asked here, whether faith requires the knowledge of Christ, or is it satisfied with a simple conviction of the mercy of God? For Cornelius appears to have known absolutely nothing about Christ. But it can be established by sound proofs that faith cannot be separated from Christ. For if the bare majesty of God is apprehended, we are overwhelmed by His glory, rather than savouring any taste of His goodness. Therefore Christ must be the intermediary so that the mind of man may grasp that God is favourable. It is not without good reason that He is called the image of the invisible God (Col. 1.15), because only in His face does the Father cause Himself to be seen. Moreover, since He is the way, the truth, and the life (John 14.6), wherever you go without Him, the snares of errors and deceptions will surround you on all sides, and death will confront you everywhere. The difficulty is easily put right in the case of Cornelius. No spiritual gifts are offered to us except in Christ. In particular from where does regeneration itself spring but from the fact that, when we are implanted into the death of Christ, our old man is crucified (Rom. 6.5, 6)? And if Cornelius was participating in the Spirit of Christ it is not for us to think that he was completely devoid of faith in Him. For he surely did not embrace the worship of the true God, whom the Jews alone used to reverence, in such a way that he did not at the same time hear something about the promised Mediator; even if his knowledge was hazy and confused, yet there was some. Anybody who had come into Judaea in those days was forced to hear something about the Messiah; and what is more, a certain amount of rumour about Him had spread through far distant lands. Accordingly, Cornelius must be placed in the category of the fathers of old who hoped for salvation by a Redeemer not yet revealed. Also, Augustine is wrong in saying that Peter laid the foundation of his faith, because it already had a firm foundation before. However, Augustine's thought agrees with ours in regard to the event itself, for he plainly affirms, in his book *Concerning the Predestination of the Saints*, and in other places, that Cornelius could not have prayed if he had not been a believer.

5. *Now send to Joppa.* With His wonderful indulgence, God orders Cornelius not to set out himself, but to send messengers to Peter, so that he may wait quietly at home, and that Peter may undertake the inconveniences of the journey for his sake. But let us not be surprised that the Lord dealt so considerately with Cornelius, since every day he forces the ministers of His Word on people who are almost unwilling; so that, without being asked, He appears to those who do not seek Him, as He reminds us through Isaiah (65.1). But why does the angel not rather fulfil the role of teacher? For it seems somewhat unreasonable that he surrenders his task to a mortal man, for an oracle would have had greater authority, than when the Gospel is preached to him on human lips. Obviously, just as Christ showed Himself to Paul in a vision, but yet left the responsibility of teaching him to Ananias, to confirm by this example the ministry of preaching the Gospel, which He has entrusted to His Church, so now the angel gives way to Peter, for the task committed to him by Christ to be carried out. Therefore, if a man wishes to be a disciple of Christ, and to be illuminated by the light of heavenly wisdom, let him not be reluctant to prove himself attentive and teachable to the external voice of men, which Christ uses as an instrument, and to which He wishes our faith to be connected. And we see by what horrible means the Lord has punished the mad pride of those who despised preaching and sought after revelations from heaven. For since God wishes to be heard among men, His ministers, to whom He has entrusted His Word, cannot be despised, without insulting Him contemptuously. At the same time I grant that the spirits must be tested, so that we may not

hear without picking out all who are pretending to be ministers of Christ. But because faith comes from hearing (Rom. 10.17), nobody, who will spurn and reject the preached Word, will attain to it.

And when the angel that spake unto him was departed, he called two of his household-servants, and a devout soldier of them that waited on him continually; and having rehearsed all things unto them, he sent them to Joppa.

Now on the morrow, as they were on their journey, and drew nigh unto the city, Peter went up upon the housetop to pray, about the sixth hour: and he became hungry, and desired to eat: but while they made ready, he fell into a trance; and he beholdeth the heaven opened, and a certain vessel descending, as it were a great sheet, let down by four corners upon the earth: wherein were all manner of four-footed beasts and creeping things of the earth and fowls of the heaven. And there came a voice to him, Rise, Peter; kill and eat. But Peter said, Not so, Lord; for I have never eaten anything that is common and unclean. And a voice came unto him again the second time, What God hath cleansed, make not thou common. And this was done thrice: and straightway the vessel was received up into heaven. (7-16)

7. *And when the angel departed.* Here Luke tells how prompt Cornelius was to obey, seeing that he does not delay even for a moment, but carefully carries out what he has been ordered. The reason for such willing promptness was that he had confidence in the promise, just as unbelief is the cause of our slowness in following God. Certainly angels do not fly to us from heaven to point out particular men to us, but that word of Christ's sounds in the ears of all, 'Seek and you will find, knock and it will be opened to you' (Matt. 7.7). How does it happen that scarcely one or two out of a hundred stir a foot, that others crawl slowly and make such little progress, except that we do not seriously believe in the promise? Therefore let us learn that there must be no procrastination, but, when each one has heard the voice of God, let him make haste to go where he is called.

Two of his household servants. Cornelius gained this reward for his diligence in instructing his household, that he had trustworthy and honest servants, who were glad to put their services at his disposal, and to whom he could also safely entrust anything. On the other hand, the Lord often inflicts just punishments on masters, who have not been concerned about the instruction of their household. For when they have neglected to educate them in piety and the fear of the Lord, they deserve to find them, in turn, disobedient and unreliable, and they even go in fear of their treachery.

A devout soldier. Since this soldier had more dealings with Cornelius, he had also imbued him, like his household servants, with the fear of the Lord. It is appropriate to recall here what I touched upon before, that there is no kind of life which excuses us from our duty to worship God purely. For military life was very corrupt at that time, because, from the discipline of former days, they had degenerated into filthy licentiousness. And yet the Spirit of God is here bearing testimony to soldiers of piety. Accordingly there is no reason for men, who would desire by any means to be free from all rectitude, to ask exemption for themselves from the worship of God, on the pretext of military service. If they say they cannot serve God because they are soldiers, they will have those two soldiers on the Last Day as sufficient witnesses and judges, by whom they will be condemned. At the same time there are also condemned the madmen who shout that it is unlawful for Christians to bear arms. For those men practise their religion along with their military life, and in accepting Christ they do not abandon their former way of life, they do not throw away their arms as if they were harmful things, and they do not renounce their own station in life.

8. The reason why Cornelius explains everything to the soldier and the servants is that it may make them more inclined to carry out the commandment, when they realize it comes from God rather than a man. And he does not hesitate to let them share the knowledge of such a great matter, when he had been frank in his instruction of them in the past.

9. *Now on the morrow, as they were on their journey*. Just as Luke told that Cornelius was advised by an oracle to summon Peter, so he now records the converse vision in which Peter is instructed to come to him. From that it appears all the clearer that this whole affair was controlled by the wonderful plan of God; for He both prepares Cornelius to be docile and, even more, inflames him with an eagerness and desire to learn, and on the other hand prepares the mind of Peter, so that he is willing to undertake the task of teaching. But nevertheless we must pay attention to the circumstances with which he lights up the story.

Peter went up onto the roof to pray privately on his own. For in prayer solitude is a great help, which even Christ did not neglect, since the mind is free of all distractions and concentrates better on God. Now the Jews used to have a different style of buildings than we are used to; for on the roofs they had space for walking. In those days *the sixth hour* was noon. And there is no doubt that it was according to custom that he devoted himself to prayer at that time. For, because almost the whole day we are distracted by a variety of occupations, and we are constantly bustling about unless we hold ourselves in check by applying the bridle, it is useful to have hours set apart for prayer, not because we are tied down to hours, but so that prayer may not escape our memory when it ought to take priority over all our concerns. Finally, the same thing must be felt about time as about place, viz. that they are remedies which assist our weakness. And if the apostles considered them appropriate for themselves, how much more assiduously must they be practised by the slow and lazy?

10. *A departure of mind* (*excessus mentis*). Because we have minds that are, so to speak, planted in the earth, so that Peter would be capable of an oracle, it was necessary for his mind, as it were, to be moved out of the place, and carried off above. And it is in this way, when he is lifted up above the world in an unaccustomed manner, that he is prepared to receive the oracle.

11. In my opinion the *opening of heaven* here means something different than in the seventh chapter (7.56). For there it is said that the heaven was opened for Stephen so that he saw the glory of Christ. Here it seems to Peter that our visible sky is rent, so that a linen cloth may come out from it.

12. If anyone asks how he could see a huge collection of animals all at once, the question is easily answered. For Luke says *every kind*, because in it different species were mixed together indiscriminately. He therefore does not start off with the first species to number them consecutively to the last. Then again, we ought not to assess this sight in human fashion, because ecstasy was giving other eyes to Peter.

But before going further we must establish what the aim of the vision was. Some men argue about that more subtly than, in my opinion, the verse demands. Therefore I think that it is shown to Peter, in a general way, that the distinction, which God had formerly imposed, is now removed. But, just as He had made a division between the animals, so, having chosen one people for Himself, He used to regard all the nations as unclean and common. The distinction between the animals having now been removed, He teaches, as a consequence, that men are no longer divided as they used to be, and that a Jew is no different from a Greek. From this, Peter is warned not to shrink, afterwards, from the Gentiles as unclean. There is no doubt that God wished to encourage Peter to come to Cornelius without fear. But He had separated one nation to Himself from the rest, as Moses says in his song (Deut. 32.9): 'When the Most High divided the nations, he made Jacob his possession[1] etc.' Therefore He used to call it His own inheritance and His private property (*peculium*).

[1] Lit. 'He placed His rope on Jacob', *posuit funiculum suum in Iacob*. Vulg.: *Jacob funiculus hereditatis eius*. *Funiculus* = a rope. Cf. Heb. לֶחֶב, a rope, measuring line, a possession. Tr.

According to this order it would not have been lawful for Peter to bring the covenant of salvation to the Gentiles, for that was to 'take the children's bread and throw it to the dogs' (Matt. 15.26); unless perchance they accept circumcision and cross over into Judaism, for it was in order to receive those who surrendered in that way. Accordingly when the apostles were first sent to preach, they were forbidden to turn aside to the Gentiles (Matt. 10.5). But since the preaching of the Gospel is the most sacred matter and of the greatest importance, Peter ought not to have approached anything in connexion with it in a doubtful and vacillating mind. Therefore, in order that he may be sure of his call, God shows him openly, as if in a picture, that the legal distinction of clean and unclean is abolished. From that he may deduce that the wall which previously stood in the middle between Jews and Gentiles is now destroyed (Eph. 2.14). Now Paul says that this is a mystery hidden for ages, that the Gentiles are sharers in the same salvation with the people of God, and ingrafted into the one body (Eph. 3.6, 9). Therefore Peter would never have dared to open the gate of heaven to the Gentiles, unless God Himself had removed the wall, and thrown open a plain way and entrance for all. I have just said that there was indeed no time when it was not permissible to admit Gentiles to the worship of God, provided that they were circumcised, but as long as they remained uncircumcised they were alienated from God. But now God has made common to the whole world the covenant of life, which He had deposited in one nation as if it were hidden treasure. And from that we conclude that this vision is of no small value for us. For when it teaches that the separation between Jews and Gentiles was only temporary, it is just as if God proclaimed from heaven that He is gathering all the peoples of the world into His grace, so that He may be God of all. Finally, we have a clear proclamation from heaven that summons us to the hope of eternal life.

But someone will object that Peter was taught about this matter before. For to him and to the others the commandment had been given to publish the Gospel throughout the whole world. Therefore he himself was ignorant of his own calling, or this vision was unnecessary. I reply that there was so much difficulty in the very newness and strangeness of it, that they could not grow used to it all at once. They did indeed grasp the predictions of the prophets, and the recent command of Christ about calling the Gentiles through the Gospel, but when it came to the actual event, nevertheless they hesitated, daunted by something in which they were inexperienced. So it is no wonder if the Lord confirms Peter by a fresh sign. On this matter something will still have to be said in the next chapter.

13. *A voice from heaven.* A voice comes down from heaven, as did

the linen sheet, so that Peter might know that both came from God, and in fact the sight would have been of no use whatever to him, unless God had cleansed, with these words, what had previously been unclean. I do not quarrel with the way that some draw out an allegory from the word to *kill*, as if God means men are sacrificed to Him by the spiritual sword of the Gospel; but I rather prefer the simple view that by these words God is abrogating the Law concerning the distinction between animals, so that He may teach, at the same time, that He rejects no people. For if sacrifice is meant by the first word what will *eat* be?

14. *Not so Lord.* This is the word, not so much of a man who is refusing, as objecting to, God's command. For he is quite rightly afraid to touch what he knows is forbidden him by the Law of God. He therefore cites to God the Law, which He Himself introduced, in case he may rashly be involved in violating it. For there was some appearance of contradiction between the vision and the Law. Therefore Peter makes no haste, but desires the removal of his scruple, before he may depart from the observation of the Law. Yet it may possibly appear strange that Peter offers more resistance in regard to food, than Abraham did in the slaying of his son, for Abraham had more things about which he might have objected to God. I dare not say here that what is exceedingly common among men happened to Peter, that they pursue external and trifling matters rather than the main points of the Law. Rather do I reply that there is no doubt at all that the mind of Abraham was so persuaded, and was immediately endowed with such power of the Spirit, that he overcame with noble and heroic courage all the things that could hinder him on his course; but in the case of Peter the Spirit of God operated slowly. And we are warned by that, that even the smallest thing may cause us anxiety unless the Lord provides us with determination and steadfastness to overcome trepidation. Yet Peter acts in a godly and conscientious way, because, hesitating between different lines of thought, he does not venture to undertake anything until it becomes clearer which he ought to follow.

Common in this verse means profane. For, because God chose the Jews to be His peculiar people, as has been said, He had laid down for them this religious usage and way of living, which would distinguish them from profane nations. They therefore called 'common' whatever was in use among the Gentiles, that was contrary to the norm of the Law, because there was nothing holy or pure, except what God had appointed for the use of His people.

15. *What God has cleansed.* This sentence certainly does deal with food, but it ought to be extended to all parts of life. It is literally,

'what God has made clean, thou wilt not profane', but the meaning is, 'It is not for us to approve or condemn anything, but just as we stand and fall by the judgment of God alone, so He is the judge of all things' (Rom. 14.4). As far as food is concerned, after the abrogation of the Law, God pronounces all to be pure and clean. If, on the other hand, a mortal man rises up who establishes a new distinction, forbidding people certain things, he is sacrilegious in audaciously seizing, and arrogating to himself, the right and authority of God. Such were the ancient heretics, Montanus, Priscillian, the Donatists, the Tatians and all the Encratites. Later on the Pope introduced a law concerning food, in order to bundle all those impious sects together. And the defenders of this impiety have no cause to gabble that they are introducing no uncleanness to foods, but that they are only prohibiting men from eating meat on certain days in order to mortify the flesh. For, since they feed on the richest foods, and those most suitable for pleasure and riotous living, why do they shrink from touching bacon fat, as if from the greatest of crimes, except that they imagine that what is forbidden by the law of their idol is polluted and unclean? The tyranny of the Pope rampages with the same pride in all parts of life, for there is nothing in which he does not insert his snares for wretched consciences. But for our part, relying on the heavenly oracle, let us spurn all his prohibitions. We must always find out what the Lord has to say, so that we may decide from that what is lawful for us, and what we are free to do, seeing that not even Peter was allowed to *make common* what was lawful according to the Word of God.

Moreover this verse is valuable for curbing the impudence of men, which makes them revel in perverse judgments. For almost everybody permits himself to pronounce judgment on the actions of others. Now, as we are peevish and spiteful we rather tend towards the unfavourable side, and in this way we snatch away from God what is His concern. This word alone ought to suffice to correct audacity of this sort, viz. that it is not lawful for us to make this or that unclean, but that this power belongs to God alone.

Finally, it is also hinted by these words, that the Jews were not God's holy people for the reason that they were distinguished by their own merit, but solely by the grace of divine adoption. Now, after God received the Gentiles into the fellowship of the covenant, all have equal rights.

16. *This was done thrice.* The repetition of the vision was effective for confirmation, so that no hesitation or anxiety or scruple might remain stuck in Peter's mind. From that we gather what old roots the observance of the Law had put down into it. Now, no other

reason occurs to me for God's leaving him in the dark until he would learn the motive of the vision from the subsequent event, except that in his astonishment he did not ask to be shown the meaning of this thing; although it was quite opportune that the messengers of Cornelius did come shortly afterwards to interpret it. Finally, *the vessel was received up into heaven* in order that Peter might be made more certain that this message came from God.

Now while Peter was much perplexed in himself what the vision which he had seen might mean, behold, the men that were sent by Cornelius, having made inquiry for Simon's house, stood before the gate, and called and asked whether Simon, which was surnamed Peter, were lodging there. And while Peter thought on the vision, the Spirit said unto him, Behold, three men seek thee. But arise, and get thee down, and go with them, nothing doubting: for I have sent them. And Peter went down to the men, and said, Behold, I am he whom ye seek: what is the cause wherefore ye are come? And they said, Cornelius a centurion, a righteous man and one that feareth God, and well reported of by all the nation of the Jews, was warned of God by a holy angel to send for thee into his house, and to hear words from thee. So he called them in and lodged them. (17-23)

17. Peter had been instructed not only by the vision but also by the Word of God; and yet he does not understand what he has seen, until the Spirit interprets to him. And of course that clearly mirrors our own slowness, although we are still far from being like Peter, for we do not even immediately comprehend what God is wanting, or why He is speaking to us, so that in the end numerous interpretations would hardly be enough for us. But at the same time we must note what Luke adds, that Peter thought about the vision intently, that is, after recovering from his bewilderment of course. For it was a sign of godly reverence that he did not negligently allow the vision to escape or vanish from him. Therefore the Lord opened to him when he knocked (Matt. 7.7). But as for us we receive just punishments for our sloth, because we do not make better progress in the Word of God, seeing that we are so indifferent about the discipline of inquiring.

20. *Go, nothing doubting.* Scripture often uses this phrase, when it wishes to express what the obedience of faith ought to be like. Thus when Paul is commending the faith of Abraham in Rom. 4.19, he says, 'He did not hesitate when God promised a child to him, when he was already without an heir and past the age for begetting one.' And in chapter 14 verse 23, where he is discussing foods, he condemns hesitant consciences. Now it is proper to judge for and against, as

they say, when we have to weigh opposing reasons, and we are driven this way and that in turn. But we must not follow God with a doubting and vacillating mind, but with one that is composed and firm. In a word, the Lord wishes us to defer to Him so much, that, when we have heard Him, we may have no further argument about what we need to do, but may decide without any question that what He commands must be done. And certainly His will is worthy to be a guiding light for us, to show us the way, when all the clouds have been scattered, and to bring the whole of our minds into ready obedience to itself, when all altercation has been brought to an end; and we gather this better from the ensuing words. For the reason why Peter is not permitted to suspend judgment on a doubtful question, is added, viz. that God is the originator of the business. For it amounts to saying that we ought to be content merely with God's nod, so that we may obey His command. Finally, we are also warned again in this verse, that men's consciences will be at peace, to perform their actions in safety, only when they have been taught by the Word of God, and they decide to undertake nothing except by His guidance and command.

21. *Behold I am he whom you seek.* Luke now tells how ready Peter was to obey; and then how he at last understood from the messengers, why the vision was shown to him. For he hears that he is called by Cornelius, a man who is a Gentile, a man whom he would have considered outside the pale, and not fit to be associated with in a friendly way, if his judgment had not been corrected by this word, 'What God calls pure, you will not consider common.' This is true wisdom, when we are emptied of all our confidence, and corrected of our obstinacy, and the will of God grasps us to itself, and takes possession of our minds in such a way that nothing is right for us except what it lays down.

22. *Cornelius, a righteous man.* The servants do not praise Cornelius in a fawning way and out of ambition, but in order that Peter may be less disinclined to meet him. And they say that he is acceptable to the Jews so that Peter may know that he is no stranger to the true and genuine religion. For even those who were superstitious boasted that they were worshippers of God, when they served idols. But Cornelius could not have had the Jews, who maintained the worship of the One God, bearing witness to his piety, if he had not professed to worship the God of Abraham along with them. Moreover as this was a rare example, so it ought to have moved Peter a great deal. However they mostly rely upon this argument, that all this is governed by the commandment of God, so that they may convince him about what they want, as if they said, that he is being called, not so much

by a mortal man, as by God, who had so commanded by His angel.

23. Peter, having also been conquered by the authority of God, is in doubt no longer, but gives the men hospitality, so that he may soon take the road with them. So we must quietly submit ourselves to God, and when His will is known, all that there is left for us to do is to run quickly to where He calls. Other things have no difficulty

And on the morrow he arose and went forth with them, and certain of the brethren from Joppa accompanied him. And on the morrow they entered into Caesarea. And Cornelius was waiting for them, having called together his kinsmen and his near friends. And when it came to pass that Peter entered, Cornelius met him, and fell down at his feet, and worshipped him. But Peter raised him up, saying, Stand up; I myself also am a man. And as he talked with him, he went in, and findeth many come together: and he said unto them, Ye yourselves know how that it is an unlawful thing for a man that is a Jew to join himself or come unto one of another nation; and yet unto me hath God shewed that I should not call any man common or unclean: wherefore also I came without gainsaying, when I was sent for. I ask therefore with what intent ye sent for me. (23b–29)

On the morrow he went forth. It is very likely that the men had arrived towards evening, because they had not yet approached the city at noon, and the vision was certainly not a mere momentary thing when it was repeated three times. Therefore, refreshed from their tiredness by a night's rest, they make themselves ready for the return journey. It was moreover an act of kindness and courtesy that some of the faithful, sent, one may well believe, by the whole Church, join themselves to Peter as companions, and accompany him right to Caesarea. And these men certainly undertake the journey along with Peter out of respect and good-will; but the Lord is bringing them, so that He may have witnesses of His grace. So they bring back the great reward of their gratitude, when they see the rule of Christ being extended to the Gentiles as confirmation of their own faith.

24. *Cornelius was waiting for them.* Luke praises Cornelius' attitude, not only in this respect, that he eagerly awaited Peter's arrival, but also in that he wished his friends and kinsmen to share the faith with him. It was certainly creating a dangerous situation to summon a crowd of men to take up a new religion. And there were grounds in plenty which he could have used as a pretext for flattering himself. For he had not been ordered to summon others into association, but rather, they had been passed over, and he alone had been chosen to be the possessor of such a great blessing. But he thought to himself how much he was under obligation both to the glory of God and to

the salvation of his brethren. He knew that it is unfair and discourteous, as it was, for everyone to look to himself as an individual, with no concern for others. He considered that it is a sign of disgraceful negligence to bury the treasure of the Gospel in the earth. He therefore fulfilled what the Lord demands of all His people through Isaiah and Micah, that individuals invite their brethren, as though grasping them by the hand, and encourage them to believe. Cornelius has therefore taught us by his example that, when God reveals Himself to us, we must not quench the light of His knowledge within us by sloth or fear, but rather we must take care to let our faith be a guiding light to show the way to others. For inheritance of the Kingdom of Heaven is not such that even a very small share in it may grow less for us, if many were admitted to share in it, but, on the contrary the addition of fellow-heirs will increase our glory.

Furthermore we must observe how far removed he is from all ostentation. For being prepared to learn himself, he calls them, so that he may have fellow-pupils. Here indeed we have the true desire for piety, when along with zeal there appears such honesty that we are not ashamed to depend upon what God says. For ambition drives many to put out effort on teaching the ignorant, and a foolish loquacity exposes their defect, when they pour out words too passionately, and earnestly strive to be the only ones to be heard. But all men ought to have this one resolution, to submit themselves and the whole world to God, so that He alone may be pre-eminent, with men reduced to true humility. Let the man, who is strong in the skill and grace of teaching, not refuse to prove himself a teacher to his brethren, only let there be no sign of boasting and a conceited desire for superiority. Let him to whom it has not been given to declare himself a teacher, keep himself within his limitations. Let neither desire the mastery, as James also warns (3.1).[1] In fact, let them so edify each other in turn, that neither learned nor ignorant may feel ashamed to be put in his place.

However, the question is asked, 'What kinsmen could he have had in Judaea, since he had come there as a foreigner on a temporary tour of military duty?' For myself, although I am not dogmatic about anything, yet I embrace this as the most likely solution, that in his company he had some of his kinsmen; for relatives and men known to each other were accustomed to join together under the same ensign. And there is no doubt that his kinsmen were only too willing to serve under the ensign of Cornelius since he was a centurion.

He calls intimate friends *ἀναγκαίους* in the same way as those who

[1] Calvin has *magisterium* whereas James 3.1 in Greek has διδάσκαλοι, Vulg. *magistri*. Cf. A.V. 'masters', but R.V., R.S.V., N.E.B., 'teachers'. Tr.

are bound together among themselves by a closer bond are called 'necessary' (*necessarii*) by the Latins.

25. *He fell down at his feet and worshipped him.* This is the word προσεκύνησεν which means to show honour and reverence, either by bending the knee, or bowing the head, or some other gesture. Now, it is asked whether Peter refuses this adoration merely on account of his modesty, or whether in fact he flatly disapproves of it as a forbidden thing. It is apparent that Cornelius' action displeased Peter, from the reason immediately added, 'Rise up, for I myself am also a man.' For one may infer from these words that there was something of a divine nature in that reverence, because he was transferring to a mortal man the honour which was due to God alone. But one is not to believe that Peter was substituted for God by Cornelius. For if he transferred God's honour to a man, what happened to that godliness and religion, with an account of which he was recently commended? I therefore think in this way, that by no means did he intend to deprive God of His legitimate worship to give it to a man, but since he wished to pay special respect to the prophet and apostle of Christ, he slipped into an extravagant sign of reverence and so sinned by excess. For words can hardly make it plain enough how easy it is to fall into superstition, when honour, which exhibits even the smallest appearance of divine worship, is conferred upon the ministers of Christ. For through imprudence we slip easily into something to which we have given very little thought. There would be less danger in the case of a king or the chief men of the world, for he who does honour to a king as a suppliant keeps himself within the bounds of civil and earthly honour. There is a different reason in the case of the ministers of Christ, since, if on the one hand their office is indeed spiritual, so on the other, if anyone falls down at their feet to worship them, this honour has something spiritual. For a distinction must be maintained between civil worship, which men use among themselves out of respect for the political order, and the worship behind which religion exists and which looks directly to the honour of God; just as there is also a distinction between laws which either are required for temporal rule or bind consciences. For some silly men are very much mistaken in thinking that genuflexion of itself is plainly condemned here. But all that I have said amounts to this: here Cornelius is not greeting his Proconsul or the Emperor with a political rite, but having been struck with admiration at the sight of Peter he confers honour on him as though he were in the presence of God. Therefore, as if he has forgotten himself, he renders to a man more than is lawful. As I have already said he had no intention at all of stripping God of any of His honour, to adorn a man with his spoils, but when the adoration of a

man has something that is mixed up and confused with the worship of God, immediately an offence that exceeds expectation and imagination creeps stealthily up, that a man, who is worshipped to show honour to God, is lifted above the human level.

The Papists disregard that distinction and lay hold of one part of it; for religious adoration alone is dealt with among them. So that they may have some decent excuse for adapting a part of it to created beings, they divide it into *latria, dulia* and *hyperdulia*. And they certainly claim *latria* for God alone, as if they were saying, that the adoration of worship is due only to Him. They make the adoration of *dulia* common to the dead and their bones, to statues and pictures. They assign *hyperdulia* to the Virgin Mary and the cross on which Christ hung. Even if I make no mention that they are gabbling from childish ignorance, how many of them grasp that offensive distinction? And I am not just speaking about the ordinary people but about their very leaders. Therefore all their forms of worship must be spoiled and corrupted by a perverse superstition, since they rashly associate creatures with God. But Luke does not say here that Cornelius showed the honour due to God to Peter, but he uses only the general word, 'adoration', and adds that he was nevertheless reproved because he wrongly exalted a man higher than was proper. Surely if there had been a place for that new dogma about the adoration of *dulia*, Peter ought to have warned Cornelius not to go beyond *dulia*. But because any adoration to which religion and respect for the divine honour is connected does not leave God His honour intact, by whatever name it is disguised in the end, Peter is therefore content with this one reason, that he is a man. What is more, I am very keen to know from the Papists if they think that John was so stupid as to give to the angel the *latria* that was taken from God? Surely nothing else drove him to the adoration of the angel but an excessive and preposterous reverence, and that indeed was to show honour to God, whose glory was shining in the angel. Nevertheless his action is condemned (Rev. 22.8, 9). Therefore so that there may be given back to God what belongs to Him, let the spiritual adoration, behind which religion exists, remain intact for Him.

28. *You yourselves know that it is an unlawful thing.* His opening remarks do not appear to be friendly, and are such as to irritate rather than conciliate them, when they hear that they are regarded as so unclean that they pollute the saints with their way of life and conversation, and that is full of grave insult against them. The truth is that Peter was bound to begin his speech in this way, lest they might suspect him of a bad conscience, because he had come contrary to the custom handed down by the fathers, and as if he were a despiser of the Law.

But when he affirms that he was sent by God, suspicion of that sort is removed and purged away. In addition, with these words he was mitigating very well the offence, which was already in possession of their minds from the ancient division between Gentiles and Jews, so that he could not have made a better opening to his speech. For he announces that those who had previously been regarded as unclean have now been given the gift of purity, so that there may now be mutual communication between them and the saints. Moreover it must be realized that his observation that it is unlawful for Jews to approach Gentiles, had its source, not so much in the Law, as in an observance of the fathers. God had certainly forbidden them to entangle themselves in marriages or contracts (Deut. 7.3), but at the same time they were never debarred from eating or transacting the ordinary affairs of life. But lest by doing that too often or by intimacy (*necessitudo*) they might be drawn to what was forbidden, they used to observe the custom handed down by the fathers, so as not to have any social intercourse. There is no point in discussing here whether that tradition was conscience-binding, for Peter is not deliberately teaching what is lawful according to the will of God, but what was generally accepted.

No man. He brings out more clearly what the substance and purpose of the vision was, when he applies to men what had been said about foods. But do not understand that his statement, that nothing is unclean, refers to individuals. For it is certain that all unbelievers are polluted by impurity of conscience, with the result that they contaminate things that are otherwise pure by the mere fact of touching them. Paul also says that their children remain unclean, until they are purified by faith (I Cor. 7.14). In a word, if faith alone purifies human hearts, unbelief makes them unclean. But here Peter is merely comparing the Jews with the Gentiles, and since the wall has been broken down, and the covenant of life and salvation is now equally common to both, he denies that those who share in God's adoption must be regarded as outsiders.

29. We must also note that he adds that he came without objection. For this is the holy silence of faith, when we do not prove an obstacle to God, but quietly undertake whatever He commands by driving far from us, whatever contrary reasons present themselves.

And Cornelius said, Four days ago, until this hour, I was[1] *keeping the ninth hour of prayer in my house; and behold, a man stood before me in bright apparel, and saith, Cornelius, thy prayer is heard, and thine*

[1] Calvin's text follows this Western reading given in R.V. margin: *From the fourth day until this hour I was fasting, and at the ninth hour I was praying*. Tr.

alms are had in remembrance in the sight of God. Send therefore to Joppa, and call unto thee Simon, who is surnamed Peter; he lodgeth in the house of Simon a tanner, by the sea side.[1] *Forthwith therefore I sent to thee; and thou has well done that thou art come. Now therefore we are all here present in the sight of God, to hear all things that have been commanded thee of the Lord.* (30–33)

Because this reply of Cornelius' contains nothing but the bare repetition of the story, there will be no need to spend too much time on it. The point is, that he called Peter by God's command.

30. *I was fasting.* Many Greek manuscripts have ἤμην,[2] I was sitting (*sic*). The Vulgate omits the word *fasting*, and I think that that happened by an error or carelessness, because it is present in all the Greek manuscripts.[3]

Moreover explicit mention is made of fasting, partly so that we may know that Cornelius did not pray in a cold or cursory fashion on that occasion, and partly so that the vision may be less suspect. For the brain of a man, who is fasting and observing reasonable moderation, does not easily admit hallucinations in the shape of apparitions. Cornelius therefore means that an angel did appear to him, when he was giving strict attention to the practice of prayer, with his mind free of all hindrances which usually leave us exposed to phantasms and apparitions. The circumstance of time also has a similar bearing, because it happened when it was still broad day-light, three hours before sunset.

A man stood in bright apparel. He calls a man, the one whom he knows to have been an angel of God. But it is usual for the name of the visible form under which they appear to be transferred to God or angels. Thus Moses is indiscriminate in his description of those who appeared to Abraham, invested with human bodies, calling them now men, now angels. The splendid clothing was an indication of heavenly glory, and, as it were, the sign of the divine majesty, which was bound to shine in an angel. The evangelists testify that there was such a splendour in the garments of Christ when He revealed His glory to the three disciples on the mountain. They say the same thing about the angels who were sent to testify to the resurrection of Christ. For just as the Lord makes concessions to our weakness to such an extent that He orders His angels to come down under the form of our flesh, so at the same time He scatters on them some rays of His glory, so as

[1] Similarly, Calvin with R.V. margin: *who when he is come will speak unto thee*. Tr.

[2] ἤμην (*I was*), is linked periphrastically with προσευχόμενος *I was praying*. Tr.

[3] This is not so; see a modern text and App. Crit. 'Fasting' and some longer Bezan readings are 'Western interpolations'. Tr.

to gain reverence for, and confidence in, the commandments, which He has entrusted them to bear.

Here the question is raised whether it was a truly natural body, or whether even the clothing was genuine, or whether it was only the appearance of such that was presented to the eyes of Cornelius. Now although it is not particularly necessary to know this, and scarcely anything can be affirmed for certain, something that tends towards conjecture yet seems quite probable to me, that God, whose property it is to create all things, gave a true body to the angel, and at the same time put clothes of magnificent splendour upon him. But it is also probable that, as soon as the angel discharged his duty as an ambassador, the body and the clothes were reduced to nothing, and he was restored to his own nature. Yet he did not appear to suffer anything human as long as he was in a human condition.

33. *Now therefore we are all here present.* In order that Peter may be the readier and more willing to teach, Cornelius is here affirming that he and the others will be ready to learn, and be prepared to obey God. For it is a great help in encouraging a teacher to be more eager to expend his efforts on his listeners, when he expects certain fruit from them.

The clause *in the sight of God* can have a double meaning, either that it is a kind of oath, or that Cornelius is simply acknowledging that that company has been gathered together in his house, as though under the sight of God, to listen to the voice of a man, exactly as if it came forth from the lips of God Himself. Whichever you choose, it will always be the same in the end. For in order to produce greater confidence in his sincerity, Cornelius testifies that he has God before his eyes, the God whom it is not right to mock by making pretence. And certainly as often as the Word of God is set before us this thought ought to suggest itself to our minds, and make a serious impression upon them, that we have not to do with a mortal man, but that God is present and calling us. For from this respect of God, the majesty of the Word and the awe of hearing it take their rise.

Yet he seems to be rash in binding others in such a serious matter. For who is fit to stand surety for the faith of another? But because each one had promised obedience for himself, he is justified in believing that they are affected in this way. And there is no doubt that they had already previously promised that, when the reality (*re*) was disclosed to them, they would be obedient to what was said; and that then they also individually confirmed what had been said by the one man.

To hear all things. We finally have this true faith, not when we embrace the Word of God merely by half, but when we yield ourselves totally to it; and yet there are in the world few examples of this full and universal faith. For, as though they may have a bargaining arrangement (*pactionem*) with God, the majority do not submit themselves to His teaching, except in so far as it pleases them, and if anything is not to their liking they do not worry about either disregarding or rejecting it.

Finally Cornelius wisely distinguishes between God and the man. For he regards God as the Author of the teaching, but leaves nothing to the man except the office of minister and ambassador. He is saying, 'You will have attentive and obedient pupils in all the things that the Lord has commanded you; so that He alone may have the authority and you may be only His minister; that He alone may speak, yet out of your mouth.' And in the person of Ezekiel, God lays this down for all His servants, saying, 'Take the word out of my mouth, and you will make it known to them for me' (33.7).

And Peter opened his mouth, and said, Of a truth I perceive that God is no respecter of persons: but in every nation he that feareth him, and worketh righteousness, is acceptable to him. The word which he sent unto the children of Israel, preaching good tidings of peace by Jesus Christ (he is Lord of all)—that saying ye yourselves know, which was published through all Judaea, beginning from Galilee, after the baptism which John preached; even Jesus of Nazareth, how that God anointed him with the Holy Ghost and with power: who went about doing good, and healing all that were oppressed of the devil; for God was with him. (34-38)

34. *Opening his mouth.* We have already pointed out that Scripture uses this expression when it means that an important and serious speech was given. In the fifth chapter of Matthew it is said that Christ *opened his mouth*, when He wished to confront His disciples, and speak about matters of the utmost importance. One may translate it as, 'He began to speak, having already of course properly thought out what He would say.'

In truth I am learning. καταλαμβάνεσθαι is to apprehend, or to gather from reasons, signs, and conjectures. Cornelius was a Gentile, yet God hears his prayers, thinks him worthy of the light of the Gospel, appoints an angel specially to him. From these things Peter grasps that all who lead godly and blameless lives are pleasing to God, without any respect of persons. For previously he never used to give it a thought that the grace of God can reach to others, for he was obsessed by this prejudice, that the Jews alone are loved by God, as they alone had been chosen out of all the nations. Indeed he was not so stupid as to think that godliness and a blameless life are rejected and condemned on account of a man being Gentile; but since he simply laid hold of the fact that all who were uncircumcised were outside the Kingdom of God and profane, he was unwisely entangling himself in that error, that is so absurd, that God despised pure worship of Himself and a holy life, in the case of a man lacking circumcision, because uncircumcision used to make all virtues unsavoury to the Jews. This example warns us how much we ought to be on our guard against prejudices, which prevent us from making right judgments.

Moreover we must note what the word *person* means, because many make a mistake about it, when they explain it in a general way, that nobody has preference over another. Thus Pelagius long ago used to deny that some are chosen, and others rejected by God, because there was no regarding of persons by God. But by this word there ought to be understood the outward state or appearance, as it is commonly called, and whatever there is about a man that procures him favour, or deprives him of it. Riches, nobility of birth, dependents, honours make a man highly respected; poverty, low birth, and anything like that, make him contemptible. The Lord continually forbids persons to be accepted on this basis, because there cannot possibly be a right judgment, as often as external considerations distract the judge from the cause. In this verse it refers to race; and the meaning is that uncircumcision does not prevent God being pleased with and approving the righteousness in a Gentile man. But in this way it will seem that respect of person did influence God for a time. For when He passed over the Gentiles and chose the Jews for His own people, did he not respect persons? I reply that the reason for this discrimination must not be sought in men, but it depends altogether on the secret purpose of God. But when He adopted Abraham to Himself, and made His covenant with him rather than with the Egyptians, He was not moved by any external consideration to do so, but the whole reason for it remained in His wonderful purpose. Therefore God was never bound to persons.

Nevertheless the difficulty is not yet resolved, because it cannot be denied that circumcision was pleasing to God, so that He counted those who used to wear that symbol of sanctification as belonging to His people. But there is also an easy reply to that, because circumcision was later than the grace of God, since it was the sign of it, and from that it follows that it was not the cause of it. At the same time it was a proof of gratuitous adoption to the Jews in this way, that uncircumcision did not prevent God from admitting any of the Gentiles, if He so wished, into the fellowship of the same salvation. But the advent of Christ brought this new and special aspect, that the dividing wall was destroyed and God embraced the whole world without distinction (Eph. 2.14). And this is the implication of the words *in every nation.* For as long as the seed of Abraham was the sacred heritage of God, the Gentiles must have seemed to be absolutely banished from His Kingdom. But when Christ was revealed as *the light of the Gentiles* the covenant of eternal life began to be common to all, on quite equal terms.

35. *He that feareth him and worketh righteousness.* The completeness of the whole of life is summed up in these two descriptive phrases. For the *fear of God* is nothing else but godliness and religion; but *righteousness* is the fair dealing which men practise among themselves, when they take care not to hurt anyone, but are yet eager to do good to all. Just as the Law of God, which is the rule for good living, consists of two parts, so nobody will make himself acceptable to God except the man who will refer all his actions to it, and direct them according to it. And all acts of service will lack any genuineness, unless the whole life is founded on the fear of God.

But this verse seems to attribute the cause of salvation to the merits of works. For if works gain us favour with God, at the same time they procure for us the life, which depends on the love of God towards us. Others also seize on the word *righteousness* to prove that we are not justified freely by faith, but by works. But this latter assertion is an extremely frivolous one. For we have already shown that this is not taken for the whole and complete observation of the Law, but that it is restricted to the second table and the services of love. It is not therefore a universal righteousness by which a man is reckoned righteous, in the eyes of God, but the honesty and uprightness which is concerned about men, when there is rendered to each what is his due.

Therefore there remains that other question, whether works may gain the favour of God for us. To explain this we must first of all note that God has a twofold consideration in loving men. For since we are all born children of wrath, God will find so little in us deserving of love, that our whole nature rather provokes Him to hatred of us (Eph. 2.3). That is why Paul says that all men are enemies to Him, until they are reconciled by Christ (Rom. 5.6, 8). Therefore God's primary acceptance, by which He embraces us within His grace, is absolutely gratuitous. For no argument for works (*operum ratio*) can be maintained, so long as they are all full of faults and perversity, and smack of their own origin. Now those, whom God has adopted to be His sons, He also regenerates by His Spirit, and recreates His own image in them. And from these things there arises that second consideration. For at that time God does not encounter a mere man, one empty and destitute of all grace, but He recognizes in every single man His own work, one should rather say, Himself. Therefore God regards the faithful as accepted because they lead godly and righteous lives. And we certainly do not deny that the good works of the saints are pleasing to God. But this gives rise to another question, whether a man may anticipate the grace of God by his merits and insinuate himself into His love, or whether in fact, since he deserves only hatred, he is, to begin with, loved out of grace, and without taking works into consideration. Moreover since a man, left to his own natural disposition, can bring forward nothing but the ground for hatred, it is necessary for him to be loved out of grace. From that it follows that God finds the cause for loving us in Himself alone (*Deum sibi ipsi causam esse*), and that He is moved by His own mercy and not by our merits. Then we must note that even if after their regeneration believers please God with good works, and by a regard for works, yet that is not done by the merit of works. For works are never thoroughly pure so that they are pleasing to God without any forgiveness; on the contrary, since they always have some imperfection mingled with them, they deserve to be rejected. Therefore it is not their own worth that determines the value of works, but faith, which borrows from Christ what works lack.

36. *Concerning the thing.*[1] Because the Greek text is disconnected some think that the accusative has been put instead of the nominative, so that the meaning is, 'This is the word which God has sent to the children of Israel.' Others link it to the verb, *you know*, which follows afterwards, and because of the transposition of the sentence they think that another word was added. For Luke puts λόγον in the first place, and ῥῆμα in the second. But since it is common and customary in Greek to supply prepositions, the meaning which I have given seems to me to suit more aptly, although if the roughness of the style can be smoothed out more skilfully I shall gladly agree.

I therefore take, by way of a preface, the phrase that refers to this memorable work of God, that He performed among the children of Israel, proclaiming peace through Christ. After that a narrative follows. Finally, in the closing part of his speech, Peter shows the purpose for which Christ has been revealed to the world.

Moreover he intentionally begins by reminding them that God has *sent His word unto the children of Israel.* Now in Hebrew *word* is used for *thing*. The fame of the eternal covenant which God had concluded with the children of Israel was widespread at that time. There was nothing more commonly known among the Jews than that, to the patriarchs of long ago, there had already been promised a Redeemer, who would restore things that had fallen down into a prosperous and

[1] Calvin's text: *De re quam misit Deus filiis Israel etc.* Greek: τὸν λόγον ὃν ἀπέστειλε τοῖς υἱοῖς Ἰσραήλ κ.τ.λ.

blessed state. All who were on friendly terms with the Jews used to know about this also. Therefore in order to gain more credence for himself Peter prefaces his speech by saying that he will not be speaking about something that is unknown or new, but about the restoration of the Church, which was dependent on the eternal covenant of God, and which has now been manifested in no obscure way, and publicly proclaimed by the talk of all.

Preaching peace. Here Peter is telling the kind of thing and rumour that was spread, viz. such as established peace. I take *peace* here for the reconciliation of God and men, which nevertheless contains within itself the complete and perfect salvation of the Church. For just as horrible confusion, and, one might say, hideous chaos, follows His separation and alienation from us, so as soon as the fatherly favour of God dawns, He gathers His Church together out of its dispersion, and true happiness springs up again. Peter therefore means by this, that in Christ God showed Himself favourable to His people, and once again embraced the sons of Abraham, whom He had appeared to have temporarily rejected, so that He might establish a prosperous and flourishing state among them. Now just as he makes God the source of this peace, so he sets forth Christ openly as its pledge, so that it may be unalterable and holy.

He expressly links *peace* to *preaching*, because this is precisely the one means by which the fruit of the reconciliation procured by Christ comes right home to us. In the same way after Paul has taught that *Christ is our peace*, he quickly adds that He has come to preach peace to those who were near and to those who were far (Eph. 2.14, 17).

37. *You know the word.* This speech of Peter's consists mainly of two parts. For in the first place he recounts a narrative of past events, and then passes on to the effect of the story. For seeing that the coming of Christ into the world, His death and resurrection, are the basis of our salvation, the only way Christ can be offered for salvation is if we first know that He put on our flesh, and lived among men in such a way that He showed Himself to be the Son of God by certain proofs; and that He was finally fastened to the cross and raised up from the dead by the power of God. Again, in case the story may cut no ice and knowledge of it be useless, at the same time we must be taught the reason why He came down to the world from the glory of heaven, why He endured the death of the cross, a death so disgraceful in the view of men, and one accursed by the mouth of God. The reason for the resurrection must be taught, for from it the effect and fruit of all these things is gathered, viz. that Christ was emptied so that He might restore us, who were lost, to complete blessedness; that together with our flesh He put on brotherly love towards us;

that taking our infirmities on Himself He relieved us of their burden; that He made atonement for our sins by the sacrifice of His death to make the Father favourable to us; that emerging victor from death He secured eternal life for us; that He opened heaven for us by His own entry; that the whole power of the Spirit was poured out on Him so that He might enrich us from His abundance.

Peter keeps this order of teaching when he begins with the story of the Gospel. Afterwards he certainly shows what the coming down of Christ to the earth, and His death and resurrection have effected for us. In the first place he relates that Christ of Nazareth came forth after the baptism of John. For seeing that John had been appointed, according to the purpose of God, to stir up the minds of the people to expect the Christ, this part ought not to have been missed out. He had been regarded as an extraordinary prophet of God, and his authority had therefore a great deal of influence in creating confidence in Christ, especially among the ignorant, and inexperienced young people.

We must note the expression *John preached baptism.* Luke is certainly including in the word *baptism* the whole ministry of John; but at the same time he is warning that it was not a dumb sign and devoid of teaching. And the chief thing in all sacraments is certainly this, that the Word of God, engraved in them, may give its light, and its voice clearly resound. That is all the more reason for detesting that impious profanation which is to be seen in the Papacy, because they have buried preaching, and intone the sacraments with merely a magical muttering.

38. *Jesus of Nazareth.* He refers to Him as *of Nazareth* here, not because He was born there, but because from there He set out to carry out His work; and, then, because this name had come into general use. He uses hypallage in saying that He was *anointed* with the Spirit and with power. For the power in which Christ excelled, was from no other source but the Spirit. Therefore when the heavenly Father anointed His Son, He equipped Him with the power of His own Spirit. Peter immediately goes on to say that this power appeared in miracles, even if he expressly mentions one kind, that Christ testified that He was endowed with the power of the Holy Spirit so that He might do good to the world. For it was not fitting that the power of God that causes terror should be put forth in Him, but the power that would draw the world, by the pleasant taste of goodness and kindness, to love Him and long for Him.

The metaphor of *anointing* is common enough, since it is used about the gifts of the Holy Spirit. Now it is applied to the person of Christ, because in this way He was consecrated by the Father, King and

Priest. Now we know that under the Law oil was the customary symbol of consecration.

The *going about* (*transitus*) of Christ is taken for the course of His calling, as though he were saying that He discharged His task for a previously determined period of time. The comparison has been taken from travellers, who continue on their journey until they arrive at an appointed place. However he is suggesting at the same time that He travelled over Judaea for three years, so that no corner was beyond the range of His well-doing.

Who were oppressed of the devil. It was an even clearer example of the power of God in Christ that He was not only curing people of ordinary diseases, but was also providing a remedy for hopeless ills. All diseases are indeed just so many whips with which God disciplines us, but when God deals with us more gently out of His fatherly tenderness, He is then said to be striking us with His hand; on the other hand in more serious scourgings He employs Satan as the minister of His wrath, and, as it were, an executioner. And this distinction must be carefully preserved, for it would be absurd to say that a man suffering from a fever, or any other common sort of disease, is tormented by the devil; but loss of reason, raving madness, and the rest of what one might call unnatural ills are appropriately and properly ascribed to Satan. That is why Scripture calls demoniacs, men who rave, and who are driven by such great violence, that they almost seem to be turned into wild beasts.

For God was with him. Peter gives a brief indication of the purpose to which the powers put forth by the hand of Christ tended, viz. to bring men, who were seeing God as if He were present, to have faith in Christ. And this was the true value of miracles, as has already been said several times, and as we shall see again afterwards at the appropriate places. For we must acquiesce in this principle that the majesty of God is diminished, unless we look up to and honour those whom He distinguishes with the mark of His servants. Accordingly, seeing that His powers made it plain that Christ came forth from heaven, His authority is placed beyond the chance decision of human judgment.

And we are witnesses of all things which he did both in the country of the Jews, and in Jerusalem; whom also they slew, hanging him on a tree. Him God raised up the third day, and gave him to be made manifest, not to all the people, but unto witnesses that were chosen before of God, even to us, who did eat and drink with him after he rose from the dead. And he charged us to preach unto the people, and to testify that this is he which is ordained of God to be the Judge of quick and dead. To him bear all the prophets witness, that through his name every one that believeth on him shall receive remission of sins. (39-43)

39. *And we are witnesses.* In order to make them believe what he is saying, he states that he and his colleagues are eye-witnesses of all the things they are teaching about Christ; and so are speaking about matters with which they have been well acquainted. A little later he uses the word *witness* in a different sense, when he says that particular witnesses were ordained by God, for by that he means, that a public role, for which they were specially chosen, was imposed upon the apostles, and that they are being led out, as it were, by God, that by their preaching they might bring men to the faith of Christ. So Paul, in I Cor. 15.15, says, 'We should be found false witnesses of God, if Christ had not risen again from the dead.' And we have already previously heard from the lips of Christ, 'You will be my witnesses in Judaea, Samaria and Jerusalem.' But now Peter is calling himself only an historical witness, because he was an observer of the events. Finally, he touches briefly on His death, because people knew about it everywhere. He dwells longer on the resurrection, about which there was more doubt, and knowledge of which possessed far more importance for faith.

41. If anyone asks here why God did not show His Son openly to all after His resurrection, my answer is that even if no reason existed, yet the purpose of God alone ought to be enough for moderate and reasonable men, so that they may persuade themselves without the shadow of a doubt that what God has resolved is best. And yet there is no doubt that God used such a temperament to the best advantage. For the certainty of the resurrection was proved enough by many and firm testimonies. But yet to believe the Gospel rather than their own eyes, was valuable for exercising the faith of the godly. As far as unbelievers and the professed enemies of Christ are concerned, since they were so often refuted and had never yielded to God, they were not deserving that Christ should admit them to see the glory of His resurrection; although those very men were also more than convinced by the report of the soldiers whom they had employed to guard the tomb. Although I am missing out other reasons, one will be at liberty to get them out of my *Harmony of the Gospels.*

Therefore, for us it is determined that the apostles were chosen by the holy decree of God, so that by their testimony to the resurrection of Christ the truth might stand. Anyone who does not acquiesce in this approbation, may pluck up and destroy, if he can, that inviolable decree of God, which Peter is commending to us here. But as for ourselves, if we desire to have God the certain source of our faith, let us learn to be content with the witnesses, whom He chose by Himself from before the foundation of the world, and in His own time led out into the open, as if by His own hand.

Who did eat. From this it is apparent how much care and concern Christ had for our ignorance, for He lowered Himself for our sake to such an extent that, although He was possessed of heavenly glory, He yet ate and drank as a mortal man. Accordingly we have no reason to ask whether there is any obscurity or doubt about the resurrection of Christ. For He allowed His disciples to be slow and find it hard to believe, so that, when they had been given fuller confirmation, they might remove every scruple of doubt from us. Yes, and what is more, we must take care that our ill-will and ingratitude do not obscure such great indulgence on the part of the Son of God towards us.

Leaving that aside, since Scripture records that Christ ate, curious men have raised the question, 'What happened to that food?' But the answer is easy, that since it had been created out of nothing, so it was easily reduced to nothing by the divine power of Christ. The food that is taken for the nourishment of the body is digested and afterwards disposed of; but we know that this food was taken by Christ for nourishing our faith, and was consumed in doing so. Now, those who think that Christ only made a show of eating are mistaken. For what good would such an appearance have done? And I do not see what point there is in looking for subterfuges of that kind. For when we say that Christ was not forced by necessity to eat, but only wished to have regard to His people, the frivolous inventions of men are left without a leg to stand on.

42. *And he charged us.* Here he begins to deal with the rule of Christ, when he says that Christ rose again so that He may judge the world on a single occasion. For by the same right the sovereignty of heaven and earth, and the perpetual government of the Church are ascribed to Him. He says that He will be *the Judge of the living and the dead*, because when the dead will have risen again, those who will be alive at that time will also be changed in a moment, as Paul teaches in I Cor. 15.51, 52 and I Thess. 4.17.

Something important underlies the word *to testify*, because, since men are naturally inclined to disbelief, the simple preaching of the Gospel would have less efficacy and force, if the Lord did not confirm it with powerful appeals to Him as witness. In particular, of course, every one of us is very well aware of how difficult it is, not only to lift our minds, caught in earthly snares as they are, above to heaven, in expectation of the coming of Christ, but also to keep them fixed on continual meditation of this, when they do not stop being swept this way and that in their fickleness.

43. *To him all the prophets.* Luke gives a brief summary of the substance of the sermon, as has been said; and that is why he is so brief, or rather concise, in noting the consequence of the narrative. Therefore let us realize that the words which Peter used are not repeated here, but only an indication is given of the things with which he dealt.

Now we must consider three things here, (1) that it is Christ's special task to destroy men's sins and reconcile them to God; (2) that we obtain remission of sins by faith; and (3) that this teaching is not new or recently invented, but ever since earliest times all the prophets of God were already bearing witness to it.

As far as the first is concerned, if God is pacified by not imputing sins to us in Christ, that makes it plain that the whole human race is hateful and hostile to Him, until it begins to be acceptable by free forgiveness. We are all therefore convicted of sin, which subjects us to the wrath of God and fetters us with the guilt of eternal death. And because we are destitute of righteousness among ourselves, we are taught to flee to the mercy of God, as to the only refuge. When he says that believers *receive remission of sins*, there is an underlying tacit antithesis between them and God; for it is necessary that it be offered by God of His own accord, in order that believers may then receive it. When he says that it is given through the *name of Christ*, he means that by the help of Christ alone we return to favour with God, and that, of course, is because He has once for all reconciled Him to us by His own death; or, as it is commonly put, by the mediation of Christ alone, and by no other mediators, do we obtain remission of sins.

Satan has never been able to wipe out from the minds of men their sense of guilt, so that they were not anxious to ask for pardon from God. But since there was one means and way of obtaining forgiveness, miserable men, deluded by the deceptions of Satan, devised wonderful labyrinths for themselves to weary themselves needlessly in their winding paths. The first error to lead them away from the right way was this, that they tried to win the pardon which is freely offered, and received by faith alone. Thereafter countless kinds of propitiations were invented, with which satisfaction was made to God. These did originally spring from the Word of God, but, since He was foreshadowing Christ when He entrusted sacrifices and offering rites to the patriarchs, blind and ungodly men put Christ aside, pursued an empty shadow, and corrupted everything of God's in the sacrifices. Accordingly all the sacrifices practised by the Gentiles from the beginning of the world, and those which are still used by the Turks and Jews today, one can set over against Christ as things that are completely contrary. The Papists are no better, except that they sprinkle the blood of Christ on their satisfactions, but in doing so they are extremely absurd, because, not being content with the one Christ, they summon a thousand modes of sacrifices to themselves from all sides. Accordingly, anyone who wishes to share in the remission of sins, is not to turn aside, even a finger's breadth, from Christ.

When we hear that remission is received by *believing* we must grasp the power and nature of faith, just as if Peter undoubtedly discussed at length how we must believe in Christ. But that amounts to nothing else but to embrace Him, as He is set before us in the Gospel, with a sincere attitude of mind. So faith depends on the promises. However Peter seems to commit an error, because, whereas Christ gave us two matters of supreme importance, he mentions only one of them. For nothing is said here about repentance and new life, which ought not to have been omitted in a summary of the Gospel. But the reply is easy, that regeneration of the Spirit is included under faith, as it is an effect of it. For we believe in Christ partly so that He may restore us to the Father's favour by the free imputation of righteousness, partly so that He may sanctify us by His Spirit. And we know that we are adopted by God as sons on this condition, that He may govern us by His Spirit. It was therefore sufficient for Peter to show how men, who were by nature alienated from God, may return to favour with Him.

As far as the third consideration is concerned, there is no need to go over all the passages of the prophets, in which they set forth Christ as the Mediator, who is to propitiate God for us by procuring forgiveness for our sins, but it was their constant method of teaching, their rule one might say, to call back all the godly to that covenant which God had made with Abraham, when the Mediator was interposed. Moreover, it is absolutely necessary for us to understand this fundamental principle, that the grace, which was finally exhibited by Christ, is the same as what the Law and the Prophets long ago taught the fathers to hope for. In particular it was of very great importance for Cornelius and those like him, who were imbued with great regard for the Law and the Prophets, to know that in actual fact there is executed and fulfilled in Christ, what had been attested by the oracles of the prophets. Therefore so that the ministers of the Church may have a pattern of teaching that agrees with the prophets, they are to be diligent in honouring Christ by their preaching; they are to testify continually that the righteousness, which consists of the free remission of sins, must be sought from Him alone. This is antiquity of quite a different kind from what the Papists uncover and boast about so much, when, in place of the price of the blood of Christ, they bring in the rotten fabrications of their own satisfactions.

While Peter yet spake these words, the Holy Ghost fell on all them which heard the word. And they of the circumcision which believed were amazed, as many as came with Peter, because that on the Gentiles also was poured out the gift of the Holy Ghost. For they heard them speak with tongues, and magnify God. Then answered Peter, Can any man forbid the water, that these should not be baptized, which have received the Holy Ghost as well as we? And he commanded them to be baptized in the name of Jesus Christ. Then prayed they him to tarry certain days. (44-48)

44. *While Peter yet spake.* God now confirms by a new miracle that the teaching of His Gospel is shared by the Gentiles equally with the Jews. And this is indeed an extraordinary sign of the call of the Gentiles; because the Lord would never have thought the Gentiles deserving of the graces of His Spirit, unless it happened to prove that those very people were also elected into the fellowship of the covenant. Indeed, these gifts mentioned by Luke are different from the grace of regeneration; nevertheless there is no doubt that in this way God put His seal, not only on the teaching of Peter, but also on the faith and godliness of those who had heard. He says that they were all endowed with the Spirit, just as we have already previously seen that they all came animated with the desire to learn and obey.

Now this visible symbol shows us, as if in a picture, how effective the preaching of the Gospel is as an instrument of the divine power. For as Peter was speaking He poured out His Spirit to show that He does not send teachers for the purpose of beating the air with the sound of empty words, but so that He might work powerfully through what they say, and quicken their words by the power of His Spirit for the salvation of the godly. According to this reasoning Paul reminds the Galatians that they received the Holy Spirit by the hearing of faith (3.2); and he states elsewhere that he is a minister, not of the letter, but of the Spirit (II Cor. 3.6). Certainly the gift of tongues and other things of that kind have long since ceased in the Church, but the Spirit of understanding and regeneration thrives and will always thrive. And the Lord unites Him with the external preaching of the Gospel so as to keep us in reverence of His Word, and obviate the fatal fantasies in which fanatics entangle themselves, when they abandon the Word and invent some sort of vague and erratic spirit.

Finally, it does not always follow that everyone whose ears seize on the words of a man, takes in the Spirit at the same time; and indeed ministers seldom meet with such listeners as Peter found, who were willing to a man, to follow God. Yet He causes the elect to feel within themselves the harmony of the external word and the secret power of the Spirit.

45. *Believers were amazed.* He calls *believers* those who were still being kept back by a perverse error. So the Lord does not banish all the clouds of ignorance from His own people at once. And yet these clouds do not obscure the commendation of faith in the eyes of God, because, overlooking its errors, He thinks it worthy of His favour as if it were pure and unclouded. Nevertheless it is strange that, although they knew that Peter was sent by God, they are now struck with astonishment, as if confounded by a new thing, because God confers the grace of His Spirit on those to whom He had already wished that Christ be preached. But the sudden change is the cause of this, because, although God had until that very day kept the Gentiles apart from His people as common outsiders, He now embraces them in the same favour, and raises them to the same level of honour. Nevertheless at the same time we are warned by this example how difficult it is, to free ourselves from the errors we have conceived, especially if they are long-standing.

46. *For they heard them.* He states what gifts of the Spirit were poured out on them, and at the same time notes their use; viz. that they were endowed with a variety of *tongues* to praise God in many languages. Yet it can be inferred from this verse that tongues were given, not only to meet a need, when the Gospel had to be preached to foreigners with a different language, but also for the adornment and honour of the Gospel itself. But ambition afterwards corrupted this second use, when many carried over to ostentation and display, what they had received for illuminating the greatness of the heavenly wisdom; as, for example, Paul has sharp things to say against this fault in the case of the Corinthians. There is, therefore, nothing strange about it, if a little later on God took away what He had given, and did not allow it to be vitiated with further abuse.

47. *Peter answered.* Peter argues from the reality to the sign. For since baptism is an appendage to the spiritual grace, a man who receives the Spirit is at the same time fit to receive baptism. And this is the proper order, so that a minister admits to the external sign those whom God has testified to be His children by the pledge and proof of His Spirit. So teaching and faith play their parts first. But the inference that ignorant men draw from this, that infants must be debarred from baptism, is absolutely groundless. I admit that those who are outside the Church must be instructed before the symbol of adoption is conferred on them; but I maintain that believers' children, who are born within the Church, are members of the family of the

Kingdom of God from the womb. Yes, and what is more, I turn back on themselves the argument which they absurdly use against us. For since God has adopted the children of believers before they are born, I establish from that, that they must not be cheated of the external sign. Otherwise men will dare to snatch from them what God has granted to them. As far as the manifest grace of the Spirit is concerned, there is nothing absurd about it, if it follows baptism in time, in their case.

But just as this testimony gives no support to their error, so it powerfully refutes the superstition of the Papists, who bind the grace of the Spirit to the signs, and think that it is lured out of heaven by 'exorcisms', just as long ago female diviners used to think that they were drawing down the moon with their incantations. But when Luke narrates that men who had not yet been initiated in baptism, were already endowed with the Holy Spirit, he is showing that the Spirit is not shut up in baptism. Finally, it must be observed that the apostles were content with water alone for administering baptism. And how one wishes that this simplicity had been retained by posterity, and that so many nonsensical things, with which baptism in the Papacy is crammed full, had not been adopted from all sides. They think that the dignity of baptism is enhanced with oil, salt, spittle, wax-tapers, when these are rather filthy abominations which corrupt the pure and genuine institution of Christ.

48. *And he commanded them to be baptized.* It was not necessary for baptism to be administered by Peter personally, just as Paul also testifies that he baptized few at Corinth, for other ministers could have undertaken this role.

His use of the words *in the name of the Lord* must not be restricted to a form of words, as we have said in the third chapter (on v. 6), but because Christ is the proper goal of baptism (*proprius Baptismi scopus*), that is why we are said to be baptized in His name.

When Luke says, finally, that Peter was asked by Cornelius and his relatives to stay for a few days, he is commending the desire they had to make progress. They were certainly endowed with the Holy Spirit, but they had not reached such a peak that confirmation would be of no further use to them. Following their example, let us make diligent use of the opportunity to make progress, as often as it presents itself to us; and let us not grow swollen with pride, for it bars the entrance of teaching.

CHAPTER ELEVEN

Now the apostles and the brethren that were in Judaea heard that the Gentiles also had received the word of God. And when Peter was come up to Jerusalem, they that were of the circumcision contended with him, saying, Thou wentest in to men uncircumcised, and didst eat with them. But Peter began, and expounded the matter unto them in order, saying,

I was in the city of Joppa praying: and in a trance I saw a vision, a certain vessel descending, as it were a great sheet let down from heaven by four corners; and it came even unto me: upon the which when I had fastened mine eyes, I considered, and saw the fourfooted beasts of the earth and wild beasts and creeping things and fowls of the heaven. And I heard also a voice saying unto me, Rise, Peter; kill and eat. But I said, Not so, Lord: for nothing common or unclean hath ever entered into my mouth. But a voice answered the second time out of heaven, What God hath cleansed, make not thou common. And this was done thrice: and all were drawn up again into heaven. And behold, forthwith three men stood before the house in which we were, having been sent from Caesarea unto me. And the Spirit bade me go with them, making no distinction. And these six brethren also accompanied me; and we entered into the man's house: and he told us how he had seen the angel standing in his house, and saying, Send to Joppa, and fetch Simon, whose surname is Peter; who shall speak unto thee words, whereby thou shalt be saved, thou and all thy house. And as I began to speak, the Holy Ghost fell on them, even as on us at the beginning. And I remembered the word of the Lord, how that he said, John indeed baptized with water; but ye shall be baptized with the Holy Ghost. If then God gave unto them the like gift as he did also unto us, when we believed on the Lord Jesus Christ, who was I, that I could withstand God?

And when they heard these things, they held their peace, and glorified God, saying, Then to the Gentiles also hath God granted repentance unto life. (1-18)

1. *Now they heard.* Luke's narrating that the report of the conversion of one household had become common knowledge among the brethren everywhere, was born of admiration; for the Jews regarded it as monstrous that Gentiles be added to them, just as if they had heard that men had been created out of stones. And their excessive love of their own nation even prevented them from acknow-

ledging the work of God. For we see that the Church was disturbed because of this ambition and pride, since equality, which was lessening their dignity, was intolerable to them. That is why they fought so stubbornly about bringing the Gentiles under the yoke. But since so many predictions of the prophets had foretold that the Church must be gathered from all the people after the coming of the Messiah, and Christ had given the commandment to the apostles about preaching the Gospel throughout the whole world, how is it possible that the conversion of a few men disturbs some as if it were something unheard of, and truly horrifies others as if it were a monstrosity? I reply that all that had been predicted about the calling of the Gentiles had been so interpreted as if the Gentiles would submit to the Law of Moses in order to have a place in the Church. But the manner of the calling, the beginnings of which they were then seeing, was not only unknown, but appeared to be inconsistent with all reason. For they were imagining that, with the ceremonies abolished, it is impossible for the Gentiles to be joined with the sons of Abraham to form one body, without grave injury being done to the sacred covenant of God. For what was the purpose of the Law except to be a middle wall to signify the division? Secondly, since they had been accustomed to that division for the whole of their lives, the unexpected newness of the thing strikes them with such consternation, as to banish from their minds everything that ought to have checked their astonishment. Finally, they do not grasp at once the mystery which Paul teaches was hidden from the angels right from the creation of the world (Eph. 3.9).

2. *They contended with him.* Stubbornness usually goes hand in hand with error. It was already due to too much stupid ignorance that they were at fault in not peacefully taking to their hearts the Gentiles, who had been united to themselves by the same Spirit of faith. But not only do they recoil, but they quarrel pertinaciously with Peter, and they make what he has done a matter of reproach, when it deserved the highest commendation. They hear that Gentiles have embraced the Word of God; what therefore prevents them from embracing them, and cultivating fellowship under the sovereignty of the one God? For what more sacred bond of union can there be than when all with one consent cleave to God together? And why should those, who assent to the Messiah of God as their Head, not grow together into one body? But because they were seeing the external form of the Law being violated, they thought that heaven was somehow being confounded with the earth.

Now, observe that, although Luke has just said that the apostles and the brethren heard this report, he has made no mention of offence; but now he introduces what looks like a new faction of men, who joined issue with Peter. *The brethren heard*, he says. He adds nothing after that. There follows, *When Peter had come to Jerusalem, they that were of the circumcision contended with him*; and these must surely be different from the former. Secondly, the description περιτομῆς does not refer simply to the Jews, but to those who were exceedingly devoted to the legal ceremonies. For at that time there were none from Jerusalem in the flock of Christ, except those who were circumcised. From whom therefore would he be distinguishing those men? Finally, it does not seem very likely that the apostles and the more moderate of the number of the believers undertook this contest. For even if they had been offended, they could have met with Peter in private, however, and demanded from him an account of what he had done. I am moved by these reasons to think that those who are said to be *of the circumcision*, are men who were gripped by such strong conscientious scruples about circumcision, that they did not allow anybody a place in the Kingdom of God, unless he undertook the profession of the Law, and laid aside impurity, when he was admitted into the Church by this sacred rite.

3. *To men uncircumcised.* This was not forbidden by the Law of God, but it was a tradition handed down by the fathers. Yet Peter does not object that he is being dealt with too severely in this connexion, and that he is not necessarily bound by a human stipulation. He totally omits that defence, but merely replies that those men came to him first, and were presented to him as though by the hand of God. Apart from that, here we see the exceptional restraint of Peter. He could have relied on the rightness of his case to spurn the inexperienced men who were being unjustly troublesome; but yet he courteously explains his position to them, something that ought to happen among brethren. Indeed this was no trivial attack, because he was being shamefully accused, simply because he had obeyed God faithfully. But because he knew that this principle was imposed on the whole Church, that each man must be prepared to render an account of his doctrine and life, as often as the situation demands it, and because he remembered that he was one of the flock, not only does he allow himself to be brought to order, but of his own accord he submits himself to the judgment of the Church. Indeed if doctrine is from God, it is placed above the hazard of human judgment, but because the Lord wishes prophecy to be assessed, this condition must not be rejected by his servants, so that they may prove themselves to be such as they wish to be regarded (I Cor. 14.29, 32). But we shall see presently how far the defence both of doctrine and actions ought to proceed. For the present we must grasp this, that Peter willingly agrees to state his case when his action is condemned.

Now if the Pope of Rome is Peter's successor why will he not be bound by the same principle? Although we grant that this was a voluntary sort of submission, yet why does his successor not imitate the example of moderation that is presented to him? However there is no need for lengthy circumlocution. For if what the Popes spew out in their sacrilegious decrees is true, Peter has treacherously abandoned the privileges of his throne (*sedis suae*), and so was a betrayer of the Roman See (*sedis*). For after they have made the Pope judge of the whole world, so that he may submit to no human judgment, after they have extolled him above the clouds, so that he may be absolved from rendering an account and may have his own will and pleasure for law, they then establish him as protector of the Apostolic See to uphold its privileges strenuously. Therefore of what sort of cowardice will Peter have to be condemned, if he threw away, by giving in easily, a right conferred on him by God? Why did he not at least object that he was not liable to law, and exempt from common order? But he starts off with nothing of the sort, but takes up his account straight away. Let us indeed remember that nothing prevents us from being allowed to condemn that idol fearlessly, since he has removed himself from the body of bishops by assuming such unbridled tyranny.

4. *But Peter began.* Because this is the same narrative as we had in the last chapter, and is repeated with almost the same words, let readers apply to it if any explanation is needed. Indeed Peter's purpose and the whole point of his speech will be clear from the conclusion. But before I come to that, we must briefly observe what makes the preaching of the Gospel the cause of salvation.

14. He says, 'You will hear words in which you may have salvation', not because salvation is confined to a man's words, but because in them God offers His Son to us for eternal life, and at the same time causes us to enjoy Him by faith. Certainly God's goodness is wonderful, for He makes men ministers of life, despite the fact that they possess nothing but the stuff of death, and are not only liable to death in themselves, but also bring death to others. At the same time disgraceful ingratitude on the part of the world reveals itself in this respect, that they disdain the true and certain salvation that is set before them, and, leaving it as if cast down at their feet, they conjure up various ineffectual salvations for themselves, and in seeking after these, they prefer to have hungry mouths hanging open, rather than be satisfied by the grace of God, that is present and easily obtained.

16. *I remembered the word of the Lord.* We have already taught fully enough in the first chapter (v. 5) that when Christ made this statement He was not making a comparison between the two baptisms, but that

He was wishing to point out how He differed from John. For just as we distinguish the sign from His reality, so it is a valuable thing to make a distinction between the minister and the author, lest a mortal man may appropriate to himself what belongs to God. A man has the sign in his hand; it is Christ alone who washes and regenerates. For it is very important where men direct their minds, when they are seeking the graces of God, for not even a drop will trickle to them apart from Christ. Therefore there is this general distinction between Christ and all the ministers of the Church; ministers certainly confer the external sign of water, but Christ is responsible for and fulfils the effect of the sign by the power of His Spirit. Readers should have been reminded about this matter again in this verse, because many wrongly infer from it that the baptism of John was different from ours, when Christ lays claim to the Spirit for Himself, and leaves nothing to John but water.

Again, if anyone, also relying on this evidence, makes baptism a pointless spectacle, and empty of every grace of the Spirit, he too is greatly mistaken. For, as has been said elsewhere, Scripture is in the habit of speaking about the sacraments in a twofold way. For since Christ does not deceive in His promises, He does not allow what He has instituted to be an empty thing. But when Scripture attributes to baptism the power of washing and regenerating, it ascribes the whole of this to Christ (Titus 3.5, 6), and teaches only what He effects by His Spirit through the agency of a man and the visible symbol. When Christ is so united with the minister, and the efficacy of the Spirit with the sign, all that is needed is attributed to the sacraments. But that conjunction ought not to be confused in such a way, that the minds of men, drawn away by what is mortal and perishing, by what is similar to themselves, and by the elements of the world, may not learn to seek for salvation in Christ alone, and to look only to the power of His Spirit; because, anyone who turns aside, even in the slightest degree, from the Spirit to the signs, is wandering away from the goal of faith (*a fidei scopo*); and anyone who diminishes the glory of Christ by a trifling fraction, in order to adorn a man with it, is sacrilegious.

Finally we must also call to mind that Christ uses the word *Spirit* to describe not only the gift of tongues and similar things, but the whole grace of our renewal. But since those gifts are a remarkable proof of the power of Christ, this sentence is very well suited to them. Let me put it more clearly. Since Christ bestowed the visible graces of the Spirit on the apostles He made it plain that the Spirit is in His hands; so in this way He testified that He is the one and only source of purity, righteousness and complete regeneration. Now Peter applies this to his plan of action in this way, that, since Christ led the way, bearing the power of baptism along with Him, he himself was bound to follow with the accessory, i.e. the outward symbol of water.

17. *Who was I?* Now we see why Peter told that story, viz. that he might bear witness that God was the Initiator and Controller of the whole affair. Therefore the point of the question turns on the authority of God, whether food carries more weight in human deliberations or not. Peter contends that he did nothing except what was proper and in order, because he obeyed God; and he shows that it was not wrong or rash of him to plant the teaching of the Gospel where Christ deposited the graces of His Spirit. The approval of everything, our teaching as well as our actions, must be judged according to this standard, as often as men call us to account. For anyone who labours at the command of God has defence enough and to spare. If men are not satisfied there is no reason why he should waste further time on their perverse opinions. And we gather from this that faithful ministers of the Word of God can give an account of their teaching in such a way as not to take away any of its trustworthiness and certitude, viz. if they show that it was entrusted to them by God. If however we shall be dealing with hostile men, who are not forced to yield by reverence for God, let us leave them to stew in their own juice, by appealing to the day of the Lord.

At the same time we must note that we resist God not only by openly opposing Him, but also by our inactivity, if we do not carry out what belongs to our calling. For here Peter says that he could not have denied baptism and the fellowship of the brethren to the Gentiles without being an enemy to God. And yet he would have undertaken nothing that was clearly contrary to the grace of God. That is, of course, true. But the man who does not receive those whom God brings forward, and closes the door that God opened, is hindering the work of God, as far as he is concerned. Similarly we say today that those who are opposing infant baptism are waging war on God, because those men are cruelly rejecting from the Church those whom the promise of God adopts into the Church, and they deprive of the external symbol those whom God honours with the name of sons. To that is related the kind of resistance when many pretenders in the office of the magistracy ought to have been assisting the martyrs of Christ by virtue of their position, but make it their business to close their mouths, and curb their freedom. For since the truth is disagreeable, they would desire its suppression.

18. *When they heard these things they held their peace.* The outcome shows that those who began the dispute with Peter were not moti-

vated by ill-will. For it is a clear sign of godliness that, having been instructed about the will of God, they immediately put a stop to contention. We are taught by this example that we must not be indifferent to those who, being offended by unthinking zeal, wrongly find fault with something, but that their consciences, which are disturbed by error, must be pacified by the Word of the Lord, and that their docility is being put to the test, as far as that is concerned at any rate. As far as we are concerned we similarly learn from this on what our judgment ought to depend, viz. solely and simply on the command of God. For this honour is due to Him, that His will is, for us, the certain and highest rule of justice and truth. As often as it is important for us to know the reason for anything, the Lord does not conceal it, but in order to accustom our faith to rightful obedience, He sometimes tells us, simply and briefly, that this or that is pleasing to Him. He who permits himself to inquire further, and lets his curiosity run away with him, brings about his own downfall by nothing else than devilish presumption. Luke certainly reports that those men not only *held their peace* but also gave glory to God. Shame forces some men to keep quiet, when all the time they are suppressing, within their minds, what they do not dare bring out. That is a false show of modesty, rather than docility. But those men submit themselves to God, so completely that they are not afraid to recant immediately.

Then to the Gentiles also . . . repentance. With these words Luke briefly shows what the Gospel contains, and what it aims at, viz. that God may reconcile men to Himself when they have been renewed by His Spirit. Indeed only the word *repentance* is used here; but the addition of *unto life* makes it clear enough that it is not separated from faith. Therefore let anyone, who wishes to make proper progress in the Gospel, put off the old man and meditate on newness of life (Eph. 4.22). Then let him know with certainty that he is not being called to repentance for nothing, but that salvation has been prepared for him in Christ. Accordingly the result will be that confidence of salvation rests only on the free mercy of God, and that the forgiveness of sins is no reason for being slothful and indifferent.

The phrase *to grant repentance* can be explained in two ways, either that God has given to the Gentiles the opportunity of repentance, since He wished His Gospel to be made known to them; or that He circumcised their hearts by His Spirit, as Moses says (Deut. 30.6); and made hearts of flesh out of their stony hearts, as Ezekiel puts it (11.19). For it is God's own work to beget men again and remake them, so that they begin to be new creatures; and this second sense[1] suits

[1] Reading *atque hoc secundum melius quadrat* with Tholuck, instead of *secundo* with C.R. French: '*et ce second sens convient mieux*'. Tr.

better; it is less forced; and is more in agreement with the phraseology of Scripture.

They therefore that were scattered abroad upon the tribulation that arose about Stephen travelled as far as Phoenicia, and Cyprus, and Antioch, speaking the word to none save only to Jews. But there were some of them, men of Cyprus and Cyrene, who, when they were come to Antioch, spake unto the Greeks also, preaching the Lord Jesus. And the hand of the Lord was with them: and a great number that believed turned unto the Lord.

And the report concerning them came to the ears of the church which was in Jerusalem: and they sent forth Barnabas as far as Antioch: who, when he was come, and had seen the grace of God, was glad; and he exhorted them all, that with purpose of heart they would cleave unto the Lord: for he was a good man, and full of the Holy Ghost, and of faith: and much people was added unto the Lord. (19-24)

19. *Who were scattered.* Luke returns to the context of a previous narrative. For he had mentioned earlier that, after the death of Stephen, when the cruelty of the ungodly was increasing, a great many had been stricken with fear, and fled in all directions. The result was that the apostles were almost the only ones remaining at Jerusalem. When the body of the Church was torn in pieces in this way, and their own fearfulness, or the contempt of outsiders, imposed silence on the fugitives, he tells of a subsequent event which no one would have expected. For just as the seed is scattered in order to bring forth a harvest, so the result of their flight and dispersion was that the Gospel, which had previously been confined within the walls of a single city, as if in a barn, was spread even to far distant regions. In the same way it came about that the name of Christ, crossing mountains and seas, reached right to the farthest bounds of the world. And in this way, according to the prophecy of Isaiah, 'destruction overflowed into righteousness' (Isa. 10.22). If so many believers had not been driven out of Jerusalem, Cyprus would have heard nothing about Christ, Phoenicia would have heard nothing, and what is more Italy and Spain, which were even farther away, would have heard nothing. But the Lord caused more bodies to be born out of some of the mangled members. For where were the churches, both at Rome and at Puteoli, gathered from, except that a few exiles and fugitives had brought the Gospel there along with them? But just as the Lord wonderfully parried the efforts of Satan at that time, so we must have no doubt that today He will procure triumphs for Himself out of the cross and persecution, so that the Church may the better grow together out of its dispersion.

Phoenicia borders on Syria, and is next to Galilee. Antioch is the most famous city of Syria, in the part in which it borders on Cilicia.

Speaking to none. Perhaps it was not only fear of persecution that was preventing them from venturing to speak to the Gentiles, but also that foolish religious scrupulousness of theirs, in thinking that the children's bread was being thrown to the dogs; even although Christ Himself had given the general commandment that the Gospel is to be preached to the whole world after His resurrection.

20. Luke finally narrates that some of them presented this treasure even to the Gentiles. But those *Greeks* are not called Hellenes (Ἕλληνες) by Luke, but Hellenists (Ἑλληνισταί).[1] Therefore many give the explanation that those men were indeed descended from Jews, but resided in Greece; a view that I do not accept at all. For it would be necessary to count in that number the Jews, whom he mentions immediately before (v. 19), since some of them were from Cyprus; because the Jews reckoned Cyprus a part of Greece. But Luke distinguishes from them, those whom he calls Hellenists (Ἑλληνιστάς) in the next sentence (v. 20). Moreover since he had said that the Word was proclaimed at first only to the Jews, and he picked out those who were living as exiles from their native land in Cyprus and Phoenicia, as if correcting this restriction, he says that Greeks were taught by some of them. That contrast surely forces one to explain it of Gentiles. For Luke means that a few spread the teaching of the Gospel more freely, because the call of the Gentiles was not unknown to them.

Leaving that aside, the perseverance of all of them deserves much praise, because although they were snatched almost out of the midst of death, yet they do not hesitate to carry out their duty to God, even in the midst of danger. From that we gather for what purpose and to what extent Christians are permitted to avoid persecution, viz. to devote the rest of their lives being active in extending the glory of God. If anyone asks what was the source of such great confidence in visitors who had recently arrived, and in men who could have been suspected by all the Jews, and been hostile to them, because of the fact that they had been banished from Jerusalem: I reply that it was created by the extraordinary influence of God, and that they made up their minds on the spot as the opportunity presented itself to them. For this deliberation is not of flesh and blood.

21. *The hand of the Lord was.* By the successful outcome Luke proves that the brethren from Cyprus and Cyrene had not been rash and thoughtless in presenting the Gospel to the Gentiles also, because their

[1] Revisers' Text has Ἕλληνας; see a modern App. Crit. for variant readings. Tr.

labour was profitable and fruitful. But such a result would never have ensued without the command and favour of God. Therefore it follows that it was pleasing to God that the Gentiles be called. *Hand*, as is well enough known, means power and virtue. Luke accordingly means that God testified, by His present help, that by His leading, the Gentiles have been called to share in the grace of Christ along with the Jews. And this blessing of God was of great value in encouraging all of them.

Now, this verse warns us that whatever work and effort ministers of God put out on teaching, it will be useless and ineffectual unless God blesses their efforts from heaven. For our task is to plant and water, as Paul teaches, but the increase comes from God alone (I Cor. 3.6), in whose hand are the hearts of men, to move and shape them as He wills. Therefore whenever faith is at stake, let us be reminded of this sentence, that God was active through His ministers, and made the teaching effectual by His *hand* i.e. by the secret inspiration of the Spirit. Accordingly let a minister not attempt anything, confident in his own abilities and diligence; but let him commend his work to the Lord on whose grace success altogether depends. On the other hand, when teaching brings results, those who have come to believe should learn to be indebted to God for their faith. Furthermore, we must note Luke's statement that 'very many were turned to God by faith', because he gives an excellent description of the power and nature of faith, that it is not cold and useless knowledge, but the thing that reinstates men, who were previously alienated from God, under His sovereignty, and binds them to His righteousness.

22. *And the report came*. If this report had been brought before Peter's apology, those good men would have been sharply rebuked by many, despite the fact that God had sealed their ministry with the grace of His Spirit; but that superstition had now been banished from their minds, when God had shown by clear signs that no nation must be regarded as common. Therefore they do not debate further, and they do not bring a charge of rashness, because some had dared to set Christ before the Gentiles, but by sending help they declare their approval of what they have done.

Furthermore the reason for sending Barnabas was this. At that time the apostles were bearing the whole burden of the Kingdom of Christ. Accordingly it was their responsibility to form churches everywhere, to retain all believers everywhere in a pure and holy unanimity of faith, to establish ministers and pastors wherever there was any number of believers. Satan's cunning is well-known. As soon as he sees a door opened for the Gospel, he tries by all sorts of means to corrupt what is pure; and so the result was that along with the teaching of Christ various heresies immediately proliferated. Accordingly the greater the gifts in which each particular church excels, the greater care it ought to take lest Satan stirs up anything among the ignorant and those still not sufficiently established in the right faith, and throw them into confusion; because there is nothing easier than for growing corn to be ruined in the early stages of growth. To sum up, Barnabas was sent to advance the rudiments of the faith further, to arrange things in some sort of order, to give shape to an uncompleted building, so that the Church might have a proper status.

23. *When he had seen the grace of God.* Luke shows by these words, first of all, that it was the genuine Gospel which those men had embraced, and secondly, that Barnabas sought nothing else but the glory of Christ. For when he reports that he *saw the grace of God*, and he exhorted them to persevere, we gather from that that they were well instructed. And his *joy* is undoubted evidence of sincere godliness. Ambition is always envious and spiteful; so we see a great many seeking to obtain commendation for themselves out of censuring others, because they are more eager for their own glory than for that of Christ. But no matter whom the Lord has used in the end to make His name illustrious, the faithful servants of Christ ought to follow the example of Barnabas and rejoice at the success of the Gospel. And certainly when men put out their efforts in common, so that they acknowledge that whatever success emerges from them is the work of God, then they will never envy each other, and will not quibble and carp at each other, but will praise the power of God with one heart and one voice.

Again it is worth noting that Luke attributes to the grace of God the faith of the people of Antioch, and whatever was deserving of praise there. He could have listed individual virtues which would bring praise to men, but all the excellence that was in that church he embraces in the one word, *grace*.

Finally we must pay attention to the exhortation of Barnabas. We have already said that Barnabas approved of the teaching which they had embraced first of all. But, in case teaching may vanish, it needs to be thoroughly imprinted on the minds of believers by constant exhortations. For since we have to wage a continuous war with so many and such powerful enemies, and our minds, on the other hand, are so slippery, unless everyone defends himself carefully, it will be lost straight away; and every day countless numbers show, by their defection, that that is all too true. We learn from his definition of the way to persevere, as continuing with *purpose of heart*, that faith has put down living roots only when it is grounded in the heart. Accordingly it is no wonder that hardly one in ten of the number of those who profess the faith perseveres right to the end, since very few know the meaning of good-will and purpose of heart.

24. *For he was a good man.* Barnabas is certainly being praised by an utterance of the Holy Spirit. Yet we must realize that it was said, not so much for his benefit, as for ours. For all who are envious of the labours of others, and are annoyed at their success are condemned of malice and badness.

We must also observe the epithet used to describe *a good man, full of the Spirit and of faith.* For after he declared him a man of integrity and uprightness, he reveals the source of this goodness, that, having dismissed the desires of the flesh, he cultivated godliness with his whole heart, under the guidance of the Spirit. But why does he separate faith from the Spirit, whose gift it is? I reply that it is not mentioned on its own as if it were something different, but is rather expressly pointed out as a particular example, from which it might be evident that Barnabas was full of the Spirit.

A multitude was added. Although the number of believers was already abundant Luke says that it grew with the coming of Barnabas. So the building of the Church makes progress when men help each other with mutual consent, and when one honestly approves what another has begun.

And he went forth to Tarsus to seek for Saul: and when he had found him, he brought him unto Antioch. And it came to pass, that even for a whole year they were gathered together with the church, and taught much people; and that the disciples were called Christians first in Antioch. (25-26)

25. For the second time the simplicity of Barnabas is commended to us, because, when he could have played a leading part at Antioch, he nevertheless set out for Cilicia to fetch Paul from there, knowing that he would be given preference over himself. Therefore we see that, having forgotten about himself, all that he is concerned about is that Christ alone may be pre-eminent, that he may have only the up-building of the Church in view, and that he may be content with the prosperity and success of the Gospel. Barnabas is therefore not afraid that the coming of Paul may take anything away from himself, so long as he glorifies Christ.

26. After this he adds that such a godly alliance was blessed by God. For it was no ordinary honour that the sacred name of *Christians* originated in that place for the whole world. Although the apostles had taught for so long at Jerusalem, nevertheless God had not yet thought the Church, which was there, deserving of this illustrious title of His Son; whether it was that many people, Gentiles as well as

Jews, had grown together into one body at Antioch, or that a better opportunity had been given to establish the church in peaceful circumstances, or that they had courage to confess their faith openly. Of course there were in fact Christians before, in both Jerusalem and Samaria; and we know that Jerusalem was the real fountain from which Christianity first flowed. And what else is being a disciple of Christ than being a Christian? But when they began, openly, to be called what they really were, the use of the name was of great value in making the glory of Christ plain, because in this way the whole of religion was being referred to Christ alone. Therefore it was an outstanding honour for the city of Antioch that from it Christ carried out His name like a standard, so that it would be made plain to the whole world that there were some people, who had Christ for Leader, and who took pride in His title.

Now, if Rome had such an excuse for being proud, who could put up with the insolent boasts of the Pope and his men? Then they would thunder, not without excuse, that Rome is the mother and head of all the churches; but, since they claim everything for themselves, it is a good thing that, when it comes to the bit, they are found out to be absolutely empty. But Antioch itself affords abundantly clear proof of how the situation of one place may not last for ever. Even if we grant to the Romans those plausible claims (*titulos*), 'We have been in existence in the past' (*fuimus aliquando*),[1] will they yet dare to take to themselves the half of what belongs to Antioch? And is the authority of Antioch any greater now for the reason that Christians derived their name from it? No! on the contrary it is a clear mirror of the horrible punishment of God. For since nothing can be seen there except unsightly devastation, it clearly remains for us to learn to humble ourselves under the mighty hand of God, and to know that ungrateful men are not given so much licence that they may mock at God with impunity.

Now in these days there came down prophets from Jerusalem unto Antioch. And there stood up one of them named Agabus, and signified by the Spirit that there should be a great famine over all the world: which came to pass in the days of Claudius. And the disciples, every man according to his ability, determined to send relief unto the brethren that dwelt in Judaea: which also they did, sending it to the elders by the hand of Barnabas and Saul. (27-30)

27. Here Luke is commending the faith of the Antioch church by its fruit, because they were eager to use their own resources in relieving

[1] French: '. . . *ces titres favourables, Autre fois nous avons este ceci et cela etc.*' 'At other times we have been this and that.' Tr.

the need of that church from which they had received the Gospel, and because they did so without being asked. Such solicitous concern for the brethren makes it plain enough how earnest they were in their reverence for Christ as Head of all. Luke indicates that the reputation of that church was widely recognized, when he says that prominent men came there from Jerusalem.

Now, since the word *prophet* is taken in different ways in the New Testament, as one may learn from the First Letter to the Corinthians,[1] the men called prophets in this verse are those who were endowed with the gift of foretelling, just as the four daughters of Philip will afterwards be distinguished by the same title (Acts 21.9). Although the prediction of the future is in fact attributed only to Agabus, one may assume from that that it was granted to each of them, to a certain degree, to know future events.

28. *He signified by the Spirit.* Luke makes it quite clear that the Spirit of God was the source of this prediction, so that we may know that this was no conjecture taken from the stars or other natural causes; and, in consequence, that Agabus did not philosophize in human fashion, but, by the secret inspiration of the Spirit, made known what God had determined. Certainly famine can sometimes be predicted from the position of the stars, but there is nothing certain in predictions of that kind, sometimes on account of conflicting combinations, sometimes, in particular, because God directs earthly affairs according to His will, far differently from what one may deduce from the stars, and He does so in order to lead men away from the wrong way of looking at the stars. Finally, even if those predictions have a standing of their own, yet the prophecies of the Spirit far surpass them.

But yet the prophecy about the famine seems to have been a calamitous and very undesirable one. For what was the point of making men miserable by the prediction of a dismal event before the time for it? I reply that, when the judgments of God and due punishments for sins are threatening, there are many reasons why it is advantageous for men to be warned well beforehand about them. I pass over others which occur all through the prophets; that an opportunity is given for men to come to their senses, so that those who are provoking His wrath against themselves may anticipate the judgment of God; that the faithful are warned in time so that they may prepare themselves for endurance; that the stubborn ill-will of the ungodly is overcome; that good men, just like bad, learn that calamities and misfortunes do not befall them by chance, but that they are punishments by which God takes vengeance on the sins of the world; that, in this way, those who are too self-satisfied, even in their faults, are aroused from their

[1] See e.g. Calvin's Commentary on I Cor. 12.28. Tr.

torpor. The value of the present prediction is perfectly plain from the context because it was a stimulus to the men of Antioch to give help to the brethren in their distress.

Which happened under Claudius. Suetonius also mentions this famine,[1] and narrates that crusts were thrown at Claudius' head in the open forum, and that he was so stricken with fear of stoning that for the whole of his life afterwards he paid particular attention to the food supply. But Josephus in the Fifteenth Book of the *Antiquities* relates that Judaea was afflicted by a serious scarcity because of a succession of droughts.

29. But here a question presents itself. Since the misfortune was common to all, why should help have been given to one particular group of people rather than to the rest? I reply that, since Judaea was exhausted by many disasters of wars and other misfortunes, the Antioch people were more disturbed, and not without effect, by the distress of the brethren who were there. Secondly, the more fiercely enemies were venting their rage on them there, the harder were their circumstances. Finally, in the Epistle to the Galatians Paul shows clearly enough that Judaea had special needs, about which all the rest were concerned, and in no off-hand way.[2] But this was gratitude deserving high praise, that the men of Antioch considered that the needy brethren, from whom they had received the Gospel, had to be helped by their efforts. For there is nothing fairer than that those who have sown spiritual things reap material things. As each one is far too intent on providing for himself, then it would be an easy matter for individuals to object, 'Why should I not rather provide and look out for myself?' But when they realize what they owe to the brethren they dismiss that immoderate anxiety, and turn to help them. To sum up, this relief had a double purpose, for the Antioch church both discharged the duty of charity towards the needy brethren, and testified to the great value they put on the Gospel by token of the fact that they bestowed honour on the place from which it had flowed.

Every man according to his ability. Here we see that the Antioch church adhere to the method which Paul prescribes (II Cor. 8.3), whether they did so of their own accord, or whether they had been informed about his direction. And it is surely not to be doubted that he was consistent in both places. Therefore this rule must be followed, that each one consider how much has been given to himself, and kindly share with the brethren, as one who is going to render an account; so the result will be that the poor man has a liberal mind, and a small gift is looked upon as a rich and splendid sacrifice.

[1] C.R. note: There is no mention of it in *The Life of Claudius.*

[2] Tholuck quotes Gal. 3, but the only possible reference is 2.10. Tr.

By the word *determined* Luke means that the giving was voluntary. And Paul also teaches that it ought to be the case that we stretch out our hand to those in need, not by force, or as if out of necessity, but cheerfully (II Cor. 9.7). When he mentions individuals, it is as though he said, that they did not impose a law on each other, and did not burden each other with their prejudices, but every single one was his own judge of what he should give. We must also note the word διακονία which teaches us that the rich are given control of greater abundance on condition that they may be servants of the poor, in a stewardship committed to them by God. Finally, Luke teaches that the blessing was sent, not to all the people, but only to those of the household of faith, not because unbelievers always ought to be cut off from our generosity and kindness, seeing that love ought to extend itself to the whole human race, but because preference is to be given to those whom God has joined to us in closer and more sacred ties.

30. *Sending it to the elders.* Two things must be noted here; first, that the Antioch church chose men who were trustworthy and of proved honesty to convey their blessing; secondly, that they sent it to the *elders*, who would disburse it wisely. For if alms are thrown to the crowd, or set out in the open, soon each one is grasping for himself as if it were free booty; and so all the boldest will cheat the needy, yes, and what is more, will cut the throats of the famishing by their greediness. Therefore let us observe these verses, which teach that not only must consideration be given to sincerity and trustworthiness, but also that a certain order and prudence are required, in making a choice, as well as in the total administration.

Elders is the name given to those in whose hands was the government of the Church, among whom the apostles held the first rank. It is to their judgment that the Antioch church submit the money that they have dedicated and appointed for the poor. If anyone objects that these were responsibilities imposed on the deacons, when the apostles said that they were not able to cope with the service of tables and the labour of teaching at the same time, the answer is easy, that the deacons were in charge of tables, but in such a way that they were still under the elders, and did nothing without their authority.

CHAPTER TWELVE

Now about that time Herod the king put forth his hands to afflict certain of the church. And he killed James the brother of John with the sword. And when he saw that it pleased the Jews, he proceeded to seize Peter also. And those were the days of unleavened bread. And when he had taken him, he put him in prison, and delivered him to four quaternions of soldiers to guard him; intending after the Passover to bring him forth to the people. Peter therefore was kept in the prison: but prayer was made earnestly of the church unto God for him. (1-5)

1. There follows a fresh persecution instigated by Herod. We see that the Church was granted a short truce, so that, for a little while, it might revive its courage for a future occasion, as though recovering its breath, and then fight another day. So today there is no reason why the faithful should expect perpetual peace for themselves when they have fought their way through one or two battles, or should seek exemption for themselves, such as veteran soldiers are accustomed to having. Let it suffice if the Lord is granting some time for them to gather their strength again.

To move on, this Herod was Agrippa the Elder, the son of Aristobulus, whom his father had slain. Josephus nowhere calls him Herod, perhaps because his brother, the King of Chalcis, was called Herod. This man was incited to trouble the Church, not so much out of concern for religion as to win over the common people to himself by this public spectacle, since they were not otherwise well-disposed towards him, or undoubtedly it was out of tyrannical cruelty, because he was afraid of innovations, of which all tyrants are suspicious, in case they disturb the peaceful state of their dominion. However, it is probable that he shed innocent blood in order to gratify a furious people, as cunning kings commonly do, because a little later Luke will tell that Peter was consigned to prison, to be a pleasing spectacle.

2. *He killed James.* There is no doubt that the cruelty of this insane man was kept back and checked by the secret power of God. For he would not have been content with one or two murders, and refrained from persecuting the rest, but, on the contrary, he would have piled up huge heaps of martyrs, if God had not intervened to protect His flock. So when we see that, though the enemies of the faith are full of fury, they do not cause fearful massacres, let us know that it does not happen because of their moderation or clemency, but because the

Lord spares His sheep and does not allow those men to do as much harm as they intended. Certainly this Herod was not so humane as to hesitate to gain peace or popular esteem by the torture of a hundred men or more. Accordingly we must come to the conclusion that his passion was held in check by a greater authority, so that he might not oppress the Church too violently.

He killed James, as it is usual, when any rebellion is raised, for the leaders and chief men to be punished, so that the common herd may be terrified by their torture. Meanwhile the Lord allowed him to be rushed to his death, after He had provided him with steadfastness, to be victorious in death as a courageous and unbeaten champion. So no matter what tyrants scheme, God nevertheless chooses sacrifices of a pleasing odour for Himself in order to confirm the faith of His Gospel.

Luke calls this James, who was killed, *the brother of John*, to distinguish him from the son of Alphaeus. I am not convinced by others who produce a third one, a kinsman of Christ's, who was only one of the disciples, because I am led by strong reasons to believe that there were no more than two. If anyone wishes to know the reasons he may look for them in Galatians chapter two. Therefore I think, that both the apostle and the son of Alphaeus were the same person, whom the Jews flung headlong from the top of the temple,[1] and whose death was so greatly honoured on account of the extraordinary reputation he had for sanctity.

3. *Seeing that it pleased the Jews.* We see more clearly from this that Herod was driven to the persecution of the Church, neither out of zeal for the Law of Moses, nor out of hatred of the Gospel, but out of concern for his own private interests, for in order to gain the esteem of the people for himself he persists in his cruelty. Therefore we must realize that there are many different causes for the Church being assailed from all sides. Indeed perverse zeal often does drive the ungodly headlong to fight eagerly for their superstitions, and to offer a sacrifice to their idols by shedding innocent blood. But the majority are led only by their private concerns. For example, when, long ago, Nero knew that, after the burning of the city, he was infamous and hateful to the people, he chased after favour by this cunning means, or at least made an effort to put an end to reproaches and complaints by murdering several thousand believers. In the same way in order to win over the people who were anything but devoted to him Herod delivers Christians to death, just as if they were a price for buying back favour. And in our day things are no different. For although

[1] Hegesippus on James the Just, brother of our Lord, see Eusebius, *Church History*, II.23. Tr.

all turn with eager rage against the members of Christ, superstition drives on few, but some sell themselves like useful slaves to the Roman Anti-Christ, while others yield to and gratify the fierce shouts of monks and the common people. But while we are bowing our poor heads to their scoffing, in the meantime there is one consolation to sustain us, that we know that our blood, which the world abuses disgracefully, is precious to God, and, what is more, that the more shamefully and contemptuously we are treated by the ungodly, the less will the goodness of God forsake us.

4. *Four quaternions guarding.* Luke shows by these circumstances that Peter was shut up as if in a tomb, so that it might appear to be all up with him. For just as they used to divide days and nights into four parts of three hours each, so Herod split up the guards so that four soldiers would always be keeping watch, and they would relieve each other every third hour. He explains why he was not carried off to execution immediately. It was because it was a religious offence (*religio*) to kill him during the days of the Feast of the Passover. Therefore Herod does not delay as if he was uncertain what to do, but is only waiting for the opportunity. But in fact he chooses a time when his spectacle would be all the more pleasing, because a great throng crowded together from every quarter for the feast.

5. *But prayers.* Here Luke is telling that in the meantime the faithful did not fail in their duty. Peter was indeed standing alone in the front line of the battle, but all the others are fighting at the same time with their prayers, and are helping him with what assistance they can. We also gather from this that they were not broken in spirit, for they testify by their prayers that they are persisting to the utmost of their ability in defending the cause for which Peter was suffering even at the risk of his life.

This verse teaches, first of all, how we ought to be affected whenever we see our brethren attacked by the ungodly because of their testimony to the Gospel. For if we do nothing, and are not made anxious by their dangers, not only do we cheat them of the rightful duty of charity, but we are also treacherously abandoning the confession of our faith. And of course if we have common cause with them, even more if they are fighting for our safety, we are failing not so much them as ourselves and Christ. And the pressing need at present is that all who wish to be counted as Christians undertake prayer with far more eagerness than we can generally see. We see some of our brethren living in exile after they have been reduced to the direst straits, others in fetters, many plunged in stinking, foul pits, many dragged off to the flames, yes, and we even see the frequent devising of new instruments of torment, on which they are tortured for a long time and feel themselves dying. If these incentives do not spur us on at least to a desire to pray we are worse than stupid. Therefore as soon as some persecution arises, we ought to have recourse to prayer.

It is also probable that the Church was the more concerned about the life of Peter because it would suffer too great a loss by his death. Luke not only says that *prayer was made* but at the same time adds *earnest* or continual. By that he means that the faithful did not pray in indifferent or cursory fashion, but as long as Peter was battling it out, they were bent on helping him, in what way they could, without flagging.

The *name of God*, which is explicit here, must always be understood when mention of praying is made in Scripture. For it is one of the basic principles of the faith that prayer is only to be directed to God, and to Him alone, as, for instance, he claims this particular act of worship for Himself, 'Call upon me in the day of trouble' (Ps. 50.15).

And when Herod was about to bring him forth, the same night Peter was sleeping between two soldiers, bound with two chains: and guards before the door kept the prison. And behold, an angel of the Lord stood by him, and a light shined in the cell: and he smote Peter on the side, and awoke him, saying, Rise up quickly. And his chains fell off from his hands. And the angel said unto him, Gird thyself, and bind on thy sandals. And he did so. And he saith unto him, Cast thy garment about thee, and follow me. And he went out, and followed; and he wist not that it was true which was done by the angel, but thought he saw a vision. And when they were past the first and the second ward, they came unto the iron gate that leadeth into the city; which opened to them of its own accord: and they went out, and passed on through one street; and straightway the angel departed from him. And when Peter was come to himself, he said, Now I know of a truth, that the Lord hath sent forth his angel and delivered me out of the hand of Herod, and from all the expectation of the people of the Jews. (6-11)

6. *When he was about to bring him forth.* At first glance the Church seems to be praying without result, for the day for Peter's execution has already been fixed previously, and only a single night stands between him and death. However the faithful do not cease praying, because they know that when the Lord intends to bring help to His own people, He has His own appointed time in the moment of greatest necessity, and that He has in His control many different ways of delivering. Finally we may believe that prayers were poured forth, not only for Peter's life, but in order that the Lord would strengthen him with invincible courage for the glory of the Gospel; and that

God would not prostitute the Gospel of His Son to the abuses of the ungodly.

On that night he was sleeping. All these details illustrate more fully the wonderful power of God. For who would not have thought that Peter was already devoured by death? For even if he is still breathing, yet he is beset by many ready to kill him, and not a crack to open a way of escape. Therefore because he escapes with deaths all about him, goes in safety with his executioners close at hand, his chains melt and are loosened, the iron gate opens itself to him, it is clear from these things that a liberation of this kind is truly of divine origin. And it was to Peter's advantage to be taught opportunely by these signs, so that afterwards he might preach with more assurance among men the grace of God that was known in this way. In fine, such a strict confinement makes it all the clearer that Herod had absolutely no intention of letting Peter get out alive.

7. *A light shone.* It is likely that this light was seen only by Peter, and that the soldiers were either asleep or senseless so that they were aware of nothing. And there could have been a twofold reason why God wished the light to shine, either that Peter might make use of it and not be hindered by the darkness, or that it might be a sign of the heavenly glory to him. For we often read that angels appeared with shining splendour even when the sun was shining. Certainly Peter ought to have concluded from the unusual light that God was present, and at the same time to have taken advantage of it for his own use.

It is evident from the angel's striking Peter's side how solicitous for His own is the God who watches for them while they sleep, and rouses them when they are lethargic. And there would certainly be nothing more wretched for us, if the only thing to keep God on guard over us was the constancy of our prayers. For, because of the weakness of our flesh, we fail, and we have the greatest need of Him when our minds are distracted elsewhere and do not seek Him. Sleep is a kind of image of death, which keeps our senses stifled and subdued. What would become of us if God ceased to look after us during it? But because believers commend their safety to God, when they retire to sleep, the consequence is that their sleep also calls on God.

Immediately after the angel's words he records that his *chains* were loosened, and from that we gather that there is enough power in the mere commandment of God to remove every kind of obstacle, when all roads seem to be completely blocked. Thus if He wishes to still the tumults of wars, even if the whole world is in arms, immediately spears and swords will fall from their hands. On the other hand if He intends to take vengeance on us and our sins with war, in a moment the minds of men, who were previously devoted to peace, will be inflamed and they will seize their swords.

The fact that Luke reports every single one of the angel's words, as well as the course of events, gives certitude to the story, so that it may be made plain from every aspect that Peter was liberated by God.

9. *He did not know that it was true.* He certainly was not supposing that it was an empty or deceptive spectre, as Satan often deceives men with illusions, but here *true* is taken for what happens naturally and humanly. For we must note the contrast between actual happening and a vision. Moreover even if he does think that it is a vision, he is nevertheless ready to obey. His obedience is shown when, content with the mere command of the angel, he does not ask or argue about what he must do, but carries out his orders.

10. *But when they had passed through.* God could have hurried Peter out in a single moment, but one after the other He overcomes various difficulties, so that the glory of the miracle might be greater. Thus He created the world in six days, not because He needed that space of time, but that He might keep us in meditation of His works. For He accommodates His method of acting to our capacity, and the progress of our faith. If Peter had been suddenly swept from prison into the house where the brethren were gathered together, one single simple delivery would have been recognized, but in fact we now see, as if with our own eyes, that he was liberated more than ten times.

11. *Then Peter came to himself.* Literally it is 'having become in himself' for previously, astonished by an unexpected and incredible happening, he was, so to speak, 'out of himself'. Now, at last, as if after an ecstasy, he realizes that he has been snatched out of death. His words, which Luke reports, contain an act of thanksgiving. For until he finds other witnesses, he praises within himself, and extols to himself, the blessing of God that he has experienced.

He says that the angel was sent by God, according to the common view of the godly, who hold that angels are appointed by God to be servants to look after their safety. For if such a conviction had not been firmly fixed in his mind he would not have mentioned the angel. And yet he does not honour the angel as the originator of the favour, but ascribes all the praise to God alone. And indeed the angels do not devote their help to us for the purpose of diverting even the smallest fraction of God's glory to themselves.

When he says that he was brought forth *out of the hand of Herod* he magnifies God's blessing in relation to the power of his enemy. What he adds about the Jews has the same bearing. For the greater the number of the enemies was, the more remarkable was the grace of God towards His servant; because it is a great thing that the hostility and animosity of the whole world ends in nothing, because God alone is favourable.

And when he had considered the thing, he came to the house of Mary the mother of John whose surname was Mark; where many were gathered together and were praying. And when he knocked at the door of the gate, a maid came to answer, named Rhoda. And when she knew Peter's voice, she opened not the gate for joy, but ran in, and told that Peter stood before the gate. And they said unto her, Thou art mad. But she confidently affirmed that it was even so. And they said, It is his angel. But Peter continued knocking: and when they had opened, they saw him, and were amazed. But he, beckoning unto them with the hand to hold their peace, declared unto them how the Lord had brought him forth out of the prison. And he said, Tell these things unto James, and to the brethren. And he departed, and went to another place. Now as soon as it was day, there was no small stir among the soldiers, what was become of Peter. And when Herod had sought for him, and found him not, he examined the guards, and commanded that they should be put to death. (12-19a)

12. *To the house of Mary.* It is evident that this was a woman of exceptional piety, whose house was a kind of temple of God, where meetings of the brethren were in the habit of being held. Now Luke says that *many were gathered together* there, because they could not all have met at the same time without the fear of a public disturbance, and so they came together in groups in different parts of the city, as it was convenient. For I have no doubt that companies were also gathered together elsewhere, because with many of the multitude of believers praying, one cannot believe that the apostles were not engaged in the same duty; and one house would not have been capable of holding such a great crowd. On the other hand the circumstances of the time must always be kept in mind, that, with their enemies burning with cruelty, the godly were still assembling together. For if this exercise is useful at any time, then it is particularly necessary when sharp conflicts are threatening.

13. *When he knocked at the door.* When they suppose that the girl, who announces Peter's arrival, is mad, we gather from that that they were not expecting the liberation of Peter. And yet we shall not say that they prayed without faith; because they were looking for other results, viz. that Peter, armed with heavenly power, would be ready to glorify the name of Christ whether by his life, or by his death; that the flock might not be scattered in terror at the violent inrush of wolves; that the weak might not give way; that the Lord might disperse that hurricane of persecution. But the Lord, with His im-

measurable goodness, outdid their prayers, granting them more than they had hoped for. Now what has happened seems incredible to them, so that they are roused to praise the power of God all the more.

15. *It is his angel.* They call *his angel* the one who has been appointed by God to be his guardian and to look after his safety. It is in this sense that Christ says that 'the angels of the little ones always behold the Father's face' (Matt. 18.10). People's common deduction from this, that individual angels are allotted to individual men, to take care of them, is too feeble. For Scripture testifies that one angel is sometimes given to a great people (Exod. 14.19), and an enormous host of them to only one man. For the eyes of Elisha's servant were opened so that he saw many fiery chariots in the air, which were drawn up for the safety and protection of the prophet (II Kings 6.17). And surely in the book of Daniel only one angel is named for the Persians and one for the Greeks (10.13, 20). And Scripture does not promise to each one his own definite and special angel, but assures us rather, in Ps. 91.11, that the Lord has commanded His angels to protect individual believers, and, similarly, to pitch their tents round about the godly (Ps. 34.7). Therefore the universal belief that each man has two genii is an unholy fabrication. Let it be enough for us that the whole heavenly host keeps watch for the safety of the Church, and therefore that, according to the need of the moment, sometimes one angel, sometimes many angels, are protecting us with their support. Certainly it is of God's inestimable goodness that He says that the angels, who are beams of the divine splendour, are our servants.

17. *Tell James and the brethren.* I understand by *brethren* not all and sundry who belonged to the Church, but the apostles and the elders. For although it was necessary for the miracle to be made known to all, yet Peter quite rightly wishes to show honour to his colleagues by informing them about it. Ecclesiastical writers after Eusebius teach almost unanimously that this *James* was one of the disciples, but since Paul includes him in the three pillars of the Church (Gal. 2.9), I do not think it likely that the apostles were put in the background and a disciple elevated to such a degree of honour. Accordingly I rather conclude that this was James the son of Alphaeus, whose sanctity had attracted the great admiration of the Jews. But there were two reasons why Peter wished this glad news to be brought to the brethren viz. that he might remove the anxiety which was tormenting them, and secondly, that they might be encouraged to greater confidence by such an example of the favour of God.

I think his departure to *another place* was done with this in mind, that, since the house was well-known through the faithful frequenting it daily, he could have lain in hiding elsewhere with less danger. He therefore sought a place that was not so suspect to their enemies, that he might spare not only himself but also his hostess and the others.

18. *When day had come.* Luke now returns to the soldiers and Herod, and says that they were in a great state of agitation. For they could not have suspected that Peter had been snatched away from them by force, or that he had escaped by some deception. Herod afterwards investigates the matter as a judge. But when he finds out that the soldiers are not to blame, he himself is forced to be a witness of the divine liberation also.

19. One may deduce from the fact that he orders them to be taken out of his sight, or to be put back to the prison,[1] that their faithfulness and diligence were laid bare, for if there had been any suspicion of negligence punishment was ready. However it was partly wicked fury mingled with tyrannical cruelty, and even partly shame, that prevented him from letting them go free. Others however give a different explanation, viz. that he wished them to be hurried off to be sentenced immediately.[2] But whether in anger he hands them over to the executioner, or whether he was content to put them in prison, there is definitely an extraordinary example of blindness here, for when he ought to be aware of the power of God, even with his eyes shut, he is not moved, and he does not soften, but continues to resist God with obstinate ill-will. Of course that is how Satan deprives the ungodly of perception, so that in seeing they do not see; and the Lord justly avenges Himself and the Church by striking them with this horrible insensibility.

And he went down from Judaea to Caesarea, and tarried there. Now he was highly displeased with them of Tyre and Sidon: and they came with one accord to him, and, having made Blastus the king's chamberlain their friend, they asked for peace, because their country was fed from the king's country. And upon a set day Herod arrayed himself in royal apparel, and sat on the throne, and made an oration unto them. And the people shouted, saying, The voice of a god, and not of a man. And immediately an angel of the Lord smote him, because he gave not God the glory: and he was eaten of worms, and gave up the ghost. But the word of God grew and multiplied. And Barnabas and Saul returned from Jerusalem, when they had fulfilled their ministration, taking with them John whose surname was Mark. (19b-25)

[1] Calvin's text, *re cognita iussit custodes abduci*. Cf. Vulg.: *iussit eos duci*. Greek: ἀνακρίνας τοὺς φύλακας ἐκέλευσεν ἀπαχθῆναι (ἀπάγω to lead to prison or punishment etc.). Cf. Western variant, ἀποκτανθῆναι (to be killed).

[2] Following Tholuck's *ad iudicium* for C.R.'s *ad supplicium*, but with C.R. and French beginning new sentence at 'But whether'. French: 'he commanded that they be led away to be punished', '*au supplice*'. Tr.

20. This is a remarkable story, which shows, as though in a mirror, not only what sort of end awaits the enemies of the Church, but how pride is hateful to God. Scripture tells us that God resists the proud (I Pet. 5.5), and God Himself has portrayed that vividly to us in the person of Herod. And indeed men cannot exalt themselves beyond what is legitimate, without joining battle with God, who orders all flesh to keep silent, so that He alone may be pre-eminent. Now if God punishes pride so severely in the case of a king, who was puffed up by his prosperous circumstances, what will happen to ordinary men who are ridiculously inflated without any justification? Furthermore we must note what the story unfolds, that everything prospers well for Herod after he has cruelly harassed the Church, and that he compels neighbouring cities, subdued by hunger, to plead humbly for his favour, as if God were recompensing him for his ungodly fury. That was a serious temptation to the faithful, on whom the suspicion could have dawned that God was not concerned about them; and who were being struck by the fear that the tyranny and cruelty of Herod would increase, step by step with his power. But God's purpose was quite different. For He raised the oppressor of His Church on high, to cast him down in greater ruin. Therefore that shadowy happiness in which he prided himself so much, was for him a kind of fattening for the day of slaughter. Similarly today when we see the bloodthirsty enemies of the Church carried high on fortune's outspread wings, that is no reason for courage to fail us. But rather let that saying of Solomon's come to mind, 'Pride goes before destruction, and a haughty spirit before a fall' (Prov. 16.18).

Herod was highly displeased. Luke uses the compound participle θυμομαχῶν denoting animosity and hatred. Herod was therefore not waging open war on these cities, but the breach was such that he tried to subdue them by covert tricks as though undermining them little by little. As Demosthenes says, rarely can there be an accord between free cities and monarchs. In addition Herod was possessed of a headstrong nature, a great deal of audacity, and insatiable cupidity. There is no doubt that Tyre and Sidon, were, so to speak, kinds of barriers to put a check on his outrageous conduct, as they were wealthy cities and not accustomed to bearing the yoke. The memory of their ancient glory could also have put spirit into them. Since it is a common-place that pride springs from riches, it is no wonder if these two cities were full of pride. Isaiah makes one of them the Queen of the Sea (23.8), saying that its merchants were princes and its traders satraps. He also says elsewhere that the pride of Sidon was derived from riches (23.2). And although they had more than once endured almost the greatest of disasters, yet the very advantageousness of their situation quickly restored them to their former state. The result of this was that they had no patience with Agrippa, a man recently despised, and of obscure circumstances, one indeed liberated from fetters and prison, especially since he domineered violently over his own subjects, and was oppressive and hurtful to his neighbours.

Because their country was fed. Since he would have gained nothing from undertaking open war against the people of Tyre and Sidon, he forbids the importing of provisions from his own kingdom. Thus, without force and an army he was putting pressure on them with a slow blockade. For the territories of both cities were small, and the ground barren, while there was a large population requiring to be fed. Therefore when hunger conquers them, they humbly sue for peace, but now it is at a price. For there is no doubt that conditions were imposed on them; and one can well believe that that Blastus, whom Luke mentions, was not persuaded with mere words, but was won over with bribes to be the negotiator of peace. I do not know why Erasmus saw fit to translate this verse differently from what the words imply.

21. *And upon a set day.* Luke has reported that peace was granted to the people of Tyre and Sidon, because this provided the king with the opportunity of delivering an oration, doubtless in order to make them subject to him afterwards. A similar account is to be found in Book Nineteen of the *Antiquities* of Josephus, except that throughout he uses the name Agrippa, while Luke calls him Herod. It is very likely that Agrippa was his proper name, and that he was called nothing else so long as he led a private life, and that, after he in fact gained possession of the kingdom, he sought to obtain royal dignity by using his grandfather's name. Josephus and Luke indeed do agree wonderfully about the actual incident and all the details. First there is agreement about the place. Josephus says that his garments were covered with gold, so that when they were struck with the rays of the sun, they glittered back in turn, and that this was seized on by the courtiers as an opportunity to hail him as a god. He says that a wound was suddenly inflicted on him, yes, indeed, and that an owl was seen sitting on a rope above his head to be the harbinger of coming disaster. And indeed he (Josephus) has no doubt that his sacrilegious insolence was being censured by this kind of punishment, so that he mentions that, even as he was suffering horrible pain, he openly acknowledged it, 'Look at me, the one whom you are honouring as a god. I am being forced to end my life in the most wretched way.' There is no mention by him about the peace made with the people of Tyre and Sidon, but he does say that he celebrated games in honour of Caesar. The celebration of the games could certainly have been organized

because of the peace, because we know that that was the practice.

23. *Immediately smote him.* As the angel was previously God's servant in liberating Peter, so now he executes His vengeance upon Herod. Now God is sometimes in the habit of using the services of the heavenly angels in inflicting punishment, but at other times He appoints the devils as executioners, and carries out His judgments at their hand. And he does this indiscriminately, to His own faithful people just as much as to the reprobate. Saul was molested by Satan (I Sam. 16.14), but the same thing also happened to holy Job (Job 1.11, 2.7). In the Psalm the plagues by which God chastises the ungodly are attributed to evil angels (78.49); but we see that the angel, who is guardian of the Church's safety, strikes the Egyptians in their firstborn. However Scripture calls evil spirits God's spirits, because they submit to His will, even if reluctantly. But when the epithet *evil* is not added, as in this verse, we ought to understand an angel who obeys God willingly. Nevertheless the figure of the owl, which Josephus mentions, was in better agreement with representing a devil than a heavenly angel.

Furthermore I am not venturing a definite assertion about what sort of disease it was. The word which Luke has used means that he was consumed by worms. Many conjecture that the disease was lice infestation. It is indeed certain that, when he was still alive, he was wasting away with rottenness and an offensive smell, so that he was, so to speak, a living corpse. So he was not only afflicted with severe pains, but exposed to the insults and mockery of all. For the Lord wished to choose a kind of punishment by which He would obliterate the ferocity of a proud man with extreme ignominy. If he had been overwhelmed by some great and powerful army, and reduced to poverty, the judgment of God would not have been so obvious, and that would have been an honourable punishment and one fitting for a king; but when he is infested by lice and worms, and that stinking putrefaction, which gnaws at him and consumes him, breaks out of his body, he is being treated according to his merits and deserts. It was like that with Pharaoh, for when he rose so often against God with ungovernable pride, he was not attacked, as befitted a king, by some neighbouring prince, but locusts and 'hoppers'[1] were God's soldiers for waging war on him. For the more anyone exalts himself in arrogance, the more does he deserve to be cast down with ignominy

[1] This is a suggested translation for *bruci*, which Lewis and Short render as 'a kind of locust without wings'. 'Hoppers' are young locusts without wings. *Bruci* does not appear in the Vulg. of the plague chapters of Exod. (7-10). Tholuck gives reference Exod. 8.17, 24, which refer to the lice and flies, whereas locusts appear in 10.4. Tr.

by God to the lowest depths. That is the reason why He left this counterfeit god Herod exposed, to be eaten by worms, and confession of this very thing was at last wrung out of him, when he said, 'Look at me, the god whom you have hailed. I am being hurried to a wretched death.' Such a striking example of a horrible punishment in the person of a king ought to fill us with great fear, lest we dare to arrogate to ourselves more than is proper, and lest we also allow ourselves to be intoxicated by the deceitful applause and the flatteries of men as if by a deadly poison.

Because he gave not God the glory. He is convicted of sacrilege not only because he allowed himself to be called 'God', but because, forgetting himself, he transferred to himself the honour due to God. We do not read that similar plaudits were given to the king of Babylon; yet the prophet reproaches him because he tried to make himself equal to God (Isa. 14.13, 14). Accordingly the offence of sacrilege is one that is common to all proud men, because, by arrogating to themselves more than is permissible, they obscure the glory of God, and so in the manner of the giants they try, as hard as they can, to remove God from His own throne. Although they may not usurp the title of 'God', and may not openly make boastful statements that they are gods, yet because they appropriate to themselves what belongs to God, they desire to be gods, and to be regarded as gods, when they have reduced Him to order. Moreover the prophet points out the source of this evil in a single word, when he introduces Nebuchadnezzar saying, 'I shall ascend' (Isa. 14.13). Accordingly there is only one remedy, if each one keeps himself in that station in which he has been placed. Let those who are poor and humble not strive for the heights. On the other hand let those at the very top, kings and all who stand over others, remember that they are still mortal men, and modestly subject their loftiness to God.

Finally we must note that it is not enough if men render half honour to God, when He claims for Himself the whole of what belongs to Him, and if men submit themselves only partly to God when He wishes them to be utterly humbled. Now, since Scripture empties us of all merit as far as wisdom, virtue and righteousness are concerned, there is not one of us who can arrogate to himself even the tiniest particle of glory without sacrilegious robbing of God. And, since Scripture pronounces that all who exalt themselves are, so to speak, making open war on God, and, on the other hand, since we all acknowledge that that cannot happen without our destruction, it is nevertheless astonishing that everywhere the majority of men rush to their own ruin with furious audacity. For there is scarcely one in a hundred who, remembering his own situation, leaves God His glory intact.

24. *But the word of God.* With the removal of the tyrant the Church was unexpectedly snatched out of the jaws of the wolf, so to speak. Therefore although the faithful are accounted sheep appointed for the slaughter (Ps. 44.22; Rom. 8.36), yet the Church always survives its enemies; and although the Word of God can repeatedly appear to be suppressed by the wicked tyranny of men, yet it soon rises up again. For it was Luke's purpose not only to report what happened after the death of Herod, but also to encourage us by this example, so that we may be quite convinced that in all ages God will do what He did then, so that the course of the Gospel may finally break through all the obstructions of its enemies, and that the more the Church is weakened, the greater it may become, with the blessing of heaven.

25. *And Barnabas and Saul.* The ministration, which, Luke writes, Paul and Barnabas discharged, ought to be referred to the alms, which were mentioned previously. For when famine and scarcity had been predicted by the prophet Agabus, money was collected by the brethren at Antioch for the relief of the needy church at Jerusalem. The duty of conveying this money was entrusted to Barnabas and Paul. Now Luke says that they returned to Antioch, to make a transition for himself to a new episode. He adds that John, surnamed Mark, whose mother was spoken of with great respect earlier, was taken by them as a companion; but later on he was the cause of a serious and damaging disagreement between them, as we shall see.

CHAPTER THIRTEEN

Now there were at Antioch, in the church that was there, prophets and teachers, Barnabas, and Symeon that was called Niger, and Lucius of Cyrene, and Manaen the foster-brother of Herod the tetrarch, and Saul. And as they ministered to the Lord, and fasted, the Holy Ghost said, Separate me Barnabas and Saul for the work whereunto I have called them. Then, when they had fasted and prayed and laid their hands on them, they sent them away. (1-3)

1. There follows a narrative that is not only worth telling, but is also very much worth knowing, viz. how Paul was ordained teacher of the Gentiles. For his calling was, as it were, the key, by which God has opened the Kingdom of Heaven to us. We know that the covenant of eternal life was especially established with the Jews, and so we had no part in the inheritance of God, since we were outsiders, and a wall was interposed, separating the members of the household from strangers. Therefore the fact that Christ brought salvation to the world would have been of no advantage to us, unless, with the division removed, an entrance into the Church had been opened for us. Certainly the apostles already had the commandment about publishing the Gospel throughout the whole world, but in fact they had so far confined themselves within the boundaries of Judaea. When Peter was sent to Cornelius it was such a novel and unaccustomed situation that it was looked upon almost like a monstrosity. Again, that could have appeared to be a privilege granted to a few men as an extraordinary thing. But now, when God specifically appoints Paul and Barnabas apostles to the Gentiles, in this way He is making them equal to the Jews, so that the Gospel may begin to be common to both without distinction. Therefore the dividing wall is now destroyed, so that those who were far off and those who were near may be equally reconciled to God, and having been gathered together under the one Head, may grow together equally into the one Body (Eph. 2.14ff). Therefore the calling of Paul ought to carry just as much weight with us as if God openly proclaimed from heaven that the salvation once promised to Abraham and his seed belongs to us today, as if we derived our origin from Abraham. Accordingly Paul takes such great pains in many passages to defend his calling, so that the Gentiles may be definitely convinced that the teaching of the Gospel was brought to them neither by chance, nor by some rash

human decision, but, first, by the wonderful purpose of God, and, secondly, by a clear command, when He made known to men what He had determined within Himself (Gal. 1.15, 2.8).

There were in the church. I have explained in Eph. 4.11 and I Cor. 12.28 how, at least in my opinion, *teachers* differ from *prophets.* In this verse these two words can be synonomous, so that Luke may mean that there were a great many men in that church endowed with the special grace of the Spirit for teaching. I certainly do not see how it suits to explain *prophets* as men who were strong in the gift of foretelling, but I rather think that outstanding interpreters of Scripture is the meaning. And such men used to perform the function of teaching and exhorting as Paul gives us to understand in I Cor. 14.29. We must observe what Luke has in his mind. Paul and Barnabas were ministers to the church at Antioch, and now God is calling them from it to go elsewhere. In case anyone might think that that church was being stripped of able and suitable ministers, so that God might look to others at its expense, Luke seeks to obviate that, and tells us that it had such numbers, that, while relieving the need of others, it had nevertheless sufficient left for its own use. It is evident from that how freely the grace of God had been poured out on that church, when streams could be drawn off from it to other places. So even in our time God enriches certain churches more than others, so that they may be nurseries for propagating the teaching of the Gospel.

Manaen, who had been brought up along with Herod, must have sprung from some noble family, to have been associated with Herod as an intimate.[1] Now Luke mentions this deliberately to bring his piety before us, because, despising worldly splendour he devoted himself to the lowly and contemptible flock of Christ. If ambition had ruled in his heart he could certainly have been one of the principal courtiers, but in order to devote himself totally to Christ he does not refuse to exchange those unsubstantial honours for reproach and disgrace. For if we reflect upon what the situation of the Church was like at that time, he could not have identified himself with the Gospel, without bringing himself into common disrepute. Therefore the Lord wished to teach us by his example to hold the world in contempt, so that Christians may learn to spurn the whole word with a brave and high heart, for the only way they can truly be Christians is to reject those things which are precious to the flesh, as damaging hindrances.

2. *And as they ministered to the Lord.* The word which Luke uses (λειτουργούντων) means not only to be occupied with holy things,

[1] Calvin's text: *Manaim qui cum Herode tetrarcha educatus fuerat.* Greek: *Μαναήν τε Ἡρώδου τοῦ τετράρχου σύντροφος.* Tr.

but sometimes also to be engaged in public duties. But, since the sacred rites of the Gentiles usually consisted of animal sacrifices and victims, it is often taken for offering sacrifices. That sense has pleased the Papists very much, in order that they might prove that the apostles made use of some sacrifice. But even if we grant what they postulate, they are nevertheless ridiculous in alleging, in defence of their Mass, that the teachers at Antioch sacrificed. In the first place, since the word is in the plural, it will follow that masses were celebrated by every one of them. But, leaving absurdities aside, I maintain that we must consider what kind of sacrifice Christ has committed to His Church. The Papists imagine that the office of the priesthood is laid upon them to sacrifice Christ, and to obtain peace with God by their offering of Him. No mention is made of that notion in Scripture, so that the Son of God may, instead, arrogate this office to Himself alone. Therefore it is another priesthood that belongs to the Christian Church, viz. that each one may offer himself and all his possessions to God, and, on the other hand, that the public ministers may sacrifice souls by the spiritual sword of the Gospel as Paul teaches in Rom. 15.16. In addition, the prayers of all the godly are the calves[1] of the lips (Hos. 14.2), with which God is well pleased, when they are offered from the holy altar, i.e. in the name of Christ (Heb. 13.15). Therefore when Luke now says that the prophets and teachers *ministered*, when the Spirit spoke to them, all I understand is that, at that time, they were carrying out their public duties (*in actione publica*).

He adds *fasting* so that we may know that their minds were freed from every hindrance, so that nothing might prevent them from being more intent on prophecy. Apart from that, it is not clear whether a fast was undertaken by them publicly, or whether Luke is only meaning that they were fasting up to that time. It is certainly beyond question that those details were brought out so that we may give all the more credence to Paul's calling.

Separate to me. God commands that Paul and Barnabas be sent out to wherever He has appointed them, by the votes of the Church. From that we gather that no election of pastors is legitimate except one in which God plays the leading part. For although He has commanded that pastors and bishops be elected by the Church, He has not, for that reason, permitted so much licence to men that He Himself does not preside as the chief Moderator. Indeed the ordinary election of pastors differs from this appointment of Paul and Barnabas, because it was fitting for those men, who were to be apostles of the Gentiles, to be appointed by a heavenly oracle, and that does not need to happen in the day-to-day ordaining of pastors. Yet they have this

[1] *Vituli* with Hebrew and A.V.; cf. LXX, R.V., R.S.V. 'fruit'. Tr.

in common, that just as God made it known that Paul and Barnabas had already been appointed by His decision to preach the Gospel, so it is not right that any others be called to the office of teaching except those whom God has already, in some way, chosen for Himself. Moreover, there is no need for the Spirit to cry to us from heaven that a man with whom we are dealing is called of God, because we receive those whom God has equipped with the necessary gifts, since they have been fashioned and prepared by His hand, and we do so, just as if they have been delivered by Him to us, from hand to hand as the saying goes.

But because Luke says here that Paul was ordained by the votes of the Church, it seems to disagree with Paul's statement, in which he denies that he was called by men or through men (Gal. 1.1). I reply that he was created an apostle long before he was sent to the Gentiles, and that not by men voting for him; and he had already discharged his apostleship for several years when he was summoned to the Gentiles by a new oracle. Accordingly in order to keep God the Originator of His apostleship, he is quite justified in excluding men. And certainly God does not instruct his ordination by the Church so that his calling may depend on the judgment of men, but He now reveals by public proclamation that decision of His, which up to then was known to a few, and orders it to be sealed by the solemn approval of the Church. The meaning of the words is therefore this: the time has now come for Paul to spread the Gospel among the Gentiles, and, because the wall has been destroyed, to gather a Church from the Gentiles, who had previously been outside the Kingdom of God. For although God had so far made use of his services at Antioch and other places, only now did He add this special task, that He wished to admit the Gentiles to the same inheritance of life along with the Jews. Now if he had been made a teacher of the Church in this way from the beginning, he certainly would not have been called by men on this occasion. For since the Lord announces that he was called by Him, what does He leave for the Church to do, but to approve obediently? For here the judgment of men is not being brought forward as in a situation of uncertainty, and they are not free to vote. But we must grasp what I have said, that Paul and Barnabas are not now, at long last, being confirmed in the order of teachers (*in ordine doctorum*), but that an extraordinary task is being laid upon them, to begin to make known the grace of God to the Gentiles everywhere. And the words *separate for the work* mean precisely that. For I am quite sure that He is indicating a new work, and one as yet strange to them.

But how is Barnabas linked with Paul as his companion and colleague, when we have never read of him carrying out the office of teaching, and, what is more, when he always remained silent and conceded to Paul the role of spokesman? I reply that more than enough opportunities for speaking were repeatedly offered to him, in Paul's absence, so that both had enough to do, for one could not always be present everywhere. Indeed there is no doubt that he faithfully carried out the duties which God had entrusted to him, and that he was no dumb spectator. And why should we wonder that Luke does not expressly report the speeches he made, seeing that he repeats scarcely one in a thousand of Paul's?

The Spirit said. Whatever objection Macedonius and his sect may make for the sake of evasion, here however we have too clear and firm a statement of the divine essence of the Spirit, than can be eluded. There is nothing that is more peculiar to God than that He alone governs the Church by His power and authority; and the Spirit arrogates this right to Himself, when He orders Paul and Barnabas to be separated to Himself, and testifies that they were called by His command. We certainly must admit that the body of the Church is mutilated and deprived of its Head, unless we acknowledge that it is God, who establishes it by His will, who places teachers over it, who governs its progress and order. Thus we shall find later, in Paul's speech in chapter 20 (v. 28) that all bishops are appointed by the Holy Spirit to govern the Church. And according to the same witness, Paul, no one must be considered a lawful pastor of the Church except the man who has been called by God; and the only sign that God gives to indicate false prophets is that He Himself has not sent them. We therefore infer that the Holy Spirit is truly God, for His authority suffices for electing pastors, and His direction (*imperium*) is the chief thing in appointing them (*creandis*). And that is also confirmed by the words of Isaiah, 'And now behold Jehovah has sent me, and His Spirit' (48.16). Furthermore, we must note from these words that He is a Person truly subsisting in God. For if we allow the fabrication of Sabellius that the name 'Spirit' does not represent a substantial reality (*hypostasis*), but is simply an epithet, then the expression that 'the Holy Spirit said' will be senseless and absurd. Isaiah would also be foolish in ascribing the mission of the prophet to Him.

3. *When they had fasted and prayed.* Out of obedience to the oracle, not only do they send Paul and Barnabas away, but they also appoint them apostles of the Gentiles with a solemn rite. There is no doubt that this fast was practised openly. Luke has previously said that they were fasting, when they were being attentive to their ministry; that could have happened as a matter of course, but now the reason is different. For they appointed a public fast, which usually took place

in situations of trouble and great difficulty, and spurred themselves and others on to serious and ardent prayer; for in Scripture this help is indeed often added to prayer. But seeing that the setting up of the Kingdom of Christ among the Gentiles was a huge task, the teachers at Antioch had every justification for anxiously asking the Lord to give His servants shoulders fit for the burden. Yet the object of their prayer was not that God might direct their judgments, by the Spirit of wisdom and discretion, in the choice they had to make, because consideration of that matter was over and done with; but that the Lord would provide with the Spirit of wisdom and courage those whom He had already chosen for Himself; that by His power He would make them invincible in the face of all the attacks of Satan and the world; that He would bless their labours so that they might not be unfruitful; and that He would open a door for the new promulgation of the Gospel.

The *laying on* of hands which Luke lists in the third place, was a kind of consecration, as has been said in chapter 6. For the apostles retained the ceremony which was practised among the Jews in accordance with the ancient custom of the Law, just as they retained kneeling and similar rites that are useful for the cultivation of piety. In a word the imposition of hands on Paul and Barnabas had no other end in view than that the Church might offer them to God, and that they might make open and unanimous witness that this office was laid on those men by God. For the call properly belonged to God, but on the other hand the external ordination belonged to the Church, and that according to the heavenly oracle.

So they, being sent forth by the Holy Ghost, went down to Seleucia; and from thence they sailed to Cyprus. And when they were at Salamis, they proclaimed the word of God in the synagogues of the Jews: and they had also John as their attendant. And when they had gone through the whole island unto Paphos, they found a certain sorcerer, a false prophet, a Jew, whose name was Bar-Jesus; which was with the proconsul, Sergius Paulus, a man of understanding. The same called unto him Barnabas and Saul, and sought to hear the word of God. But Elymas the sorcerer (for so is his name by interpretation) withstood them, seeking to turn aside the proconsul from the faith. But Saul, who is also called Paul, filled with the Holy Ghost, fastened his eyes on him, and said, O full of all guile and all villany, thou son of the devil, thou enemy of all righteousness, wilt thou not cease to pervert the right ways of the Lord? And now, behold, the hand of the Lord is upon thee, and thou shalt be blind, not seeing the sun for a season. And immediately there fell on him a mist and a darkness; and he went about seeking some to lead him by the hand. Then the proconsul, when he saw what was done, believed, being astonished at the teaching of the Lord. (4-12)

4. *Being sent forth by the Spirit.* There is no mention here of the election made by the Church, because their call was entirely from God. The Church merely embraced those presented to it by the hand of God. He says first of all that they came to *Seleucia*, which was a city of Syria. There was indeed a district of the same name, but it is more likely that Luke is speaking about the city from which there was a short crossing to Cyprus.

5. He says that they began their task of teaching at *Salamis*, which is quite a well-known and populous city of Cyprus. Yet they seem to be beginning in the wrong way; for, whereas they have been sent specifically to the Gentiles, yet they are proclaiming the Word of God to Jews. I reply that they were not so bound to the Gentiles, that they had to set the Jews aside and devote themselves to the Gentiles all the time. For when God assigned them to the Gentiles as teachers, He did not strip them of the function which they had exercised previously. So there was no reason to prevent them from bestowing their labour on Jews and Gentiles without distinction, and, what is more, a beginning ought to have been made with the Jews, as we shall see at the end of the chapter. Luke also adds in passing that they were helped by John. For he does not mean that he served them in a private capacity, or their physical needs, but is rather commending his godly zeal and diligence, because he assisted in the preaching of the Gospel. This did not mean that they were on an equality as far as office (*honoris*) was concerned, but the work was common to all of them; and that is why there was all the less excuse for him later on when he abandoned the holy calling.

6. *When they had gone through.* One may well believe that this journey did not lack fruit altogether. And Luke would certainly not have kept quiet about a general repulse, but he considered it enough to say that they did not rest from the duty of teaching while on the road, for he is hurrying on to a memorable incident, which he will narrate at once.

Apart from that, since Salamis was on the east coast looking towards Syria, Paul and Barnabas had to make their way through the middle of the island to the opposite coast in order to reach *Paphos.* For Paphos was a city on the coast facing south. Moreover while the whole island was sacred to Venus, Paphos was however the principal seat of the idol. Therefore the goodness of God is all the more wonderful, because He wished the light of His Gospel to penetrate into such a filthy and abominable den. For we may guess what sort of integrity and chastity, honesty and sobriety flourished in that city, from the fact that religion granted its inhabitants the greatest licence for all sorts of unchaste behaviour and shameful acts.

They found a certain false prophet. Since religion was thoroughly corrupt among the Jews, it is no wonder if they fell into many ungodly superstitions. Now, since they had up to then professed to be worshipping some God of their own, it was a plausible excuse for deceiving, since they might freely make use of the name of this unknown God as a pretext, but it is a wonder how Elymas could mislead a serious and wise man with his illusions. For we know that at that time the Jews were hateful to the whole world, and particularly among the Romans indeed, extreme contempt for them went hand in hand with hate.

Now Luke is quite right in explicitly commending the prudence of Sergius, in case anyone supposes that he was susceptible to the sorcerer's impostures through foolishness and shallow-mindedness. He undoubtedly wished to show in a clear mirror how frail and worthless the wisdom of the flesh is, for it cannot guard itself from such clumsy stratagems of Satan. And certainly where the truth of God does not shine, the wiser men appear to be, the more foolish and scandalous is their behaviour. We see how filthy and monstrous superstition raged among Gentiles of the most acute minds, and replete with learning of every kind. Therefore there is neither judgment nor prudence except from the Spirit of God. And this is God's just vengeance on all idolaters, that they are given over to a reprobate mind, and they discern nothing (Rom. 1.28). However, it may be that Sergius Paulus, disgusted with the old superstitions, aspired to a purer worship of God just at the time when he fell in with that sorcerer. Now, if we accept that, it was certainly an astonishing judgment of God, that He allowed a man touched by a desire for godliness, to put himself into the deadly snares of Satan. But God sometimes disciplines His elect in this way, driving them in circles through a variety of errors, before they are directed on to the way.

7. Now since Sergius Paulus desired something better than what he had learnt from boyhood, but was unfortunately attracted to different superstitions, I gather from this verse that he summoned Paul and Barnabas to instruct him. Therefore he had acquired a certain reverence for the true God, although He was as yet unknown to Him, and when He was persuaded that the God, worshipped by the Jews, is the true God, he desired to learn a pure and certain rule of godliness from His Word, but having got a taste of the fantasies of the false prophet he was in a state of perplexity. And there is no doubt that God fills him with apprehension in case he may find

complete satisfaction in an empty thing, even although he allowed himself to be deceived for a time by a dishonest fellow.

8. *To turn aside the proconsul from the faith.* It is no wonder if the impostor tries to ward off the light, for he saw his darkness being scattered by it. We have a similar struggle today with innumerable wranglers who are accustomed to make empty promises, and blind the eyes of the simple with whatever tricks and deceptions they can, so that they may not perceive that the Sun of Righteousness has arisen. We must wrestle with such hindrances. For although sorcerers are not present always and everywhere to cause us trouble, Satan brings in many allurements which take possession of our minds to the exclusion of Christ; and the flesh is far too ready to receive such things. In a word, both the attractions of the world, and the perverse passions of our flesh are just so many enchantments with which Satan does not cease to subvert the faith.

9. *But Saul who is also Paul.* Luke now shows how God burst the knot by which the proconsul was bound. For since he was too devoted to the sorcerer, he could not have embraced the true teaching as an independent and free man, for in an incredible way the devil holds minds, which he has entrapped, in subjection to himself, so that they do not see the plainest of truth, but when he was overthrown it was easy for Paul to make an approach to the proconsul. But observe what Luke says, that faith is destroyed when the Word of God is attacked. From that we may conclude that faith is founded on the Word in such a way that without this support it totters at the first attacks that come, yes, and what is more, it is nothing else but the spiritual building of the Word of God.

10. *Full of all guile.* It was not for nothing that such a fierce and passionate outburst suddenly overtook Paul. For he could not look for any success, if he were to act in a moderate and gentle way. A beginning must indeed always be made with teaching, but, clearly, those who are not yet utterly inflexible must also be warned, encouraged and spurred on. And certainly Paul does not fulminate so vehemently against the sorcerer straight away at the very beginning, but when he sees him maliciously and openly waging war on the teaching of the faith, he treats him just like a slave of Satan's. That is what must be done with the abandoned enemies of the Gospel, in whom plain obstinacy and impious contempt of God are conspicuous, especially when they block the way for others. And in case anyone may think that Paul was far too hot-tempered, Luke expressly states that the Spirit was his guide, driving him on. Accordingly this fervour of zeal is not only above reproach, but it ought to strike with horrible fear the impious despisers of God, who do not hesitate to

rise up against His Word, seeing that this judgment is brought against all of them not by a mortal man, but by the Holy Spirit through the lips of Paul.

As far as the words are concerned this verse refutes the error of those who think that Saul adopted the proconsul's name for himself, as if he were setting up a monument to his victory. Indeed there are many reasons, and quite strong ones at that, in contradiction of that; but this passage alone is sufficient for in it Luke shows that before the proconsul was brought to the faith he had two names. There is no doubt that he retained his family name among the Jews. On the other hand we know that it was a customary thing for those who were Roman citizens to take some Italian name for their own use.

Luke links *craftiness* with *guile*; and that is the opposite of sincerity, for it means sly men changing their versatile characters into different forms, so that they have no unity or simplicity. Although the Greek word which Luke uses means an audacity that finds it easy to do harm, yet the former meaning suits better.

By *son of the devil* is to be understood a man who is corrupt and given up for lost. Such are all who maliciously and, as it were purposely, fight against what is just and right. Therefore Paul adds that the sorcerer is an *enemy of all righteousness.*

Wilt thou not cease to pervert? He calls the *ways of the Lord* all the means by which God brings us to Himself. He asserts that this way is plain and straight, but he complains that the sorcerer is making it crooked, twisted and involved by his evasions and artifices. A useful doctrine can be got out of that, viz. that it is due to the cunning of the devil that we do not make our way to the Lord by an easy course. For He shows us in His Word a way that is easy and by no means thorny. Accordingly we have to be very much on our guard against impostors who block the way or make it hard for us, either with their pot-holes or thorns. Indeed it is appropriate to repeat here once again what I mentioned before, that fault must not always be found with the servants of Christ, if they are driven with violent force against professed enemies of sound doctrine, unless one is perhaps disposed to accuse the Holy Spirit of lack of moderation. Yet I am not unaware of how easy it is for a man to lapse in this respect. That is why pious teachers need to be all the more alert and on their guard, first, not to yield to the passions of the flesh under pretext of zeal, secondly, when there is still room for moderation, not to boil over in hasty and inopportune fervour, thirdly, not to give free rein to futile and unbecoming abuses, but only to give expression to the enormity of the situation with the gravity of their words. The vehemence of holy zeal and of the Spirit in the prophets was like that, and if soft, effeminate men think it stormy, they do not consider how dear and precious God's truth is to Him.

Nowadays it is not one Elymas who rises up to subvert the faith, but a countless number, far more vicious than he was. For we see how they strip God of all honour by sacrilegious presumption, how they profane the whole of religion with filthy corruptions, how cruelly they hasten wretched souls to eternal destruction, how shamefully they mock at Christ, how horribly they deform the whole worship of God, how they tear the sacred truth of God to pieces with savage insults, how they lay waste the Church of God with barbarous tyranny, so that you may say that they trample God under their feet. Moreover there are a great many peevish philosophers who would wish those frenzied giants to be appeased with flatteries. But since it is quite plain that such men have never experienced what this means for them, 'The zeal of thy house has eaten me up' (Ps. 69.9), let us, having nothing more to do with their coldness, or, rather, their sloth, be carried away, as we ought, to the eager defence of the glory of God, even to the highest pitch of ardour.

11. *Behold the hand. Hand* is employed here for inflicting a blow; and he means by it that it is God who is responsible for this punishment, while he is only the agent. Moreover this ability seems to me to be what Paul himself calls *δύναμις, power,* in I Cor. 12.28.[1] For just as they were able by the power of the Spirit to heal believers with miracles, so they had a whip in their hands with which to tame the rebellious and obstinate. Peter made use of such a punishment of God in the case of Ananias and Sapphira (Acts 5.5). But such miracles ought, as far as possible, to have been representing the nature of Christ, who is utterly kind (*humanus*), pleasing (*suavis*), generous and merciful. He therefore intended the apostles to produce examples of the opposite power but rarely. And it must not be supposed that they were endowed with this ability to take vengeance on anyone whenever they liked, but the same Spirit of God, who was equipping them in this way, was directing them as to its right and proper use. Therefore we must keep in mind what we found before, that Paul spoke by the inspiration of the Spirit. Moreover the kind of punishment was very suitable. For since the sorcerer attempted to darken the sun and to deprive others of the benefit of the light, he was rightly plunged into horrible darkness.

But today when many of the Papists are surpassing that sorcerer in impiety, it may appear to be a strange thing why the boldness, in which they boast so insolently, comes to them with impunity. Has the hand of God begun to be weakened? Is He less concerned about His glory?

[1] Greek δυνάμεις translated, R.V., *miracles.* Tr.

Or has He abandoned His zeal to avenge the Gospel? I reply that this visible punishment, which was once inflicted on the sorcerer, and similar ones, are examples of the perpetual wrath of God on all those who are not afraid either to corrupt and adulterate the pure teaching of the Gospel, or openly to fight against it with their calumnies. For we know that, for a time, miracles were performed for this purpose, that they may be held in esteem for ever, and that they may remain before our eyes and give us light to look at the judgments of God, which are not so obvious to our eyes. But it is not for us to prescribe to God this or that method of punishing His enemies. Sergius Paulus who had had no experience of the true religion before manhood, who, imbued from boyhood with many different superstitions, had very hard obstacles which kept him back from the faith, who, finally, fascinated by the ravings of the sorcerer, could hardly accede to the faith, had need of aids that were anything but trivial. As a result of that it came about that God, so to speak, stretched forth His hand openly from heaven. However He helped us all in the person of this man; for the same Gospel whose authority was confirmed on that occasion is being preached to us today. Yet God is not so idle that He does not put forth His formidable power in different ways against the enemies of the Gospel, unless our eyes were too dull for us to look closely[1] at His judgments.

12. *Then the proconsul when he saw.* This is what I have said, that the snares, in which Elymas held him fast, were broken. For he was brought to faith by the miracle, because respect for teaching is the beginning of, and the preparation for, faith. Therefore when he saw with his own eyes a very clear example of the power of God he knew that Paul was sent by God, and so he began to receive his teaching, which he had previously been hesitant to believe. If the Lord is now marvellously maintaining in many hearts the faith of the Gospel, which everywhere is shaken by so many and such powerful engines of war, if in an incredible way He causes the course of faith to surmount a thousand obstacles, let us, content with this favour of His, not murmur against Him or expostulate with Him, as if our circumstances would be poorer if fresh miracles were not performed every day at our request.

Now Paul and his company set sail from Paphos, and came to Perga in Pamphylia: and John departed from them and returned to Jerusalem. But they, passing through from Perga, came to Antioch of Pisidia; and they went into the synagogue on the sabbath day, and sat down. And after the reading of the law and the prophets the rulers of the synagogue

[1] *ad eius iudicia.* Adopting C.R. footnote *ad consideranda.* Tr.

sent unto them, saying, Brethren, if ye have any word of exhortation for the people, say on. (13-15)

13. Here an account is given of Paul's second stopping-place (*altera statio*).[1] For when he had left Paphos and come to *Antioch of Pisidia*, there he delivered a memorable address, which Luke will report along with its outcome. Before that, however, he mentions, in passing, the departure of John, because later on he will be the cause of an unhappy disagreement. When he says *the companions of Paul* set sail from Paphos he means, in the first place, Paul himself, secondly, the others, with one exception. So by taking note of his weakness he is commending the others, who followed Paul with untiring steadfastness.

14. *Entering on the day of the Sabbaths.* He has employed the plural instead of the singular, as often occurs elsewhere in Scripture. For they were accustomed to meeting together on the Sabbaths so that their rest would not be a useless and lazy occasion. The institution of the Sabbath had indeed another purpose also, to be a figure of the spiritual rest, when believers, having died to the world and the flesh, renounce their own will and cease from their own works. Because the truth of this is established in Christ for us, when, having been buried along with Him, we put off the old man, the old figure has therefore been superseded. But at the same time God looked to the civil usage, that the Jews, being released from all other concerns and business affairs, might hold their sacred assemblies, so that cessation from earthly labours used to give an opportunity for their heavenly exercises. In the same way even today we must make use of festivals, for it is fitting to set everything else aside, so that we may devote ourselves to God with more freedom.

15. *After the reading of the Law.* No mention is made of prayers, yet it is certain that they were not omitted or neglected. But because Luke's first thought was to report the sermon which Paul delivered there, it is no wonder if he only recounts those things which had to do with the order of teaching. But this is a verse worth noting because from it we learn what sort of method of carrying out teaching was in use among the Jews at that time. First place was given to the Law and the Prophets, because it is not lawful to set anything before the Church, that has not been drawn from that fountain. From this we also gather that Scripture was not kept within the circle of a few men, but all, without distinction, were allowed to come and hear it being read. Afterwards those who were strong in the grace of teaching and exhorting had to fulfil a second role, as interpreters of the scripture that had been read. However Luke finally makes it clear that per-

[1] French: '*une autre sejour*'. Tr.

mission to speak was not given to everybody, in case confusion was born out of licence, but the office of exhortation was committed to certain men, whom he calls the rulers or masters of the synagogue. Accordingly Paul and Barnabas do not burst out into speech straight away, so as not to disturb the accustomed order by excessive haste, but they wait quietly until the opportunity of speaking is granted, and that by the permission of those who were given the authority by general consent.

We know how corrupt the condition of that people was at that time, and Luke will finally show at the close of the chapter that those at Antioch were exceedingly proud and inflexible in rejecting the grace of Christ, and yet there was this amount of good left among them, that their meetings were conducted in a proper and decent way. Accordingly such unseemly confusion as is seen today among those who wish to be regarded as Christians is all the more disgraceful. Certainly the Papists chant Scripture in their temples in a high and sonorous voice, but in an unknown language, with the result that the people derive no benefit from it. Rarely is any teaching added, and it would be better then too for the impious wranglers to keep quiet, for they pour out their own vile fabrications instead of the Word of God, and contaminate everything that is sacred by the filthiness of their impieties.

If there is in you any word. This expression denotes that whatever grace men may have for edifying the Church, it is, so to speak, deposited. However the preposition, *in*, following the Hebrew idiom, can be superfluous. Therefore I do not lay too great stress on that, because the meaning can be a simple one, 'If you have any exhortation suitable and useful for the people'. Now exhortation does not exclude teaching. But it seems that this word was accepted by common use among them, because the proper office of a teacher is not to produce some novel thing out of his own head, but to adapt Scripture to the people's immediate need, for the total wisdom of the godly is contained in it. In this way they are not so much teaching, as adapting teaching taken from another source, for the edification of the Church. And that, I think, is what is meant by the word *exhortation*.

And Paul stood up, and beckoning with the hand said, Men of Israel, and ye that fear God, hearken. The God of this people Israel chose our fathers, and exalted the people when they sojourned in the land of Egypt, and with a high arm led he them forth out of it. And for about the time of forty years suffered he their manners in the wilderness. And when he had destroyed seven nations in the land of Canaan, he gave them their land for an inheritance, for about four hundred and fifty years: and after these things he gave them judges until Samuel the prophet. And afterward they asked for a king; and God gave unto them Saul the son of Kish, a man of the tribe of Benjamin, for the space of forty years. And when he had removed him, he raised up David to be their king; to whom also he bare witness, and said, I have found David the son of Jesse, a man after my heart, who shall do all my will. Of this man's seed hath God according to promise brought unto Israel a Saviour, Jesus; (16–23)

16. First of all we must note the theme of the speech, so that we may not think that words are being senselessly wasted on the air. Indeed Paul seems to start by going right back to the beginning, but he says nothing that does not suit his present purpose very well. For his intention is to lead the Jews to the faith of Christ, and that that may be done, they must be shown that they themselves surpass other nations in this one respect, that to them was promised a Saviour, whose rule is to be their[1] greatest and only happiness. Paul therefore begins in this way: that they were once chosen to be God's peculiar people, and that so many blessings were bestowed on them continually for generations on end, however unworthy they proved themselves. Those things, he says, are dependent on the promise of the Messiah, and have this end in view, that God may govern them at the hand of the Messiah; and accordingly there is nothing for them to glory in, unless they are gathered together under their Head. Yes, and he says further that unless they receive Him, when He is presented to them, the covenant of life, which God had made with their fathers, will be void, and their adoption will be null.

The first part of the sermon has this aim, that this is the main point of the Law, and the foundation of God's covenant, that they may have Christ as Leader and Governor, to restore everything in their midst, and that without Him religion cannot continue, and they will be most wretched. From that Paul moves on to the second part, that that Jesus whom he preaches is in fact the Christ, through whom salvation is presented to the people. He also explains the kind of redemption procured by Him. Further on he deals with His power and function, so that they may know what good things are to be expected from Him. The closing sentence contains a reproof. For a horrible judgment threatens them if they reject the Author of salvation, who offers Himself of His own accord, and this the one whom the Law and the Prophets urge them to seek after eagerly. That is, more or less, what it amounts to. Now I shall examine the individual points in their order.

[1] Reading *eorum* for *eius*. French has no possessive. Tr.

Men and brethren. Because Paul was well enough aware that many were not genuine descendants of Abraham, he addresses the Jews, to whom he is speaking, by two names. In the first place he calls them *brethren*, out of regard for their common origin; yet at the same time he reminds them that they will be true Israelites if they *fear God*, and only then will they also be proper listeners, because 'the fear of the Lord is the beginning of wisdom'. In the same way he causes the faithful to be attentive, and procures an audience for himself from among them, as if he were saying, 'Although many may boast that they are sons of Abraham, when they have no title at all to such a great honour, show that you are not impure seed.' Let us learn from this that it is not a defect of just one generation, that honest and genuine worshippers are mixed up with hypocrites and share the name of the Church in common with them. But we must take care to be in fact what we are said to be, and the true fear of God will guarantee that, and not merely external profession.

17. *The God of this people.* This preface was evidence that Paul was not introducing some new thing, which might lead the people away from the Law of Moses. There is indeed one God of all the nations, but he calls Him God of that people to whom He had united Himself, the God who was worshipped among the descendants of Abraham, and among them alone was pure and sound religion flourishing. The words immediately following, *He chose our fathers*, refer to the same thing. For by these words he asserts that he desires nothing less than for them to depart from the true and living God, who has separated them from the rest of the world. I am certainly quite sure that he made it pretty clear that he was not preaching to them an unknown or new God, but the One who had long ago made Himself known to their fathers. So he briefly sums up the whole knowledge of God which was based on the Law, so that their faith, acquired from the Law and the Prophets, may remain firm.

At the same time however he is commending the free love of God towards that people. For how did it come about that only the sons of Abraham were the Church and inheritance of God, except that it pleased God to separate them from the rest of the nations? For there was no merit to distinguish them, but the distinction originated with the love of God, by which he embraced Abraham out of favour. Moses often reminds the Jews of this gratuitous favour of God's, e.g. in Deut. chapters 4.37, 7.8, 10.15, 14.2, 32.8ff and other places, in which God has set before us a clear mirror of His wonderful purpose, for although He found nothing outstanding in Abraham, an obscure man and a wretched idolater, He yet gave him preference over the whole world. Moreover like circumcision, this election was common to the whole people, for by it God chose the seed of Abraham for Himself. But there was also another, more secret, election, by which God separated to Himself a few of the sons of Abraham, and made it evident that not all who are descendants from Abraham according to the flesh are to be regarded in the spiritual descent.

And exalted the people. Paul teaches that all the blessings God later bestowed on the Jews flowed from that gratuitous favour of God, by which He had embraced the fathers. For it was due to it that they were redeemed by the wonderful power of God, and led by His hand into possession of the land of Canaan, with so many nations overthrown for their sake. For it was no common thing for a land to be stripped of its inhabitants in order to take in sojourners. God's election of the fathers is the spring and root of all the blessings to which Paul calls us. It was also the reason for God's wonderful tolerance in not rejecting that rebellious people, who would otherwise have destroyed themselves a thousand times by their own perversity. Similarly when Scripture mentions that they received pardon for their sins, it says that God remembered His covenant. He says that, when they were *sojourners*, they were *exalted*, so that they may recall to mind how splendid and magnificent their deliverance was.

18. *Suffered their manners.* The Greek compound verb, expressing God's indulgence in putting up with a people whom He knew to be obstinate and disobedient, is more emphatic and pleasing (ἐτροποφόρησαν). Now Paul again means that God's election was responsible for His goodness struggling with the wickedness of the people. However we must note that although God intends to stand firm in His purpose, He took pity on His chosen people in such a way that He yet punished the rebellious and the wicked severely. Indeed He spared the people, so as not to wipe them out completely, as He could quite rightly have done, but He also found a way not to let their offences go unpunished. And so that word of Isaiah's is fulfilled, 'If the people will be as the sand of the sea, a remnant will be saved' (10.22).

20. *He gave them judges.* By this word Scripture means commanders and governors. Now it is further evidence of God's clemency towards the Jews, that He pardoned so many of their defections. For it is likely that the things which Luke summarizes briefly, were expounded more fully and clearly by Paul. But we do know what the condition of the people was like during all that time, when, again and again, they were shaking off the yoke because of their unsubdued insolence. Often they were afflicted with the severest disasters, yet when they had been humbled, God soon snatched them out of the tyranny of their enemies. So through a thousand deaths He saved the body of the people for four hundred and fifty years. And it is evident from that

how undeserving they were of the favour of God, which they spurned and rejected so often, if the enduring nature of their election had not triumphed. For how did God never weary, but keep faith with those who broke the covenant a hundred times, except that, turning His eyes on His Christ, He did not allow the covenant, founded on Him, to perish?

21. *Then they asked for.* This change in fact amounted to their openly rejecting the government which He had constituted; and even God Himself complains of this to Samuel (I Sam. 8.5, 7). But the firmness and durability of their election prevented them from suffering the punishment such madness deserved; yes, and what is more, the wicked and unlawful desire of the people provided God with a new and unbelievable opportunity for setting up a Kingdom out of which Christ would afterwards come. For how did it happen that the sceptre came to the tribe of Judah (Gen. 49.10) except that the people cherished the desire to make a king? And the people certainly acted improperly, but the Lord, who knows to make good use of evil things, turned that offence into their salvation. When Saul was dispossessed of the kingdom it tended to expose the people's fault, but when the kingdom was soon afterwards established in the family of David, confidence in the prophecy of Jacob remained firm (Gen. 49.10).

22. *I have found David my servant.* This saying was quoted by Paul, not so much to praise the man, as to make the Jews more intent on receiving Christ. For the Lord asserts that it was for no trivial reason that His heart was completely devoted to David, but He commends something remarkable in him, and in praising him so highly He wishes to lift up the minds of the faithful to Christ in his person. Now this verse is taken from Ps. 89 (v. 20). Only, Paul has inserted what is not found there, that *David* was *the son of Jesse*, because it makes the grace of God clearer. For seeing that Jesse was a cattle-farmer, it was a marvellous thing for God to do, to take the youngest of his sons out of the sheepfold and place him on the throne of the kingdom. By the word *find* God means that He obtained or came across a man of the kind that He wanted. Not of course that David by his own exertions and diligence made himself fit and suitable to meet God, but the expression is taken from men's everyday usage.

But, it is asked, since David lapsed so seriously how does God testify to his continual obedience? The reply is twofold. For God looked to the continuous tenor of David's life rather than to his particular actions, and, secondly, He did not praise him in this way for any merit of his own so much as for the sake of His Christ. He certainly had deserved eternal destruction for himself and his family, because of a single offence, and as far as he was responsible the way had been barred to the blessing of God, so that he would raise nothing but viper's seed from Bathsheba. And yet, by the wonderful purpose of God, such a filthy crime as the death of Uriah results in the very opposite, for from that union, inauspicious as it was, full of treachery as it was, and, finally, defiled with many stains as it was, Solomon is born. And despite the fact that David sinned most grievously, yet, because he followed God all his life through, he is given unqualified praise, because he proved himself obedient to God in all things. While it is true that the Spirit has brought us to a higher level, yet the common calling of all the faithful in Christ, the Head, is portrayed for us here.

23. *According to promise.* This clause also confirms what has already been said several times, that in sending Christ, the Lord was considering only His own faithfulness and goodness. For He sent Him, because He had promised Him. But just as the promise is evidence that salvation was free, so at the same time it gains no ordinary confidence for the Gospel, because it is plain from this that Christ did not come forth unexpectedly, never having been heard about before, but that He, who had been promised right from the beginning, has shown Himself now, in His own time. Finally, the promises which Luke mentions here in passing are famous and well enough known. But among the Jews they were so familiar in daily conversation that everywhere they called the Christ nothing else but the Son of David (Matt. 22.42). He says that Jesus was *brought to Israel*, because, even if salvation does belong to the whole world, yet first of all He was a servant of the circumcision, to fulfil the promises which were given to the fathers (Rom. 15.8).

The Hebrew name, *Jesus*, he has translated into the Greek *Saviour* (σωτήρ). So he has said the same thing twice. But it is not tautologous, because he wished to teach that Christ is in fact, and fulfils, what the name, given Him by God by the words of the angel, means (Matt. 1.21).

when John had first preached before his coming the baptism of repentance to all the people of Israel. And as John was fulfilling his course, he said, What suppose ye that I am? I am not he. But behold, there cometh one after me the shoes of whose feet I am not worthy to unloose. Brethren, children of the stock of Abraham, and those among you that fear God, to us is the word of this salvation sent forth. (24-26)

24. We know the nature of John's task, viz. to prepare the way of the Lord. Paul therefore brings in his testimony to prove to the Jews that he is preaching no fictitious Christ, but the true Christ of God, whom that most famous of heralds had already previously com-

mended. Not that the witness of a man is sufficient for proving a matter of such importance, but there was another consideration in John's case, for, everywhere, nearly all were convinced that he was a prophet of God. Therefore the authority of the testimony comes from the fact that a herald sent from heaven, not some private individual, has things to say about Christ. Now Paul briefly repeats two things about John, that he taught *the baptism of repentance* before the coming of Christ, and, secondly, that voluntarily rejecting the title and honour of Messiah for himself, he yielded them to Christ.

The baptism of repentance. The baptism was introduced contrary to the rite and practice of the Law, and was the sign of a great change. For it was not lawful to change anything before the coming of Christ. Certainly the Jews used to have their own baptisms in the Law, and there were also exercises of penitence. But John was the originator or rather the minister, of a new and unaccustomed baptism, to give hope of the restoration that had long been expected and desired. When he calls it the *baptism of repentance* he does not exclude the remission of sins, but he is speaking out of regard for the circumstances of the time, because that baptism was a preparation for the faith of Christ.

And we must note the expression that he *preached the baptism.* We are taught by this that the sacraments are properly administered only when teaching is also added to the visible figure. For the mouth of the baptizer ought not to be silent, because without teaching the sign is worthless.

25. *When John fulfilled his own.* The second part of the testimony is that John, being near the end of his course, sent his disciples off to Christ. For he had already prepared them with the first step, baptism, but then he passed them on to Christ, from hand to hand, as the saying goes. On the other hand, this question 'Whom do you suppose me to be?' is not one that comes from a man in doubt. For John rebukes and blames the Jews because they wrongly confer the office of the Messiah on him. Although in one text it can be read, 'I am not he whom you think me to be', yet the other reading is the more usual one, while it has also more weight for refuting error. Moreover his testimony deserves far more credence because of his own accord he refuses the office that is offered to him, one that he could have accepted with complete approbation, and gives it up to another. In his case there certainly cannot be any suspicion of ambition or any self-seeking, to take away confidence in his words.

Behold he comes, i.e. He will come. This Hebraism is also quite common in the New Testament. When he confesses his unworthiness to loosen the ties of Christ's sandals, this is a proverbial figure, by which he minimizes himself as much as he can, so that his own greatness may not obscure the glory of Christ. For he wished to carry out faithfully what had been entrusted to him, so that Christ alone might be pre-eminent. Therefore, however great he is, he says that he is nothing compared with Christ. For although the servants of Christ may have their own greatness, yet when it comes to comparison with Christ, they must all be reduced to nothing so that He alone may be the outstanding one, just as we see all the stars vanish, to give place to the splendour of the sun.

26. *Men and brethren.* Again Paul urges the Jews to embrace Christ. For it ought to have raised a good deal of interest and attention in their minds to hear that their own salvation is the question at issue, and that he is properly appointed to be the messenger of salvation to them.

He calls them the *children of Abraham* not only to honour them, but that they may realize that they are heirs of eternal life. And he urges them so persuasively, that it may not be hard for them to break with the high priest and the scribes, whom they venerated, because of their need to receive Christ. Further, we must remember what I have taught previously, that, although the door of the Kingdom of Heaven was open to the Gentiles, the Jews, nevertheless, were not yet deprived of their own standing, but were considered the firstborn in the family of God. He therefore says that *salvation was sent* to them, because they had a priority in order. However because carnal descent was of no great importance in itself, and the impiety of many was revealing itself, Paul particularly appeals to the true worshippers of God, pointing out that words are spoken in vain, unless the fear of God reigns in their hearts, to receive them, and to cherish them when they have been received. We must note this way of speaking of the Gospel as the *word of salvation.* Therefore those who are not attracted by its delights must be harder than iron. Finally, although its nature is like that, it becomes, accidentally, the 'savour of death to death' for the reprobate (II Cor. 2.16).

For they that dwell in Jerusalem, and their rulers, because they knew him not, nor the voices of the prophets which are read every sabbath, fulfilled them by condemning him. And though they found no cause of death in him, yet asked they of Pilate that he should be slain. And when they had fulfilled all things that were written of him, they took him down from the tree, and laid him in a tomb. But God raised him from the dead: and he was seen for many days of them that came up with him from Galilee to Jerusalem, who are now his witnesses unto the people. (27-31)

27. Wisely and opportunely he removes a stumbling-block, which could have kept them back from believing. For Jerusalem was God's sanctuary, the royal seat, the fountain of truth, the light of the whole world; but there Christ had been killed. Moreover, nothing could have seemed more absurd than to accept a man who had been put out of the temple of God, and to look for the teaching of salvation anywhere else than the place from which God Himself had declared it would spring. Add to that the fact that by believing in Christ a rift seemed to have been created in the Church. And so this one objection was strong enough to refute what Paul was saying, 'Why do you use the excuse of God's covenant to force upon us a man whom the leading group of the holy people condemned?' Paul removes this stumbling-block so that it may not impede the course of the Gospel. Not only does he do that, but he even turns it round the other way. For, seeing that the Author of life was despised and rejected at Jerusalem, Paul urges the men of Antioch, at least those of them who fear God, to accept Him all the more eagerly. For the causal clause amounts to his saying, 'Seeing that Jerusalem did not recognize its own good, it is to your advantage that you be made more wide-awake and alert, so that the same ingratitude and perversity may not be found in you.'

But he uses another argument to remove the stumbling-block, viz. that so far from having taken anything away from the divine superiority of Christ, their high-handedness (*impietas*) is rather bound to have the effect of proving and establishing it. For what gives better proof of Christ than the fact that everything that had been predicted in the Law and the Prophets has been fulfilled in Him (Luke 24.25, 26)? Moreover what did the enemies of Christ perceive, but that the striking truth of the Scripture shone brightly in Him? It was necessary for Christ to be rejected by the principal men, for it had been so predicted in Ps. 118.22, 'the stone which the builders rejected God has set in the head of the corner'. It was necessary for Christ to be condemned along with criminals, to clear us in the eyes of God; for our sins to be laid upon Him, that He might atone for them for us; for Him to be sacrificed on the Cross so that the shadowy victims of the Law might come to an end. For the Scripture also contained these things in Isa. 53.4ff and Dan. 9.26. Therefore the more violently the leaders of the people tried to annihilate Christ, they in fact proved that He is the Christ, and the Lord frustrated them in a wonderful way so that their stubborn disobedience establishes, rather than destroys, the faith of the godly.

All scandals which lead away weak and fickle souls from Christ are almost of the same kind. For if they would consider more closely the total progress of the work of God, there would be grounds for strengthening them, when they are collapsing. It is therefore mostly due to our own negligence that we are troubled by stumbling-blocks, because, looking on those things which belong to Christ with wild or purblind eyes, we imagine that what is white is black. On the other hand we see that Paul hides nothing, but frankly confesses what the truth is, that Christ was detested not only by the common people but also by the chief men, and that He was not driven out by a few, but destroyed by the wicked conspiracy of the whole people. That was hard and offensive for an opening shot, but Paul brings forward a more powerful weapon, that God used them against their wills as a touchstone on which to prove His Son. Since the situation of the Gospel is also like that today, let us not be ashamed to confess with Paul that the proud rulers of the world and those who hold the primacy in the Church are the deadly enemies of Christ, inasmuch as that is turned to the glory of Christ rather than to His reproach. For Scripture is fulfilled in this way.

Since they knew him not. Even if deliberate malice drove the chief men to destroy Christ, yet Paul rightly puts it down to ignorance, as he does elsewhere, when he says that the wisdom of the Gospel was hidden from the rulers of this world, because otherwise they would never have crucified the Lord of glory (I Cor. 2.8). For the ill-will of the ungodly is like raging madness, and in seeing does not see. There is absolutely no doubt that those who did not hesitate to wage war with God to their own destruction were deprived of soundness of mind and the light of the Spirit. He also charges them with ignorance of Scripture. And in case anyone objects that he is speaking about something unknown or obscure, he adds at the same time, that he is talking about those very prophecies which are read every sabbath. It is as if he said, that the oracles of Scripture, which were unknown to them, are clear and known even to all the ignorant. In this way Paul warns how unnatural their disbelief was, to make it detestable to his hearers. But we are taught by such an example that even if the Lord reveals Himself to us through Scripture, yet all men do not have eyes for Him. Later on the stupidity of the people was even more dense, just as Paul says elsewhere that a veil is placed before their eyes, so that they do not see the presence of Moses (*ut praesentem Mosen non videant*, II Cor. 3.15). At the same time we must observe that we are called back to Scripture, so that the authority of great men may not deceive us. And there is no occasion for anyone, prejudiced through the corrupt outlook of others, to think that he is freed from it. For Paul encourages the men of Antioch to judge from Scripture against the bewitched directors of the Church. For it has been given for the purpose of being read. But the reading of it has not been instituted by God for nothing, but so that all the godly may benefit from it and judge what is right.

They fulfilled them. Thus we see that it is not only creatures lacking understanding who are under the providence of God, but also the devil and all the ungodly, so that He may execute among them what He has determined in His own mind. Similarly we find in chapters 3.17ff and 4.28, that, when the enemies of Christ were absolutely mad for His destruction, they nevertheless did not get what they wanted, but rather they brought into being by their own efforts what God had determined according to His own purpose. Indeed it does a great deal for the commendation of the divine truth, that not only is He powerful enough to fulfil what He has promised, but those, who try to reduce His purposes to nothing, put out their labour in establishing them, albeit against their will. For how would the truth of God not stand, when its greatest enemies are forced to fulfil it? Yet here we need prudence lest we confuse Satan with God. For the Jews are not to be excused because they fulfilled Scripture, because it is their corrupt will that must be considered, and not the outcome, which was not what they expected, no indeed, when it ought to be regarded like a miracle. If their action is looked at in itself, it is completely contrary to God. But just as with wonderful skill God controls movements in the sun and the other planets that are contrary and in conflict with each other, so by His secret influence, He directs the perverse efforts of the ungodly towards a different end than they thought and intended, so that they may do nothing but what He has willed. As far as they are concerned those men indeed act against His will, but the outcome is according to the will of God, in some sort of incomprehensible way. Since this procedure is contrary to nature, it is no wonder if it is not visible to carnal wisdom. Accordingly it must be perceived by the eye of faith, or rather it must be treated with reverence and adoration; but the dogs who carp at it must be rejected along with their petulance.

28. *And though they found no cause of death.* It made a great difference to the matter for them to know that Christ was put to death without deserving it. For He would not have obtained righteousness for us by His death, if He had suffered it for His own misdeeds. Therefore it was necessary for Him, whose death is an atonement for the sins of the world, to be innocent. There is no doubt indeed that Paul has made it quite clear that Pilate did not condemn Christ by virtue of his office as a judge, but that, when he was prevailed upon by the outrageous demands of the people, he granted permission for Him to be handed over to death; and that at the same time the Jews were driven by wilfulness and not by reason to desire the death of Christ. For his listeners

had to be frightened into not associating themselves with such an abominable crime as accomplices. But in his usual way Luke is now condensing into a few words what Paul, at the time, covered with a complete narration.

29. *When they had fulfilled all things* i.e. those things which God allowed to be done through them. For they handled Christ in such a way that not one of the prophecies of Scripture was neglected. In this way the stumbling-block, which the carnal mind imagines from the ignominy of the Cross, is removed, viz. that the Son of God was not given up to the raging fury of his enemies, but met death in accordance with the Father's decision. Moreover it is clear from the Scriptures what sort of circumstances were appointed for him long before.

Luke's statement that Christ was buried by the same men as had killed Him seems to conflict with the Gospel story, but it may be that Luke took the word for burying in an indefinite way. Even if you wish to apply it to those same men, it will be synecdoche. For He was buried by Pilate's permission, but on the other hand guards were placed at the sepulchre by the decision of the priests. Therefore even if Joseph and Nicodemus committed Christ to the sepulchre, it is incorrect, but yet not absurd, to attribute that to the Jews, because Paul's intention here is not to praise the act of kindness, but to prove the resurrection of Christ, since God brought Him out of the sepulchre in which His enemies had shut Him up, and on which they kept guard. He is therefore pointing out that the body of Christ was not removed in secret or by stealth, but was put in a place that was much frequented and known to His enemies, that they even set a guard over it, and that, nevertheless, it was not found. The deduction from that is the certainty of the resurrection.

30. *God raised him.* The death of Christ was certainly the salvation of the godly, but in conjunction with the resurrection. Therefore Paul dwells longer on this second aspect. For he would never have convinced his hearers that salvation must be sought from His death, unless the power of God had been evident in raising Christ up.

31. After he has said that Christ came out of the tomb, which was under the eyes of the hired servants of His enemies, he now adds that He was seen by many disciples, who gave faithful testimony to the people. But he calls them *witnesses*, either out of regard for their office, since they were chosen for this purpose, as has been said in the first chapter (1.8); or because he is simply showing that they declared publicly and freely what they knew about Christ. It follows from that that the event was made well known in Jerusalem. But proving it was no easy matter, in this way, because it was in the midst of the

formidable power of enemies who were ready and eager to resist, and were leaving no stone unturned, that there had come on the scene those who openly maintained that Christ rose again, and were also eye-witnesses of that event. For if any refutation had been available, the scribes would not have neglected it.

And we bring you good tidings of the promise made unto the fathers, how that God hath fulfilled the same unto our children,[1] *in that he raised up Jesus; as also it is written in the second psalm, Thou art my Son, this day have I begotten thee. And as concerning that he raised him up from the dead, now no more to return to corruption, he hath spoken on this wise, I will give you the holy and sure blessings of David. Because he saith also in another psalm, Thou wilt not give thy Holy One to see corruption. For David, after he had in his own generation served the counsel of God, fell on sleep, and was laid unto his fathers, and saw corruption: but he whom God raised up saw no corruption.* (32-37)

32. *We bring you good tidings.* He now assumes the task and office of an apostle, so that he may be heard as a lawful minister of God. And he says that the substance of the embassy imposed on him is that what God had long ago promised has now been revealed to their generation. But in a few words he embraces many important matters. In the first place he points out that he is introducing nothing new, or different from the Law and the Prophets, but that he is revealing the fulfilment of that teaching, which, according to their own acknowledgment and conviction, was delivered to them by God. The consequence is that they cannot reject what he is presenting to them without abrogating, so far as they will be concerned, the covenant which God had made with the fathers. Secondly he commends the faithfulness of God, because now at last it is in fact quite evident that the promises made long ago had nothing rash or meaningless about them. But principally he extols the magnitude of the grace finally revealed in Christ. For we must observe the comparison between them and the fathers, when he says that they have obtained what was promised to the fathers. For, since the grace of God has been poured out more liberally on them, their ingratitude will be all the more disgraceful, if they were to spurn or despise this inestimable good. For what else would they be doing, but throwing down at their feet the treasure held out for them to grasp, and even put in their laps; the very treasure, the hope of which the fathers saw from far off, embraced with reverence, and cherished throughout their lives?

But the question is asked if those who lived under the Law were

[1] R.V. margin and Calvin's text read, *us their children*. Tr.

not also sharers of the promises. I reply that the fellowship between us of the same grace is such that it does not however prevent there being a great difference between us. But Paul means here this one thing, that their faith was, so to speak, in a state of suspense, until Christ appeared, in whom all the promises of God are Yea and Amen, as he teaches in II Cor. 1.19, 20. Therefore we are heirs of the same heavenly kingdom, and sharers of the spiritual blessings with which God provides His sons; and God also gave them the taste of His love in this present life, just as we now enjoy it. But Christ, who is the substance of eternal life and of all blessings, was only promised to them, while He has been given to us; and they used to long for Him, when He was absent and far off, while we have His presence.

33. *To their children viz. us.* It is certain that Paul is speaking about the natural children, who derived their origin from the holy fathers. And we must pay attention to that, because certain fanatics, who make allegories out of everything, imagine that no account is to be taken here of descendants but only of faith. But with a fiction like that they are making meaningless the sacred covenant of God, which says, 'I will be your God, and the God of your seed' (Gen. 17.7). They say that it is faith alone that makes children of Abraham. But I take the opposite view that those who are born children of Abraham according to the flesh, are also to be regarded as God's spiritual children, unless they cut themselves off by their own unfaithfulness. For the branches are holy by nature, because they have been produced from a holy root, until they are polluted by their own fault (Rom. 11.16). And it is certainly Paul's intention to draw the Jews to Christ. But for that to happen they must be separated and removed from the common order by privilege. But it does not follow from that, what those scoundrels throw out in a hateful way, that the grace of God is bound to the carnal seed; because, even if the promise of life was an inheritance for the descendants of Abraham, yet many lost it because of their unbelief. Therefore it is due to faith that few out of a great multitude are regarded as children. Indeed it is by faith that God separates His own. And that is the twofold election which I have mentioned previously. The one is the common election of the whole nation quite equally; because God's first adoption embraces the whole family of Abraham. The other is the one which is limited according to the purpose of God, and is finally confirmed by faith, to be men's sure possession (*ut penes homines rata sit*).

Therefore Paul is quite right in maintaining that what God promised to the fathers was fulfilled for the Jews. For the promise had been made to them also; as Zacharias says in his song, 'The oath which He swore to Abraham our father, that He would grant to us etc.' (Luke

1.73). Yet the worthiness of that nation does not prevent the grace of Christ spreading itself out into the whole world at the same time; because the eldest occupies the chief position of honour in such a way that he yet leaves the second place to his brothers. For, seeing that the ancient people were disinherited, and the Church's possession was left vacant for strangers, a new opportunity began for gathering a Church from the Gentiles. But even if that people had continued in the faith, the Gentiles would have been added to the common fellowship of honour.

When Christ had been raised. In my opinion the word for *raising* has a wider meaning here than in the verse immediately after where it is repeated. For he is not only saying that Christ rose from the dead, but that He was appointed by God, and brought forward into public view by the hand of God so to speak, to fulfil the role of Messiah, just as Scripture teaches everywhere that kings and prophets are raised up by the Lord. For the verb ἀναστῆσαι is sometimes taken in that sense. But the reason that influences me is this, that in sending His Son into the world God sustained the promise given to His servants long before, by the actual accomplishment.

As also in the second psalm. Although the Greek manuscripts agree about the number, yet we ought not to overlook what Erasmus says, that many of the ancient writers have read the first Psalm. And perhaps Luke wrote that. For the Psalm which today is regarded as the second Psalm could have been called the first, and with good reason, since it is probable that the first Psalm was added instead of a preface by the scribes and priests, by whose efforts the Psalms were collected into a single corpus. For the author's name is not added to it; and it merely gives an exhortation to meditate on the Law of God. But there is nothing momentous in that. For the chief thing is for us to realize how suitably and in what way Paul adapts the testimony taken from the Psalm to the present situation. We do not deny that in it, when David saw himself attacked on all sides, and that he was no match to resist more powerful and stronger enemies, he set over against them the protection of God, whom he knew to be the One responsible for putting him on the throne. But since he was a figure of the true Messiah we know that in his person there were foreshadowed for us those things which apply in fulness only to the Messiah. And the context makes it plain enough that it does contain no mere simple thanksgiving, that applies to David's kingdom, but a profounder prophecy. For it is quite well known that in his life-time David enjoyed scarcely the hundredth part of the glory which is described in it. We have already said a good deal more about this in chapter 4.

Let us now consider the words more closely. Kings are indeed generally called *sons of God* (Ps. 82.6). But since it is God's purpose to prefer David to other kings, and isolate him out of their number, this title of honour is pre-eminently (κατ' ἐξοχήν) ascribed to him above all others; but that does not mean that such a great honour resides in his person, because in that way he would also be more superior to the angels, as it is put in Heb. 1.4. Therefore it was out of regard for Christ, whose image he was, that he is distinguished so magnificently, that God acknowledges him not as an ordinary man, or one out of the crowd, but as if he were His only begotten Son. Proof follows, because God begot him when He established the kingdom in his hand. For that did not come about by the activity of men, but God stretched forth the invincible power of His hand from heaven, and from that it was openly established that he reigned according to God's purpose. Therefore that begetting which was mentioned ought to be referred to the understanding and knowledge of men, viz. that it was openly known at that time that he was begotten by God, since he ascended the throne of the kingdom in a wonderful way, contrary to the expectation of all, and broke innumerable conspiracies by the power of the heavenly Spirit; because he could not reign without bringing all the neighbouring nations to submission, as if in a kind of world conquest.

Now let us come to Christ. Certainly He did not come forth into the world without evidence to prove Himself the Son of God. For His glory was visible, as became the only-begotten of the Father, as it is put in John 1.14, and in different places He asserts that He has God as Witness and the Vindicator of this honour. Therefore God begot Christ when He engraved on Him certain marks by which He might be recognized as the true and express likeness of Himself and His Son. Yet that does not prevent Christ being the Word begotten by the eternal Father before time. But that is the secret generation. But David now declares that it was revealed to men. So the reference is, as we have said, to men and not to God; because what was hidden in the heart of God was made plainly known to men. And it is a well-chosen figure, because the divinity of Christ was proved and established just as clearly as if God had actually begotten Him before the eyes of men. I know that the ingenuity of Augustine is rather pleasing to a great many, that by *today* is meant *perpetually*. But when the Spirit of God Himself is His own interpreter, and explains through the lips of Paul what He had said through David, we have no right to invent another meaning. Besides, since, according to the same witness, Paul (Rom. 1.4), Christ was manifested the Son of God in power when He rose from the dead, we gather that that was the principal proof of His heavenly perfection, and that the Father then properly brought Him into view, so that the world might know that He was begotten by Him. Therefore although Christ began to be raised by God, when He came into the world, yet the resurrection was, so to speak, the perfect and complete raising, because although He had previously emptied Himself and taken the form of a servant (Phil. 2.7), He then emerged as the conqueror of death and the Lord of Life, so that He lacked nothing of the majesty suitable to the Son, and indeed the only-begotten Son, of God.

34. *Now no more to return.* Now he adds another aspect, that Christ was raised from the dead once, to live for ever, as Paul teaches in Rom. 6.9, 10, 'He dies no more, and death will have no more dominion over him, because he lives to God.' For the assurance derived from the resurrection of Christ would be slight and pointless in the extreme, if destruction or any change still awaited Him. He is therefore said to have entered into the Kingdom of God so that, being alive for ever, He may endow His own also with eternal felicity. For seeing that Christ rose for us rather than for Himself, the perpetuity of life which the Father conferred on Him is extended to all of us, and is ours.

Yet the verse from Isa. 55.3, which is added here, seems to have nothing to do with proving the immortality of Christ, *I will give you the holy and sure blessings of David.* But that is not so. For since Isaiah is speaking of the redemption promised to David, and maintains that it will be firm and enduring, we are right to deduce from this the imperishable Kingdom of Christ, on which eternal salvation is founded. But Paul has followed the Septuagint in putting *holy things* for mercies. The Greeks usually translate חָסִיד (*chasid*), which means gentle, kind and merciful, as holy. Therefore in this verse they translated חַסְדֵי of David, *the holy things of David* (τὰ ὅσια Δαυὶδ τὰ πιστά), whereas the prophet rather means the grace promised to David. But Paul conceded this to the ignorant and weak, who were more accustomed to the Greek reading, especially since the weight of the testimony was placed elsewhere. For what Paul means in substance is this, that if the grace, which God says He will give in His Son, is eternal, the life of the Son is similarly eternal, and not subject to change. For we must grasp the principle that all the promises of God are Yea and Amen in Christ (II Cor. 1.20), and accordingly they cannot be effective unless He gives life to them.

35. *Thou shalt not permit.* This verse was also adduced by Peter in his first sermon, which Luke reported in chapter 2.27, where I have explained it. Readers should therefore refer to it. I shall merely say briefly that two Hebrew words are used by David for the grave, as repetitions are common with him. The first of these (שְׁאוֹל) is de-

rived from longing for things, because the grave, like an insatiable abyss, devours everything; the other is really derived from corruption (שַׁחַת, *pit*). David's meaning is faithfully expressed in Greek according to this etymology. For the nature of the grave is noted, when it receives the dead body, and as it were devours it, so that it may rot there and finally be consumed and perish. Paul affirms that it belongs to Christ alone that He has been preserved free from corruption. For despite the fact that His body was buried in the sepulchre, corruption had no right to it on that account, since it lay in it untouched, as if in a bed, until the day of His resurrection.

36. *David after he had in his own generation served.* In case anyone might object that it is David who is being dealt with in that Psalm, Paul quickly counters that by saying that this does not fit David in every respect, for his body was consumed with rottenness in the sepulchre. It therefore remains that, since that is a privilege belonging to Christ alone, David prophesied about Him in the Spirit. At the same time we must note the similarity between Head and members. For just as the full and absolute truth of this prophecy appeared in Christ alone as in the Head, so it takes place in the individual members according to the manner and order of each. But since Christ rose for this purpose, 'to make the body of our humiliation conform to His glorious body' (Phil. 3.21), the godly go down into the pit on this condition, that rottenness may not consume their bodies. Therefore in accordance with the hope of the deliverance to come, David is justified in declaring that he himself will not see corruption. In fact corruption ought not to be thought of as complete for the man for whom a better renewal has been prepared, for the bodies of believers rot in order that they may put on blessed incorruption in their time. Yet this does not prevent the situation of Head and members being very different, and our following the Son of God slowly and at a distance. We now see that both things are true and properly stated, that David and the rest of believers are not to see corruption, seeing that they will be conformed to their Head; and yet that the Son of God alone will be totally free and immune from corruption.

We must note this expression that David *served his own generation*, or the men of his time. The Vulgate punctuates it differently,[1] and certain Greek manuscripts agree, viz. that David served the will of God in his own day. Even if that is a probable reading, yet it has not the effect of weaning me from the opposing one. For it is no useless or pointless thing that he slept by the will or purpose of God, because he means that God did not forget that prophecy when David

[1] Calvin: *David quidem quum suae aetati inservisset, consilio Dei obdormivit, etc.* Vulg. punctuates as R.V. Tr.

died. It is as if he said that it was not apart from the will of God that the body of David lay in the grave, until he would rise again, to put on the effects of the prophecy, held in suspense until Christ. If what I bring forward is not displeasing, we are taught by this how men are to live in the world, viz. helping each other in their mutual dealings. For each man is not born to live for himself; but the human race is bound together as if by a sacred chain. Therefore unless our intention is to overthrow the laws of nature, let us remember that we must not live privately for ourselves, but for our neighbours.

But the question is asked, must we not also be concerned about posterity? I reply that the ministry of the godly is indeed beneficial for posterity also, just as today we realize that David, who is dead, does more good for us than the majority of those who live alongside us. But Paul simply means that believers devote themselves and their services to their neighbours all through the course of their lives, and that for them death is really the goal, so to speak, because they are discharged only when the Lord calls them out of the world. To sum up, in the first place we must be concerned about our own generation, so that we may serve our brethren with whom we have the fellowship of life, but, secondly, we must take care that the fruits of our service also redound to those coming after us. Since God lays down this principle for His servants, there can be no excuse for the thoughtlessness of those who imagine that the dead are praying for us, and that they are serving the Church just as much as when they were alive.

By the counsel of God fell asleep. Paul could simply have said that David died. He adds by *the counsel of God*, so that we may know that what we read in the Psalm was not fulfilled in the person of the prophet. Yet we are warned that the boundary of life and death is similarly fixed at the end for us by God, as we have it in Ps. 90.3, 'thou sendest men forth, and dost make them go over; afterwards thou dost say, Return, O children of men'. And even Plato shrewdly teaches that it is right that men do not depart from the earth except by the will of God, by whose hand they are placed in it for a time, as at a post. But when speaking about the death of David he expressly mentions *the counsel of God* for this reason, that we may know that corruption did not befall him by chance, as if God had forgotten His promise, but that it happened by the providence of God, so that the faithful might know that the prophecy must be transferred to another.

To *sleep* and to be *laid unto his fathers* are expressions too well known and too common to require explanation.

Be it known unto you therefore, brethren, that through this man is proclaimed unto you remission of sins: and by him every one that believeth is justified from all things, from which ye could not be justified by the law of Moses. Beware therefore, lest that come upon you, which is spoken in the prophets;

Behold, ye despisers, and wonder, and perish;
For I work a work in your days,
A work which ye shall in no wise believe, if one declare it unto you.
(38-41)

38. *Be it known unto you therefore.* After he has explained the manner by which salvation is procured through Christ, he now deals with His function and power. And the main point to grasp is what blessings the coming of Christ has brought to us, and what one must expect from Him. Now although Luke mentions in a single sentence that Paul preached about the benefits of Christ, yet there is no reason for anyone to doubt that such great matters were dealt with seriously and splendidly in accordance with their grandeur.

By the phrase *let it be known unto you* Paul means that only indolence will prevent such a clear and open matter becoming known to them, and therefore that it is absurd for those benefits of God, which were revealed through Christ, to be concealed from the faithful. For he was sent with the resounding publication of the Gospel, which our faith ought to hear so that it may enter upon the sure possession of His blessings. For we must grasp what He is like in order to enjoy Him properly.

Remission of sins is put in the first place, for by it God reconciles us to Himself. Since God wishes it to be announced to all His people, He is showing that it is needed by all men. For Paul does not address one or two, but all the Jews who were at Antioch. Therefore in the first place we must hold that we are all hostile to God on account of sins (Col. 2.13). It follows from that that all are shut out of the Kingdom of God, and abandoned to eternal death, until God receives us into His grace by the free remission of sins. We must also note this, that God forgives our sins and is made favourable through the Mediator because, apart from Him, just as there is no expiation, so there is no pardon, or release from guilt. These are the rudiments of our faith, and they are not learnt in the philosophic schools: that the whole human race is condemned and overwhelmed by sins; that we possess no righteousness to reconcile ourselves to God; that the only hope of salvation remains in His mercy, when He acquits us out of His favour; that, on the other hand, men remain under condemnation except those who flee to Christ and seek expiation for sins in His death.

39. *And from all things.* He is tacitly anticipating what could appear to be contrary to the preceding teaching. For however many cere-

monies of the Law there were, they were just so many procedures for obtaining remission of sins. It was therefore easy for the Jews to object: 'If this man alone propitiates God for us, having abolished sins, what is the purpose of so many washings and sacrifices, which we have made use of up to now in accordance with the Law's prescription?' Therefore so that the ceremonies of the Law might not hold the Jews back, Paul teaches that Christ carries out what those things could not do. It is not the case that Paul spoke so briefly and concisely, for there was no hope of the Jews abandoning their confidence in legal righteousness suddenly and coming to Christ; but it was enough for Luke to glance at the substance of the things which he taught on that occasion in their proper order. But the meaning is that that obstacle, on which the Jews stuck, was removed by the Mediator. Indeed the ceremonial law ought to have been a tutor to lead them by the hand to Christ; and all rites enjoined by God were aids given for supporting and increasing their faith. But as it is customary for men to be perverse and corrupt the sacred institutions of God, they were blocking the way for themselves with ceremonies, and were closing the gate of faith, to prevent them from coming to Christ. They thought that they possessed righteousness in sacrifices; that they acquired true cleanliness by washings (*baptismis*); that God was pleased with them when they had gone through their external displays; in a word, they forsook the substance and were laying hold of empty shadows. Certainly God had instituted nothing useless or futile in the Law. Accordingly ceremonies were reliable and certain testimonies of the remission of sins. For God had not lied with these words, 'Let the sinner sacrifice, and his iniquity will be purged.' But as Christ was the end of the Law (Rom. 10.4), and the heavenly pattern of the tabernacle (Heb. 8.5), so the force and effect of all ceremonies depended on Him. The deduction from that is that apart from Him (*eo remoto*) they were fleeting shadows. Therefore Paul properly takes away the cause of righteousness from the Law in order to ascribe it to Christ. Now we know Paul's intention, viz. that he wished to draw the Jews away from a false and wrong confidence in the Law, so that they might not be swollen-headed and think that they had no need of Christ's help, or merely look for external happiness in Him.

Be justified in the Law. This verse makes it quite clear what the word *justifying* means everywhere else, viz. to be delivered and forgiven. Mention had been made of remission of sins: Paul has denied that it can be obtained any other way than by the grace of Christ. In case someone might object that remedies are available in the Law he replies that there is nothing effectual in any one of them. The meaning is therefore clear, that a man cannot be justified from sins in the Law, because legal rites were neither the right nor proper payments for removing guilt; they were worthless in themselves for promoting righteousness; and they were not proper compensations for pleasing God. It really cannot be denied, except wrongly, that this justification is connected to remission of sins, as the means and grounds of obtaining it. For what is Paul doing except removing contrary objections to confirm that statement, that our sins are forgiven by the benefit of Christ? On the other hand he does show that neither sacrifices nor all the rites of the Law justify us from sins. Therefore a man who is freely released from guilt and the judgment of eternal death, to which he was liable, is justified through Christ. This is the righteousness of faith when God regards us as righteous, by not imputing our sins.

The proper meaning of this word alone suffices to refute the cavils of the Papists who contend that we are righteous, not by forgiveness and gracious acceptance, but by character (*habitu*) and infused righteousness. Accordingly we do not allow this text of Paul's to be shamefully and viciously mangled by them; for in it he has said that we are *justified from all things*, so that the remission of sins is assured for us.

Now indeed we must realize that the Law of Moses is set over against Christ as the chief means of acquiring righteousness, that is, if there might have been anything other than, or different from, Christ. Paul does indeed discuss ceremonies, but it must be noted that they included everything that would make for expiating sins and placating the wrath of God. Yet there was not one of all the ceremonies of the Law, which did not fetter a man with the guilt of sin, as if it were a newly written bond, as Paul teaches in Col. 2.14. What then? God certainly wished to make it known that men are justified by the death of His Son, and that alone, because 'He made him, who knew no sin, to be sin for us, so that we may have righteousness in him' (II Cor. 5.21). It follows from this that whatever satisfactions men devise tend to strip Christ of His honour.

In the law[1] and *in Christ* mean the same thing as *by the law* and *by Christ*, according to the Hebrew idiom.

From all. This phrase refutes the impious invention of the Papists, by which they teach that only original sin, and actual sins which were committed before baptism, are unconditionally and freely forgiven by Christ, and that others are atoned for by satisfactions. But Paul clearly states that throughout the whole course of our lives we are justified from sins by Christ. Indeed it must be borne in mind that the rites of the Law were entrusted to the Jews, so that their usefulness as well as their use might flourish daily in the Church; in other words, that the Jews might in fact realize that the continual repetition of their

[1] Calvin's text: *in lege Mosis justificari*. Tr.

expiations and washings was not in vain. If the reality and substance of all of them is found in Christ, it follows that there is no other sacrifice for the destruction of sins than His death. Otherwise no resemblance (*analogia*) would exist between it and the ancient figures. The Papists call us back to penitence and the keys, as if the legal ceremonies were not in fact exercises for meditating on penitence, as if the power of the keys was not also connected to them. But the faith of the godly was helped by such aids, to flee to the grace of the Mediator alone. Therefore let it remain a determined principle that the righteousness which we are given in Christ, is not the thing of a single day or a moment, but is permanent, so that the sacrifice of His death daily reconciles us to God.

Everyone who believes. Paul declares how men obtain the righteousness of Christ, viz. when they receive it by faith. But what faith procures, we do not get by any merits of works. Accordingly there is no ambiguity in Paul's statement, that we are justified by faith alone. However the Papists oppose that with as much obstinacy as zeal. At the same time it is proper to know what is the meaning of the word believing, which ignorance makes distasteful to the Papists. Indeed there are other benefits of Christ which we also obtain by faith. For, regenerating us by His Spirit, He restores the image of God in us, and when our old man has been crucified He remakes us in newness of life. But it was enough for Luke to deal with this one thing, how men return to favour with God, from whom they have been alienated through sin, because the transition from that to the other things is easy.

40. *Beware lest that come upon you.* Because he had to deal with men who were inflexible, or at least because many mingling in the crowd were stiff-necked, he adds reproof to his teaching, as if he intended to hammer their stubbornness into pliableness. For if the Jews had been obedient and ready to submit, there is no doubt that he would have tried to draw them to Christ in a pleasing way. But either their torpor or their obstinacy forced him to be more heated and vehement, inasmuch as all those who are contemptuous of the grace of Christ, must be summoned to God's judgment-seat, and the horrible judgment of eternal death must be declared to them. He certainly means that there is still room for repentance, when he urges them to *beware*; yet at the same time he warns that, unless they are quickly on their guard, the horrible vengeance of God is not far away.

Which is spoken in the prophets. The verse that is quoted is taken from the first chapter of Hab. (v. 5). But because all the prophets were collected into one corpus or volume, Paul says that it is written *in the prophets.*

41. He does not repeat Habakkuk's statement word for word. It goes like this: 'Behold ye among the nations, and see, and be astonished, and amazed; because a work will be done in your days, which nobody will believe when it will be told.'[1] Paul says: *Behold, ye despisers* so that the Jews may know that the punishment that was once inflicted on their fathers is one common to despisers of the Word. It is as if he said, 'God, who once punished contempt of His Word so severely, today values it just as highly.' Therefore the prophet's warning applies to all ages, so that despisers may not expect that they can now escape the punishment which others have experienced. They were taking pride in the temple, they were boasting that they were the people of God, elated with impious arrogance, they were rejecting all warnings. Therefore Paul reminds them how God threatens despisers through His prophets.

A work in your days. The meaning is that those, who refuse to have faith in the Word of God, will feel His hand, so that, when they have at last been convinced by punishment, they may know that He spoke seriously. The common proverb says, 'Experience is the mistress of fools.' Similarly the Lord brings it home to the ungodly by hard fact so that, when they have been subdued by misfortunes, they may begin to acknowledge His power. But what kind of punishment does He announce? 'Because', He says, 'you do not believe my Word, I shall produce an example in your case, which will be incredible to all.' He means by these words that He will inflict punishment on them, that will strike the world with horror. For as rebellion against God is a detestable monster, so it is no wonder if it brings forth monsters of punishment from itself. Therefore if we put an end to belief in the Word of God, we must be on our guard in case we feel His hand more powerful than all our senses are capable of, and even to the point where the whole world is stupefied, and indeed we ourselves are also struck dumb with fear. Habakkuk is prophesying about the disaster inflicted by the Chaldeans, but the punishment with which the Lord has avenged contempt of His Gospel is far more severe. Accordingly, let us get used to fearing God, and embracing His Word reverently, so that nothing like that may happen to us.

And as they went out, they[2] besought that these words might be spoken to them the next sabbath. Now when the synagogue broke up, many of the Jews and of the devout proselytes followed Paul and Barnabas: who, speaking to them, urged them to continue in the grace of God.

[1] Translation of Calvin's text. Tr.

[2] Calvin's text as R.V. margin: *And when the Jews were gone out of the synagogue, the Gentiles besought.* Tr.

And the next sabbath almost the whole city was gathered together to hear the word of God. But when the Jews saw the multitudes, they were filled with jealousy, and contradicted the things which were spoken by Paul, and blasphemed. (42-45)

42. *And as they went out of the synagogue.* It can be read *from the synagogue of the Jews*, and perhaps that is better. For it is likely that they went out before the congregation dispersed; and one gathers that from the context, because immediately afterwards Luke adds that some of the Jews followed Paul and Barnabas *when the synagogue broke up.* The meaning therefore is that Paul and Barnabas left, while the Jews were still holding their meeting, and were then asked by the Gentiles to give them assistance in the meantime; and afterwards certain of the *Jews* and *proselytes* came to Paul both out of a desire to learn, and in order to profess their faith. The Vulgate and Erasmus, in translating it 'on the following sabbath', have not followed what Luke meant. For since it is Gentiles who are being dealt with here, it does not seem to me a likely thing for them to choose a sabbath on which to hear Paul and Barnabas. For that day was fixed for the Jews, but the Gentiles had as much opportunity on other days. Why therefore should they put off their desire and requests for eight days? And what is more, they wish to hear Paul when he is free and not involved with (*ferias habet cum*) the Jews. So the Lord does not allow them to be idle until the sabbath comes round, giving them in the Gentiles material with which to busy themselves.

They would speak the words. I have translated what Luke has, although the article τὰ can be taken as τὰ αὖτα as in some other passages. Then the meaning would be that they were asked to speak to the Gentiles about the same matters during that week. Moreover, while the Gentiles eagerly seize the first possible opportunity, the Jews are filled with contempt, and neglect what has been presented to them, apart from a few of them who do join themselves to Paul and Barnabas. Luke expressly mentions *proselytes* who, since they had embraced the teaching of the Law, and were worshipping the God of Israel, were not swollen with that pride which was a barrier to the Jews, who boasted of their long lineage.

43. *Who speaking.* The meaning is ambiguous, for it can be applied to the Jews and proselytes, that they urged Paul and Barnabas not to lose courage, but whole-heartedly to persist in the grace of God. And they certainly did not lack the opportunity for they saw preparations being made to involve them in fights, and that they needed strenuous perseverance to sustain the attacks of the opposing faction. Accordingly it would suit very well that they were burning with the desire

to make progress[1] and strove to encourage Paul and Barnabas to continue. If you refer it to Paul and Barnabas the meaning will be that those who had come were not repulsed by them, but were received kindly and courteously, and were encouraged by a godly exhortation to continue *in the grace* they had received. Finally, the word *grace* includes first of all the faith of the Gospel, and secondly, the blessings which come to us from it; or, to put it in a nut-shell, the calling to the hope of eternal salvation.

44. *And when the sabbath came*. The gathering of the people is proof that Paul and Barnabas were not idle in the week before that sabbath, and that their work among the Gentiles was not in vain. For the people had been so prepared in their studies that they all desired to have a surer grasp of the whole matter, and they hoped that that would be the case if it were discussed along with the Jews. For we may conjecture that, although they were attracted by some pleasant taste, they were nevertheless not yet completely persuaded to accept the teaching of the Gospel without question, but that they came into the synagogue suspended between expectation and desire.

45. *They were filled*. It is no new thing for the fury of the ungodly to be inflamed when the light of the Gospel is brought too near. In particular when they see the progress of sound doctrine they leap to resist with a more frenzied attack. But it is not clear whether Luke means by the word *zeal*, that they were moved by some sort of perverse emulation to set themselves against Paul and Barnabas, as ambition is the mother of envy as well as all contentions; or whether he takes zeal for the indignation conceived from the fact that they deplored the Gentiles being equal to the people of God. For they thought it intolerable in the extreme that the holy treasure of teaching, that was the proper inheritance of the sons, should lie, as it were, under the feet of all.

Contradicted and blasphemed. Carried away by the passion to resist they finally break out in blasphemies. And Satan generally drives the ungodly to this point of madness, where, defeated and broken by arguments, they become more and more obdurate, and, knowingly and willingly, they finally spew out blasphemies against God and the truth. Accordingly we must be all the more anxiously on our guard so that, if the passion to contradict carries us away, we may not rush at once towards that precipice.

And Paul and Barnabas spake out boldly, and said, It was necessary that the word of God should first be spoken to you. Seeing ye thrust it from you, and judge yourselves unworthy of eternal life, lo, we turn to

[1] Or, be helpful (*proficiendi*). Tr.

the Gentiles. For so hath the Lord commanded us, saying,
I have set thee for a light of the Gentiles,
That thou shouldest be for salvation unto the uttermost part of the earth.
And as the Gentiles heard this, they were glad, and glorified the word of God: and as many as were ordained to eternal life believed. And the word of the Lord was spread abroad throughout all the region. But the Jews urged on the devout women of honourable estate, and the chief men of the city, and stirred up a persecution against Paul and Barnabas, and cast them out of their borders. But they shook off the dust of their feet against them, and came unto Iconium. And the disciples were filled with joy and with the Holy Ghost. (46–52)

46. *And when they took the liberty.* Luke shows that far from being broken by the inflexibility of their enemies the servants of Christ begin to inveigh against them afresh because of it. For although they had already goaded them sharply, yet they were still sparing them to some extent. But now when they see that they are obstinate in rejecting Christ, they, in turn, excommunicate them and disinherit them from the Kingdom of God. Now we are taught by this example that we must not use extreme severity except against those who are given up for lost. Finally, the more boldly and exultantly the reprobate oppress the truth, the more we ought to take heart. For the servants of God ought to be equipped with the unconquerable steadfastness of the Spirit, so that they may never submit to the devil or his ministers, just as the Lord orders Jeremiah to contend with the reprobate with a countenance of iron.

It was necessary . . . first to you. He accuses them of ingratitude, because, although they had been chosen from all nations by God, so that Christ might present Himself to them, they are maliciously rejecting so great a blessing. But in the first sentence he reminds them of the level of honour and pre-eminence into which God had raised them. Afterwards there follows the reproach that they are rejecting so great a favour by their own free will. From that he concludes that it is now the time for the Gospel to be transferred to the Gentiles. His statement that it ought to have been *first preached to them,* strictly refers to the time of the Kingdom of Christ. For under the Law, before Christ was revealed, the Jews were not only first, but were also the only ones. Accordingly Moses called them a kingdom of priests and God's peculiar people (Exod. 19.5, 6). But at that time the adoption of God remained their possession, and only theirs, with the Gentiles passed over, on condition that with the coming of Christ they still ought to have the preference over the Gentiles. For although Christ reconciled the world to the Father, yet those who were already near to God, and belonged to His family, were first in order. It was therefore the proper order for the apostles to gather the Church first from the Jews, and then from the Gentiles, as we have seen in chapter 1 verse 8, and other passages. Thus the association of the Gentiles did not remove the right of the firstborn from the Jews, but they would always be pre-eminent in the Church of God. Following this reasoning Paul says (Rom. 1.16) that the righteousness of God is manifested in the Gospel first to the Jews and secondly to the Greeks. When God had thought them worthy of a favour of such magnitude, it underlines the seriousness of their sin, when they reject what is offered to them so benevolently. He therefore adds that they pronounce judgment on themselves of being unworthy of eternal life. For since rejection of the Gospel is the denial of the righteousness of God there is no need of any other judge to condemn the unbelieving.

But after you reject. Paul does not appear to be arguing correctly. For in the first place, in order that the Gentiles might be admitted into the hope of salvation, it was not necessary for the Jews to be excluded from it. Secondly what was more suitable was for the Jews, once they had embraced the Gospel, to grant the second place to the Gentiles. But Paul speaks as if they could not grow together into the one body, and that the Gospel could not come to the Gentiles unless it was rejected by the Jews. Before he had experienced such stubbornness had he not in fact already been ordained the apostle of the Gentiles? Why then does he turn to the Gentiles now, at last, as if their election depended on the unfaithfulness of the chosen people? I reply that the emphasis is on the words *we are turned* (*convertimur*). For he means that he is now turning away from the Jews in order to devote himself entirely to the Gentiles. If the Jews had remained in their own position, then such a turning would not have ensued, but with the Jews received into the bosom of the Church, he would have drawn the Gentiles along with them in an unbroken connexion, and embraced them both equally. Now, when the Jews turn their backs, and cut themselves off from his ministry, he cannot cast his eyes on them and the Gentiles at one and the same time.[1] Therefore having bidden them farewell, he is forced to transfer his concern to the Gentiles. Accordingly if the Jews had not alienated themselves from the Church, the call of the Gentiles would have been such as the prophets describe, 'On that day seven foreigners will seize a Jew's mantle, and say, "We shall walk with you, because God is with

[1] Reading C.R. *uno intuito eos cum gentibus respicere*; but Tholuck's reading is also possible, *uno intuito eos cum gentibus recipere*, 'accept them along with the Gentiles on any consideration.' Tr.

you." ' (cf. Zech. 8.23). But now the Gentiles have been called by a new and accidental way, because, with the rejection of the Jews, they have entered into the vacant possession. They ought to have been added to the Jews, but after the latter fell out and were put aside, they were substituted in their place. So the death of the Jews was the life of the Gentiles, as Paul says (Rom. 11.12, 15, 24); and when the natural branches had been cut off, the wild olive trees were grafted into the holy root, until God at last also restores them to life, when they are grafted back into the original root, so that the Israel of God, having been gathered from every quarter, may be saved.

47. *So He commanded.* The verse is taken from Isa. 49.6, where God is speaking to His Son rather than to the apostles. But we must note that many things that Scripture ascribes to Christ, apply to His ministers. I say 'many things', not everything, for certain descriptions are peculiar to the person of Christ, and it would be impious sacrilege to honour his ministers with them. Christ is called our Righteousness, because He was the only atoning sacrifice (*victima expiatrix*), and has reconciled the Father to us by His death, and afterwards rose again, having conquered death, to procure eternal life for us. Therefore the whole substance of our salvation subsists in the person of Christ. But since He acts through His ministers transferring His own functions to them, He also shares His descriptions with them. The preaching of the Gospel is in this class. He alone, indeed, has been appointed our Teacher by the Father, but He has put pastors and ministers in His place to speak as if out of His mouth. Thus the authority remains entirely with Him, and He is heard nevertheless in His ministers. Therefore Paul skilfully adapts the testimony of Isaiah to himself, when it is a question of the preaching of the Gospel.

I have set thee for a light. The calling of the Gentiles seems to be announced there in such a way as not to carry with it the disowning of the ancient people. Indeed God is rather associating foreigners with the Jews, who had previously belonged to His household. He says, 'It is not enough for you to be a servant to me in teaching Israel, because I have appointed you a light to the Gentiles.' Certainly God appears to make a beginning with His Church from the sons of Abraham, and afterwards to stretch out His hand to the Gentiles, so that they may both form the same Church with complete unanimity of faith. But yet Paul adduces the prophecy in such a way as if it could not be fulfilled without the rejection of the Jews. For he indicates that the light of Christ has been kindled for the Gentiles after the Jews have been cast into the darkness of death. I reply that it cannot necessarily be proved from the context that Paul affirms that the Gentiles were not to be enlightened until the light had been extinguished for the Jews. For the meaning can be this, 'Since you have deprived yourselves of eternal life, that is no reason for you to think that the grace of God is profaned, if you are set aside and we begin to be concerned about the Gentiles. For the Messiah has not been given for you alone, but was appointed for the salvation of the whole world, as it is written, *I have set thee for a light of the Gentiles* etc.' However if you consider the passage in the prophet more closely you will find the rejection of the ancient people included in it. For God announces that He will be glorious and magnificent in the ministry of Christ, *though Israel be not gathered* (Isa. 49.5).[1] Afterwards He adds, as if by way of explanation, that the power of Christ is not going to be restricted to one people, because His light is to be sending out its beams for salvation right to the uttermost ends of the earth. This occasion of the call of the Gentiles seems to be noted by Paul, clearly because he devoted his efforts to the Gentiles completely, when he found no ground for occupying himself among the Jews.

Incidentally we ought to notice in the words of the prophet that *salvation* is placed after *light*, in accordance with that saying of Christ's, 'This is life eternal, to know thee the true God' etc. (John 17.3). For if the knowledge of God is the only saving thing for us, similarly the only resurrection from the annihilation of eternal death is for us to be snatched out of the darkness of ignorance and be enlightened in the faith of Christ.

48. *And the Gentiles hearing*. The Gentiles had ground for rejoicing when they heard that they were not being called to the hope of salvation suddenly, as if this had not been determined previously by God, but that what had been predicted many generations before was now at last being fulfilled. For the fact that salvation had been promised to them with the advent of Christ, was an extraordinary confirmation of their faith, and the reason why it came about that they were embracing the Gospel with greater desire and reverence.

To *glorify the word of God* can be explained in two ways, either that they acknowledge the truth of the prophecy of Isaiah, or that they faithfully embraced the teaching that was set before them. Certainly full approbation (*subscriptio*) is indicated, inasmuch as they do not discuss or argue any further once they have observed Paul's victory. And surely we bestow on the Word of God the honour due to it only when we submit ourselves to it in trust and obedience, just as no greater dishonour can be inflicted upon it than when men refuse to believe it.

Finally we see that the obstinacy which they saw in the Jews did

[1] But contrast R.V. and R.S.V., and Kittel, *Biblica Hebraica, ad loc.*, which reads לא but gives variant לו. Tr.

not prevent the Gentiles from surrendering to Christ. With similar greatness of mind we ought to spurn and scorn the pride of the ungodly when they try to block the way for us by their obstinacy.

And they believed. This, in my opinion at any rate, is an explanation of the preceding sentence. For Luke shows what sort of *glory* they ascribed to the Word of God. However we must note the limitation, when he records that they did not all, to a man, believe, but those who *were ordained to eternal life.* Now there is no doubt that Luke calls τεταγμένοι those who were elected by the free adoption of God. For it is a ridiculous cavil to make this refer to the attitude of believers, as if those who had the proper disposition of mind received the Gospel. For this particular ordaining can only be understood of the eternal purpose of God. And Luke does not say that they were ordained to faith, but to life, because God predestines His own to the inheritance of eternal life. On the other hand this verse teaches that faith depends on the election of God. And since the whole human race is blind and obstinate, those faults certainly remain fixed in our nature until they are corrected by the grace of the Spirit; but the correction flows only from the fountain of election. For of two men who hear the same teaching together, the one proves himself docile, while the other persists in his ill-will; yet that does not happen because they differ in nature, but because God enlightens the former and does not think the latter worthy of the same grace. We are certainly made sons of God by faith (Gal. 3.26), and faith, so far as we are concerned, is the door and commencement of salvation. But there is a profounder consideration as far as God is concerned; for He does not begin to choose us after we have believed; but He seals His adoption, which was hidden, by the gift of faith in our hearts, so that it may be plain and sure. For if it is the particular property of the sons of God alone to be His disciples, it follows that it does not apply to all the sons of Adam without distinction. Therefore it is no wonder if all, without distinction, do not receive the Gospel, because, even if the Heavenly Father calls all men to faith by the external voice of a man, yet He calls effectually by His Spirit only those whom He has determined to save. Now if God's election, by which He ordains us to life, is the cause of faith and salvation, the result is that no room is left for worthiness or merits. Let us therefore grasp what Luke says, that those, who have been engrafted into the Body of Christ by faith, and receive the earnest and pledge of their adoption in Christ, were previously ordained to life.

From this we also gather what effect the preaching of the Gospel has by itself. For it does not find faith in men until God inwardly calls those whom He has chosen, and draws to Christ those who were previously His own. At the same time Luke teaches by these words that it is not possible for any one of the elect to perish. For he says, not that one or a few of the elect believed, but as many as were chosen. For although we may know nothing about God's adoption until we grasp it by faith, yet there is no dubiety or hesitation about it in His secret purpose; because all whom He has for His own He entrusts to the protection or care of His Son, who will remain a faithful Guardian right to the end.

It is necessary to know both aspects. When election is established as antecedent to faith, there is no cause for men to arrogate anything to themselves in any part of their salvation. For, if faith in which salvation consists, which is evidence to us of God's gracious adoption, which unites us to Christ and makes His life ours, by which we possess God along with His righteousness, by which, finally, we receive the gift of sanctification, if that faith has its foundations outside ourselves in the eternal purpose of God, then we must of necessity give the credit for whatever blessings we have, to the grace of God, which precedes us without being asked. Again, because many get themselves involved in confused and thorny speculations, when they search out their salvation in the hidden purpose of God, let us learn that the election of God is confirmed by faith for this purpose, that our minds may be turned to Christ, as the earnest of our election, and let them seek for no other certitude than that which is disclosed to us in the Gospel. Let this, I say, be a sufficient sign to us, that 'whoever believes in the only-begotten Son of God has eternal life' (John 3.36).

49. *The word of the Lord was spread abroad.* Here Luke is reporting the progress of the Gospel. In this the truth of Christ's parable is apparent, when He says that it is like leaven (Luke 13.21). We have learned above that there was a great concourse of people, so that the seed of the true teaching was scattered through the whole city. Now Luke says that it was spread more extensively, viz. throughout the whole region.

50. Nevertheless he mentions that it was not done without sweat and trouble. Therefore the beginnings of the call of the Gentiles were favourable and auspicious, and Satan could not impede the course of the grace of God. But at the same time Paul and Barnabas, whom God had brought forward into the arena as athletes, had to fight. But we must take note of Luke's statement that the *devout and honourable women* were instigated along with *the chief men of the city* to persecute the servants of Christ. For it was a considerable stumbling-block for the ignorant and those who were scarcely yet begotten in Christ, to see all the men and women, who were highly regarded and praiseworthy in men's eyes, in opposition to Christ. A great crowd of men

had received Christ, but they were the crowd, and nothing but the dregs of humanity. At the other extreme stood the chief men of the city, who easily overwhelmed the low-born and insignificant crowd with their splendour. Also the fact that matrons who were devout and honourable to all appearances, were hostile towards the teaching, could also have rendered it suspect, even hateful. If good-for-nothing, shameless and dissolute men had risen up from their debaucheries or taverns, if droves of harlots had burst out of a brothel, it would have been no disgrace to the Gospel, on the contrary in that way its grandeur would have shone forth all the clearer. Now what can occur to the weak-minded but that teaching that has such adversaries is not from God? Therefore it was necessary not only that believers, who were still tender novices, be confirmed by the Lord, so that their faith might not collapse, but also that a hand be stretched out to Paul and Barnabas, so that they might not be disheartened and give up.

Finally by this example God wished to teach us that we must vigorously resist such stumbling-blocks, and be on our guard so that worthless masks of virtues do not blind our eyes and we do not see the glory of Christ shining in the Gospel. For it is certain that all the virtues and honesty that can be conceived of in men, are mere hypocrisy when they set themselves in opposition to Christ. Although it is possible for men, who are thoughtlessly carried against Christ for a time, afterwards to come to their senses, nevertheless it must be established that no matter with what kind of sanctity they shine, those who resist the Gospel are not endowed with genuine fear of God, and all the virtues they display are nothing else but a deceptive shadow. For it is not for nothing that this description is given to Christ, that He 'reveals the thoughts of many hearts' (Luke 2.35).

Religious women. What sort of religion could that in fact have been, in which there was no reverence for the Word of God? We must observe that there are four kinds of people. As the number of those who worship God sincerely and from the heart is few, so there are few of those who profess open and gross contempt of Him. Now those are two of the classes. On the other hand the majority are not completely devoid of religion, and are not completely alienated from the common worship of God; but yet if they are given a penetrating examination, they are nothing less than religionless, as though they play with God in a cold and perfunctory way. Similarly today the ungodliness of many is in one way or another concealed under ceremonies, and a spurious profession of the worship of God. Thus in all generations there have existed play-acting worshippers of God, whose total sanctity consisted in gesticulations and empty displays. In the time of Paul, just as in the present day, a particular devotion to piety was conspicuous in a certain few; and even if their religion was impure, and their heart false, deceitful and double, yet they are somehow looked upon as religious, out of regard for their zeal, misguided though it is. But it is plain from this incident what the value of bare religion is, when it drives its worshippers headlong and with heedless vehemence to fight against the Kingdom of God, and suppress His glory. Moreover one may well believe that, although those matrons had not come over to Judaism completely, and were not imbued with the teaching of the Law, yet they were semi-Jewesses, and that was the reason why they undertook the defence of the nation so willingly. For, according to the witness of Paul, women are driven about in circles in this way, held captive by the burden of their sins.

51. *Having shaken off the dust of their feet.* We may also gather from the commandment of Christ (Matt. 10.14, Luke 9.5 and 10.11) that this was a sign of cursing among the Jews. For it is not likely that Christ wished His men to use an unknown sign, since it was His intention to strike the gross and self-professed despisers of His teaching with terror. Moreover in this way He wished to make it known that the ungodly are so abominable to God that we must take great care not to have anything in common with them, so that no contagion from their uncleanness may reach us. Indeed all the wicked are said to pollute the earth on which they walk, but the Lord has nowhere directed that any but the despiser of His Word be rejected with so great a curse. If any adulterer or fornicator, if any perjurer, if any drunkard, if any murderer had to be excommunicated, this sign would not have been used. It is therefore clear how intolerable contempt of His Word is to God; because, when He orders the dust to be shaken from their feet, it is just as if He were pronouncing that they are the bond-slaves of Satan, lost and hopeless men, and deserving to be exterminated from the earth. Accordingly, let severity as great as this teach us to reverence the Gospel. Ministers of the Word are also taught how the majesty of the Word must be affirmed by them with great ardour and zeal, so that they may not be indifferent and let contempt of it pass unnoticed.

52. *The disciples were filled with joy.* This sentence, that *they were filled with joy and the Spirit,* can be explained in two ways. The first is by hypallage in this way, 'with the joy of the Spirit', or, what amounts to the same thing, 'with spiritual joy', because there is no clearness of conscience, peace or joy except from the Spirit of God. That is why Paul says that the Kingdom of God is righteousness, peace and joy in the Spirit (Rom. 14.17). Or, secondly, it may mean that the word *Spirit* includes in itself other virtues and gifts. Yet I prefer it that *they were filled with joy,* because the grace of the Holy

Spirit was ruling within them, and this alone makes us so genuinely and thoroughly joyous that we are exalted high above the whole world. For we must pay attention to what Luke had in mind viz. that far from being agitated or upset by those serious hindrances, by the ignominy of their teachers, by the disturbance of the city, by alarms and threats, even by the fear of imminent dangers, the faithful, out of the depth of their faith, strongly despised the showiness of their spurious sanctity as well as of their power. And there is no doubt that if our faith is properly founded on God, and strikes its roots deep in His Word, and, finally, if it is made thoroughly secure by the protection of the Spirit, as it ought to be, it will foster peace and spiritual joy in our minds, even with the whole world in an uproar.

INDEX OF SCRIPTURE REFERENCES

INDEX OF SCRIPTURE REFERENCES

INDEX OF SCRIPTURE REFERENCES

INDEX OF SCRIPTURE REFERENCES

INDEX OF SCRIPTURE REFERENCES

INDEX OF NAMES

INDEX OF NAMES

INDEX OF NAMES

GENERAL INDEX